CW00816346

# Karl Barth and the Strange New World within the Bible

## Barth, Wittgenstein, and the Metadilemmas of the Enlightenment

Karl Barth and his family (taken in 1918/early 1919)

(photograph/Hans-Anton Drewes, Karl Barth-Archive

PATERNOSTER BIBLICAL AND THEOLOGICAL MONOGRAPHS

# Karl Barth and the Strange New World within the Bible

## Barth, Wittgenstein, and the Metadilemmas of the Enlightenment

Neil B MacDonald

Foreword By Christopher R. Seitz

paternoster
press

First published in 2000 by Paternoster Press

04 03 02 01 00   7 6 5 4 3 2 1

Paternoster Press is an imprint of Paternoster Publishing,
P.O. Box 300, Carlisle, Cumbria, CA3 OQS, U.K.
http://www.paternoster-publishing.com
and
P.O. Box 1047, Waynesboro, GA 30830-2047, U.S.A.

**British Library Cataloguing in Publication Data**
A catalogue record for this book is available from the British Library

ISBN 0-85364-970-7

Printed and bound in Great Britain
by Nottingham Alpha Graphics

*For my mother and father,*
*and in memory of my brother John (1953-1977)*

# Contents

# PART II
## The Metatheological Dilemma and the *Church Dogmatics*:
## The Historical Truth-Claims of the Strange New World within the Bible

# PART III
## The Enlightenment's Final Epistemological Reckoning With the Bible:
## Kant's 'Measure of God' *Versus* Barth's Conception of the Reformers'
## *Analogia Fidei*

**PART IV**
**Barth Against the Enlightenment's Final Reckoning:**
**The Creation History, the Resurrection-Appearances History, and the Pre-Easter Gospel Narrative**

Contents                                                                                    xi

# Foreword

Neil MacDonald has written three books within the confines of one. All three are necessary and all are of equal, sterling quality.

One book is on Barth, Wittgenstein and what he terms the "meta-dilemma" facing, respectively, theology and philosophy. Barth and Wittgenstein reinstated theology and philosophy as disciplines unto themselves, thus responding effectively to various challengers from various eras (from Hume to Overbeck). Much imaginative and disciplined labour goes into analysing how it is appropriate to speak of Barth and Wittgenstein as comparable figures in the history of ideas, in that they did not know one another personally and because they were acting independently of one another on behalf of disciplines each likely judged to be properly independent of one another.

The second book is on Karl Barth as theologian. The reader will come away with a clearer picture of Barth as an Enlightenment figure. MacDonald rejects efforts to see in Barth unconscious pre-modernity. So, famously, Barth's rejection of natural theology is nuanced, modern, and fully conscious of the difference and the distance lying between himself and Calvin, Augustine, or Thomas.

Neither is Barth a post-modern thinker. His categories and concerns are Enlightenment ones, and in Barth there is no hint of a retreat into "post-conceptualities." Barth believed the Bible anticipated the self-same concerns and challenges that the Enlightenment believed it was bringing to light for the very first time. MacDonald shows that, if Barth is right, the Bible understood the Enlightenment better than it understood the Bible, and, indeed, better than the Enlightenment understood itself: according to its *own* canons of inquiry it ought not to have lost faith in the Bible in the way that it did.

The third book is on Barth as reader of scripture. Specifically, MacDonald pursues what Barth meant by history. One comes away with a sense (developed in book two from the standpoint of the history of ideas) that, come modernity, scholars of the Bible deployed a term "history" they believed was exhaustive and self-evident. In reality, it meant by "history" a certain specific genre of inquiry into the past. In a brilliant and nuanced and sustained manner, MacDonald shows how Barth never gave up on the idea that the Bible's account of things (MacDonald focuses on two difficult cases, creation and resurrection) is historical, in that it has to do with reality that exists in time and space. But because the word "historical" was made to do duty in the wake of the Enlightenment for a certain sort of factual accounting, the Bible's way of doing history was unappreciated, deprecated, seen as naïve or mythical or poetical; or, what is worse, appreciated, but then archaeologised, reclassified, demythologised, distilled for this or that purity (in Frei's phrase, of "ostensive reference") - all this amounting to an eclipse of the final form of Scripture and its claim truthfully to tell about reality in time. Theology, as an independent discipline with its own integrity, was therefore eclipsed as well (the subject of MacDonald's book one). By reinstating what MacDonald refers to as *sui generis* historicality as a species of historical realism ("a historical sphere of a different kind", *Church Dogmatics* IV/1, 334), theology was reinstated.

It is important to underscore the significance of this "book three." Many have been the recent efforts to insist that the Bible has a genuine claim on the modern (or post-modern) account of reality, whether aesthetic (Alter, Frye), metalinguistic-poetic (Milbank), poetic-real (Sternberg), history-like (Frei), imaginative (Ricoeur), linguistic (Wolterstorff, Vanhoozer), mythical (Thompson), canonical or literal (Childs, Greene-McCreight), figural (Radner), or even historical in the "thin" or "thick" versions of modernity (viz., the many tribes of historical-critical endeavour, with their various *sachems*). Many of these have their counterparts in the earlier post-Enlightenment rationality (Herder, Semler, Ewald, and even Bishop Ussher).

MacDonald's achievement is in bringing greater clarity to Barth's understanding of the Bible's claim to speak the truth about historical reality, as that which constitutes its own unique and quite unparalleled inner nerve. As he puts it in an early footnote, "Good ideas on what is in the Bible have to have their day. Perhaps the Barth of the *Dogmatics* is still in front of us, not behind us." MacDonald makes good on showing that this is so. What is in the Bible is a strange new world. Barth's argument is not that we are absorbed into that world, as some more recent "post-conceptualities" might conceive it. The strange world within the Bible is historical and it speaks of and refers to genuine realities outwith its linguistic expression, even as the historical reality to which it refers is not what is meant by modernity. The point is not that we are absorbed into anything, nor is it that our imaginations are stirred (though that may well happen). The Bible's unique truth-claiming form (what Barth calls *Sage*) serves the purpose of locating us in time and under the judgement of God as reconciler. In so doing the Bible reveals God as God, and His reality in this world as reconciler. (Here again, we are in MacDonald's debt for showing how and where Barth differed from Calvin or Thomas on believing God to be visible in the theatre of the created world. We do not know God in creation; we know God as reconciler of creation. I cannot improve on or adequately paraphrase MacDonald's own careful formulation.)

*****

I was fortunate to have studied, and then taught, at Yale, while Hans Frei was still alive and teaching. I watched the transition to a new period, and especially the subtle shift expressed by the arrival of Nicholas Wolterstorff and the later work of George Lindbeck (see now his essay in the Childs Festschrift, *Theological Exegesis*, Eerdmans, 1998) and of Frei himself (in his "Will it Stretch or Break?" essay in response to Ricoeur and others). I watched the interpreters of Brevard Childs seek to understand (Noble, Brett), and on occasion correct (Barton) or angrily rebuke (Barr) him. It appeared that the sharp edge of Barth's own thinking was being dulled, taxonomised, transformed, or misunderstood, as a new wave of hermeneutical proposals sought to assess the damage done by modernity and make their attendant contributions (Fowl, Watson, Vanhoozer, Hays). Of course, Barth has himself been the subject of much recent resourcement (Wolterstorff, Rogers, Ward, Webster, Hart, McCormack).

What has been needed is a more comprehensive investigation into the history of ideas (what Childs used to call, "the history of history"), into which could then be fitted the contribution of Barth. Not for the purposes of becoming a Barthian, God forbid; but for the purpose of coming to terms with Barth as a reader of scripture. I concur with MacDonald: Barth is in this sense not behind but ahead of us.

MacDonald has paid Karl Barth the highest tribute by locating him within the logic represented by Barth's own favoured tableau of the Isenheim Altar. Insofar as the strange new world becomes visible in Barth's analysis, he decreases, and it, or God as God, increases. MacDonald has given such clarity to Barth's work that the ultimate honour has been bestowed: Barth has decreased and the strange new world of the Bible has come into sharp focus.

Christopher R Seitz

# Acknowledgements

I would like to thank: Professors Christopher Seitz and Trevor Hart of the University of St Andrews for encouraging me to bring this project to completion; Martin Dotterweich of Crichton College, Memphis, USA for bringing his sharp mind to bear on what I have tried to say in the book (not least his efforts as regarding proof-reading an early draft). In respect of the latter, I should also thank Ronald Kerr for his assiduous deliberations on the letter of the typescript, and also Dr James L MacLeod of the University of Evansville, Indiana, USA. Others who deserve mention for their involvement at various stages in this work are Professor James P Mackey, Fergus Kerr, and Professor David Wright of New College, Edinburgh. Finally, I would like to thank the students of New College for many stimulating theological and biblical discussions during the year I have been there. They have encouraged me to think that some of the problems raised and faced in this book are the common concern of those who persist in wishing to take the Bible seriously as a claim upon reality. Five of the chapters - Chapters 1, 2, 3, 4, and 14 bear a resemblance to the PhD submitted to the University of Edinburgh in 1994. The other chapters are later developments.

Neil B MacDonald

# Introduction

The thesis of this book is simple. Karl Barth anticipated - in the true sense of the word - the reaction of the Enlightenment to the Bible. He forestalled its critique before it 'got going.' One may put it this way. The Enlightenment *esprit* manifested in the optimistic, positive, not to say discriminating, demeanour of that period was one with which the Bible was very much in harmony. One might go so far to say that, since the Bible had 'got there first', historically as it were, the Enlightenment *esprit*, though clearly not derivative in any plagiaristic sense, was a decidedly less original spirit than its advocates thought. It was not really new. Not without a certain irony did Barth conclude this, but he did conclude it. The Bible had 'got there first': it was as if there on its pages could be found the self-same criticisms that the Enlightenment had directed against the Bible itself. Barth's reaction to Franz Overbeck was instructive in this respect. When Overbeck rejected the possibility of a non-eschatological Christianity, Barth's response was precisely one of blithe accord: "Quite so, Overbeck!: a Christianity which is not utterly and absolutely eschatological has nothing to do with Christ!" This of course is one of many famous aphorisms Barth uttered on the pages of *Romans* II. The utterance - with all its ironic implications - set a pattern of response that pervaded the later, and (in my mind) greater work, the *Church Dogmatics*.[1]

---

[1] When I started work on this book I intended to recreate a vision of the past, to recreate in words a certain epoch in the history of theological ideas. I hope it is this; but I hope it is more too. As I made progress I realised that this history of ideas was not confined to the past but had enduring worth in face of the present. Accordingly, if there is a tension in the book it lies in the fact that, among other things, we seem to emerge from the past into the present when we move from *Romans* II to the *Church Dogmatics*. It seems to me that, notwithstanding current 'post-modern' analyses, *Romans* II is more firmly attached to the past - the specific past of the first two decades of Central European history this century - than the *Dogmatics* (a similar point can be made when comparing Wittgenstein's *Tractatus* with his *Philosophical Investigations*). The *Dogmatics* has

Barth's response to Overbeck was primarily a matter of the truth of the Bible. It was also a matter of resolving what I call Overbeck's metatheological dilemma. If the historical truth-claims of the Bible were true then it followed that historical truth-claims pertaining to events of a particular *theological* historicality were true. But if this was the case then it further followed that Overbeck's dilemma was resolved. Theology remained unalterably and irreducibly itself and did not become some other subject, anthropology or some other social or psychological science. Most importantly it was not to be assimilated to history of a certain kind, the kind of history that investigated the historical truth of the Bible with definite preconceptions regarding what it could and could not be claiming. It was not that Barth was against history *per se* (he is perhaps the most thorough-going historical truth-claiming theologian who has ever existed). Rather, he was against a conception of it which precluded exploring the historical truth-claims that were actually in the Bible. A blind-spot such as this had mistakenly led to the conclusion that theology did not exist in itself (retrospectively from the perspective of the *Church Dogmatics* this was Overbeck's fundamental error). The existence of theology ultimately depended on a category of historical truth that could be called *sui generis* historical truth. The best that could be said of principles such as those of Troeltsch – particularly his principle of analogy – was that they had neglected such historical truths. But according to Barth they were there in the Bible, and they were crucial to the existence of theology 'in and for itself.'

The matter of Barth's reaction to Overbeck has a decided Enlightenment precedent in philosophy. Kant claimed that Hume woke him from his "dogmatic slumber". One might say that Overbeck stirred Barth in just this way too. If Hume was right then according to Kant there was no such subject as philosophy. If Overbeck was right then there was no such subject as theology. Kant's response to Hume was this: the existence of philosophy 'in and for itself' depended on the existence of a certain class of truths, *a priori* synthetic truths. Such truths exist, *ergo* philosophy exists. Essentially Barth was to reason in the same way about *sui generis* historical truth – authentic theological truth.

Nevertheless, notwithstanding the philosopher Saul Kripke's ingenious argument about *a priori* contingent truths, the existence of *a priori* syntbetic truths has never been secure. It may be that Kant did not succeed to resolve the metaphilosophical dilemma. I believe this to be so. Though Kant's reaction to Hume provides the ready-made means of historical comparison and conceptual analysis – it is in this sense that Kant can be read as a theological counterpart to Barth - it was really Ludwig

---

enduring worth in the face of the present. Good ideas on what is in the Bible have to have their day. Perhaps the Barth of the *Dogmatics* is still in front of us, not behind us.

Wittgenstein who resolved the metaphilosophical dilemma. In this sense it can be argued that Wittgenstein is the true philosophical counterpart to Barth.

To read Barth as the theological counterpart to Kant, and most especially of Wittgenstein may seem problematic given a certain exclusively "neo-orthodox" reading of Barth. Nevertheless I am forced to conclude that it is justified. Not that Barth was not neo-orthodox in some ways: it has rightly been pointed out that his preference in Christology was to engage with the sixteenth and seventeenth centuries and not the twentieth. He also, like the Reformers, affirmed the canonical (final) form of the biblical text. Nevertheless, Barth can rightly be seen in the context of the Reformation only if he is first refracted through the lens of the Enlightenment. For only then can one understand how Barth, as a man of his time, was able to share with the earlier centuries a moral desire to take the final form of the biblical text seriously, both religiously and intellectually.

A man of his time. Barth was certainly this; not only in the obvious sense that is true of us all but in the more important sense that he did not feel the need to turn his back on the intellectual ethos of his age: the cultural, scientific, historical investigations and discoveries of his time. Rather, his task as he saw it was essentially a simple one. In essence it meant that he set out what the Bible actually said and - without any hint of apologetic - juxtaposed this understanding to the essence of what the Enlightenment had to say. He did not find the two incompatible. The Bible was true because there was a crucial though historically neglected sense in which what it claimed was historically true; it therefore anticipated the valid things - philosophical, historical, scientific, methodological, etc. - the Enlightenment had to say. Not to understand this is gravely to underestimate the cogency of Barth's theology, not least his view of the reasonableness of the Bible.

The other thing I wish to say is a corollary of the above. Barth did not pour cold water on the achievements of the theological tradition of the nineteenth century. He did not do this. He thought that the representatives of this tradition were people of the highest integrity, drawing the conclusions they felt morally compelled to draw, from premises they thought were unavoidable. Overbeck is perhaps the most radical figure in this respect, though Barth had great respect for other, perhaps less gifted, figures of nineteenth-century theological thought. One may put it this way: he had more in common with traditions that faced the problems of the Bible and theology with intellectual honesty, with passion and rigour, than he did with those movements, past and present, which sought to move desired conclusions by side-stepping, through dubious meta-argument, the critical apparatus of the Enlightenment. To be sure, he did not agree with the conclusions of those who had embarked on a scientific study of the historical Jesus but he thought their reasoning on the whole had been sound. It was, to repeat, simply that they had reasoned from false premises, false premises as regards, for example, what historical truth-claims the Bible was actually making. It was as a result of this judgement that he did not concur with the pathos that had emerged from this study, the pathos that was anticipated in such as Arnold's "Dover Beach" and came to fulfilment in Schweitzer's *The Quest of the Historical Jesus*. When Barth said at the end of his life, "Our God will reign!", he said nothing that was out of joint with the Enlightenment legacy.

Bruce McCormack wonders whether Barth needed Kantian epistemology to describe his understanding of revelation. "To that question", McCormack replies, "I would say, it may indeed prove possible to improve on Kant; to retain Barth's theological epistemology while making adjustments in the philosophical conceptuality he employed to explicate it."[2] This book goes some way to showing that such an improvement might be possible. *Inter alia*, it provides a twentieth-century conceptuality for Barth's theology in the form of Ludwig Wittgenstein, establishing Barth's current relevance by positing his connections with more recent philosophical developments. But it is not for that reason an anachronistic reading of Barth. The reading remains faithful to Barth's historical antecedents: the Enlightenment and the Reformed tradition; Wittgenstein too can be understood within the bounds of this joint legacy. Nevertheless, while it affirms the historical and conceptual relevance of Wittgenstein's philosophy to Barth's theology, it makes no apology for the fact that it is neither a post-modern reading nor essentially a narrative reading though, in respect of the latter, it seeks to satisfy contemporary concerns in biblical hermeneutics. What is critical for Barth is the presence of "the strange new world within the Bible" (the phrase is taken from the title of a lecture he gave in 1917), intimating *a sui generis* historicality, what Barth calls in *Church Dogmatics* IV/1, "a historical sphere of a different kind [*ein Geschichtsbereich anderer, eigener Art*]" differing formally from 'critical-historical' history in the way in which it took place in the human sphere and human time, and therefore in the way in which it had to be understood as history.[3] *Sui generis* historicality - the concept (and actuality) of *a historical event whose only means of measurement is it itself* - is the fundamental rationale behind his position on the Bible as regards historical truth-claims, literal sense, and the final form of the text.

The book opens with an account of the historical rationale behind Barth's discovery of the strange new world within the Bible. The strange new world within the Bible is Barth's attempt to seize the horns of Franz Overbeck's metatheological dilemma: since modern theology was in fact a species of non-theology (religious or 'non-unique' history, anthropology, the social and

---

[2] Bruce L McCormack, "Barth in Context: A Response to Professor Gunton", *The Scottish Journal of Theology* 49 4 (1996), 498.
[3] Barth, *Church Dogmatics* IV/1, 334.

psychological sciences in general), the choice theologians faced was that of doing non-theology or nothing. Barth's relation to Overbeck is illuminated in terms of Kant's relation to Hume's metaphilosophical dilemma: since philosophy was reducible to non-philosophy (the empirical sciences), philosophers were faced with non-philosophy or nothing (Chapter 1). Chapter 2 introduces Barth and Wittgenstein in the context of the possible influence each could have had on the other. Notwithstanding the apparent lack of cross-fertilisation, the larger historical picture of Chapter 3 integrates Barth's metatheological concerns with Wittgenstein's metaphilosophical ones in the *Tractatus Logico-Philosophicus*: the origin of Wittgenstein's historical and cultural relevance to Barth is traced from the tradition of the *Tractatus* represented by key figures of "Wittgenstein's Vienna" - the satirist Karl Kraus, the composer Arnold Schoenberg and the architect Adolf Loos.

The strange new world within the Bible (whose character is the subject of Chapters 4 and 5) is the rationale behind a new reading of Barth's conception of the *analogia fidei* in the *Church Dogmatics* (Chapter 6). Barth's conception is assimilated to the Reformed tradition's understanding of the *analogia fidei* as a 'measure of faith' - a means of measurement of truth and meaning. This interpretation breaks with the received view of the *analogia fidei* as essentially a matter of analogical correspondence. By combining the consequences of the presence of the strange new world within the Bible with his conception of the *analogia fidei* (a conception fundamentally in continuity with the Reformed tradition), Barth was able to tackle the Enlightenment's conception of the problem of God, as exemplified by Kant's immanent 'measure of the divine' in the latter's *Religion Within the Limits of Reason Alone*. The relevance of Troeltsch's principle of analogy is also a primary focus. The fact that the strange new world within the Bible is a 'measure of faith' whose only point of comparison is it itself - that it can be measured only against itself - proves to be crucial to affirmation of the historical truth of the Bible. Chapters 7 and 8, respectively, elucidate the *sui generis* historicality of the creation history and the resurrection-appearances history. Chapter 9 completes the analysis of the latter: in particular it clarifies a crucial aspect as regards the historical status of the resurrection-appearances history. Chapter 10 completes the understanding of Barth's position on historical epistemology focussing on the non-Kantian transcendental argument at the heart of it. Chapter 11 examines Barth's view of the relation between, on the one hand, the historicity of the resurrection-appearances stories, and, on the other, the validity of a specifically theological interpretation of the pre-Easter Gospel narratives. This involves a new slant on the question of the historical Jesus as conceived by the nineteenth and the twentieth century.

It is at this point (Chapter 12) that the book restates its commitment to the comparative history of theological ideas as regards Barth and Wittgenstein. A new 'Reformed' interpretation of the later Wittgenstein is proposed as a corrective to the one traditionally represented in the theological literature, for example, in George Lindbeck's *The Nature of Doctrine*. The key argument of the 'Reformed' Wittgenstein is that doubt, for example, can only make sense measured against a pre-existing criterion of measurement - a philosophical *analogia fidei*, if you will. Meaning presupposes a foundational truth of some kind or another (hence the rationale behind the use of the phrase conceptual foundationalism as a description of the later philosophy). There is no doubt that the logical structure of Wittgenstein's key argument requires a substantive measure of old-fashioned mental labour before one can be confident one has successfully assimilated it. But the hard work will not be vain. It will reveal a stringency of rational argument not normally associated with the later Wittgenstein in theological circles. It will also by analogy reveal the cogency of Barth's argument as regards an event as an object of measurement whose only means of measurement is it itself.

The penultimate chapter is a postscript (Chapter 13). It shows how Barth and Wittgenstein can be assimilated into the epoch of history continuing on from the Enlightenment - the age of Hegel. This adds further credence to the view that the Enlightenment provides the point of departure for both thinkers. *Contra* post-modern proposals, Barth and Wittgenstein are best understood within the context of the age of Hegel and its own attempt to resolve the conflict between two ostensibly opposing historic aspirations: reason and 'desire.' The metadilemmas of the Enlightenment - and Barth's and Wittgenstein's respective solutions - constitute the fundamental rationale behind the manner of their resolution of the great problem of the age of Hegel. Finally, I bring the book to a close with an epilogue.

All in all, what I hope emerges from the book is not only a striking interpretation of Barth's theology; more importantly, what I hope emerges from Barth's theology is the most cogent argument since the Enlightenment, an argument he expounded on behalf of the rationality of the Christian faith in the face of a loss of belief in the truth of the Bible in the modern age.

# Abbreviations

## Barth

**CR II**   *Romans 1922*, translated by Sir Edwyn Hoskyns, (London: Oxford University Press, 1933).

**CD**   *Church Dogmatics*, edited by G W Bromiley and T F Torrance, (Edinburgh: T&T Clark, 1936-1969).

**FQI**   *Anselm: Fides Quaerens Intellectum. Anselm's Proof of the Existence of God in the Context of his Theological Scheme*, translated by Ian Robertson, (London: 1960; reprinted, Pittsburgh: The Pickwick Press, 1975).

**PT**   *Protestant Theology in the Nineteenth Century. Its Background and History*, translated by B Cozen and J Bowden, (London: SCM Press, 1972).

## Wittgenstein

**BB**   *Blue and Brown Books Preliminary Studies for the 'Philosophical Investigations'* (Oxford: Basil Blackwell, 1978).

**CV**   *Culture and Value*, edited by G H von Wright in collaboration with Heiki Nyman, (Oxford: Basil Blackwell, 1980).

**NB**   *Notebooks 1914-1916*, edited by G H von Wright and G E M Anscombe, translated by G E M Anscombe, (Oxford: Basil Blackwell, 1961).

**OC**   *On Certainty*, edited by G E M Anscombe and G H von Wright, translated by Denis Paul and G E M Anscombe, (Oxford: Basil Blackwell, 1969).

**PG**   *Philosophical Grammar*, edited by R Rhees and translated by A Kenny, (Oxford: Blackwell, 1974).

**PI**   *Philosophical Investigations*, edited by G E M Anscombe, (Oxford: Basil Blackwell, 1953).

**TLP**   *Tractatus Logico-Philosphicus*, translated by D F Pears and B F McGuinness, (London: Routledge and Kegan Paul, 1961).

**Z**   *Zettel*, edited by G E M Anscombe and G H Von Wright, (Oxford: Basil Blackwell, 1981).

... it is surely possible that even the most obstinate of unbelievers, whether or not they can come to a knowledge of the truth, can at least come to appreciate the inner consistency and to that extent the meaning of the evangelical message. If they do not, the community is well advised to ask itself whether this is not because of a deficiency in its own attention to the inner clarity, rationality, and perspicuity of the Gospel on the one side and neglect of the human means at its disposal on the other. It is thus advised to seek the fault in itself rather than the wicked world, and therefore with new zest and seriousness to make new and more energetic efforts in this direction. The Gospel is not generally knowable. But it is generally intelligible and explicable. For its content is rational and not irrational.

Karl Barth, *Church Dogmatics* IV/3.

It is much easier to point out the faults and errors in the work of a great mind than to give a distinct and full exposition of its value.

Schopenhauer, *Criticism of the Kantian Philosophy*

# PART I

## The MetaDilemmas of the Enlightenment:

## Karl Barth, Ludwig Wittgenstein, and "Wittgenstein's Vienna"

# Chapter 1
# Karl Barth and the Metatheological Dilemma

## 1. Introduction

To many, the assertion that the theology of Karl Barth was ultimately loyal to the Enlightenment legacy, must seem *prima facie* implausible. But it is possible to identify Barth's theology, rather than, for example, Schleiermacher's, as the true heir of the Enlightenment legacy. Indeed, not only does Barth take up the challenge of the Enlightenment legacy: to the extent that his theology cannot be understood apart from the *metatheological dilemma* of Franz Overbeck, it cannot be understood apart from the Enlightenment. Kant defined autonomy as the self-determination of the will, apart from any object willed; the autonomy of theology implies the self-determination of theology apart from objects external to theological truth, i.e., non-theology (history, anthropology, psychology, and the social sciences in general).[1]

## 2. Kant's Response to Hume's Metaphilosophical Dilemma

Not only is there nothing about the Enlightenment that patently precludes Barth from being theological heir to its legacy, the definitive parameters of the problematic which Barth's theology made its own, the underlying historical dynamic without which the identity of Barth's theology remains hidden, have no historical precedent other than the later stages of the Enlightenment, and,

---

[1] In referring to history as non-theology I am referring to the *discipline* of history not the realm of historical *event* (I shall have more to say about this distinction in Chapter 7 where the former is understood as *Historie*, the latter *Geschichte*). The discipline of history is defined by Barth specifically as a commitment to particular historical *methodological presuppositions* characteristic of the critical-historical method. What these are will be seen in Chapters 6, 7, and 8.

in particular, Hume and Kant. Indeed, though it was Hume who inadvertently or otherwise[2] posed the problematic, it was not until Kant that the Enlightenment became truly self-conscious, which is to say, came face to face with the truly 'modern' predicament of metaphilosophical and metatheological dilemma.[3]

Some years before Kant's declaration of *Sapere Audere!* Hume had stated the case for the forces of reason somewhat more dramatically. However he intended the concluding paragraph of his *Enquiry Concerning Human Understanding* to have been read, it was subsequently interpreted as a clarion call for all enlightened thinkers to unleash the forces of reason on dogmatism wherever it existed:

> When we run over libraries, persuaded of these principles, what havoc must we make? If we take in our hand any volume; of divinity or school metaphysics, for instance; let us ask, Does it contain any abstract reasoning concerning quantity or number? No. Does it contain any experimental reasoning concerning matter of fact or existence? No. Commit it then to the flames: for it can contain nothing but sophistry and illusion.[4]

---

[2] G J Warnock writes: "[Kant] held that when [Hume] stated it, Hume had simply not realized the extent of the havoc that its acceptance would occasion." See G J Warnock, "Kant", in D J O'Connor (ed), *A Critical History of Western Philosophy* (New York: The Free Press of Glencoe, 1964), 299.

[3] Although the etymology of the word 'metaphysics' has the meaning 'after' (Aristotle's *Metaphysics*, and later the subject itself, was so-called because it came after the *Physics*), the customary meaning of 'meta' is 'about' as in 'meta-ethics', 'metahistory', and 'metalanguage'. Accordingly, where (Christian) theology is 'about' God, Jesus Christ, etc., (which constitute the 'objects' of theology), 'metatheological' is 'about' theology (i.e., theology itself constitutes the object of metatheological discourse); exactly the same distinction holds in the case of 'metaphilosophical': metaphilosophy is about philosophy, which in turn is 'about' mind, rationality, etc. Thus, for example, where philosophy might enquire into the existence of mind, metaphilosophy would enquire into the existence of philosophy itself. Accordingly, if it were demonstrated that philosophy did not exist then the question of the existence of mind would not be a philosophical question though it might well be a scientific (psychological or physiological) one. Similarly, if theology did not exist then questions related to the nature and existence of God would not be theological though it might be appropriate for science to study them.

[4] D Hume, *Enquiry Concerning Human Understanding and Concerning the Principles of Morals*, ed. by P H Nidditch, (Oxford: Oxford University Press, 1975), 165. That Hume's indictment should have cut at the very heart of theology ("divinity") is obviously of momentous importance. But for the moment I will focus on his reaction to "school metaphysics" only, since it is the consequence of "Hume's fork" for philosophy that concerns us here. A J Ayer cited "Hume's fork" as the basis for the position he took in *Language, Truth and Logic*, the Anglo-Saxon manifesto for logical positivism. A J

Corresponding to these two kinds of reasoning, abstract and experimental, were two types of truth, relations of ideas and matters of fact or real existence:

> All objects of human reason or enquiry may naturally be divided into two kinds, to whit, *relations of ideas*, and *matters of fact*. Of the first kind are the sciences of Geometry, Algebra, and Arithmetic .... [5]

The second are represented by the empirical sciences of physics, chemistry, history, etc. This justly celebrated classification of two types of truth, between on the one hand relations of ideas and, on the other, matters of fact - what has become known as "Hume's fork" - is what Kant speaks of when crediting Hume with waking him from his "dogmatic slumber".[6] Kant believed that philosophy was the one truly autonomous subject, subject only to the dictates of reason, because unlike the faculties of theology, law and medicine, it was free from the meddling of authority. But now, ironically, as a consequence of Hume's peerless example of criticism in action, philosophy as the very embodiment of reason appeared to have done away with itself. For Kant saw that if Hume's fork was an exhaustive and mutually exclusive scheme for the classification of truth and truths, no space was left for philosophy. Analytic truths aside (truths which were simply true by definition), all that was left were the truths of history, geography, astronomy, politics, natural philosophy, physics, chemistry, etc. In other words, if all substantive truths were *a posteriori* truths then the realm of truth was completely accounted for in terms of non-philosophy; there simply were no truths that philosophy could claim as its own. In other words, Hume had announced the end of philosophy as an autonomous subject. Every truth formerly cited as an example of philosophy was in

---

Ayer, *Language, Truth and Logic*, revised edition, (London: Victor Gollancz, 1946), 2. Stroud points out the difference between Ayer's logical positivism and Humean empiricism. Where Ayer condemns all theological statements to the realm of semantic meaninglessness, Hume concludes that they are not appropriate topics for reasoning. See B Stroud, *Hume*, (London: Routledge and Kegan Paul, 1981), 220. For a history of positivism from Hume to the logical positivists, see L Kolakowski, *Positivist Philosophy. From Hume to the Vienna Circle* (Middlesex: Penguin Books Ltd, 1972).

[5] Hume, *Enquiry*, 25.

[6] Kant, *Prolegomena to Any Future Metaphysics*, translated by P G Lucas, (Manchester: Manchester University Press, 1953), 9. A Flew points out that though such a distinction is present in Leibniz, Hume is the philosopher who made its epistemological implications clear to Kant. See A Flew, *David Hume: Philosopher of Moral Science* (Oxford: Blackwell, 1986), 45.

actual fact either meaningless,[7] or a function of, and hence reducible to, a truth of non-philosophy, (natural philosophy, physics, chemistry, history, etc.).

Kant's resolution of the dilemma posed by Hume for philosophy was to add to Hume's truths of matters of fact and existence what for him was the patent existence of *a priori* synthetic truths.[8] As Körner puts it he "does not accept the Humean dichotomy of meaningful propositions because he believes that as a matter of fact we are in possession of propositions which fall into neither of Hume's two classes; they form a third class whose logical nature, function, and systematic connexion, with each other and with other types of proposition is the main topic of his own philosophy."[9] Hume's bipartite classification becomes a tripartite classification. This third class is in fact a second sub-class of the class of Hume's truths of matters of fact and existence. Not all synthetic truths are *a posteriori*; some are *a priori*. Therefore while Kant accepts Hume's general concept of truth, he augments this general class of truths to include truths that while known *a priori* (before experience) were yet synthetic (truths whose negation was not a contradiction in terms) and accordingly informative about the world.

Yet, as Körner puts it, the mere fact that we use *a priori* synthetic principles in our judgements "does not by itself imply that we have a 'right' to use them, since it may well be that we thereby in some sense misrepresent reality. [...] Thus there arises the problem of going beyond the fact of our use of the categories, and of proving the validity of this use or rightfulness."[10] Such proof cannot be experimental (or abstract), so Kant introduces an additional mode of reasoning, namely what he calls the *transcendental deduction*.[11] This mode of reasoning has to show that "without the Categories [i.e., the *a priori* synthetic principles], the experience of objects, i.e., objective experience (*Erfahrung*] as opposed to the mere occurrence of impressions, would be impossible."[12] By this means Kant attempted to resecure philosophy's own special identity by recasting it as a *transcendental* science specifying the conditions of the possibility of all experience. Such conditions constituted both a framework and a boundary

---

[7] Flew writes that one of the items of "divinity and school metaphysics" that Hume must have had in mind was the 'Arguments for the existence of God' drawn up in geometric fashion, which Descartes had appended to the set of objections to his meditations. *Ibid*, 69-70.

[8] Warnock, "Kant", 299.

[9] S Körner, *Kant* (Middlesex: Penguin Books, 1955), 18.

[10] *Ibid*, 57.

[11] Kant, *The Critique of Pure Reason*, translated by N Kemp Smith, (London, MacMillan, 1933), 120-175.

[12] Körner, *Kant*, 57.

within which empirical truth was apprehended. Thus the *a priori* synthetic principle 'Every event has a cause' specified both a framework and a boundary within which empirical science established its truths. Philosophy was in that sense restored to its rightful place as queen of all the sciences.

Philosophy was no longer threatened with redundancy and extinction; on the contrary, Kant had apparently imbued it with a new life of its own such that philosophy is once more philosophy in its own right.

### 3. Barth's Response to Overbeck's Metatheological Dilemma

Historically, the theological response to the Enlightenment was to Kant, not Hume. After Kant, theology took an anthropocentric turn. Kant's critical philosophy not only made room for itself, it made room for faith: "I have found it necessary to deny knowledge, in order to make room for faith."[13] Theologians occupied this space in various ways, the most influential being Schleiermacher's advocacy of faith as feeling [*Gefühl*]. While Barth does not dispute, and indeed is a proponent of, the *historical* thesis that Schleiermacher was the principal theological *Endstation* of the Enlightenment, he sets himself against the view that Schleiermacher is the *inevitable* legatee of the Enlightenment:

> Positively or negatively we can draw lines from everywhere leading to Schleiermacher, from every point we can come to understand that for his century he was not only one among many others, with his theology and philosophy of religion, but that it was possible for him to have the significance of the fullness of time. I do not say it was inevitable but possible. Whether the century understood itself rightly in thinking it heard the liberating world from Schleiermacher, whether it might not have been possible to gain further insights of an entirely different kind from all the points which Schleiermacher had touched upon - that is a different question.[14]

It is not the Enlightenment legacy *per se* that Barth is against but rather the particular historical twist Schleiermacher gives it.[15] Schleiermacher,

---

[13] Kant, *Critique*, 29.

[14] Barth, *Protestant Theology*, 427-428.

[15] Barth took a resolutely 'anti-historicist' view of the Enlightenment. That is, he believed that the Enlightenment could have developed in ways other than it did. For example, he wrote: "Despite the great stress that has been placed on the significance of the change in the picture of the world and the rise of scientific and mathematical thought, it should not be over-estimated here: a man like Leibnitz, who occupies so

rather than the Enlightenment, is Barth's alter-ego. Moreover, it does not strain the bounds of credulity to suggest that, however faintly, Barth hints that he himself is the true legatee of the Enlightenment. Can we take him seriously? Can we amplify Barth's faint hint into an assertion worthy of serious consideration?[16]

Claude Welch categorises Barth as one more major theological reaction, and in this sense, variation on Kant:

> Kant ... is above all the philosopher with whom the nineteenth century theologians had to reckon. After him, four possible routes may be distinguished, all of which were travelled to a greater or lesser extent. One was to question the validity of the first critique's restriction of theoretical

---

exalted a place in modern intellectual history and who incorporates its results so consistently into his system, shows that it is quite possible to know everything that could be known of philosophy and science at the time without the necessity of taking the offensive even against dogma, let alone the Bible. He was able to struggle in his own way to combine the traditional church doctrine of the Trinity and even the specifically Protestant dogmas of predestination and justification within his theory of monads and of pre-established harmony. Things did not *necessarily* (from that point at any rate) have to come out differently. That they did come out differently was only a matter of fact, or rather, was governed by a necessity which had its grounds elsewhere." *Ibid,* 102. Indeed, it is striking that when speaking of Enlightenment reason, Barth is never anything other than complementary. As if calling into question the rival interpretations of rationalist and traditional Barthian alike, Barth begins Chapter 3 of *Dogmatics in Outline* with a statement that is eminently Enlightenment philosophy: "Possibly you may be struck by the emergence of the concept of reason. I use it deliberately. The saying 'Despise only reason and science, man's supremest power of all', was uttered not by a prophet, but by Goethe's Mephisto. Christendom and the theological world were always ill-advised in thinking it their duty for some reason or other, either of enthusiasm or of theological conception, to betake themselves to the camp of an opposition to reason." Barth, *Dogmatics in Outline*, translated by G T Thomson, (London: SCM Press, 1949), 22.

[16] Trutz Rendorff has advanced the thesis that the historical significance of Barth consists in his positing the radical autonomy of God. According to Rendorff this is how Barth satisfies the Enlightenment principle. As J Macken puts it, according to Rendorff: "The Enlightenment with its principle of autonomy, must be radically adopted or not at all. Barth chose to adopt the principle of autonomy in a radical sense, but instead of accommodating himself to the historical event of the Enlightenment, as liberal theology had done, he presented the principle of autonomy in a new systematic construction as a challenge at every point to the accepted self-understanding of the Enlightenment. What Barth represented was a new Enlightenment that turned on the Enlightenment itself the same critical weaponry which the Enlightenment had formerly used against religion. He replaced the freedom and autonomy of man with the freedom and autonomy of God." J Macken S.J., *The Autonomy Theme in the Church Dogmatics. Karl Barth and his Critics* (Cambridge: Cambridge University Press, 1990), 125.

knowledge or cognition, either (as in the idealistic philosophy) by "more consistently" and "courageously" following out Kant's speculative principle and overcoming the phenomenal-noumenal "dualism" or by some revised program of natural theology that would take account of Kant's work (e.g. in more recent neo-Thomism). The second, a minor stream in the nineteenth century which was renewed in the twentieth by Karl Barth, was the acceptance of reason's criticism of its limits and thereby the denial of reason's right to establish the point of departure for theology. [...] The third, which was to be taken up most dramatically in the Ritschlian school, was the full acceptance of the Kantian critique of theoretical reason and adoption of the moral as the basis of proceeding. The fourth, by far the most widely followed, was to enlarge the category of direct experience by turning to *Gefühl* (Schleiermacher), *Abhang* (De Witte), or by finding in a fuller "reason" the possibility of knowing the spiritual (Coleridge). In all these ways however there was reflected a Socratic turn to the role of the subject, in faith and knowledge, a turn which had its epistemological expression in Kant's analysis in the *Critique of Pure Reason.*[17]

But not only is it a mistake to assimilate Barth to Kierkegaard in this way (the preeminent example of the "minor stream in the nineteenth century"), there is yet a deeper fault with this analysis, one which ironically serves to obfuscate the real significance of Kant for Barth. Had Barth's theology really participated in the turn to the subject prevalent at the time, it could not have escaped being a function of philosophy (and hence a second-order response to Hume). But where in Kant theology is a second-order function of Hume's problematic, and hence a (first-order) function of philosophy,[18] Barth's theology, like Kant's philosophy itself, is a *direct first-order* response to Hume.[19]

---

[17] Welch, *Protestant Thought*, vol 1 (New Haven: Yale, 1972), 47-48.

[18] Thus Kant's rational theology is in the precise sense of the term a *philosophical* theology, i.e., theology as a function of philosophy. See A W Wood, *Kant's Rational Theology* ((Ithaca: Cornell University Press, 1978), 22-23.

[19] Bruce McCormack's rightly acclaimed book, *Karl Barth's Critically Realistic Dialectical Theology* implicitly endorses the conclusion that Kant did not resolve the metatheological dilemma. Kant's focus was firmly on the metaphilosophical dilemma articulated by Hume. Since theology for him was firmly a function of his philosophy, his theology could not in principle resolve the metatheological dilemma. But, as McCormack rightly notes, one way of characterising Barth's resolution of the dilemma is to say that he stated his resolution in terms of Kantian conceptuality. Indeed, McCormack argues that Barth's theological epistemology and the philosophical conceptuality he employed to explicate it remained basically unchanged from *Romans* II through *Anselm: Fides Quaerens Intellectum* to the *Church Dogmatics*. Bruce Lindley McCormack, *Karl Barth's*

Accordingly, Barth's theology, unlike Schleiermacher's, is not a turn to the subject at all. (Kant's faith-knowledge demarcation is neither a necessary nor a sufficient condition of the *sui generis* identity of theology.)[20] His theology makes a qualitatively different response. Instead

---

*Critically Realist Dialectical Theology* (Oxford: Oxford University Press, 1995). In a recent review article he presents a succinct and penetrating statement of Barth's theological epistemology expressed in this conceptuality. It is, as he implies, an unambiguously Kantian conceptuality. He wrote: "... God is the one noumenal reality which - precisely because He is the omnipotent divine Subject who created all things and is therefore Lord even over the subject-object split - is capable of grasping us through the phenomena from the other side. Without setting aside or altering the cognitive apparatus as it is given in the human knower, God makes Himself the object of our knowledge by giving Himself to be known in and through a creaturely veil and granting to us the eyes of faith to see what there is to see in this veil." McCormack, "Review Article: Graham Ward's *Barth, Derrida and the Language of Theology*" *The Scottish Journal of Theology* 49 1 (1996), 105-106. It goes without saying that this is not Kant's position (it could not be), but Barth's. Hence once again there is here corroboration that Kant and the metatheological dilemma have only a negative, and not a positive, relation to each other. The question remains whether characterising Barth's response to the metatheological dilemma in terms of Kantian conceptuality commits one to the conclusion that Barth's response is a second-order response, and not a first-order one. Given that I understand Barth's response as a first-order response to Hume - through the medium of Overbeck - obviously I am committed to the conclusion that it does not. My argument that the intellectual impetus of Barth's response is antecedent to the Kantian revolution, the anthropocentric turn, and has its origins in Hume, is based on the following premise. Overbeck's critique of theology assumes nothing of Kant's critique. Overbeck's critique of theology, based as it is on unfulfilled hopes of a future eschatological event (the *parousia*), challenges theology on the grounds of false historical fact or truth. That is, rather than shunt theology off into the side-track of miracle, Overbeck's critique presupposes the kind of analysis Hume brings to bear on the fact of the sun rising every morning (inductive reasoning); he anticipates the Popperian principle of falsifiability, observes the 'event' of falsification, and concludes that Christianity and hence theology has been falsified. One characterisation of Barth's response to this in *Romans* II for example, is to say that he stated the eschatological event in terms of Kant's concept of noumenal reality thereby evading Overbeck's critical-historical strictures. But the response, I submit, remains a first-order response to Overbeck.

[20] Barth readily agreed with Kant that the "biblical theologian proves that God exists by means of the fact that he has spoken in the Bible." See Barth, *Protestant Theology*, 312. But Kant's philosophical scheme implicitly allows for the possibility that the resultant theology can be theology as a function of philosophy. Therefore it is not a sufficient condition of the autonomy of theology. But neither is it a necessary condition. In other words, *pace* Welch, it does not follow that Barth's theology accepted "reason's criticism of its limits" and "*thereby* [my italics] the denial of reason's right to establish the point of departure for theology." See Welch, *Protestant Theology*, vol i, (New Haven: Yale University Press, 1972), 47. Whether Barth accepted the former or not was independent

Barth, in making a first-order response, seeks, again like Kant, to deal with Hume's dilemma at the first-order level of *truth*. Historically, of course Barth did not, as Kant did, deal with Hume directly (Barth's is an indirect direct first-order response); rather it was in the form and figure of Franz Overbeck (1837-1905) that Barth encountered Hume. Overbeck's critique of theology, like Barth's theology itself, is not dependent on Kant's anthropocentric turn implicit in his critique of the bounds of reason.

Overbeck's reputation in Basel was - as Hume's had been in Edinburgh - that of a dissenter from, and despoiler of, mainstream opinion on Christianity. It is surely no historical accident that both Overbeck and Hume were in their respective life times castigated, even reviled, as objects of anxiety, fear and trepidation for exercising the most trenchant and iconoclastic criticism of religion. (Yet Bernoulli describes Overbeck in terms that would not have been inappropriate had he been speaking of Hume: Overbeck the sceptic is "'a happy, loving, doubter'".)[21] Overbeck the learned historian and scholar was "the diagnostician of the end of Christianity, not a proclaimer like his friend Nietzsche."[22] But though in Basel "the mere mention of Overbeck's name was enough to make everyone's hair stand on end",[23] Overbeck was treated somewhat less prejudicially than Hume in that where Hume was twice denied a university chair (in philosophy) for his "atheistic" or "aggressively agnostic" views, Overbeck, though perceived as an *enfant terrible*, became Professor of Church History at the University of Basel.

Though Overbeck was separated from Hume by more than a century, he pushed the metatheological dilemma implicit in Hume to its explicit logical conclusion.[24] For once again, just as in the case of philosophy, if Hume was

---

of the implicit affirmation in his work of the latter. That is, he could accept the antecedent without *deriving* the consequent (which latter he could implicitly affirm on other grounds).

[21] *Ibid*, 58.

[22] E Jüngel, *Karl Barth. A Theological Legacy*, translated by G Paul, (Pennsylvania: Westminster Press, 1986), 56.

[23] E Busch, *His Life From Letters and Autobiographical Texts*, translated by J Bowden, (London: SCM Press, 1976), 115.

[24] I have come across one other citation of the term "metatheological" in the literature: Raeburn S Heimbeck, *Theology and Meaning: A Critique of Metatheological Scepticism* (London: Allen and Unwin Ltd, 1969). As the metatheological consequence of logical positivism, the position of metatheological scepticism is that God-talk is meaningless, not true (e.g., theological realism) or false (theological scepticism). Hence, it is no surprise that Heimbeck cites A J Ayer's *Language Truth and Logic* as the earliest and pre-eminent example of this species of scepticism. *Ibid*, 22. Resolving Overbeck's dilemma is a more demanding task than disproving metatheological scepticism since to show that terms such as 'God' or 'Jesus Christ' are meaningful does

right theology was in actual fact a function of, and hence reducible to, non-theology. The domain of Hume's truths of matter of fact and existence is constituted by reasonings concerning either *particular* or *general facts*:

> Moral reasonings are either concerning particular or general facts. All deliberations regard the former, as are disquisitions of history, chronology, geography and astronomy.
>
> The sciences, which treat general facts, are comprised of politics, natural philosophy, physic, chemistry, &c ....
>
> Divinity or Theology as it proves the existence of a Deity and the immortality of souls, is composed partly of reasons concerning particular, partly concerning general facts.[25]

But though Hume goes on to reaffirm that theology "has a foundation in *reason*",[26] he quickly inserts the qualification that this is "so far as it is supported by experience."[27] It is clear he thinks it is *not* supported by experience, hence not by reason either. Thus in order to restore the situation and appease conventional religious sensibility[28] he (perhaps even more

---

not resolve this dilemma, i.e., it is not a sufficient condition of the existence of theology. Conversely, to resolve Overbeck's dilemma is a sufficient condition of the meaningfulness of these terms. This is why Barth is better understood as responding to Hume rather than to the logical positivists.

[25] Hume, *Enquiries*, 164-5.

[26] *Ibid*, 165.

[27] *Ibid*, 165. "All our reasonings concerning matters of fact are founded on a species of Analogy, which lead us to expect from any cause the same events, which we have observed from similar causes." (*Ibid*, 104) For Hume reasoning is either experimental and therefore what we would call inductive reasoning, or abstract reasoning and therefore what we would call deductive reasoning. Given that constant conjunction - for Hume the basis of science - is the basis of experimental reasoning, insofar as revelatory theology was based on a non-replicable event, it was not a suitable subject of reason. Thus according to Flew: "Theology was even prepared to concede a little to natural science, if in exchange it could be assured the mark of scientific method." See Flew, *David Hume*, 16. Hendel writes: "He [Hume] wants to evaluate natural theology according to the criterion of natural science." See C W Hendel, *Studies in the Philosophy of David Hume* (New York: Bobbs-Merrill, 1963), 267.

[28] According to N Kemp Smith, Hume, as in the *Dialogues concerning Natural Religion*, makes mention of, but certainly does not take refuge in, "revealed truth" as a "conventionally required proviso". N Kemp Smith (ed), *Hume's Dialogues Concerning Natural Religion*, 2nd ed., edited with an introduction by Kemp Smith, (New York: Social Science Publishers, 1948), 74. Nor does he make "the conventionally required concessions in regard to faith and revelation." *Ibid*, 63. Similarly, Hume appears to have second thoughts on the rationality of revealed religion at the close of Section X 'Of Miracles' in the *Enquiry*. See Hume, *Enquiries*, 131. A E Taylor describes this as a

quickly than before) adds: "But its best and most solid foundation is *faith and divine revelation*."[29]

But even had Hume been more positive, even had he answered the question of the existence of a Deity in the affirmative, theology would still have been dissolved in the process. In other words, Hume had dispatched and dispersed theology throughout the domain of non-theology, assimilating it here as natural science, there as history or anthropology. To echo what was said of philosophy: theology was no longer an autonomous subject; every truth formerly cited as an example of theology was in actual fact either meaningless, or a function of, and hence reducible to, a truth of non-theology (natural philosophy, physics, history, anthropology, etc.); there simply were no truths that theology could claim as its own. One either did non-theology or nothing.

Overbeck, like Hume, is a trenchant and radical critic of Christianity; but it is as an inspired metatheological critic rather than a sceptic that he accordingly inspires Barth.[30]

---

"volte-face". See A E Taylor, *Philosophical Studies* (London: MacMillan, 1934), 341. Flew describes it as "blisteringly sardonic". See Flew, *Hume's Philosophy of Belief: a study of his first 'Inquiry'* (London: Routledge and Kegan Paul, 1961), 210.

[29] Hume, *Enquiries*, 165. According to Flew the most powerful case in Hume's day for the existence of God was developed in two stages: (1) arguments of natural reason supplemented by (2) particular revelation constituting sufficient historical evidence to prove the constitutive and enduring miracles of Christianity. See Flew, *David Hume*, 61-62. Flew writes: "Hume is engaged in a question of evidence rather than a question of fact. What he means to establish is not that miracles do not occur, although he does make it plain that this was his own view as well as that of all other men of sense; but that, whether or not they did or did not occur, this is not something we can any of us ever be in a position to know." *Ibid*, 80. But for Hume not only is it something we are not in a position to know, it is something we are not in a position to reason about. In other words, given Hume's definition of experimental reasoning as constant conjunction, miracles are not an appropriate subject of rational discourse. That a miracle has occurred is a question for faith since the former is a particular fact one cannot reason about.

[30] Barth writes that Overbeck "stands just on the boundary between" "sceptic" and "inspired critic". "And one side of his nature (if one can speak of two sides) will be comprehensible through the other." Barth, "Unsettled Questions in Theology Today", in Karl Barth, *Theology and Church*, with an introduction by T F Torrance, translated by L Pettibone Smith, (London: SCM Press Ltd, 1962), 58. Jüngel, quoting Overbeck, also reads his critique of Christianity and the Christian-ness of theology as indicative of a metatheological dilemma: "an eschatological faith cannot tolerate any theology; on the other hand, 'theology insofar as it is a scholarly discipline, does not itself possess any proper principles of knowledge.' And since theology can no longer dictate to other disciplines as it did in the Middle Ages, it must derive from them, so that 'even the delusion that [theology] is Christian is no longer possible.' 'Theology can demonstrate

Barth's essay on Overbeck, "Unsettled Questions for Theology Today", is in fact a review of Overbeck's work posthumously published under the title "Christianity and Culture". This work he judged to be

> an inconceivably impressive sharpening of the commandment 'Thou shalt not take the name of the Lord thy God in vain.' If it is read and understood, the normal effect would be that ninety-nine percent of us ... will make the discovery that it is impossible for anyone really to be such a thing as a theologian.[31]

According to Barth, Overbeck's great virtue is that he questioned the continued existence of theology. Though for Overbeck the burning issue revolves round the Christian-ness and hence religiousness of theology,[32] for Barth this signifies no less than the fate of theology itself: "How radically Overbeck questions the possibility of theology dominant today (and for him that meant questioning its *Christian-ness*,) and with what earnestness he renounced it .... Theology still owes the answer to the inquiry made to it in 1873 [in Overbeck's essay 'The Christian-ness of modern theology']."[33] Barth himself was under no illusion as to the answer: in its present condition theology was "now in a house built on sand."[34]

---

that it is an academic discipline only by selling out completely.'" See Jüngel, *Karl Barth,* 57. Unfortunately, "modern theology does not see through its self-deception. It does not recognise its own 'unhappy, hybrid, internally fragmented nature' and 'does not comprehend the confusion in which it is entangled.' According to Overbeck, this is its essential characteristic. He knows how distant he is from it, because he can see through it and recognized its essential inability to be a Christian theology." *Ibid*, 58.

[31] Barth, "Unsettled Questions for Theology Today", 57. Commenting on Barth's judgement, Jüngel writes: "Indeed, this was already evident in the polemical essay that Overbeck did publish during his lifetime. And Barth was also amazed 'that the theology that is dominant today could ... remain so indifferent to and untroubled by the questions he [Overbeck] put to it.'" Jüngel, *Karl Barth,* 59.

[32] Jüngel too sees Overbeck's critique of theology this way. Quoting Overbeck, he writes: "'As long as a religion is alive among us, everything connected with it is taken for granted, and it is not defended, because it needs no defence. As soon as it moves out into our culture, however, it dies as a religion and must draw its life from the vitality of the culture.' But theology belongs to culture insofar as it wishes to be scholarly. 'Therefore every theology, insofar as it relates faith to knowledge, is itself irreligious.'" *Ibid*, 57.

[33] *Ibid*, 71.

[34] *Ibid*, 57.

Overbeck claimed with some justification to be the only theologian of his generation who had looked into the mirror and faced reality.[35] Such veridical self-perception coupled to honest self-understanding consisted in the fact that when theology had looked in the mirror it had not recognised itself; for what had stared back at it was history, anthropology, etc.[36] In other words, Overbeck perceived that if there was no alternative to what his theological peers were doing, there was no subject called "theology". The eventual assimilation and absorption of theology to non-theology, reaching its apogee in the second half of the nineteenth century and culminating in the methodological programmes of von Harnack and Troeltsch,[37] had seen to that. Accordingly, Overbeck's conclusion amounted to the charge that if theology had any intellectual integrity at all it would acknowledge it no longer existed and had in fact ceased to exist some time before.

But, according to Barth, that Overbeck was never anything but a theologian explains why more positive statements - "which deal with the possibility of a theology of greater insight and more caution" -[38] "escaped the author almost against his will".[39] Examples Barth cites are:

---

[35] Jüngel observes: "His claim to be the only one who has realised this makes his remarks seem pointed and bold." See Jüngel, *Ibid*, 58. And Barth asks: "Why did no one listen to Overbeck?" See Barth, "Unsettled Questions for Theology Today", 56.

[36] Barth's interest in and positive appraisal of, Ludwig Feuerbach, is likewise explained by this theme of the autonomy of theology and the implied tension *vis-á-vis* non-theology. According to Barth, Feuerbach plays an identical role to Overbeck in the history of theology on the grounds that where Overbeck derived the non-existence of theology from the perspective of history, especially church history, Feuerbach derived the formally equivalent result from the perspective of anthropology. Theology is a function of anthropology, is therefore a function of non-theology. See Barth, "Introductory Essay", translated by J L Adams, in L Feuerbach, *The Essence of Christianity* (New York: Harper Torchbooks, 1957), x-xxxii. Barth especially singles out the liberal theology originating in Schleiermacher as an appropriate target for Feuerbach's critique. *Ibid*, xxii. Barth offered a similar appraisal of the significance of Feuerbach in his history of nineteenth-century Protestant theology. See Barth, *Protestant Theology*, 534-540. Notwithstanding the fact that Nietzsche is often bracketed with Overbeck (see for example Jenson, "Karl Barth", in D F Ford, *The Modern Theologians. An Introduction to Christian Theology in the Twentieth Century* (Oxford: Basil Blackwell, 1989), 28), Barth's lesser appreciation of the former is surely attributable to the fact that, unlike Overbeck, he has nothing substantial to say about the metatheological dilemma. Nietzsche, as Jüngel puts it, is simply a proclaimer not a diagnostician of the end of Christianity. Jüngel, *Karl Barth*, 56.

[37] See the collection of essays in J P Clayton, (ed), *Ernst Troeltsch and the future of theology* (Cambridge: Cambridge University Press, 1976).

[38] Barth, "Unsettled Questions for Theology Today", 72.

[39] *Ibid*, 72.

'Theology cannot be re-established except by audacity.' [...] 'Only a heroic Christianity which takes its position without regard to any era and establishes itself on itself alone can escape the fate of Jesuitizing.' [...] No presentation which attempts to 'establish Christianity historically will ever be possible; only that composed from the heart of the matter itself, the non-historical Christianity.'[40]

But as Barth is only too well aware, Overbeck's diagnosis of the condition of modern theology spares no prospect of cure:

I have no intention of reforming theology. I admit its nullity in and of itself and I am not merely attacking its temporary decay and its present basis.[41]

And Barth adds (not without irony):

An end to Christianity! (*Finis Christianismi!*) rings his prophetic imprecation - still more an end to theology![42]

Indeed, as Jüngel points out, Barth's understanding of the first remark missed Overbeck's point and was in fact rather a "grotesque misunderstanding."[43] For what Overbeck had actually said was: "It may be true that theology can no longer be re-established except by audacity. But what help is that to a person who has already lost faith in theology as a result of studying early church history!"[44] In other words, since it is none other than non-theology that leads to his loss of faith in the existence of theology, Overbeck's final submission to the thesis of the "nullity of theology in and of itself" is a corollary of endorsing the thesis that theology cannot be *other than* non-theology. Overbeck believed that one did non-theology or nothing. It is in this sense that he made explicit what was implicit in Hume. Do non-theology or nothing: this

---

[40] *Ibid*, 72.

[41] Quoted by Barth, *Ibid*, 71.

[42] *Ibid*, 71.

[43] Jüngel, *Karl Barth*, 54

[44] *Ibid*, 55. Jüngel writes: "Overbeck in one of his numerous sketches, as malicious as they were apt ... had sneered at the announcement of his Berlin colleague G Runze, who was publicizing his upcoming lectures on no less a topic than 'The Best That There Is to Know in the History of Religions'. By no means then, did Overbeck ever think that theology could - even with audacity - be 're-established'. The bitter irony of his remark makes it an argument *ad absurdum*. Either Barth did not notice this irony or he consciously ignored it." *Ibid*, 54-55. Whether Barth did not notice the undoubted irony or consciously ignored it, his response to Overbeck in both *Romans* II and the *Church Dogmatics* (as we shall see in Chapters 3 and 4) out-does Overbeck for irony.

is the metatheological dilemma, implicit in Hume, made explicit in Overbeck. Overbeck's dilemma is of immense importance to understanding Barth's theology: not only does it inform *Romans* II, it is the key to *Fides Quaerens Intellectum* and the *Church Dogmatics*. It is the key to *what it is* Barth is doing as theologian.[45]

---

[45] Ingolf Dalferth has discerned the relevance of such a dilemma for theology. Ingolf Dalferth, *Theology and Philosophy* (Oxford: Basil Blackwell, 1988), 13-17. In the course of a discussion on the existence of theology and its problems, he articulates his own version of the dilemma: "The argument so far has assumed that there are theological problems. But precisely this has been questioned. The problems which theology attempts to solve - as Hegel, Freud and logical empiricists have argued in their different ways - are said either to be unintelligible and thus unsolvable or, if they are intelligible, they are not specifically theological and cannot be solved by theology. Under the philosophical microscope they turn out to be the result of conceptual confusion or dissolve into a set of historical, philosophical, psychological and sociological problems which fall into the domain of these disciplines but do not require any specifically theological treatment. What traditionally has been taken to be a theological problem really is an unanalysed complex of spurious and/or non-theological problems. It follows that theology can be reduced without loss to science and philosophy and, therefore, no longer claim to be an autonomous and intellectually respectable discipline. I shall call this the *reductionist argument*." *Ibid*, 13. Like Barth, Dalferth contends that the "intelligibility of theological problems and claims is a necessary, not a sufficient condition" for avoiding the consequences of the reductionist argument. *Ibid*, 13. He continues: "What we also need to show is that those problems are such that they withstand reduction to non-theological problems, i.e. that they raise genuinely *theological* and not merely historical, philosophical, psychological or sociological issues." *Ibid*, 13-14. But when Dalferth claims there is "sufficient reason to reject the reductionist argument" (*Ibid*, 16), the weakness of his position becomes clear. His rejection of reductionism consists of no more than the assertion that it is *not proven* that theological problems are impossible. He argues that, even if the sceptic's arguments against genuine experiential, philosophical, and revelational theological problems "were sound and cogent, they would not suffice to show that the three sets described can include no genuine theological problems; and as long as this is not shown, we are justified in presuming that at least some of the problems of traditional theology are innocent of incoherence and reducibility until proven guilty." *Ibid*, 16. The problem with this position is that, even if we are justified in presuming some of these problems to be genuine theological problems, it does not follow, as he implicitly acknowledges, that theological problems are possible. That is, from the premise, *it is not proven that theological problems are impossible*, it does not follow that *theological problems are possible*. Or, in other words, from the premise that, (1) premises a,b,c,d, ..., do not entail theological problems are impossible, it does not follow that, (2) theological problems are possible. It is clear that Dalferth attempts to resolve the dilemma to theology's satisfaction from a philosophical perspective. This is the source of the weakness of his position. Had he realised (a) that the dilemma he articulates did not surface in the history of ideas until Hume and Kant, and, (b) was *particularly* pressing

*Contra* Overbeck and Hume, Barth's response is really that *theology* must be re-established with audacity or more simply: *theology* must be re-established (for audacity is after all no guarantee that it is not non-theology that will once more be re-established!). Barth's thesis is, *inter alia*, the possibility of the *sui generis* autonomy of theology. The Enlightenment, and Kant in particular, defined autonomy as the self-determination of the will, apart from any object willed; the autonomy of theology implies the self-determination of theology apart from any objects external to *theological* truth, i.e., the truths of non-theology.

Barth agreed with Overbeck's premise that modern theology was a species of non-theology, but he did not thereby affirm the thesis of the (necessary) non-existence of theology "in and of itself". (For all that Overbeck's acumen is not in doubt, the meaning of his "theology in and of itself" does not anticipate Barth's.) Barth did not affirm Overbeck's thesis because he discovered something in the Bible that resolved the dilemma and resisted the reduction of theology to non-theology. He discovered: the *strange new world of the Bible*; he discovered theological truth which, in the fullness of time, he characterised as a *sui generis* historicality constitutive of a *theological* historicality.

## Concluding Remarks

The scene is set: Overbeck's dilemma is of immense importance to understanding Barth's theology and, in particular, how the above concepts manifest themselves in Barth's theological writings, in "The Strange New World Within the Bible", in *Romans* II, and in the *Church Dogmatics*. As will be seen in the following chapters, not only does the metatheological dilemma inform *Romans* II, it is the key to the *Church Dogmatics*. Moreover, it is the key to his association with "Wittgenstein's Vienna" and, of course, Wittgenstein himself.

---

for theology from then on (rather than assuming Barth's relation to the dilemma to be no different in kind from that of the thought of Aristotle, Augustine, St. Thomas, Calvin and Luther. *Ibid*, 15-17), he may well have looked for its resolution in the first-order discipline, theology itself. Nevertheless, that Dalferth does not derive *Barth's theology proves theological problems are possible* is not an incredible oversight on his part, it is that his own interpretation of Barth cannot in principle resolve the dilemma. In other words, Dalferth does not provide sufficient conditions for resolving the dilemma because his interpretation of Barth does not provide sufficient conditions. But unlike the pre-Enlightenment theologians, I will argue, Barth *does* provide sufficient conditions. For Dalferth's interpretation of Barth, see *Ibid*, 112-148; see also Dalferth, "Karl Barth's Eschatological Realism", in S Sykes (ed), *Karl Barth Centenary Essays* (Cambridge: Cambridge University Press, 1989), 14-45.

# Chapter 2
# Prologue to Barth and Wittgenstein

Karl Barth (1886-1968) and Ludwig Wittgenstein (1889-1951) did not meet during their lives. The closest they might have come would have been Berlin in 1906-7 when both studied in the then capital city of Germany, Wittgenstein an engineering student at the *Technische Hochschule*, Barth studying theology at the university. Otherwise, their paths did not cross. Barth's life was spent for the most part in Basel as university professor amidst an academic theological fraternity. Wittgenstein's domicile was less settled, but in the main it alternated between Vienna and Cambridge in England. He too was a university professor - at Cambridge - but in philosophy.

Barth did not at any time read Wittgenstein the philosopher. There is no evidence he was even aware that such a philosopher existed, or after 1951, had existed. To be sure, Barth possessed a scholarly appreciation of certain philosophers of the classical tradition. He knew Descartes' *Meditations*, Leibniz's *Theodicy* and Kant's *Critique of Pure Reason* (a book he had gone through twice with a fine-tooth comb).[1] Of the post-Kantian philosophers he had read Hegel and his *Lectures on the Philosophy of Religion*, Schopenhauer, and Nietzsche.[2] Yet while it is true to say that Barth absorbed - however unconsciously - something material from these past philosophical masters, when it comes to his contemporaries he seems to have learned little, digested next to nothing. Certainly, he knew Husserl, Jaspers, Jean-Paul Sartre and Heidegger, but this knowledge at no time ever pretended to be anything other than one of mere acquaintance. Indeed, unless through personal acquaintance and accident of circumstances, unless

---

[1] Barth refers to and discusses such philosophers throughout the *Church Dogmatics*. See: K Barth, *CD* III/1, 350ff for Descartes; Barth, *CD* III/4, 316ff for Leibniz; Barth, *CD* II/1, 183, 270, 310f, 464 for Kant.

[2] For Barth's knowledge of Hegel, see M Welker, "Barth und Hegel. Zur Erkenntnis eines methodischen Verfarhens bei Barth", *Evangelischen Theologie* (1983), 307-328. See Barth, *CD* III/I 334ff, 337ff, 405 for discussion of Schopenhauer; Barth, *CD* III/2 231ff, 277, 290 for Nietzsche.

his theological mission dovetailed with another's philosophical project at a particular moment in time - as in the case of Heinrich Scholz regarding Anselm - Barth had no genuine desire to learn from his philosopher contemporaries. And that, I am sure, would have precluded Barth learning from, or being influenced by, Wittgenstein had he read him.

On the other hand, Wittgenstein was in a position where he could have been influenced by Barth. He *had* read some Barth. His first impression of the Swiss theologian had been based on hearing, in 1930, some of *The Word of God and the Word of Man*. The immediate impression then conveyed was "one of great arrogance".[3] Ten years later, he himself was reading Barth, most probably the first half-volume of the *Church Dogmatics*. This time he thought the "writing must have come from a remarkable religious experience".[4] Although it was an altogether more positive reaction it seems probable that all that had changed in the intervening years was Wittgenstein's evaluation. It was as if what had once provoked a charge of arrogance was now attributed to a religious experience. Finally, in 1950 Wittgenstein wrote down a remark in which Barth is mentioned by name. Again it is clear that he has *CD* I/1 in mind. And again, it is as if what had been attributed to a religious experience reverted once more to being a cause for complaint:

> How do I know that two people mean the same when each says he believes in God? And just the same goes for belief in the Trinity. A theology which insists on the use of certain particular words and phrases, and outlaws others, does not make anything clearer (Karl Barth). It gesticulates with words, as one might say, because it wants to say something and does not know how to express it. Practice gives words their sense.[5]

---

[3] M O'C Drury, "Conversations with Wittgenstein", in R Rhees (ed), *Recollections of Wittgenstein* (Oxford: Oxford University Press, 1984), 119.

[4] *Ibid*, 146. Were it not for the fact that Wittgenstein had in the past told Drury that Moore and he once tried to read Barth's Commentary on the Epistle to the Romans together but "didn't get far with it and gave it up", (*Ibid*, 119) it would have been more reasonable - given the "ecstatic" nature of the text - to infer that Wittgenstein was speaking of Barth's *Römerbrief* or - given Drury's uncertainty over the date of this particular conversation - Sir Edwyn Hoskyns' translation of it. But unless he simply overlooked what appears to be his (and Moore's) earlier indifference to *Romans* II, it is more likely he was speaking of *Church Dogmatics* I/1.

[5] L Wittgenstein, *CV*, 85. It is conceivable that Wittgenstein cites Barth *approvingly*, as a *counterexample* to, rather than an example of, the 'solipsists' he attacks in this remark. See Barth, *CD* I/1, 78. Yet it seems more likely that Wittgenstein read Barth's exposition of the doctrine of the Trinity in I/1 § 8 and concluded that such trinitarian language was fraught with interpersonal translation difficulties.

There is more here than a simple declaration of 'arrogance' or 'religious experience'. Wittgenstein appears to be critical of Barth's doctrine of the Trinity, a doctrine which Barth held very dear to his theological heart. And he criticises it from the vantage-point of one of his *own* central philosophical contentions, namely the impossibility of a private language and the consequent necessity for language to be grounded in communal use. Far from receiving him as a kindred spirit, Wittgenstein appears to have rejected Barth's trinitarian assertions for reasons that were central to his own philosophy.

Whether Wittgenstein would have made a more appreciative response to Barth's exposition of the Trinity in I/1, had he read all of the *Church Dogmatics* is, alas, a matter for speculation. It has been said that I/1 is not the optimum volume with which to begin one's understanding of the *Church Dogmatics*, especially with regard to its hermeneutical content.[6] It could be said with equal justification that I/1 ("a preliminary leap into the subject-matter itself") is not the optimum volume with which to begin one's understanding of I/1. It is commonly assumed that an answer to the question, whether Barth and Wittgenstein *do* share fundamental themes in common can only be ascertained on the basis of an examination of what it is each actually said, independently of the other. According to this view, whether Wittgenstein saw fundamental affinities and resemblances to his own work is irrelevant: he could have completely rejected the idea and it still be the case that there *are* fundamental affinities and resemblances. By and large, this assumption is valid.

There is, however, a limiting case, one Wittgenstein himself would have recognised.[7] In principle, what it is Wittgenstein actually said would indeed be a function of (or our understanding of him would be affected by) what Barth said if, after it being demonstrated that he understood Barth, he still maintained that what he himself had said was different, and radically so. However, since I can do no other than take the position that understanding Barth is understanding the content of the following (and indeed, previous) pages, I am, perforce, committed to the view that, had Wittgenstein understood Barth, he would have recognised the affinities, the resemblances to his own ideas.

---

[6] David F Ford, "The Interpretation of the Bible", in S Sykes (ed), *Karl Barth. Studies of his Theological Method* ((Oxford: Clarendon Press, 1979), 59-60.

[7] It is implicit in *PI* § 241: "'So you are saying that human agreement decides what is true and what is false?' - It is what human beings *say* that is true and false; and they agree in the *language* they use. That is not agreement in opinions but in form of life."

The story of Barth and Wittgenstein begins with the metatheological dilemma, *Romans* II and "Wittgenstein's Vienna" - the Vienna of Kraus, Schoenberg, Loos and, of course, Wittgenstein and the *Tractatus Logico-Philosphicus*. It ends with the same metadilemma, the *Church Dogmatics* and the central themes of the later philosophy, particularly those of the *Philosophical Investigations* and *On Certainty*. A comparative study on this scale will show, not only that the central ideas of Barth and Wittgenstein's earlier works endure into the respective later works, but that the ideas themselves are kindred spirits. And though the study is not in essence a developmental study it does testify to the fact that there is mileage in the following thesis. This is that there is an analogy between, on the one hand, the   modification and augmentation of these ideas manifest in the development of Barth's thought (from the lecture, "The Strange New World Within the Bible", to *Romans* II, through to the *Church Dogmatics*) and, on the other, the modification and augmentation of the same ideas manifest in Wittgenstein's thought (in respect of the *Tractatus* and the *Philosophical Investigations*). In a fundamental respect, historically and conceptually, Barth and Wittgenstein were 'making for and meaning' the same thing.

## Chapter 3
# "Wittgenstein's Vienna" and Barth as Metatheological Critic: *Romans* II and Overbeck's Dilemma

## 1. Introduction

That all of Barth's theology is best understood within the horizon of the specific Enlightenment legacy of Hume and Overbeck's metatheological dilemma sets a constraint on the answer to the following question: into which cultural peer-group can *Romans* II be best assimilated? For that cultural peer-group must of necessity be assimilated for the same or similar reason into this specific legacy. Otherwise, whatever characteristics the peer-group has in common with *Romans* II cannot be regarded as absolutely integral to this work.

To assimilate Barth into the tradition of Ludwig Wittgenstein, and at one remove, Karl Kraus (1874-1936), Arnold Schoenberg (1874-1951) and Adolf Loos (1874-1933) - key figures of "Wittgenstein's Vienna" - is a move not without attendant difficulties.[1] Yet such difficulties must be

---

[1] It should be made clear from at outset of this chapter that a distinction is to be made between "Wittgenstein's Vienna" (as I use the term) and *"fin-de-siècle* Vienna". *Fin-de-siècle* Vienna was, as Ray Monk points out, a "place of doubt, tension and conflict ... the birth-place of both Zionism and Nazism, the place where Freud developed psychoanalysis, where Klimt, Schiele and Kokoschka inaugurated the *Jugenstil* movement in art, where Schoenberg developed atonal music and Adolf Loos introduced the starkly functional, unadorned style of architecture that characterizes the buildings of the modern age." Ray Monk, *Ludwig Wittgenstein. The Duty of Genius* (London, Vintage, 1991), 9. To take just one example: though both Klimt and Loos belong to *fin-de-siècle* Vienna, Loos' criticism of Klimt's style reveals a fundamental difference between the two that goes to the heart of the matter. Klimt's "lavish use of ornamentation" is anathema to Loos's principles of architecture. Alan Janik and Stephen Toulmin, *Wittgenstein's Vienna* (London: Weidenfeld and Nicholson, 1973), 93-98. Thus, it is not that Wittgenstein, Kraus, Schoenberg and Loos do not belong to *fin-de-siècle* Vienna; it is that they constitute a distinct grouping among other potential distinct groupings. The theme that separates them from Viennese

judged in the light of the unsatisfactory nature of attempts to place Barth in alternative traditions. The objection that Barth is Swiss and not Austrian can be countered with two observations. First, Wittgenstein, Kraus, Loos and Schoenberg can themselves be subsumed into a larger tradition beyond their immediate Viennese *milieu* and indeed beyond an indigenous Austrian tradition. Second, though Barth himself was conscious of his "Swissness",[2] it is hard to see into which specific Swiss tradition he could be assimilated.[3] The implication is that there is no such *a priori* argument against the possibility of assimilating *Romans* II into "Wittgenstein's Vienna".

---

peers, who may or may not belong to other distinct groupings, I describe as a unique form of objectivism. Not only is it irreconcilable with Klimt's art, it is irreconcilable with the subjectivism, and indeed, Romanticism, at the heart of the later artistic movement of expressionism. Wittgenstein's *Tractatus*, for example, is not to be assimilated to Kraus, Schoenberg and Loos on the basis of a common expressionist spirit - nor is Barth's *Romans* II.

[2]  Barth was born in Basel in 1886. It was in the Swiss canton of Aargau, in the village of Safenwil that Barth was to write *Romans* I and II. And from 1935 until his death he lived in Basel, where all but the first two half volumes of the *Church Dogmatics* were written. Perhaps more importantly, he was a citizen of Basel. Basel was his family's city. Both Barth's grandfathers had been pastors in Basel; hence Barth's parents had been born and grew up there. Barth himself was to live the greater part of his life in Basel, and an even greater part in Switzerland. He also felt that to belong to Basel was something special. "We breathe a distinctive kind of air here" and "there is a particular spiritual tradition here, which probably has something to do with climate of the place", he said. Quoted in Busch, *Barth*, 5. Yet Barth was to counter the accusation that he was not (to use Emmanuel Hirsch's phrase) "a German from boot to bonnet" with a deeply felt sense of "dual nationality". That is, he was certainly Swiss, but he also thought he knew what it was to "feel like a German": "I am well aware of the Swiss element in me, but at the same time want to remain totally and unflinchingly in the centre of German theology and the German Church. [...] And if there is to be talk of my certificate of origin. I cannot think of a better way of showing my love of Germany and my identification with it than by remaining in the heart of Germany, even if I differ from so many Germans by being Swiss." Quoted in Busch, *Barth*, 217.

[3]  Though the eighteenth century, for example, is a great century for Switzerland in intellectual and cultural matters - Albrecht von Haller, poet, anatomist, physiologist; Jean-Jacques Rousseau; the Bernoulli family of mathematicians - it is difficult to see what Barth has in common with them (and indeed what each has in common with the other) except at a most general level. See: J R de Salis, *Switzerland and Empire: essays and reflections*, translated by A and E Henderson, (London: Wolff, 1971), 29-30; Oechli, *History of Switzerland, 1499-1914*, translated by E and C Paul, (Cambridge: Cambridge University Press, 1922), 245-7; G Thürer, *Free and Swiss: the Story of Switzerland*, adapted and translated by R P Heller and E Long, (London: Wolff, 1970), 73-77. Of Rousseau, de Salis observes that "his feeling for nature and his democratic ideas are quite Swiss." De Salis, *Switzerland*, 29.

Still more encouraging is the fact that the most successful attempt to date to assimilate Barth straightforwardly into a German theological tradition is based on a criterion of membership involving no more than an implicit acknowledgement of what it is the tradition opposes, rather than what it is for. Gerhard Ebeling's study "The Significance of the Critical Historical Method for Church and Theology in Protestantism" puts the case for this tradition this way:

It is characteristic of the nature of Protestantism that this new factor has proceeded from theology and has remained confined, in the first instance at least, to the work of the theologians. Authors and works so far apart to our way of thinking as Rudolf Otto with his book on the Holy, Karl Barth with his *Romans*, Karl Holl with his collection of Luther essays, Wilhelm Lutgert with his work on the Religion of German Idealism and its End, Emil Brunner with his Schleiermacher book *Die Mystik und das Wort*, Friedrich Gogarten with his controversy with cultural idealism in *Illusionen*, Rudolf Bultmann with his book on Jesus - they all form, in that more or less accidental chronological order, a chain of effective impulses toward a thorough-going new orientation of theological thinking. The right to join their names together like that rests above all merely on the fact that at roughly the same time and in relative independence from each other they threw theology into a ferment. And yet surely more than that can be said of their mutual affinity, be it ever so limited. Even the one most strongly indebted to the nineteenth century in his method and his way of thinking, Rudolf Otto, certainly also had his share in contributing from the religious-historical standpoint toward the unsettling of a popular theological liberalism, and in his own way likewise towards the pointing up of elements grown unfamiliar in the Reformers' faith. For the consciousness of being unable simply to continue on the nineteenth century's line of theological development, and of being called to subject church and theology to a thorough-going critical revision that takes its bearing from the Reformation, is the basic tendency that has established itself since the end of the First World War with surprising speed and power of appeal.[4]

But what is the common link to this "thorough-going new orientation of theological thinking" beyond the negative one that they all in their various ways opposed one or another strand or school of nineteenth-century liberal theology? Beyond this assertion, Ebeling is left with very little, acknowledging that "it is very difficult to give more precise substance to

---

[4] Ebeling, "The Significance of the Critical Historical Method for Church and Theology in Protestantism" in *Word and Faith*, translated by J Leitch, (London: SCM Press, 1963), 23.

the common factor which comes to expression here."[5] And of Barth specifically and the 'dialectical theology' group to which he belonged, Ebeling acknowledges the fact that the group broke up after a relatively short time  and "no sharply definable groupings have resulted from this process."[6] He concludes that it is only "the immediate entourage of Karl Barth  - though his actual influence extends far beyond it and indisputably sounds the dominant note in the present theological situation - [that] forms a more or less firmly outlined unity."[7]

Such historical facts are of course to be expected if there is no positive bond holding together the elements of a new theological orientation. Once the common enemy, so to speak, had been defeated (more or less), such common cause as there had been was no more (hence Barth's parting from Gogarten and the other 'dialectical theologians'). Therefore we are left with a straightforward choice: Barth left to himself unless one can assimilate him into a tradition based on a positive affinity.

Over and against  the 'negative' company of Otto, Holl, Lutgert, Brunner, Gogarten and Bultmann, it is submitted that the company of Wittgenstein, Kraus, Loos, and Schoenberg represent a more resonant interpretative perspective. Just as Wittgenstein is a metaphilosophical critic, Kraus a metalinguistic critic, Loos a meta-art, meta-architectural and meta-design critic, Schoenberg a metamusical critic, Barth's *Romans* II is the work of a metatheological critic whose blue-print for the possibility of theology "in and of itself" is the life-long proclamation 'God is *God*'.[8] 'God

---

[5] *Ibid*, 23.

[6] *Ibid*, 23-4.

[7] *Ibid*, 24.

[8] 'God is *God*' can be understood in two ways: as a description or as a definition. According to Robert Brecher, "God could in both its instances function as a proper name. But since definitions cannot be given of proper names or their bearers, the formula should have to be treated as a description, and not a definition, of God." Robert Brecher, *Anselm's Argument. The Logic of Divine Existence* (Aldershot: Grover Publishing Ltd, 1985), 108. This, as Brecher points out in the context of Barth's interpretation of Anselm, is not how Barth understands the assertion. He understood it throughout his life as a definition. Again, I am indebted to Brecher for the clarification of the implications of construing 'God is *God*' as a definition: "If the formula is taken as a definition ... then it must be a definition of God as a descriptive predicable." *Ibid*, 108. The first instance (God) functions as a proper name but the second (*God*) functions as a descriptive predicable. Hence we get: God (proper name) is *God* (descriptive predicable). If one thinks of the analogous statement, 'Jones is *Jones*', one can see that when one makes this assertion one is saying or alluding to the fact that Jones has characteristics peculiar to him, and that these characteristics make him what he is. Thus an exchange about Jones might go as follows: One person says, "I'm surprised Jones did what he did." Another responds, "I'm not. After all, Jones is *Jones*!" - meaning that the action is the kind of thing Jones would do, given who he is. In other words, the

is *God*' is the blue-print for a *sui generis* theological realm belonging to theology "in and of itself'. In that sense it is a blueprint for *sui generis* theological truth and the resolution of Overbeck's dilemma. Thus as the guarantee of theological truth, 'God is *God*' entails the possibility of theology "in and of itself" and the existence of theology entails 'God is *God*'.

According to Barth, the age through which Overbeck had lived, essentially the second half of the nineteenth century, had been incapable in principle of resolving the metatheological dilemma. The failure of theology in this respect stemmed from the fact that it had subordinated itself to the principles of positivism formulated at the same time in other intellectual fields, in particular, science and philosophy. From the perspective of Wittgenstein's *Tractatus*, the philosophy to be found in German-speaking central Europe during the second half of the nineteenth century suffered from the same fundamental deficiency. Far from being philosophy at all, it was in essence no more than a species of positivist non-philosophy. The supreme irony was that those contemporaries of Wittgenstein who could be identified as the genuine legatees of this tradition interpreted the *Tractatus* as if it too had sprung from the same tradition.

## 2. The *Tractatus Logico-Philosophicus* and Hume's Metaphilosophical Dilemma

Continuous with the bourgeois and nationalist ethos of the second half of the nineteenth century is a positivist ethos that manifests itself in most intellectual and artistic activity of that period, including philosophy, theology, and music. The theology of the German world of the second half of the nineteenth century betrayed - in the words of Paul Tillich - "an attitude of self-sufficient finitude".[9] It was the attitude of the self-satisfied bourgeois man, satisfied with who he was and what belonged to him as a member of this or that nation. In theology it was Albrecht Ritschl whose theology, with all due propriety, flew this particular flag. This was how Barth saw it:

---

action is characteristic of his identity. Similarly, God is to be designated with properties peculiar to Him. In the context of *Romans* II, it means that one should not be surprised that God is not apprehensible by critical-historical or psychological methods. After all, God is *God*!

[9] Welch, *Nineteenth Century Theology*, vol 1, 4.

He stands  with incredible clearness and firmness (truly with both feet)
upon the ground of his 'ideal of life', the very epitome of the national-
liberal German *bourgeois* of the age of Bismarck.[10]

Ritschl's "ideal of life" - that which in theology served as the epitome of
*bourgeois* national society - was heavily charged with Kant's conception of
the highest good, the animating force behind Kant's notions of duty and
moral law. Thus Ritschl's theology is an anti-metaphysical moralism which
observes, is content to remain within, the finite boundaries circumscribed
by the transcendental analytic. Ritschl's theology conforms to "the pressure
of the positivism prevailing in the second half of the nineteenth century."[11]
It conforms to the positivist ethos prevailing in German, inclusive of
Austrian, science. Indeed the ethos then burgeoning close to home and with
which the nineteenth century was drawing to a close was, in the wake of the
1848 revolutions, at once *bourgeois* and nationalist and as such its prime
motivating force the spirit of Prussian militarism which prospered under
Bismarck and proceeded to more ambitious things under Wilhelm II.[12]  The
German population  of the Habsburg Empire whose dominance became
increasingly undermined by the diplomatic compromises of the Habsburg
dynasty in the face of Slav and Czech nationalist discontent and tension
within its borders, turned more and more to Berlin and Germany. The
growth of German nationalism, the emergence of the Pan-German
movement under Georg Schönerer whose aim was the union of Austrian
Germans with the powerful German Reich of Wilhelm II, the Christian
Socialist programme led by Karl Lueger, whose appeal lay in the lower
middle classes, were all manifestations of this phenomenon.[13]  It is
noteworthy that German nationalism also took hold of the mind of Barth's
Germanic Switzerland toward the end of the  nineteenth century:

---

[10] Barth, *Protestant Theology*, 656.

[11] Barth, "Evangelical Theology  in the 19th Century", *Scottish Journal of Theology
Occasional Papers*, No 8, translated by J S McNab, (Edinburgh: Oliver and Boyd, 1959),
56.

[12] See: W Carr, *A History of Germany, 1815-1945* (London: Edward Arnold, 1987); G A
Craig, *Germany 1866-1945* (Oxford: Oxford University Press, 1981).

[13] See: C A McCartney, *The Habsburg Empire 1790-1918* (London: Weidenfeld and
Nicholson, 1968); McCartney, *The House of Austria: The Later Phase, 1790-1918*
(Edinburgh: Edinburgh University Press, 1978); A J P Taylor, *The Habsburg Monarchy,
1809-1918: A History of the Austrian Empire and Austria-Hungary* (Harmondsworth:
Middlesex, Penguin Books, 1981); R A Kann, *The Multinational Empire: Nationalism and
Natural Reform in the Habsburg Monarchy 1848-1918*, 2 vols, (New York: Octogon,
1950); F Field, *The Last Days of Mankind: Karl Kraus and his Vienna* (London: St.
Martin's Press, 1967).

If the first half of the nineteenth century had been characterised by Switzerland's emancipation from French, and then, generally, from foreign influence; if the four decades which followed 1848 were a period of national expansion and self-assertion of a newly established Swiss confederation, the last ten years of the century and the period 1900-1918 saw a very peculiar development. With astonishing rapidity and without any apparent resistance, Germanic Switzerland slipped into complete cultural, economic, and even moral, but not political subservience to Imperial Germany. [...] The fascination which Imperial Germany, the Kaiser, his people and their institutions exerted over the liberal and libertarian Swiss democrats of German stock between the 90s and 1918 was so strong that at the time eventual complete absorption appeared by no means impossible. In fact the Pan-German league had as one of its declared aims incorporation of Germanic Switzerland into a greater *Reich*, along with Austria and the Netherlands.[14]

That a positivist ethos manifested itself in philosophy in the second half of the nineteenth century and, in particular, in the most influential school in philosophy in Central Europe is one essential ingredient of the paradox that Wittgenstein's *Tractatus Logico-Philosophicus* (1922) was assimilated into a positivist legacy (and hence to his way of thinking assimilated to non-philosophy).[15] All Wittgenstein's writings, excepting the manuscripts which became *The Blue and Brown Books*, were written in German. But they did not find a receptive ear in twentieth-century German philosophy. German philosophy both before and after the war remained loyal on the whole to its Kantian heritage and transcendental philosophy. The influence of the later Husserl, and later of Heidegger remained dominant right up to the sixties.[16] In Austria the situation was different. There Wittgenstein's *Tractatus Logico-Philosophicus* was one, if not the, major influence on the Vienna Circle and logical positivism. The phenomenon of the Vienna Circle and logical positivism in the 1930s was the culmination of a homogeneous tradition of Austrian philosophy which had begun with Brentano's

---

[14] G Soloveytchik, *Switzerland in Perspective* (Oxford, Oxford University Press, 1954), 208-9. That Barth was aware of this historical phenomenon, see Barth, *The Germans and Ourselves* (London: Nisbet and Co., 1945).

[15] For an account of this particular history, see Peter Alexander, "The Philosophy of Science, 1850-1910", in D J O'Connor, *A Critical History of Western Philosophy*, 402-425. For a more general account, see Herbert Schädelbach, *Philosophy in Germany 1831-1933*, translated by Eric Matthews, (Cambridge: Cambridge University Press, 1984), esp. 3-4.

[16] R Haller, "Wittgenstein and Austrian Philosophy", in J C Nyíri (ed), *Austrian Philosophy: Studies and Texts* (Munich: Philosophia-Verlag, 1981), 97.

*Psychology From an Empirical Standpoint* in 1874.[17] This tradition had more in common with German science, with the science of Helmholtz, Hertz, and Kirchnoff at Berlin, than it had with German philosophy. *Vera philosophiae methodus nulla alia nisi scientiae naturalis est* ('the true method of philosophy is none other than that of natural science') was Brentano's guiding philosophical principle.[18] Mach, Brentano's successor at Vienna, continued the empirical tradition originating in Hume and defended a presuppositionless, in the sense of antimetaphysical, positivism.[19] In the Vienna Circle's eyes the seminal achievement of *Tractatus* had been to provide a criterion of meaningfulness that demarcated science from non-science. From this perspective it naturally followed that Wittgenstein's objective had been to protect the whole body of meaningful statements, which is to say, the propositions of natural science, from the encroachment of the pseudo-statements of metaphysics and theology. Otto Neurath, a member of the Vienna Circle, attributed the following view to Wittgenstein:

> The increase of metaphysical and theological leanings which shows itself today in the many associations and sects, in books and journals, in talks and university lectures seems to be based upon the fierce social and economic struggles of the present: one group of combatants, holding fast to traditional social forms, cultivate traditional attitudes of metaphysics and theology whose content has long since been superseded; while the other group, especially in Central Europe, faces modern times, rejects these views and takes its stand upon the ground of empirical science. This development is connected with that of the modern process of production, which leaves ever less room for metaphysical ideas. It is also connected with the disappointment of people with the attitude of those who preach traditional metaphysical and theological doctrines.[20]

Rudolf Carnap, another member of the Vienna Circle, also spoke about the influence the *Tractatus* had on him:

> The most important insight I gained from his work was the conception that the truth of logical statements is based only on their logical structure and on the meaning of the terms. Logical statements are true under all conceivable circumstances; thus their truth is independent of the contingent facts of the world. On the other hand, it follows that these

---

[17] *Ibid*, 92.
[18] *Ibid*, 93.
[19] *Ibid*, 98.
[20] Quoted, *ibid*, 76.

statements do not say anything about the world and thus have no factual content.

Another influential idea of Wittgenstein's was the insight that many philosophical sentences, especially in traditional metaphysics, are pseudo-sentences, devoid of cognitive content. I found Wittgenstein's view on this point close to the one I had previously developed under the influence of anti-metaphysical scientists and philosophers [21]

The logical positivists also read the *Tractatus* as advocating a verifiability principle of meaning against which the meaningfulness of scientific propositions had to be measured. Epistemologically this converged with the supposition that the mode of verifiability lay in sense experience. Thus Wittgenstein's *Tractatus* was ultimately read as a positivist tract entering into the legacy of Hume. It was what was said that was important and not that which could not be said. The latter was simply nonsense.

The immediate *milieu* into which Wittgenstein's works were born was England where they were received into the academic tradition of Anglo-Saxon philosophy. This was as true of the *Tractatus Logico-Philosophicus* as it was of the *Philosophical Investigations*. Just as the Vienna Circle adopted the attitude that true philosophy was to be identified with the Enlightenment generally and with David Hume's empiricism in particular, so Bertrand Russell judged Wittgenstein by the canons of the Enlightenment. He too praised the *Tractatus* and viewed its achievement as that of providing the foundations of a general philosophy of the scientific conception of the world. The success of science in the nineteenth century had led philosophers to borrow from the methods of science in their pursuit of truth. Accordingly, Russell conceived philosophy as almost continuous with the natural sciences, its distinguishing feature being that its function was to theorise on the most general features of the world using the methods of science:

... there are two different ways in which a philosophy may seek to base itself upon science. It may emphasise the most general results of science and seek to give greater generality and unity to these results ... or it may study the methods of science, and seek to apply these methods with the necessary adaptation to its own particular province. Much philosophy inspired by science has gone astray through preoccupation with results

---

[21] Quoted in Fann, *Wittgenstein's Conception of Philosophy* (Oxford: Blackwell, 1969), 34.

momentarily supposed to have been achieved. It is not results but methods
that can be transferred with profit to the sphere of philosophy.[22]

Russell applied this methodological principle to the metaphysical
problem of the ultimate constituents of the world. Hence, though Russell's
"Lectures on Logical Atomism" owed much to the metaphysical apparatus
propounded in the *Tractatus*,[23] he coincided with the logical positivists in
assuming that the fundamental point of the *Tractatus* resided in what could
be positively said. Indeed he paid scant respect to Wittgenstein's showing
and saying distinction, declaring that "Mr Wittgenstein seems to be able to
say a great deal about what can't be said."[24]

Here then is the paradox: the *Tractatus* was assimilated into the tradition
of Austrian scientific positivistic philosophy as represented by Brentano
and Mach (Stern takes the view that "if Wittgenstein's philosophy is to be
placed in a tradition, then the one summed up in the old story of the
Austrian railway line - from Bolzano to Brentano, Meinong, and Husserl to
*Endstation* Wittgenstein - is undoubtedly more relevant than any other");[25]
it was hailed as the Bible of the logical positivists; it was accordingly
perceived as continuing the philosophy of David Hume. In other words, not
only was it perceived as an epistemological treatise,[26] it was taken to be a
more formal (because stated in the language of formal logic) restatement of
Hume's dilemma. Yet though the limits of meaningful discourse drawn by
the *Tractatus* coincide, more or less, with Hume's definition of factual
discourse,[27] paradoxically it is as a resolution rather than as a restatement of
Hume's dilemma that the *Tractatus* should be read.

---

[22] B Russell, "On Scientific Method in Philosophy", in *Mysticism and logic and other essays*, (London: Longmans Green, 1918), 98.

[23] See B Russell, "Logical Atomism", in *The Monist* 1918-1919, nos 28-29, in B Russell, *The Collected Papers of Bertrand Russell*, vol 8, (London: G Allen & Unwin Ltd, 1986).

[24] Russell, "Introduction", in Wittgenstein, *TLP*, xxi.

[25] Stern, "Wittgenstein in Context", 166.

[26] W B Bartley III writes: "Readers of the *Tractatus* - including, conspicuously, most of the logical positivists - have often supposed that elementary propositions report sense experiences." See Bartley III, *Wittgenstein* (London: Quartet Books, 1977), 45. Unfortunately, he adds that "it is probably safe to assume that Wittgenstein did have, and must have had, *some* such idea in mind." *Ibid*, 45. This is precisely what it is not safe to assume since the admission of sense-experience would have, as a species of non-philosophy, compromised the *sui generis* philosophical realm that it will be argued was Wittgenstein's objective.

[27] Wittgenstein writes: "The correct method in philosophy would really be the following: to say nothing except what can be said i.e. propositions of natural science - i.e. something that has nothing to do with philosophy - and then, whenever someone else wanted to say

In this respect, it is the comparison with Kant rather than Hume that suggests itself. Yet while there is no contradiction involved in asserting that both Kant and Wittgenstein resolved Hume's dilemma,[28] Wittgenstein's resolution differs markedly from, and indeed conflicts with, Kant's. First, unlike Kant's, Wittgenstein's resolution does not involve positing the existence of *a priori* synthetic truths. Second, what he does posit excludes the possibility of such an existence. Indeed, the manner in which Wittgenstein resolves Hume's dilemma does not follow the path taken by Kant's transcendental question.[29] To be sure, just as Kant's critique set a limit to reason, the *Tractatus* "set a limit to thought, or rather not to thought

---

something metaphysical, to demonstrate to him that he had failed to give meaning to certain signs in his propositions." Wittgenstein, *TLP*, 6.53.

[28] That Barth resolves Hume's metatheological dilemma is obviously not dependent on whether Wittgenstein resolves Hume's metaphilosophical dilemma. Moreover, that Wittgenstein plays the role of metanarrative to Barth does not entail that Hume's metaphilosophical dilemma is resolved by Wittgenstein *but not Kant*. They may both have resolved it. Yet I do in fact take the view that it is Wittgenstein and not Kant who resolves Hume's metaphilosophical dilemma, that it is his conception of philosophy rather than the Kantian conception that restores the *sui generis* autonomy of philosophy. That Kant failed to solve Hume's metaphilosophical dilemma is obviously a thesis in itself. Yet it would, I believe, include the following reasons why any claim for Kant's success can be viewed with some doubt. It can be argued that Kant saving philosophy from extinction is not a sufficient condition or guarantee of autonomy. In other words, the Critical Philosophy does not sufficiently distinguish itself from science; philosophy remains compromised by non-philosophy. First, its concept of truth is in fact the most general concept of truth possible and therefore criterial for all the sciences assumed to be under its stewardship. Second, for all that the Critical Philosophy initiated a famous 'turn to the subject', it would not do Kant an injustice to call his transcendental philosophy a transcendental science since his objective - to map out the necessary structure of metaphysical reality via the transcendental categories - presupposed an investigative approach to the number and nature of these categories. Third, like his immediate predecessors, Kant thought philosophy like science proves things. Thus, for example, he thought it was the task of philosophy to prove the existence of the external world. See Hacker, *Insight*, 208. The assertion that the Enlightenment legacy had to wait until Wittgenstein's *Tractatus* before Hume's metaphilosophical dilemma was resolved implies that though historically speaking Kant's critical philosophy was the exemplar and culmination par excellence of Enlightenment Philosophy in that it discharged its critical duty, it did not embody the legacy of the Enlightenment with respect to autonomy. Hence the chair of *sui generis* philosophy was vacant pending.

[29] This I believe is the rationale behind Pears' remark that the Kantian explanation works rather better for the form of the *Tractatus* rather than its content. See D F Pears, *The False Prison. A Study of the Development of Wittgenstein's Philosophy*, vol 1, (Oxford: Oxford University Press, 1987), 20.

but to the expression of thoughts".[30] But where in Kant the bounds of sense are described by *a priori* synthetic truths, in Wittgenstein this is determined by the essential nature of representation, which in turn is determined by mind-independent logical forms of reality.[31] In other words, Wittgenstein is closer to Hume than to Kant here (thus the rejection of *a priori* synthetic truths and the identification of meaningfulness with scientific discourse at *TLP* 6.53). Somewhat ironically, the intersection with Kant occurs where Wittgenstein *restates* rather than resolves Hume's metaphilosophical dilemma.[32] Third, and most important, unlike Kant's, Wittgenstein's critique holds that the "description of the limits of language lies beyond the realm of what can be said. Language can no more describe its own essence than it can describe the essence of the world."[33]

Yet reinforcing "Hume's fork" is not the same as resolving Hume's dilemma. Indeed, where Hume states his dilemma on the basis of an empiricist epistemology, Wittgenstein's resolution rests on matters of pure logic, principally the propositions of logic.[34] These latter propositions are in the Wittgensteinian imagination bearers of tautology, autotelism and utter self-sufficiency.[35] In that sense they mirror the autonomous safe haven that Wittgenstein finds for philosophy, though paradoxically philosophical speech is dialectically undermined as a result.[36]

---

[30] Wittgenstein, *TLP*, 3. See also Pears, *Wittgenstein* (Glasgow: Fontana, 1971), 12.

[31] Hacker, *Insight*, 23. Thus Bartley is right to say that this doctrine is "not only *non*-Kantian but *pre*-Kantian in spirit. [...] Before Kant it was commonly assumed that some sort of harmony existed between the human mind and the external world so that the human mind could apprehend ... the nature of reality." Bartley, *Wittgenstein*, 46.

[32] Thus the assertion that the *Tractatus* set out to answer a Kantian-style question: `How is langauge possible?' (A Quinton, "Contemporary British Philosophy", in O'Connor (ed), *A Critical History of Western Philosophy* (New York: The Free Press of Glencoe, 1964), 536) does justice only to the dimension in the *Tractatus* devoted to restating Hume's dilemma. For an exposition of the main differences between Kant and the *Tractatus*, see Hacker, *Insight*, 22f.

[33] Hacker, *Insight*, 23.

[34] Though Wittgenstein calls logic "transcendental" he does not mean that the propositions of logic state "transcendental truths, it means that they like other propositions, shew something that pervades everything sayable and is itself unsayable." See Anscombe, *An Introduction to Wittgenstein's Tractatus*, 1st edition, (London: Hutchinson, 1959), 166.

[35] Thus Wittgenstein writes: "In logic every proposition is in the form of a proof." Wittgenstein, *TLP* 6.1264. Thus "It is always possible to construe logic in such a way that every proposition is its own proof." *Ibid*, 6.1265.

[36] Hence the famous words at the end of the *Tractatus*: "My propositions serve as elucidations in the following way: anyone who understands me eventually recognises them as nonsensical, when he has used them - as steps - to climb up beyond them. (He must, so to speak, throw away the ladder after he has climbed up it.) He must transcend these propositions and then he will see the world aright. Whereof one cannot speak thereof one

Those very same origins of the *Tractatus* - tautology, autotelism and utter self-sufficiency - are quickly usurped by Wittgenstein's distinction between showing and saying,[37] which is why he can say to Russell:

> Now I'm afraid that you haven't really got hold of my main contention to which the whole business of logical propositions is only corollary. The main point is the theory of what can be expressed (*gesagt*) by propositions, i.e., by language (and which comes to the same thing, what can be thought) and what cannot be expressed by propositions, but only shown (*gezeigt*); which I believe is the cardinal problem of philosophy.[38]

That logic shows its properties, that is, reveals *itself* (logic reveals itself as *logic*),[39] circumvents the accusation that it is merely autotelic (though "logic looks after itself").[40] Just as "the unutterable is - unutterably -

---

must be silent." *Ibid*, 6.54-7. Hacker describes Wittgenstein's attitude here as espousing a conception of philosophy that is negative and dialectical. See Hacker, *Insight*, 24-27.

[37] There are a number of commentators who take the view that the showing and distinction is the fundamental rationale behind the *Tractatus*. See: R Rhees, "Miss Anscombe on the Tractatus" *Philosophical Quarterly*, 10, (1960), 21-31; M Black, *A Companion to Wittgenstein's `Tractatus'* (Cambridge: Cambridge University Press, 1964), 190; J Griffin, *Wittgenstein's Logical Atomism* (London: Oxford University Press, 1964), 18; A Kenny, *Wittgenstein* (Harmondsworth: Middlesex, Penguin Books, 1975), 45; Pears, *Wittgenstein*, 87; M O Mounce, *Wittgenstein's Tractatus: An Introduction* (Oxford: Basil Blackwell, 1981), 12; Hacker, *Insight*, 19; McGuinness, *Wittgenstein*, 199.

[38] Letter to Russell, 18.8.19. See Wittgenstein, *Letters to Russell, Keynes and Moore* (Oxford: Basil Blackwell, 1974). Anscombe infers that this passage refers to *Russell's* interest in logical propositions. See Anscombe, *Introduction*, 164. Yet insofar as the distinction between showing and saying can be shown to emerge from Wittgenstein's reflections on the propositions of logic, it may also (if not exclusively) be his own preoccupation with the propositions of logic he speaks of here.

[39] 'Logic reveals itself as *logic*' - 'logic is *logic*' - like 'God is *God*', is to be understood as a definition of logic and not as a description. (This, of course, coincides with Wittgenstein's own explicit conclusion that logic cannot be described.) The first instance, 'logic', is analogous to the proper name, 'God', and functions as the name of what it is we are talking about, namely logic. The second instance, '*logic*', functions as a descriptive predicable. Hence we get: 'Logic (= proper name) is *logic* (= descriptive predicable)'. As in the case of 'God is *God*', this can be elucidated by the analogous statement, 'Jones is *Jones*'. As was said earlier in this chapter (footnote 8), when one makes this assertion one is saying or alluding to the fact that Jones has characteristics peculiar to him, and that these characteristics make him what he is. Similarly, logic has characteristics that make *it* what it is. It reveals itself - its *sui generis* identity - to be such that it is not apprehensible through or representable in language itself.

[40] Wittgenstein, *TLP* 5.473.

contained", which is to say, revealed, in what is "uttered", so logic shows itself,[41] though what it shows cannot be said:[42]

> Propositions cannot represent what they must have in common with reality in order to be able to represent it - logical form.[43]

> Propositions cannot represent logical form: it is mirrored in them.
> What finds its reflection in language, language cannot represent.
> What expresses itself in language, we cannot express by means of language.
> Propositions show the logical form of reality.
> They display it.[44]

This is a thought to which Wittgenstein had already given vent in the *Notebooks*:

> But is *language* the *only* language?
> Why should there not be a mode of language through which I can talk *about* language in such a way that it can appear in coordination with something else?[45]

There was no sense in which logic could "appear in coordination with something else"; it was itself, *sui generis*.

---

[41] It is not we who show logical structure in our use of factual language: it expresses itself. Black conceives of the distinction in this respect as follows: "The intended opposition comes out neatly in a point of diction. It is we, the users of language, who 'say' things, make assertions, by means of the arbitrary coordinations we have assigned to words; but whatever is shown, shows itself (*zeigen sich*, as Wittgenstein often says), independently of any arbitrary conventions we may have adopted - what is shown is not something 'we express' (6.124g)." See Black, *Companion*, 190. He is aware that "unhappily Wittgenstein does once or twice use the expression 'we show', in the sense of 'we prove or demonstrate' - as at 6.126" *Ibid*, 190. But he goes on to say: "We can usually see whether Wittgenstein uses, or might as well have used, the reflexive form. For example, the important remark that a proposition shows itself, 4.022a, can be legitimately transformed into a: 'A proposition's sense shows itself in the proposition.'" *Ibid*, 190. The point is: the *sui generis* objectivity of logic is such that we (and human subjectivity) have no role in its showing of itself. *It* shows itself.

[42] "What can be shown, cannot be said." Wittgenstein, *TLP* 4.1212.

[43] *Ibid*, 4.12

[44] *Ibid*, 4.121. For a list of things that Wittgenstein says show themselves but cannot be said - the sense of a proposition (4.022 a), that a proposition is about a certain object (4.1211 a), etc. - see Black, *Companion*, 190-191.

[45] Wittgenstein, *NB*, entry dated 29.5.15.

That Wittgenstein's solution to Hume's metaphilosophical dilemma originates in the propositions of logic is confirmed by the rationale behind the first recorded expression of the distinction between showing and saying:

> Logical so-called propositions show the logical properties of language and therefore of the universe, but say nothing.
> This means that by merely looking at them you can see these properties; whereas, in a proposition proper, you cannot see what is true by looking at it.[46]

That is, if logical propositions are analytically or tautologically true, then it follows that they say nothing about the world. *Ceteris paribus*, it therefore follows that the same logical properties manifest in "propositions proper" (factual propositions) are not the representatives of anything either. We find this idea expressed in the *Tractatus* thus:

> My fundamental idea is that the 'logical constants' are not representatives; that there can be no representatives of the logic of facts.[47]

The German logician Gottlieb Frege had thought the logical particles (the logical connectives of propositional logic '→' ('if...then...'), '&' ('...and...'), 'v' ('either...or...')[48] were names of literal functions: thus 'not' was the name of the concept of negation (which in turn was a unary function); the binary connectives 'and' 'if...then...' were names of relations; and the quantifiers in the predicate calculus were names of second-level functions. These functions themselves were also taken to be names, names of logical objects which existed in a Platonic realm. Russell's answer had been slightly different but tended in the same direction. Science, he argued, had its objects - matter, energy etc. - so logic, being another substantive science, must be about some other category of objects. Russell, then, thought of philosophy as a science, differing only from the other sciences in that it was 'the science of the most general', the science of the properties and relations of logical objects. In other words, Frege and Russell thought

---

[46] Wittgenstein, *NB*, 107. That Wittgenstein had not solved the problem of logical constants or provided a solution to the need for a Theory of Types in 'Notes on Logic' (a document which charted Wittgenstein's progress up to Autumn 1913) makes it all the more certain that his reflection on the nature of logical propositions constitute the key explanatory variable of the presence of the doctrine of showing and saying in the *Tractatus*.
[47] *TLP* 4.0312.
[48] There is a useful glossary of the vocabulary of logic in Anscombe, *Introduction*, 21-24.

of the propositions of logic as expressing general (*a priori*) realist truths about logical entities.

Wittgenstein early on disagreed with both Frege and Russell. The first philosophical remark of his that has been preserved is in a letter to Russell dated 22 June 1912. In it Wittgenstein starts out as he means to end:

> Logic is still in the melting pot, but one thing gets clearer: the propositions of logic contain only apparent variables and whatever may turn out to be the proper explanation of apparent variables, its consequence must be that there are no logical constants.
>
> Logic must be completely different from any other science.[49]

'Logic must be completely different from science.' It must be *sui generis*. Yet had Wittgenstein adhered to the definition of philosophy formulated in the appendix to the *Notebooks* - philosophy as the *description* of logical form[50] - such description would have been one more description assimilable to science and hence to non-philosophy. In other words, Wittgenstein's credentials as a metaphilosophical critic who resolves Hume's dilemma would not have been genuine. Accordingly, logical analysis cannot be a sufficient condition of the autonomy of philosophy (which is not surprising since, as the logical positivists knew, it is a means

---

[49] Wittgenstein, *Letters*, 10. To the extent that Wittgenstein's resolution of the problem of logical constants led to the dissolution of any need for Russell's Theory of Types, one can agree with Griffin's conclusion that the theory of showing and saying is in part a reaction to Frege's *Grundgesetze*, in part a reaction to Russell's Theory of Types, and in part the result of Wittgenstein's own deliberations about the unique character of the propositions of logic. See Griffin, *Atomism*, 9. Indeed, Hacker's four historical `theses' describe the development of his early philosophy: (1) Wittgenstein's rejection of logical constants led to his repudiation of any need for Russell's Theory of Types. Hacker, *Insight*, 11. (2) "[Wittgenstein's] repudiation of the theory of Types played a major role in moulding his conception of the nature and limits of philosophy, from 'Notes on Logic' in 1913 to the *Tractatus*.", *Ibid*, 12. (3)) "The extent to which his conception of philosophy changed can be gauged by comparing 'Notes on Logic' with the *Tractatus*." *Ibid*, 11. (4) "The cause of the change can be attributed to the emergence of the distinction between showing and saying." *Ibid*, 12.

[50] As Wittgenstein writes: "In philosophy there are no deductions; it is purely descriptive. The word 'philosophy' ought always to designate something over or under, but not beside, the natural sciences. Philosophy gives no pictures of reality, and can neither confirm nor confute scientific investigations. It consists of logic and metaphysics, the former its basis. Epistemology is the philosophy of psychology. Distrust of grammar is the first requisite for philosophising. Philosophy is the doctrine of logical form of scientific propositions (not primitive propositions only). A correct explanation of the logical propositions must give then a unique position as against all other propositions." Wittgenstein, *NB*, Appendix I, 93.

of stating Hume's dilemma). Wittgenstein's demarcation of philosophy from species of non-philosophy follows from the wholesale identification of philosophy with logic as *logic*[51] establishing a genuine philosophical realm:[52]

Philosophy is not one of the natural sciences.
(The word "philosophy" must mean something whose place is above or below the natural sciences, not beside them.)
Philosophy aims at the logical clarification of thoughts.
Philosophy is not a body of doctrine but an activity.
A philosophical work consists essentially of elucidations.
Philosophy does not result in 'philosophical propositions', but rather in the clarification of propositions.
Without philosophy thoughts are, as it were, cloudy and indistinct: its task is to make them clear and to give them sharp boundaries.[53]

And on the specific sciences that constitute the natural sciences he goes on:

Psychology is no more closely related to philosophy than any other natural science.[54]

Also:

---

[51] In 1912 Wittgenstein presented a paper entitled "What is Philosophy?". In it he attempted to argue for the thesis that philosophy is to be identified entirely with logic. Indeed, in the later 'Notes on Logic' he represents himself as a logician and not at all as a philosopher in the classical sense. See McGuinness, *Wittgenstein*, 144.

[52] In the *Tractatus* neither logical form or the sense of a proposition are nonsense but they lack sense; they are *sinnlos* but not *insinnig*, which is to say neither can be brought in under the wraps of our language to the realm of apprehensability. This makes for a fundamental distinction in the *Tractatus* between *talk* about something and *that which we talk about*. It is talk about logic which is nonsense, but not the logical form or the sense of a proposition itself. This puts it on a different plane altogether from Russell's Theory of Types, perhaps the most perfect example of a philosophical theory Wittgenstein could have cited during his *Tractatus* period. Talk about the Theory of Types is nonsense because the Theory of Types is nonsense, albeit disguised philosophical nonsense. (It is nonsense both because it talks nonsense about logic and because it attempts to talk about that which we cannot talk in the first place.) In other words, talk about logic is nonsense, not because logic is nonsense but because it is such that it cannot be talked about. See Hacker, *Insight*, 18.

[53] Wittgenstein, *TLP* 4.111-4.112.

[54] *Ibid*, 4.1121.

Darwin's theory has no more to do with philosophy than any other hypothesis in natural science.[55]

And:

Philosophy sets limits to the much disputed sphere of natural science.[56]

David Pears writes that all Wittgenstein's philosophy "expresses his strong feeling that the great danger to philosophy to which modern thought is exposed is domination by science."[57] Wittgenstein certainly saw it this way. In a remark from the draft to the preface to the later posthumously published *Philosophical Remarks* he wrote:

> ... I have no sympathy for the current of European civilisation and do not understand its goals. [...] It is all one to me whether the typical western scientist understands or appreciates my work, since he will not in any case understand the spirit in which I write. Our civilisation is characterised by the word 'progress'.[58]

It would be a neat answer to say that the tide against which Wittgenstein swam was the tide of science. But it was not as simple as that. Wittgenstein was not against science in itself. He maintained a life-long interest in engineering, in the construction and development of new technology, in the functional principles of all kinds of machinery. He had at one time contemplated becoming an engineer and during his time at Manchester in the years 1908-11 attempted to make contributions to the then experimental stages of aeronautical engineering. He did, however, think that mankind had misread the implications of scientific and technological progress. "By its very nature progress always seems greater that it actually is" was the epigram he chose as the motto of the *Philosophical Investigations*. While progress was perfectly acceptable within the limits of science, what was not was the implication that in virtue of undeniable success of science, the criterion of progress should be accepted as the final adjudicator on all areas of human life, including philosophy. This was what Wittgenstein found unacceptable.

---

[55] *Ibid*, 4.1122.

[56] Wittgenstein, *Ibid*, 4.113.

[57] Pears, *The False Prison. A Study of the Development of Wittgenstein's Philosophy*, vol 2, (Oxford: Oxford University Press, 1987), 221. Pears gives a perceptive account of the nature of Wittgenstein's antipathy to the encroachment of science on philosophy. *Ibid*, 199-225. See also Pears, *Wittgenstein*, 1971.

[58] Wittgenstein, *CV*, 6.

## 3. "Wittgenstein's Vienna"

Thus that the central ideas of the *Tractatus* were conceived through reflection on logic is not in the least irreconcilable[59] with the fact that the history of its publication reveals that Wittgenstein viewed the work as an ethical deed continuous with the preoccupations of some of the outstanding figures of Viennese culture during the last twenty-five to thirty years of Habsburg Austria.[60] *Inter alia*, the preoccupations of this culture revolved

---

[59] Thus Stern writes that there is no "dual" Wittgenstein: no Wittgenstein the rigorously "scientific" Anglo-Saxon logician or Wittgenstein the Austrian or Continental philosopher with "mystical" leanings. See Stern, "Wittgenstein in Context", 150.

[60] The *Tractatus* is a text which cannot be fully understood simply by looking at what is in it. Otherwise one would be committed to rejecting the most convincing explanation behind the history of Wittgenstein's attempt to publish it, namely that he identified the *Tractatus* with the work of certain key *cultural* figures of *fin-de-siècle* Vienna and not with a *scientific* Austrian philosophical tradition. The first publisher to whom Wittgenstein submitted the *Tractatus* was the firm which published Karl Kraus. It was rejected. Wittgenstein was prompted to write a letter to Engelmann, part of which is quoted below: "Today I received notification from Jahoda that he cannot publish my treatise. Allegedly for technical reasons. But I would dearly like to know what Kraus said about it. If there were an opportunity for you to find out, I should be very glad. Perhaps Loos knows something about it." Letter dated 25.10.18, Engelmann, *Letters*, 15. It is difficult to understand Wittgenstein's desire that Kraus should see it in any other light than that he thought it dealt with matters close to the latter's heart - even though it was extremely unlikely the literary Kraus would have thought the *Tractatus* had anything in common with his critique of modern (Viennese) culture and society. The second publisher Wittgenstein approached published the work of Otto Weininger, a fellow Viennese, whose work Wittgenstein respected. Wittgenstein later said that this was the reason he had made the approach. This second attempt, likewise, came to nothing. See Janik, "Wittgenstein: an Austrian Enigma", 80. The third attempt involved a professor in Germany who has been identified as Frege. (von Wright, "The Origin of the *Tractatus*", *Wittgenstein* (Oxford: Basil Blackwell, 1982), 80. What stands out from this encounter is Wittgenstein's reaction to the conditions of publication. Frege was prepared to publish the book as long as Wittgenstein rewrote it in the form of a treatise. For Wittgenstein this was nothing less than to 'mutilate' the work, so important did he consider the form in which he had written the *Tractatus* to the point of the book. Janik, "Wittgenstein: an Austrian Enigma", 80. The fourth and final attempt Wittgenstein made in person was to Karl Von Ficker. Von Ficker was the editor of the periodical *Der Brenner* of which Karl Kraus had said: "That the only honest review in Austria appears in Innsbruck, should be known in Germany, if not in Austria, because the only honest review in Germany appears there too." *Ibid*, 83. *Der Brenner* was also known for its defence of Kraus. *Ibid*, 82. Wittgenstein for his part seems to have selected Von Ficker

around a critique of the shortcomings of Habsburg Viennese society. In this respect, it was a critique that found its most vociferous voice in the work of Karl Kraus. Kraus's life-long mission was embodied in a journal called *Die Fackel*.[61] Just as Kierkegaard before him had lambasted "*bourgeois* Copenhagen" with his street pamphlet *The Instant*, so from 1899 onwards Kraus engaged in an unrelenting attack on - and exposure of - what he perceived as the duplicity, hypocrisy and corruption at the   heart of Viennese society. Kraus's ethical personality has been likened to an Old Testament prophet, a "Jeremiah"[62]; his artistic personality has been described as an "apocalyptic satirist".[63] In truth, the ethical and the artistic were fused in the one man who accordingly evaded classification into the standard literary or artistic categories of Impressionist, Expressionist, Social Realist, etc. Since for Kraus what mattered in art as in life was integrity or ethical wholeness and not the particular art-form in which it was cast, his artistic standards transcended artistic allegiances.[64] Thus Kraus's place in the history of Austrian Expressionism 1890-1914 is not as straightforward as, say, Schiele's or Kokoschka's. Indeed Kraus, like Wittgenstein, looked back to the age of Goethe as the golden age of artistic achievement and to this extent shared Wittgenstein's aesthetic conservatism.

Correlatively, it could be said of Wittgenstein's *Tractatus* that while it itself did  not engage these shortcomings on the very streets of Vienna as did Kraus's polemics, it articulated, both in its form and content, an ethical-philosophical blue-print that did justice to Krausian polemics.

---

because of the good things Kraus had said about him and his journal *Der Brenner* in *Die Fackel*. *Ibid*, 83. Janik sums up the reception of the *Tractatus* as follows: "The reception of Wittgenstein's *Tractatus* in Austria presents a paradox: those Austrians who considered himself to be his disciples interpreted his work in a manner that Wittgenstein himself considered unacceptable, while those intellectuals with whom he identified himself in his own time could neither appreciate nor understand the *Tractatus*." *Ibid*, 75. In other words, the very people whom Wittgenstein hoped would see the true message of the *Tractatus* only succeeded in adding  a final ironical twist to the history of the assimilation of the *Tractatus* to the tradition of Austrian scientific positivistic philosophy.

[61] Sources for Kraus are: W A Iggers, *Karl Kraus: a Viennese Critic of the Twentieth Century* (The Hague: Martinus Nijhoff, 1967); H Zohn, *Karl Kraus* (New York: Twayne Publishers, 1971). For a more general history in which Kraus is a central character see: Field, *The Last Days of Mankind: Karl Kraus and his Vienna*; Janik and Toulmin, *Wittgenstein's Vienna*.

[62] Janik and Toulmin, *Vienna*, 67.

[63] Timms, *Karl Kraus, Apocalyptic Satirist: Culture and Catastrophe in Habsburg Vienna* (New Haven: Yale University Press, 1986).

[64] Janik and Toulmin, *Vienna*, 80.

It is the following passage from a letter which Wittgenstein wrote to Ficker in October 1919 which casts light on what Wittgenstein intended by the *Tractatus*:

> The book's point is an ethical one. I once meant to include in the preface a sentence that is not in fact there now but which I will write for you here for it will be perhaps a key to the work for you. What I then meant to write, then, was this: My work consists of two parts: the one presented here plus all I have not written. And it is precisely this second part that is the important one . My book draws limits to the sphere of the ethical from the inside as it were, and I am convinced this is the ONLY rigorous way of drawing these limits. In short, I believe that where many others are just gassing, I have managed in my book to put everything into place by being silent about it.[65]

And earlier on in the same letter Wittgenstein made the following revealing comment:

> For the present I will only say this much: the work is strictly philosophical and at the same time literary: but there's no gassing in it.[66]

The objective of the *Tractatus* coincided with that of Kraus's to the extent that, like Kraus, Wittgenstein was concerned with the integrity and wholeness of a statement rather than the effect it had on the hearer. Hence there was on the one hand the autonomy or *sui generis* identity of the statement and on the other hand the implicit critique of language that failed to satisfy this criterion. For Kraus the most conspicuous failure in this respect was that of the Viennese Press, one of *Die Fackel's* main targets. As Stern has written of Kraus:

> Gradually, after 1905, it is borne in upon him that language - that is, the way a statement is made - bears within itself all the signs he needs to understand the ethical quality of that statement and of him that made it. Conversely, it is necessary to read a statement in a way that is supremely sensitive to all its linguistic qualities, in order to discover the truth.[67]

Here it is the object - the statement - that is of primary importance to Kraus. He inveighed against the tendency to make everything subject to the criterion of effect, especially where truth was handed over to, and hence

---

[65] Quoted in von Wright, "Origin", 83.

[66] *Ibid*, 81.

[67] Stern, "Karl Kraus's Vision of Language", *Modern Language Review* (1966), 73-74.

compromised by, the lie, as in the Viennese newspapers' attitude to the
Great War, and war in general.[68] His objection to technology was based on
the same rationale. He objected to its invasion of nature, of progress
invading nature, of it failing to remain within its own realm. Just as
Wittgenstein objected to a culture pervaded and swamped by science, so
Kraus objected to the invasion of nature by technology. Hence when the
Great War came, he viewed it as an invasion of nature (and man) by the
destructive weapons of war.[69]

---

[68] The Viennese press are implicated in the 'mystification of war' Timms, *Kraus*, 145-
165. Instead of war as the bloody inhuman confrontation it is in reality, it is imbued with
heroism and glory. Come 1914, Kraus writes: "Through decades of practice, the
newspaper reporter has brought us to that degree of impoverishment of the imagination,
which make it possible to fight a war of annihilation against ourselves. The boundless
efficiency of this apparatus has deprived us of all capacity of experience and for the
mental development of that experience .... He has the images of heroic quality at his
disposal, and this abuse of language embellishes the abuse of life." Quoted, *Ibid*, 276.
But it is not just the press's abuse of language and of moral truth that *Die Fackel* takes
to task during the great War. The niney-three signatories on Kaiser's "Appeal to the
Civilised World" constitutes for Kraus as it did for Barth, an appalling intellectual *volte
face*. Kraus witnessed the phenomenon of some of the finest literary spirits in the
German language commit their talents to the service of war propaganda. *Ibid*, 290.
Kraus was particularly outraged by Gerhard Hauptmann, a German writer and Nobel
Prize Winner, whom he had greatly admired. As Kraus saw it, the German academic
community found it easy to interpret the war as promotion and defence of the idealism
of German culture. Kraus himself had sought to keep separate the 'two Germanies': the
Germany of Goethe and Beethoven and the Germany of Prussian militarism. But this
distinction went unobserved by the German academic community. *Ibid*, 304-308.
[69] E Timms, *Kraus*, 149. Thus it was that when the Great War came, it constituted for
Barth the most terrible metaphor for the translation of theology into non-theology.
Barth's reaction to the war is both well-known and well-documented. He was totally
against it. The German theological establishment was in the main not. And to Barth's
dismay, he discovered most of the names of his own theological teachers on the
manifesto issued by ninety-three intellectuals in support of the Kaisers' war policy.
Barth described this event thus. On the very day the First World War broke out "ninety
three German intellectuals issued a terrible manifesto, identifying themselves before all
the world with the war policy of Kaiser Wilhelm the Second and Chancellor Bethmann-
Holweg. For me it was almost worse than the violation of Belgian neutrality. And to my
dismay, among the signatories I discovered almost all my German teachers (with the
honourable exception of Martin Rade)." Quoted in Busch, *Barth*, 81. As Barth put it, it
"was like the twilight of the gods when I saw the reaction of Harnack, Herrmann, Rade,
Eucken and company to the new situation". Barth discovered how religion  and
scholarship could be changed completely into "intellectual 42cm cannons". Quoted in
Busch, *Barth*, 81. As a result Barth did not know what to make of "the teaching of all
my theological masters in Germany. To me they seemed to have been hopelessly
compromised by what I regarded as their failure in the face of the ideology of war."

Kraus was one of a brilliant galaxy of stars who populated Vienna just at a time when Habsburg Austria's own star was about to be extinguished in the cataclysm that was the First World War. There was Kraus, but also Adolf Loos, Arnold Schoenberg, Robert Musil, Rainer Maria Rilke, Sigmund Freud, Egon Schiele, Oscar Kokoschka. The two that stood closest to Kraus were Loos and Schoenberg. The architecture of Loos and the music of Schoenberg were intimately and consciously related to, and even extensions of, the critique of language and society conducted by Kraus.[70] But more fundamentally - and in this the three are to be distinguished both from the merely "languorous aestheticism" of Vienna and the alienated, *angst*-ridden elements of German expressionistic art-forms -[71] the rationale behind their respective critiques can be traced to a

---

Their "ethical failure" indicated that "their exegetical and dogmatic presuppositions could not be in order". Quoted in Busch, *Barth*, 81. Thus "a whole world of exegesis, ethics, dogmatics, and preaching, which I had hitherto held to as essentially trustworthy, was shaken to the foundations, and with it, all the other writings of the German theologians." Barth, *Schleiermacher*, 264. The war is perceived as the most appalling *reductio ad absurdum* of theology to non-theology: thus the translation of theology into 42cm cannons. Standing amidst the scene of this appalling hermeneutic of death and destruction, Barth did not miss what was now in retrospect the oddly prophetic voice of Overbeck: "Do the modern theologians think that they can put us off much longer with their absurd delusion that Christianity's best defence to insure its continued existence is its unlimited capacity for change?" Barth quoting Overbeck, "Unsettled Questions for Theology Today", 69. And if von Clausewitz was not wholly wrong in saying that diplomacy is only war by other means, then, most ominously of all: "Moses, Christ, Paul, and Luther are still given a place in world history, but only as a kind of ornamentation for display in public exhibitions .... But at the bottom of their hearts they are the best of 'believers in new things' and their master is Bismarck." Barth quoting Overbeck, *ibid*, 69-70. In fact, Overbeck's oddly prophetic voice is not odd at all: it is only the voice of an inspired metatheological critic who has witnessed the first stage of the eventual translation, pending Bismark's dismissal from office by Wilhelm II, of theology into 42cm cannons.

[70] "Kraus's insistence that he is trying to effect, by a polemical analysis of grammar and language, the same "creative separation" between the sphere of reason (or fact) and that of fantasy (or value) as Adolf Loos was doing in his critique of bourgeois Viennese taste, by distinguishing merely functional artifacts from genuine objets d'art, should be taken quite literally." Janik and Toulmin, *Vienna*, 89. On the cover of Kraus's copy of *The Theory of Harmony*, Schoenberg wrote: "I have learned more from you, perhaps than a man should learn, if he wants to remain independent." Regarding Loos, Kraus wrote: "Adolf Loos and I - he literally and I grammatically - have done nothing more than show that there is an essential distinction between an urn and a chamber pot and that it is this distinction that above all provides culture with elbow room." *Ibid*, 89.

[71] E Lunn distinguishes quite correctly between, on the one hand, the "languorous aestheticism" of Vienna, and, on the other, the "nervous, agitated and suffering" art

positive (though not positivistic and indeed anti-positivistic) aspiration to resolve Hume's dilemma transposed, as it were, to their respective fields.[72]

Transposed to the sphere of Adolf Loos, such an aspiration embodied as it was in his aesthetic theories of architecture and design, inevitably opposed the canons of late nineteenth-century popular taste[73] on the grounds that art as *art* was being sacrificed on the altar of impressionistic and therefore positivistic "good taste". In opposition to the practice of ornamenting articles of every-day use, a practice obliterating the essential distinction between an *objet d'art* and a purely functional item, Loos in his architecture "desired to eliminate all forms of decoration from functional

---

produced by German expressionism. See E Lunn, *Marxism and Modernism* (Berkeley: University of California Press, 1982), 58.

[72] Thus that the *Tractatus* cannot be assimilated to the expressionist movement of the first two decades of the twentieth century is of no of material importance to the thesis. The important fact is that Kraus, Loos and Schoenberg all participate in an attempt to restate the Enlightenment legacy, all continue to look back. Expressionism was a movement whose ethos was one of revolt from the bourgeois ethos prevailing at the close of the nineteenth century. (Thus just as the second half of the nineteenth century recapitulated the positivism of Hume then so expressionism, with its emphasis on solitariness of the individual alienated from society, was a recapitulation of Romanticism.) Wittgenstein did not embrace this revolt: if anything, he thought it a further disintegration from, and deterioration of, the great culture that had come to an end by the end of first half of the nineteenth century. In other words, it was a critique of bourgeois society and aesthetic that was itself badly in need of critique. Thus in the words of McGuinness, he was a "stranger to young Vienna". McGuinness, *Wittgenstein*, 33. During the First World War, at a time when Wittgenstein was stationed at the Eastern Front, he received two works by Albert Ehrenstein, a then-contemporary expressionist writer. Wittgenstein's reaction was undisguisedly hostile. In a letter to Paul Engelmann he wrote: "I received from Zurich two books by Albert Ehrenstein - the one who used to write in *Die Fackel* (once I helped him financially without really wanting to). Now he returns the favour by sending me his 'Tubutsch' and 'Man Screams'. It's just muck if I'm not mistaken. And such stuff is sent to me out here! Please send me as an antidote, Goethe's poems, the second volume, which has the *Venetian Epigrams*, the *Elegies*, and the *Epistles*! Also Morike's poems." Letter to Paul Engelmann 31.3.17 in Engelmann, *Letters*, 4. Wittgenstein's scathingly expressed distaste is not simply the reaction of a man who, in the midst of war, longed for something other than the aesthetic of expressionist angst. His judgement was rather, as Paul Engelmann put it some half a century later, "a judgement on an entire literary epoch, on what was then proclaimed as expressionism." *Ibid*, 85. The antidote with which Wittgenstein seeks to counter expressionist disequilibrium and instability is the classical beauty, serenity and simplicity of the classics of German literature. As Engelmann puts it, Wittgenstein asks for the "most severely classical verse of Goethe and Morike." He "draws on the purest well of classical German poetry." *Ibid*, 86.

[73] Janik and Toulmin, *Vienna*, 93-4.

items .... He put this notion into effect himself by designing buildings that entirely lacked the conventional elaborate facade."[74] Once again art and non-art stood as unsynthesisable thesis and antithesis such that the assimilation of the former into the realm of the latter was to be resisted at all costs.

Arnold Schoenberg, his music and the ideas underlying it, Schoenberg not merely as musicologist, but as metamusical critic, extended Kraus's polemic into yet another domain of the cultural life of *fin-de-siècle* Vienna just as  Loos had done in architecture. Schoenberg saw clearly that Viennese society demanded in music "conformity to conventional tastes", "elaboration of orchestration", and perhaps the most damaging demand of all: conformity to the principle that music was to be measured by "the effects which [it] produced in the listener".[75] For Schoenberg the cardinal question was whether music was "'self-sufficient' - that is, merely a coherent assemblage of sounds, and a language unto itself - or whether it was essential for it to express ideas or feelings - that is, to express something other than the musical" and thus be assimilated to the realm of the subjective.[76] As Janik and Toulmin remind us:

---

[74] *Ibid*, 93.

[75] *Ibid*, 103.

[76] *Ibid*, 103. Although Wittgenstein did not say explicitly that a meaner age had ushered in the end of the great golden European past of Mozart, Goethe, Schiller and Beethoven, it is clear that this is what he thought. McGuinness observes that Wittgenstein was not obsessed with the thought that the culture which he himself represented was a thing of the past. He accepted it more simply - as the medium in which to form his understanding of life. B F McGuinness, *Wittgenstein: A Life. Young Ludwig, 1899-1921* (London: Duckworth, 1987), 33. Thus Wittgenstein writes: "I often wonder whether my cultural ideal is a new one, i.e. contemporary, or whether it derives from Schumann's time. It does at least strike me as continuing that ideal, though not in the way it was actually continued at the time. That is to say, the second half of the nineteenth century has been left out. This I ought to say has been a purely instinctive development and not the result of reflection. Wittgenstein, *CV*, 2. In this remark on Schumann Wittgenstein implicitly dissociates himself from the music of the second half of the nineteenth century. Indeed, the origins of Schoenberg's question - whether music was "self-sufficient" or should express other than itself, ideas or feelings - can be traced to this period. At the time there were two opposing camps on this issue, the music of Brahms representing one school of thought and Wagner the other. That Brahms was regarded as an exponent of *sui generis* music would have made sense to Wittgenstein since for him Brahms was the last representative of the first Viennese school. See McGuinness, *Wittgenstein*, 19f. In contrast, Wagner is never viewed as such for the reason that his music fails the autonomy criterion. As McGuinness perceptively puts it: according to Wittgenstein, Wagner "was an imitator of Beethoven and in him Beethoven's terrible or cosmic irony had become earthly and *bourgeois* ...." *Ibid*, 56. More than anything else, it is the programmatic element in Wagner to which Wittgenstein is sensitive. As McGuinness

Schoenberg used to defend his so-called "atonal" music - while disavowing the term - against those who attacked it for its dissonance, by reminding them that the musically untutored had similarly attacked all the classical Viennese composers, whom they considered to be writing dissonant monstrosities. But Haydn and Mozart did not write for the untutored and never aimed at "sounding good."[77]

And as Schoenberg himself put it:

To be musical means to have an ear in the *musical* sense, not in the *natural* sense. A musical ear must have assimilated the tempered scale. And a singer who produces natural pitches is unmusical, just as someone who acts "naturally" in the street may be immoral.[78]

In other words, Schoenberg perceived himself to be taking the music of the first Viennese school to its logical conclusion. His objective was nothing other than to eliminate all traces of the natural to leave behind pure *sui generis* music. Music was now to be itself completely and exclusively - it was not to be a function of, or measured by, anything else, not the natural ear (not nature), and not demeaned for the sake of effect. Schoenberg, then, shared another quality with Kraus, Loos and Wittgenstein. If he was a revolutionary at all, then he was a conservative revolutionary. His objection to the music of the second half of the nineteenth century was that it, unlike the music of the classical Viennese school, had succumbed to the criterion of effect.[79] In opposition to his immediate predecessors, Schoenberg

---

puts it: "Perhaps we can read something more into his critical remark - that we cannot translate word for word from one language in to another. ... the literary goals, the message desired are too mechanically rendered in music by Wagner: a move away this from Wittgenstein's youthful identification with the *Meistersingers* and a move toward an inexpressive art, where what matters is not what is said but how it is said." *Ibid*, 272.) As Wittgenstein puts it himself: "where Genius wears thin, skill may show through (Overture to the *Meistersingers*)." Wittgenstein, *CV*, 43. The skill in question is precisely the skill of the human, the creator who fails to remove himself from his work of art and had therefore compromised the identity of art.

[77] *Ibid*, 111.

[78] Janik and Toulmin, *Vienna*, 111.

[79] Indeed there is no better spokesman for Schoenberg's (and Wittgenstein's) aesthetic ideal than the Abbé in Goethe's *Wilhelm Meisters Lehrjahre* (bk viii, ch 7): "Most people treat finished works of art as though there are made of putty. According to their own preferences, prejudices and whims, they would have the chiselled marble remodelled, massive walls pulled out or in; a painting must teach, a drama edify, and everything must be anything but what it is. [...] They reduce it all to what they call effect

claimed time and time again that he was only working through in a strictly logical fashion the purely musical ideas of Bach, Mozart and Beethoven.[80] Accordingly, all his compositions can be viewed as attacks on the pseudo-sophistication of *bourgeois* aestheticism.[81] In fact, when viewed as a whole, the positivist aesthetic ethos of the second half of the nineteenth century is a recapitulation of Hume's aesthetic in the eighteenth century.[82] This constitutes one more reason why it is erroneous to assimilate Wittgenstein to a Humean tradition if he can be assimilated to Schoenberg.[83]

---

and everything is relative to their own feeling and taste." Quoted in E M Wilkinson, *Goethe's Conception of Form*, (London: Oxford University Press, 1951), 191.

[80] Janik and Toulmin, *Vienna*, 107.

[81] Janik and Toulmin, *Vienna*, 111-112.

[82] In a section entitled "Taste and The Trend Toward Subjectivism", Cassirer writes: "Thus taste is no longer classified with the logical processes of inference and conclusion [as in the earlier Cartesian Geometric paradigm] but placed on a par with the immediacy of the pure acts of perception - with seeing and hearing, tasting and smelling. This transition has now brought us to the way which Hume follows through to its logical conclusion." Cassirer, *Enlightenment*, 304-5.

[83] Schoenberg can also be seen as providing the key to the deepest impulse behind Barth's objection to natural theology (and perhaps the allergic reaction shown by some to what appears as the lack of air - the lack of the human - in Barth's theology). Schoenberg's metamusical analysis leads him to reject music assimilated to natural sound, natural pitch, as *unmusical*. The composer, insofar as it is *music* he wishes to compose, is obliged to exclude the natural, and, at one remove, nature itself. Transposed to the realm of music, natural theology is a contradiction in terms - there it becomes *natural* music, *naturally* apprehended; there it becomes *natural* theology, assimilated to *natural* (and hence non-theological) categories. Schoenberg's advocacy of *sui generis* music - a specifically *musical* truth - makes him the legatee of the greatest composer of the late Enlightenment, Wolfgang Amadeus Mozart. Accordingly, the explanation of Barth's exclusive love of Mozart is not that it is attributable, as John Bowden believes, to some kind of personality flaw in Barth, (J Bowden, *Karl Barth, Theologian* (London: SCM Press, 1983), 103-4); nor that Mozart's musical dynamic structure mirrors in some way the developing structure of the *Church Dogmatics* as Theodore Gill asserts (T Gill, *Barth and Mozart*, 409); rather Mozart's music embodied as parable, not simply a theological ideal to which theology as *theology* can approximate, but a *sui generis* theological identity identifiable as theological truth and expressed by 'God is *God*'. It is such a rationale that underlies Barth's attitude toward Mozart *vis-à-vis*, for example, Bach and Beethoven: "Mozart does not wish to say anything at all, he just sings and sounds. So he does not intrude a thing upon the hearer, he does not ask decisions of or comments of him, he just lets him alone." (Barth, "Wolfgang Amadeus Mozart", translated by W M Mosse, in W Leibrecht (ed), *Religion and Culture: Essays in Honour of Paul Tillich* (London: SCM Press, 1959), 69.) According to Barth, Mozart's music is not to be judged by the criterion of *effect*, the effect it has on the listener. (This of course shadows Schoenberg's metamusical conclusions). He does not wish his music to translate into the realm of the non-musical, in this case the human. In other words,

The clash between on the one hand Wittgenstein, Kraus, Loos and Schoenberg and, on the other, the dominant cultural and social tendencies of Central Europe toward the end of the nineteenth century was essentially a clash between a unique form of objectivism and a ubiquitous subjectivism. One took its point of departure from the external object in that it followed on from the autonomy of the object in question. The other was the culture  whose aesthetic criterion was decorativeness and effect such that it amounted to a superficial sensationalism where art was reduced to the sensations it evoked.  Thus what separates "Wittgenstein's Vienna" from the second half of the nineteenth century also separates it from the subjectivism at the heart of the German Expressionist movement. *Romans* II was also separated from these two traditions, and for the same reasons.

### 4. Barth as Metatheological Critic:
### *Romans* II and Overbeck's Dilemma

Paul's letter to the Romans is by common consensus one of the greatest New Testament writings. Of all the Pauline epistles it has more often than not been Romans that has had the greatest evangelical impact, even on its most theologically literate readers (as was attested by Augustine and Luther). In other words, the response the epistle demanded could not be contained within, and indeed transcended assimilation to, the ordinary canons of 'grammarian' scholarship. This was no less true of Barth, modern

---

Barth's attitude to Bach and Beethoven is precisely that they compromise music as *music*: "Mozart's music, in contrast to that of Bach's, has no message and, contrary to that of Beethoven, involves no personal confession. His music does not give rules, even less does it reveal the composer himself. (Barth, *Mozart*, 69.) And in a criticism of the development  of music through the nineteenth century: "It must be said that the later music from Beethoven onwards, desired and loved the world of sound too little for its own sake." (Barth, *Protestant Theology*, 72.) In other words, Mozart's music had an autonomy both Bach and Beethoven (and the rest of the nineteenth century) lacked: Bach's preached, (Barth's objection to Bach, "otherwise so loved by theologians, was his all too deliberate, all too artificial desire to preach, while Mozart attracted him because he was free from such intentions and simply played." *Ibid*, 362.); Beethoven's is a barely concealed confession. In contrast, Mozart's stood its ground on its own terms: it possessed self-contained musical autonomy, which is to say, it did not stray into the human realm, either linguistically as sermon or emotionally as personal confession. It therefore exemplified as in Wittgenstein the standard against which all music can and should be criticised as *music*. Music is *music*, not sermon, not emotion, but music. The similarity between Barth and Wittgenstein's  respective aesthetic criteria as described in Chapter 13 section 8 - and the relation between the criteria and their views of, respectively, theology and philosophy - is unmistakable!

as he was. To say that Barth's commentary on Paul's letter to the Romans "remains the greatest Pauline study of our time"[84] overestimates the extent to which it was a study at all in the traditional scholarly sense. This is above all true of the second of the two commentaries Barth wrote on Romans. Where the first manifested "knowledge in the mode of contemplation",[85] knowledge belonging to a "relatively secure contemplative subject",[86] the second is replete with a self subject to dialectical fragmentation. This has led scholars to reconstitute *Romans* II as a theological postmodernity thematically coincident with the expressionist movement which undoubtedly formed part of its cultural *milieu*.[87]

That *Romans* II shares characteristics in common with Oswald Spengler's *Decline of the West*, Ernst Bloch's *Geist der Utopie* (1918), Karl Jasper's *Psychologie der Weltanschauungen*, Graf Keyserling's *Reise-Tagebuch eines Philosophen*, Theodore Lessing's *Geschichte als Sinngebung des Sinnlosen* ('*History as giving meaning to the meaningless*') (1919), Leopold Ziegler's *Gestaltwandel der Götter* (1920), Max Brod's *Heidentum, Judentum, Christentum* (1921), Ludwig Klage's *Vom kosmogensichen Eros* (1922), Sigmund Freud's *The I and the Id*, Fritz Mauthner's *Der Atheismus und seine Geschichte im Abendlande* (1923) - that *Romans* II shares characteristics in common with some or of all of these books cannot be gainsaid.[88] Yet neither *Romans* II nor Barth's theology can be understood properly inside this particular cultural context.[89]

Though in *Romans* II Barth will use a language that shares in the expressionistic art-forms of the time,[90] it is not, as in the case of the expressionists in order to respond to "the times." To be sure, there are

---

[84] P Minear, *The Obedience of Faith: The Purposes of Paul in the Epistle to the Romans* (London: SCM Press Ltd, 1971), ix.

[85] R H Roberts, "Barth and the Eschatology of Weimar: A Theology on its Way?", R H Roberts, *A Theology on its Way? Essays on Karl Barth* (Edinburgh: T & T Clark, 1991), 193.

[86] *Ibid*, 192.

[87] *Ibid*, 184-185.

[88] I am indebted to J C O'Neill's book, *The Bible's Authority. A Portrait Gallery of Thinkers from Lessing to Bultmann* (Edinburgh: T & T Clark, 1991), 227-278 for bringing this list of books to my attention. Roberts has also argued the affinity between *Romans* II and Bloch's work.

[89] O'Neill, *The Bible's Authority*, 278.

[90] Even so, it is possible to view the "expressionist" literary style of *Romans* II - a combination of hyperbole (Nietzsche) and irony (Kierkegaard) - as more or less continuous with Barth's "dialectical meanderings". See S H Webb, *Re-Figuring Theology: The Rhetoric of Karl Barth* (New York: University of New York, 1991). Once again, we are back with Overbeck's dilemma: as we shall see, Barth took the view that his various dialectical "meanderings" were merely ways of expressing `God is *God*'.

themes coinciding with the expressionist spirit of the times - nihilism (annihilation), the shattering of *bourgeois* reality, etc.;[91] but to emphasise an expressionist dimension participating in *angst* and alienation in relation to a decadent bourgeois society is to assimilate *Romans* II to a specific Romantic (and hence post-modern) tradition that is not finally appropriate.

---

[91] See K-J Kuschel, *Born Before All Time? The Dispute over Christ's Origin*, translated by John Bowden, (London: SCM Press, 1992), 68-81; R H Roberts, "Barth and the Eschatology of Weimar", 193. To be sure, as Kuschel notes, (*Born Before All Time?*, 81), Barth declared that "[h]owever strong our aversion may be to the work of the modern expressionists, it is more than clear that for these men the chief concern is the essence, the content, the referring of the beautiful to life's unity, in contrast to that *art for its own sake* which prevailed during the last generation, but which, after all, can cite precedent with certainty in neither Raphael or Dürer." Barth, "The Christian's Place in Society", *The Word of God and the Word of Man*, translated by D Horton, (New York: Harper, 1957), 292. Yet though this is the testimony of a man who thought more of expressionist art than that which Schoenberg scorned as *bourgeois* aestheticism, it is certainly not a whole-hearted approval of expressionism. The context of the statement is precisely that, given the *art for art's sake* movement (the English equivalent would have been the life and work of Oscar Wilde), it is not surprising that there has been such a reaction in the form of expressionist excess. That his own theology is a reaction against *religion for its own sake* is corroboration of the fact that the *art for art's sake* movement was not the aesthetic equivalent of his own theology, (*Ibid*, 293); rather, it represented an utterly self-centred aesthetic ethos aimed at the 'aestheticification' of everything human. It was aesthetic *effect par excellence*. Though Barth, ultimately, could not countenance expressionism positively, his attitude was that one could not be surprised that aestheticism had been attacked, as indeed had been *authority for its own sake, the family for its own sake, work for its own sake*, and of course, *religion for its own sake*. *Ibid*, 291-293. Barth had no expressionist sympathies other than the "sympathy" he expressed for the movement as a reaction to the previous generation's art. *Ibid*, 291-292. Indeed, late in his life Barth, speaking specifically of literature, was to admit to the poet Carl Zuckmayer that on reading a novel from the modernist tradition he could not make head or tail of it: "I am unfortunately a child of the nineteenth century and there is nothing I can do about it." C Zuckmayer, *A Late Friendship, the Letters of Barl Barth and Carl Zuckmayer*, translated by G W Bromiley, (Grand Rapids: Michigan, 1983), 1. Indeed, his attitude toward modernity mirrored Wittgenstein's. Barth, like Wittgenstein, admitted he could not understand its language. In 1956 a pianist and musicologist friend of Barth's had attempted in vain to make him interested in Paul Hindemith. In a letter Barth wrote to a friend in 1963 he conceded that "unfortunately I simply cannot make sense of any modern art (in all three of its forms). I am in no position to pass a negative judgement, which is why I don't think I have ever said a bad word against it. But it is a sad fact that I have no understanding of it, no eye or ear for it. Perhaps I shall discover in heaven what is so hidden from me now. But it is lamentable that it has not happened to me yet." (Quoted in Busch, *Barth*, 411). To be sure, where Wittgenstein seems to have dismissed modern art forms out of hand, Barth located the problem in himself rather than, as Wittgenstein did, in the art!

It is to confuse the literary means with the theological end, the form in which the content is expressed with the content itself.[92] *Romans* II may have been a product of the times but it was not primarily a response to the times.

*Prima facie*, assimilating the cacophonous chord of discord struck by *Romans* II to a "reworking" of the history of the Enlightenment legacy may appear to work only at the expense of 're-editing' the message of the text to the point of distortion. Yet if its final hermeneutical horizon is Overbeck's and Hume's dilemma[93] then the themes coinciding with the expressionist spirit of the times - nihilism (annihilation), the shattering of *bourgeois* reality, etc. - must be taken as rather more incidental than essential to the

---

[92] It is noteworthy that Roberts makes such a case for *Romans* II in an essay in which the only reference made to Overbeck occurs within the context of the Weiss-Schweitzer consistent eschatology thesis. Roberts, "Barth and the Eschatology of Weimar", 191. Overbeck's influence went far beyond this. Barth wrote "Unsettled Questions for Theology" between writing his first and second commentaries on Paul's letter to the Romans. Indeed, it was his encounter with Overbeck that precipitated writing the second commentary from a 'consistent eschatology' perspective. See Bruce L McCormack, *Karl Barth's Critically Realistic Dialectical Theology. Its Genesis and Development 1909-1936* (Oxford: Clarendon, 1995), 231-232. Moreover, the expressionist influence that prevailed between the autumn of 1921 and the summer of 1922 - the period in which Barth wrote *Romans* II - (Busch, *Barth*, 118) was as strong if not stronger during the period in which *Romans* I was written. This begs the question why the expressionist ('dialectical') style was not utilised in *Romans* I. Roberts himself demonstrates just this difference when he shows how *Romans* II's exegesis of 8.24-5 differs from that of *Romans* I. *Ibid*, 191-196. My own view is that one can make best sense of these facts if one assumes the expressionist style was brought in with the eschatological theme, which in turn was due to Barth's encounter with Overbeck's dilemma.

[93] This does not mean there are no Kantian elements in *Romans* II. Barth himself refers to "closer acquaintance with Plato and Kant" as one of the reasons for rewriting *Romans*. See *CR* II, 4. Hendry has shown how Barth combined Plato and Kant (utilising the latter's concept of 'transcendental condition') in his treatment of the Fall of the world. See G S Hendry, "The Transcendental Method in the Theology of Karl Barth", *The Scottish Journal of Theology*, (1984), 216-9. Yet once again all this takes place within the horizon of Hume and Overbeck's dilemma as it is resolved by 'God is *God*'. Pears' remark that Kant fits the form rather than the content of the *Tractatus* applies equally well to *Romans* II. McCormack cites Barth's statement that the revelation does not become intuitable next to the other intuitable objects; it becomes intuitable [*anschaulich*] as the Unintuitable [*das Unanschauliche*] (McCormack, *Karl Barth's Critically Realistic Dialectical Theology*, 249) as the launching pad for a distinctly Kantian interpretation of *Romans* II. It is just conceivable that this mistakes what is only form for content (the form being what Barth uses to express the content). The Kantian language is, as McCormack acknowledges, used as a metaphor (*Ibid*, 249), notwithstanding the fact that Barth affirmed Kantian epistemological conceptuality.

expression of the message (thought this is not to say it is not intrinsic to the identity of *Romans* II).

The crisis to which Barth responded in *Romans* II was fundamentally a *theological* crisis.[94] But in which precise sense was it theological? Was the crisis, for example, one of judgement about all things human (human religion, culture, ethics, etc.)? To be sure, Barth does sound such a judgement in *Romans* II, but there is a very specific 'human thing' which constituted the theological crisis to which Barth responded in *Romans* II. This was the crisis brought about by the practice of theology as non-theology. The theological crisis to which Barth responded in *Romans* II was that which he had articulated in "Unsettled Questions for Theology Today" after reading Overbeck's *Christentum und Kultur*. The theological crisis was nothing other than the metatheological dilemma.

This latter conclusion depends upon a premise which is, at present, unsubstantiated, namely: is there any evidence in *Romans* II itself that the identity of the crisis to which Barth responded was in the nature of a dilemma? The answer to this question must be derived from an analysis of the text itself. Nevertheless, what it is Barth intended by the text is indicated in his remark on Overbeck in the second preface to *Romans*. McCormack agrees that Overbeck is the undoubted catalyst behind Barth rewriting *Romans* I in the form of *Romans* II.[95] In January 1920 Barth read *Christentum und Kultur*. The following month he wrote "Unsettled Questions". But it is not merely that (when Barth lists the influences which brought him to rewrite the first edition), Overbeck is placed on his own and receives attention before the next group of influences - Plato, Kant, Kierkegaard and Dostoyevsky. In other words, it is not merely that Barth asserts Overbeck influenced him; it is that Barth is quite precise about the nature of this influence. Overbeck's book is "filled with the apocalyptic air of judgement."[96] Judgement on whom? In the second preface to *Romans*,

---

[94] Hence, neither the Great War nor the failure of socialism were in themselves the *cause of* Barth's theology. The crisis is that articulated by Overbeck.

[95] McCormack, *Karl Barth's Critically Realistic Dialectical Theology*, 231-232. One could argue that when Barth encountered Overbeck he realised that Overbeck had articulated the problem far more precisely than he had when he wrote *Romans* I. And since *Romans* I did not adequately deal with Overbeck's "riddle", he rewrote it. This is why Barth could say that where *Romans* I "had been written in a still very nebulous and speculative form' ... the second edition ... presented the reader with 'sharply contoured antitheses' ... 'I think I am a *bit* nearer the truth of the matter than before'." Busch, *Barth*, 118. Again: "... the second edition represented much more clearly than the first bold attempt to introduce a theology 'which may be better than that of the nineteenth century and the beginning of the twentieth in that it is concerned quite simply with *God* ....'" *Ibid*, 119.

[96] Barth, "Unsettled Questions", 57.

Barth refers to "the warning addressed by Overbeck to all theologians." He continues:

> This warning I have first applied to myself, and then directed upon the enemy. Whether I have dealt at all adequately with the questions raised by this eminent and pious man I must leave to the judgement of those who are able to perceive the nature of the riddle [*das Rätsel*] he has formulated so precisely, and are willing to attempt at least its solution. To the judgement of men like Eberhardt Vischer I cannot submit myself! He sees in the riddle no more than a biographical and psychological problem.[97]

It is reasonable to assume that this "riddle" is precisely what Barth articulated in "Unsettled Questions for Theology Today". If this is so, and it can be shown from the text itself that *Romans* II is an attempt to resolve this riddle, it must follow that *Romans* II is an attempt to resolve the metatheological dilemma. Though one could still have maintained that *Romans* II deals with Overbeck's dilemma in the *absence* of the fact that Overbeck is referred to in terms of the "riddle he has formulated so precisely" for theology,[98] the fact that there *is* such a reference serves to strengthen the validity of my conclusion: *Romans* II is an attempt to resolve the metatheological dilemma.[99] It was the judgement of the nineteenth

---

[97] Barth, *CR* II, 3-4.

[98] The preface in which Barth uses the term *das Rätsel* is dated September 1921. It is not a term he uses in the essay "Unsettled Questions for Theology Today" written in the early part of 1920. Busch, *Barth*, 115. One can surmise that when Barth spoke of *das Rätsel* in the later preface he had further interpreted what he had written in his essay on Overbeck in terms of "Overbeck's riddle for theology".

[99] To be sure, in a passage from the text of *Romans* II itself Barth appears to depict Overbeck's riddle in a way that is not immediately identifiable with the concept of metatheological dilemma: "The paradox must be maintained absolutely, in order that the scandal may not be obscured, and in order that Christianity may be disclosed in its true nature as `a problem which is itself essentially a riddle, and which sets a question-mark against every human achievement in history' (Overbeck)." Barth *CR* II, 100. Yet in the context of the question whether Christianity has the possibility of an historical development, Barth construes Overbeck's answer in terms of the metathcological dilemma: "Overbeck denies such a possibility categorically. Inflexibly he confronts us with the choice: If Christianity, then not history; if history then not Christianity. 'Historic Christianity - that is Christianity subjected to time - is an absurdity' .... History is precisely the basis on which Christianity can *not* be established; for 'neither Christ himself nor the faith which he found among his disciples has ever had any historical existence under the name of Christianity' .... 'History is an abyss into which Christianity has been thrown against its will'...." Barth, "Unsettled Questions for Theology Today", 61.

century that any crisis was Overbeck's own; Barth's judgement was that the
crisis is precisely a crisis for theology and for men like Vischer.[100] This
crisis Barth dated to Overbeck, but in fact it was one that had been in
perpetual motion, so to speak, since even before Overbeck and 1873 -
namely, since Hume. Barth, the lone prophetic theological voice of the
time, put Paul's letter to the Romans to distinctly theological use. It was, as
he put it, "a bomb dropped into the playground of the theologians".[101] In
other words, it was primarily aimed at theologians, not merely *all* things
human.

It is thus that *Romans* II must be understood. To repeat: Barth is a
metatheological critic whose blueprint for the possibility of theology "in
and of itself" is the life-long proclamation "God is *God*". 'God is *God*' is
the blue-print for a *sui generis* theological realm belonging to theology " in
and of itself'. In that sense it is a blue-print for theological truth. As the
guarantee of theological truth, 'God is *God*' entails the possibility of
theology "in and of itself' and the existence of theology entails 'God is
*God*'.

Eberhard Busch writes that: "There are those who believe that to his very
end Barth repeated only 'God is God'. But as time went on, another aspect
is claimed to have been more characteristic of his theology, namely its
*Christocentrism*. That view is not altogether false."[102] In opposition to the
somewhat stronger thesis that the later Christocentric presence *overcame*
Barth's earlier 'God is *God*' theology,[103] Busch counters with the assertion
that the "theological principle not only does NOT exclude the later
Christocentric theology but was *and* remained its *premise*, a premise which
neither dropped nor even corrected the basic structure of the principle."[104]
But Barth as a Christian theologian was a Christocentric theologian before
the *Church Dogmatics*. He was in fact a Christocentric theologian in
*Romans* II.[105] Hence if 'God is *God*' is a blueprint for the earlier theology,
Christocentricity is no bar to it being present with the same force in the later
theology. Whether Christocentrism became more characteristic (in the
precise sense of the term) is not the issue here. Indeed, as will be seen,

---

[100] Barth described Vischer, later a colleague at Basel, as "a sturdy embodiment of the
extraordinary academic spirit to be found at the end of the nineteenth century." Quoted in
Busch, *Barth*, 268. Thus it was to be expected that he would seek the source of the riddle in
Overbeck rather than in theology as it was practised at the time.

[101] Quoted in Barth, *How I Changed my Mind*, translated by M E Bratcher, (Edinburgh:
Saint Andrew Press, 1969), 25.

[102] Busch, "God is God: The Meaning of a Controversial Formula and the Fundamental
Problem of Speaking About God", *The Princeton Seminary Bulletin* 7 (1986), 102.

[103] *Ibid*, 102.

[104] *Ibid*, 103.

[105] McCormack, *Karl Barth's Critically Realistic Dialectical Theology*, 250.

'God is *God*' is no less apparent in the later work. Barth did repeat 'God is *God*' to the very end.

The affirmation of a blueprint for a theological truth that is authentically *sui generis* is finally the issue at stake and the rationale behind the proclamation 'God is *God*' in *Romans* II. *Romans* II constitutes both a blueprint for the *sui generis* identity of theology and proceeds to propound an eschatological instantiation of it.

Is affirming the *sui generis* identity of theology incompatible with historical truth-claiming? Is such an affirmation anti-historical in essence? No. One outstanding reason Barth resolves Overbeck's dilemma in the realm of the eschatological is because it was there that Overbeck thought the existence of theology "in and of itself" was nullified. According to Barth, Overbeck is an inspired metatheological critic who left the theology of the time with the stark choice: either do non-theology or nothing. This conclusion Overbeck based on premises derived from early Church history, in particular the unfulfilled expectation of the *parousia* in the lifetime of the early Church. (That is why he had lost faith through the study of early Church history.) The historical event of the imminent end of the world required to fulfil the eschatological expectation of the early church had not materialised.

Certainly if Overbeck is right, Barth will give up the ghost on the prospect of "theology in and of itself". His proclamation that any Christianity "which is not utterly and absolutely [*ganz und gar und restlos*] eschatological has utterly and absolutely nothing to do with Christ"[106] informs us that such a condition was no less than a necessary condition of theology. It also announces the advent of that characteristic Barthian voice of dialectical irony missing in *Romans* I and "The Strange New World Within the Bible": "Quite so, Overbeck! Any Christianity which is not utterly and absolutely eschatological has utterly and absolutely nothing to do with Christ."[107]

---

[106] Barth, *CR* II, 314.

[107] Thus Jüngel writes: "The end of Barth's theological beginnings, and the dawn of the so-called dialectical theology, can be seen most clearly in Barth's lecture 'Unsettled Questions for Theology Today' which took the form of a review of Overbeck's aphorisms in *Christentum und Kultur*." See Jüngel, *Barth*, 56. *Pace* M Beintker's determination to show that a dialectical theology of a kind exists in Barth's so-called "pre-dialectical" phase (M Beintker, *Die Dialectik in der `dialektischen Theologie' Karl Barths* (Munich: Chr Kaiser Verlag, 1987), 109-117), there is little doubt that, from now on, Overbeck's metatheological dilemma constitutes the fundamental rationale behind the characteristic contours of Barth's dialectical irony. The period of Barth's theology encompassed by this study begins with "The Strange New World Within the Bible". This lecture anticipates the theme of *sui generis* theological truth, though without the characteristic dialectical irony which informs Barth's theology from his encounter with Overbeck's metatheological

So Barth agrees with Overbeck: the resolution of the metatheological dilemma must be in the realm of the eschatological. But In *Romans* II the eschatological dimension is identified with the resurrection (the identity of the resurrection is "absolutely and utterly" eschatological, not to say "absolutely and utterly" theological). And since theology "in and of itself" entails 'God is *God*', the assertion that "The resurrection is the revelation of the disclosing of Jesus as the Christ, the appearing of God, and the apprehending of God in Jesus."[108] attests to 'God is *God*' revealed in the eschatological.[109] In other words, there is now "absolute and utter" identity (an identity Barth will later retract)[110] between, on the one hand, 'God is *God*', and, on the other, His revelation of Himself in the eschatological event.

According to Barth, this means that eschatological event - and by this Barth means the resurrection - cannot be a historical event of the kind evaluated by historians. As he put it himself later: "Last *things*, as such, are not *last* things, however great and significant they may be." [111] Last *things* are the subject-matter of non-theology, *last* things as the revelation of God as *God* belong to theology proper.[112]

*But it is not that Barth thought that revelation - the resurrection - was not a historical event.* It was. When he spoke of the resurrection as a de-historicized eschatological event, he did not mean that he had taken it out of the realm of history; he meant that it must be a historical event that left "theology in and of itself" intact. As McCormack puts it, it had to be an event "*in* history but not *of* history",[113] which is to say: it had to be the kind

---

dilemma onwards. Thus not only does Overbeck inform *Romans* II, it is also the final horizon of *Fides Quaerens Intellectum* and the *Church Dogmatics*.

[108] Barth, *CR* II, 30. As we shall see, throughout Barth's theological life, the resurrection is God's self-revelation.

[109] Thus Jüngel's thesis that 'God is *God*' is to be construed as a proposition of natural theology (Jungel, *Barth*, 78) is to rejected.

[110] Later, in the *Church Dogmatics*, Barth will retract this assertion and reverse the functional relationship, making the eschatological a function of the resurrection. See Barth *CD* II/1, 631-638. Later still in the *Dogmatics* the resurrection is constituted by pre-temporal, post-temporal and supra-temporal properties, (not merely the post-temporal alone). Barth, *CD* III/2, 488ff.

[111] Barth, *The Resurrection of the Dead*, 110.

[112] Jüngel, *Barth*, 35. . Barth appropriated the term "primal history" [*Urgeschichte*] from Overbeck, but used it, in a sense Overbeck never intended, to retheologise the eschatological dimension, (in the process tying protology to eschatology). But this appropriation of *Urgechichte*, as McCormack points out, is precisely a reaffirmation of history, it is not remotely anti-historical. It is *Urgeschichte* as *Geschichte*. McCormack, *Karl Barth's Critically Realistic Dialectical Theology*, 229.

[113] *Ibid*, 252.

of historical event faithful to the truth of 'God is *God.*' Otherwise, the possibility of resolving Overbeck's dilemma vouchsafing the existence of theology as *theology* would be nullified. Barth's proclamation 'God is *God*', coinciding as it must with the deliverance of the resurrection from non-theology[114] and reinstantiation of it in the realm of the *sui generis* historical, has no horizon other than Overbeck's metatheological dilemma, itself also articulated in language whose subject-matter is the realm of eschatological phenomena.

### 5. Barth's `Position on Epistemology' in *Romans* II: the Principle Behind Dialectical Speech

That the resurrection was a historical event in this sense - one not susceptible to the discipline of history and its accompanying critical-historical methodological principles - is the rationale behind the necessity of dialectical speech when speaking of God's revelation. Barth took the view that his various dialectical "meanderings" were merely ways of expressing 'God is *God*'.[115] McCormack is of the opinion that the eschatological demands dialectical thinking understood in terms of contradiction and antithesis.[116] Given the identity between 'God is *God*' and the eschatological, it is no surprise that the same `property' is predicated of both.[117]

---

[114] Thus for Barth, believing historicism is just as much a species of non-theology as unbelieving historicism: "... in spite of all believing and unbelieving historicism and psychologising, we encounter in Jesus the scandal of an eternal revelation .... The truth of God is not liable to the 'flux of history'. His action can neither be perceived everywhere nor be dismissed as being nowhere. In Jesus, and precisely in him, the Love of God breaks through all historical and psychological analysis and in directness and mediation transcends both, for it is bound neither to this or that thing nor to this or that place." Barth, *CR* II, 277. Later, historicism (and psychologism) as tokens of non-theology became a "shorthand" for what it is Barth opposed on behalf of theology. McCormack writes: "These two targets of Barth's criticism are attacked separately but at times are coupled together. This will occur with increasing frequency during the course of the 1920s, becoming a shorthand for that which he opposes." McCormack, *Karl Barth's Critically Realistic Dialectical Theology*, 249.

[115] Quoted in Busch, *Barth*, 119.

[116] McCormack, *Karl Barth's Critically Realistic Dialectical Theology*, 165.

[117] Overbeck's dilemma is *the* final horizon of *Romans* II and not just *a* horizon. Given: (1) the identity of 'God is *God*' and the eschatological; (2) the fact that Barth's use of dialectic whether between time and eternity or Christ and Adam, the Old Man and the New Man (in Christ) is logically subordinate to his futuristic yet historical (and retheologised) eschatology, it follows that dialectic *must* be logically subordinate to

It is precisely because, as McCormack puts it, the resurrection as revelation was "*in* history but not *of* history" that speech about God must be dialectical. Therein lies the need for paradox. If it were neither *in* history nor *of* history there would be no need for paradoxical language. But since it was in history, it demanded a method of statement and counter-statement caught in the spiral of an unstable equilibrium. As Barth famously wrote: "If I have a system," he wrote, "it is a system limited to a recognition of what Kierkegaard called the 'infinite qualitative distinction' between time and eternity, and to my regarding this as possessing negative as well as positive significance."[118]

Barth uses the word "System" not without ironic connotation. In both the *Philosophical Fragments* and *Concluding Unscientific Postscript*, Kierkegaard castigated those indices of supreme self-confidence integral to Hegel's system: completeness, equilibrium, unity. To be sure, Kierkegaard's reaction to Hegel was based on the view that it was human existence which evaded every attempt to represent it in a system. For Barth, it was God who could not be represented in a system - not in spite of but because of revelation. The infinite qualitative distinction (revealed in revelation) rules out such a system.[119] Accordingly, if Barth has a system it is one that rules out completeness, equilibrium and unity etc. In other words, he declares that if he has a system it is one that rules out all systems in so far as they possess the aforementioned properties!

It is not Hegel *per se* that Barth is against but rather any system which entailed completeness, equilibrium and unity - a (stable) human position on

---

'God is *God*'. Given the identity of 'God is *God*' and the eschatological, it follows that dialectical speech is no less in force in face of the latter: "In the resurrection the new world of the Holy Spirit touches the old world of the flesh, but touches it as a tangent touching a circle, that is without touching it. And precisely because it does not touch it, it touches it as its frontier - as the new world. The resurrection is therefore an occurrence in history, which took place outside the gates of Jerusalem in the year 30 AD, inasmuch as it there 'came to pass', was discovered and recognised. But inasmuch as the occurrence was conditioned by the resurrection, insofar as it was not the 'coming to pass', or the discovery, or the recognition, which conditioned its necessity and appearance and revelation, the Resurrection is not an event in history at all." Barth, *CR* II, 30.

[118] Barth, "Preface to the Second Edition", *CR* II, 10.

[119] Yet *Romans* II is not a species of theological subjectivism. The subjectivism only emerges as a by-product of the first-order exposition of 'God is *God*'. As McCormack shows, Barth's concern in his use of dialectic is to "secure the objectivity of revelation" not to tackle "the problem of how revelation is subjectively appropriated by the individual." McCormack, *Karl Barth's Critically Realistic Dialectical Theology*, 238. He is concerned with divine subjectivity not human subjectivity, divine freedom not human freedom. He is concerned with the problem of how God can reveal Himself without ceasing to be God.

God. Non-dialectical modes of apprehension implied a (stable) human position on God. 'God is *God*' implied that there could be no such position. Hence, such modes of apprehension were deemed incompatible with the Godness of God - and with the resolution of the metatheological dilemma. In other words, any such species of language deemed worthy of expressing man's acknowledgement of 'God is *God*' logically had to exclude any such human position on God.[120] We have, *in nuce*, the principle behind dialectical speech. Given the identity between, on the one hand, 'God is *God*' and, on the other, the eschatological, it is no surprise that Barth will pronounce on the resurrection in terms that exclude the possibility of taking up a position on it. Even the assertion of miracle is invalid because such a characterisation still implies 'taking up a position'. If the resurrection:

> were a 'historical', that is, a psychical, or super-physical event, it would have taken place on a plane which would render legitimate those many weighty and sophisticated hypotheses which are nowadays held to be more or less compatible with 'belief'.[121]

However, according to Barth, the truth of the resurrection must be:

> sought not merely beyond all negation, beyond death, and beyond men, but beyond 'Yes' and 'No', life and death, God and the world, or of ranging them in a causal sequence, and so playing them off one against the other. The conception of the Resurrection ... wholly forbids this method of procedure ....[122]

---

[120] Hence Barth writes: "Does the general demand for simplicity mean more than a desire - intelligible enough, and shared by most theologians - that truth should be expressed directly, without paradox, and in such a way that it can be received otherwise than by faith alone? I am thinking here of an experience in relation to that earnest and upright man, Wernle. As a modern man he is deeply hurt when I say, for example, plainly and simply - Christ is risen. He complains that I have made use of an eschatological phrase, and have ridden rough-shod over very, very difficult problems of thought. However when I endeavour to say the same thing in the language of thought, that is, in dialectical fashion, he protests in the name of the simple believer that the doctrine of the Resurrection is wonderful, spiritual, and hard to understand. How can I answer him? He would be satisfied only if I were to surrender the broken threads of faith, and to speak directly, concretely, and without paradox." Barth, *CR* II, 3-4.

[121] *Ibid*, 203.

[122] *Ibid*, 204-205.

The resurrection is not even, to adapt a phrase that Barth used of Jesus Himself, "the most supreme event of our imaginings."[123] It is simply beyond the possibility of taking up *any* position as regards to it.

I now look at the principle in more depth. McCormack notes that "interestingly enough, Barth devotes very little consideration to the formal problem of [dialectical] method in *Romans* II."[124] Interesting, but not surprising: *Romans* II is a relentless first-order exposition of the theme of 'God is *God*' such that a human position is impossible. The second-order exposition comes in "The Word of God and the Task of the Ministry". Where *Romans* II continually *uses* - rather than speaks of, i.e., *mentions* - dialectical speech, "The Word of God and the Task of the Ministry" speaks of dialectical speech non-dialectically.

After having exposed the inadequacies of the dogmatic method and what he calls the method of self-criticism, Barth goes on to speak of dialectic as the "way of Paul and the Reformers", adding "intrinsically it is by far the best."[125] Speaking of God as truth standing in the centre Barth declares:

> The genuine dialectician knows that this centre cannot be apprehended or beheld, and he will not if he can help it allow himself to be drawn into giving direct information about it, knowing that *all* such information, whether it be positive or negative, is *not* really information, but always *either* dogma *or* self-criticism. On this narrow ridge of rock one can only walk: if he attempts to stand still, he will fall either to the right or to the left, but fall he must - an appalling performance for those who are not free from dizziness - looking *from one side to the other*, from negative to positive and from positive to negative.[126]

As McCormack puts it: it is precisely because God reveals Himself as *God* that we *cannot* speak of God except by means of "the continuous negation of every theological statement through the immediate affirmation of its opposite."[127] In other words, any statement which constituted a *stable human position* on God was antithetical to the *Godness* of God. This entailed that even such a self-effacing statement as "We have no basis on which to make statements about God" intimated an aspiration to completeness which was irreconcilable with God is *God*. Completeness - even the Gödelian kind decreeing as it did completely, as it were, on

[123] *Ibid*, 98.

[124] McCormack, *Karl Barth's Critically Realistic Dialectical Theology*, 270.

[125] Barth, "The Word of God and the Task of the Ministry", *The Word of God and the Word of Man*, 206.

[126] *Ibid*, 207.

[127] McCormack, *Karl Barth's Critically Realistic Dialectical Theology*, 311.

incompleteness - implied a break with a dialectical form of speech; for it presumed that even in the case of a system of dialectically-related utterances there was some vantage-point outside this system where one could take a non-dialectical perspective. Taking up such a vantage-point was impossible. No such stable equilibrium existed. Indeed, since the assertion itself that no such stable equilibrium existed presupposed a stable equilibrium (in the sense that it represented something that we could say was *true* in relation to God) it was no less able to halt the movement of a spiralling dialectic; which is to say, it itself was not exempt from the consequences of its own truth.[128]

We can apply the insights of "The Word of God and the Task of the Ministry" to a statement Barth makes in the process of interpreting Romans 1.16: "Exactly because God's No is so complete, it is also His Yes." This is integral to Barth's view of God's relation to man in *Romans* II.[129] Yet it does not, in spite of its appearance, represent something we could say was *true* in relation to God. Were this the case this would imply convergence to a non-dialectical point-of-view on dialectical speech. Barth's epistemological position in *Romans* II was that this is impossible. We cannot take a position on God. The reason is quite simple and reveals the need for dialectical speech; or to put it more precisely, explains why dialectical speech is necessarily generated. If "Exactly because God's No is so complete, it is also His Yes" is affirmed as something we can say is true in relation to God then this would undermine the very truth of "God's No is so complete that ...." In effect, we would have taken refuge in the illusion that the crisis was over, or at least, had temporarily ceased.

As H R Mackintosh put it, "Barth contends that ... we can do no otherwise in theology than proceed by using the method of statement of statement and counter-statement; we dare not pronounce absolutely 'the last word'".[130] Indeed, we cannot.

Barth has not so much an epistemology as a position on epistemology in *Romans* II. That there is no non-dialectical perspective coincides with the discovery Barth made in 1915, namely that the basic difficulty in speaking of God is in itself relevant knowledge of *God*.[131] In "The Word of God and the Task of the Ministry" Barth makes the famous utterance: "As theologians we ought to speak of God. We are human, however, and so

---

[128] Later Barth will say that his theology was "not a *stand-point*, as one might demand as the most minimal requirement of a proper theology. Rather it is a *mathematical* point on which one cannot stand." Barth, "The Need of Christian Preaching", *The Word of God and the Word of Man*, 143.

[129] Barth, *CR* II, 38.

[130] H R Mackintosh, *Types of Modern Theology*, 266f.

[131] Busch, *Karl Barth*, 91.

cannot speak of God. We ought therefore to recognise both our obligation and our inability and by that very recognition give God the glory."[132] The truth is of such a nature - God is *God* - that it cannot be asserted directly; but it can be conveyed. "If you ask me about *God*, and if I am ready to tell about Him, dialectic is all that can be expected of *me*. Neither is more than a *witness* to that Truth which stands at the centre between every Yes and No."[133] But it does witness; and it is in this witnessing that knowledge of God is manifested - though, that this is so, cannot be said without violating the principle of dialectical speech.


## 6. "Wittgenstein's Vienna" Again

To be sure, the theme of the eschatological is not present in Wittgenstein's *Tractatus*, nor in Schoenberg or Loos, though it is present in Kraus's *Die Letzten Tage der Menscheit*, his monumental satire on the Great War. But to the extent that Wittgenstein thought he had brought philosophy to an end, he had appointed himself the last judge (as Hegel had before). There was, in this sense, an apocalyptic undertone to the *Tractatus* - even though that this was so could not be said.

Roberts refers to the "double crisis of self and of language" at the turn of the twentieth century, a historical crisis he terms the "first postmodernity."[134] There may or may not have been a crisis in the German language during this time;[135] yet Weimar Germany is characterised by the dissolution of the individual, self-determining modern subject and the

---

[132] Barth, "The Word of God and the Task of the Ministry", 186. If we attempt to formulate a position on God (by definition a non-dialectical stance) we are doing non-theology (we are human); but if we say nothing, we are left with the fact that we must say something (we are theologians). Non-dialectical theology is non-theology because it violates 'God is *God*.' It attempts to take up a stable position on God. Once again, the spectre of Overbeck's metatheological dilemma hovers over ostensibly theological thinking: either do non-theology or nothing. To use the word "God" does not entail one is doing theology, simply because using this word does not mean that one is talking about *God*. As Busch puts it: "it implies the critical thesis that our speaking of God does not automatically speak of *God*." Busch, "God is God", 104. What is perhaps less obvious from Busch is Barth's parallel thesis that our speaking Christocentrically does not automatically speak *Christocentrically*. For Barth, speaking of *God* entails speaking *Christocentrically* and speaking *Christocentrically* entails speaking of *God*.
[133] Barth, "The Word of God", 209.
[134] Roberts, "Barth and the Eschatology of Weimar", 184-185.
[135] The conclusion that can be drawn from William Bartley's analysis of the relevant facts is that the evidence for such a crisis is, at best, ambiguous. Bartley, *Wittgenstein*, 36-40.

subversion of logocentricity.[136] Nevertheless, if "Wittgenstein's Vienna" is, in the words of Kraus, the "testing ground of world destruction" (the House of Habsburg, an ancient dynasty come to ruin in 1918), then not only is it conceivably the paradigm-case of such a phenomenon, it illuminates, in a way that Weimar Germany does not, the more complex historical forces at work in the thought of Barth (and Wittgenstein) - specifically the relationship between resolution of the metadilemma and the implications this had for a direct representational object-language.

It is not only that Wittgenstein is a metaphilosophical critic, Kraus a metalinguistic critic, Loos a meta-art, -architectural and -design critic, Schoenberg a metamusical critic, and Barth a metatheological critic. Stern wrote that preoccupation with language was peculiarly Viennese.[137] Kraus, he said, insisted that it is "necessary to read a statement in a way that is supremely sensitive to all its linguistic qualities, in order to discover the truth."[138] Conversely, one could say it is necessary to *write* a statement in a way that is supremely sensitive to all its linguistic qualities, in order to *convey* the truth. Henceforth, since truth can only be conveyed, it is a function both of the genre of what is said and the genre of how it is said (hence the proliferation of philosophical and theological interest in genres of linguistic devices, e.g. irony, hyperbole, etc.).

Hitherto, this had not been so: it had not been necessary to be supremely sensitive to *all* linguistic qualities, in order to convey the truth. If truth was something one *asserted*, it was almost exclusively dependent on the linguistic quality of *what is said*. Barth's *Romans* II affirms - in unity with Kraus, Wittgenstein, Schoenberg, and Loos - the closest possible connection between form and content. Direct expression manifested a position on God; an indirect self-referential metalinguistic mode of expression was testimony to our inability to take up a position on God; as such, it was witness to the truth of 'God is *God*', (witnessing is the theological counterpart to Wittgenstein's doctrine of showing and saying). Kierkegaard's doctrine of indirect communication is the direct ancestor to this mode of thought.[139]

---

[136] Roberts, "Barth and the Eschatology of Weimar", 184-185.

[137] See Stern, "Grillparzer's Vienna"; *Re-interpretations*.

[138] See this chapter, note 67.

[139] On the resemblance between Wittgenstein and Kierkegaard on this point, see Janik and Toulmin, *Wittgenstein's Vienna*; Charles Creegan, *Wittgenstein and Kierkegaard: religion, individuality, and philosophical method* (London: Routledge, 1989). On the resemblance as it occurs between Barth and Kierkegaard, see Torrance, *Karl Barth: An Introduction to His Early Theology, 1910-1931* (London: SCM Press, 1962), 83f.

## Concluding Remarks

Roberts characterises the development of Barth's theological strategy in the following terms:

> Barth, having abandoned the subject [of *Romans I*], was obliged to create an eschatological discourse, a rhetoric of the dialectics of God and negation, which answered immediate contemporary needs with extraordinary efficacy. This discourse was, however, subject to the normal conditions of rhetorical success (that is the power to persuade and to establish an enduring commonplace), which depends upon the continuing congruence of the *ethos* of the originator of discourse and the *pathos* of the audience addressed. It becomes apparent that Barth fell victim of the overwhelming logocentric power of his own renewal of primal discourse. After the second *Romerbrief* and supremely in the *Church Dogmatics* he became the entextualised but no longer context-bound mouth of 'God', a god once tied to the catastrophic circumstances of the Weimar era but then emancipated into its own temporality.[140]

This, as we shall see, is a distortion. *Pace* George Steiner, the *Church Dogmatics* is no more a "partial reconciliation with institutional Christianity" than *Romans* II.[141] The principle behind the dialectical speech of *Romans* II continued, in its later *sui generis* form, to play an essential role in defining Barth's position on epistemology in the *Church Dogmatics*. For Barth did not abandon the principle that one could not take up a position, a stand-point, on God. In the *Church Dogmatics*, it was not possible to take up a position on God because doing so was to imply that one knew *what it is* God's revelation is independently of revelation itself. Taking up a position on God would imply one possessed a criterion of *what it is* revelation is independently of (and hence prior to) revelation. Moreover, rather than withdraw from the realm of the metalinguistic, Barth became even more convinced that it was in terms of meaning that the truth about *sui generis* theological truth had to be articulated.

Barth described the question "Don't things become dangerous only *if* and *because* God is?" as the question which "came down on [him] like a ton of bricks around 1915":

> Don't things become dangerous only *if* and *because* God is. In that case does not the decisive question recoil on one, because then setting out *and*

---

[140] Roberts, "The Eschatology of Weimar", 175.

[141] George Steiner, Review of Bruce McCormack's *Karl Barth's Critically Realistic Dialectical Theology*, *Times Literary Supplement*, May 19, 1995, 7.

continuing, scepticism *and* the supposed courage of faith ... in short the whole of human independence and self-assurance, are weighed in the balance and finally found wanting. This is notoriously not the case with the sceptics' question. That is the question which I failed to recognise as a student or a young pastor. It is *the* question, which came down on me like a ton of bricks round about 1915.[142]

The sceptical question presupposed the possibility of a vantage-point, a (human) position on God from which one could discuss, in the spirit of 'human independence' and 'self-assurance', the existence of God. That Barth made this comment in April 1932 - *after* he had written *Fides Quaerens Intellectum* and *Church Dogmatics* I/1 - is testimony to the fact that from 1915 onwards Barth's objective on epistemology remained unchanged: to formulate what exactly it meant to be in a position where one could not take up a position on God independently of God's self-revelation itself.

It is precisely because Overbeck's rueful judgement on theology arose from the unfulfilled eschatological hopes of the early church that Barth uses the eschatological motif in *Romans* II - his instantiation of *sui generis* historical truth - to resolve the metatheological dilemma. Yet though the exclusively post-temporal dimension of the eschatological is one way of guaranteeing a *sui generis* historical realm peculiar to theology - and therefore of vouchsafing that one cannot take up a position on God - it is not a necessary and sufficient condition. That Barth will reaffirm revelation as temporal and still manage to resolve (in fact, improve on his resolution of) the metatheological dilemma, is one of the hallmarks of the genius of the *Church Dogmatics*. It is to this work that we now turn.

---

[142] Quoted in Busch, *Barth,* 115.

# PART II

## The Metatheological Dilemma
## and the *Church Dogmatics*:

## The Historical Truth-Claims of the
## the Strange New World within the Bible

# Chapter 4
# Overbeck's Dilemma
# and the *Church Dogmatics*

## 1. Introduction

I have argued that the central theme of "Unsettled Questions for Theology To-day" is what I call the metatheological dilemma - the existence of theology or the ubiquitous presence of non-theology. I then argued that *Romans* II is an attempt to resolve this dilemma; and that one main reason Barth resolves this dilemma in the realm of the eschatological (in such a way that crisis - and judgement - is engendered *illic et nunc*) is because it was there that Overbeck thought the existence of theology 'in and of itself' was nullified. (As we shall see, one other central motivation is that Barth sees the realm of the eschatological - like that of angelology later - as no less than a test-case, perhaps *the* test-case, for the existence of theology 'in and of itself'.)

However, these arguments are not inconsistent with the view that Barth's resolution of the metatheological dilemma was *restricted* to the eschatological. *Hence, according to this view, to the extent he no longer concerned himself exclusively with the eschatological, he no longer concerned himself very much with the resolution of Overbeck's dilemma* (and thereafter turned his mind to matters altogether less modern and more traditional, in the form of classical doctrinal orthodoxy.) This deduction I believe to be invalid. Nevertheless, it is widely held that Overbeck ceased to be of any great importance to Barth after *Romans* II; that, like Kierkegaard, his influence was restricted to this work. It is held that Barth moved from an exclusively eschatological position - "Christianity which is not utterly and absolutely eschatological has utterly and absolutely nothing to do with Christ" - to embrace the whole Christian story and its constituent parts (and indeed espouse a view of theological time that encompassed, but was not exclusively defined by, the future). The view allows that there is more to Overbeck's influence on *Romans* II than that contained in the

Schweitzer-Weiss 'consistent eschatology' thesis; but it still confines their
encounter to the realm of the eschatological. Hence - so this argument
concludes - insofar as the impact of Overbeck carried over to the later
theology, it was as the genesis of a simple chain reaction; it therefore had
diminishing effect at an ever-increasing distance (through the intervening
works); and, as time went on, settled into becoming one, though not
insignificant, background circumstance to the making of the later theology.

It is undoubtedly true that in the later works - notably the *Church
Dogmatics* - Barth did not concern himself exclusively with the
eschatological. But it does not follow that he was any the less concerned
with the resolution of Overbeck's dilemma;[1] it does not follow that he
thereafter turned his mind to matters altogether less modern and more
traditional, in the form of classical doctrinal orthodoxy. As we shall see, in
the *Church Dogmatics*, the primary theme of "Unsettled Questions for
Theology Today" - matters metatheological - is instantiated in phenomena
other than the eschatological. Overbeck's dilemma remains the horizon.

A short time - approximately two months - after writing "Unsettled
Questions for Theology Today", Barth delivered a lecture entitled "Biblical
Questions, Insights and Vistas" (date of delivery April 1920).[2] In it are
references to eschatological themes one might have expected in the wake of
an encounter with Overbeck.[3] But, prior to these references, Barth makes
the following comment:

> ... when we now turn our serious though somewhat dispassionate attention
> to the objective content of the Bible, we shall not do so in a way to
> provoke religious enthusiasm and scientific indignation to another battle
> against "stark orthodoxy" and "dead belief in the letter." For it is too clear
> that intelligent and fruitful discussion of the Bible begins when the
> judgement as to its human, its historical and psychological character has

---

[1] McCormack notes something of great potential influence in Overbeck which Barth did
not discuss in "Unsettled Questions in Theology Today." This is Overbeck's reflections on
the philosophy of history as regards *Urgeschichte* as a *geschichtsphilosophische* category.
*Urgeschichte* as 'originating history' is for Overbeck 'incomparable'. As such it "cannot be
evaluated by the normal principles of analogy, criticism, and correlation." McCormack,
*Karl Barth's Critically Realistic Dialectical Theology*, 228-229. There is little doubt, as we
will see, that in the *Church Dogmatics* Barth understood the creation history and the
resurrection-appearances history in these terms. Whether it is Overbeck's concept of
*Urgeschichte* which decisively determined Barth's understanding of these respective
histories is unclear. But the possibility that it was should warn us off from dismissing
Overbeck's influence on the historical ontology of the *Church Dogmatics* out of hand.

[2] Barth, "Biblical Questions, Insights, and Vistas", *The Word of God and the Word of
Man*, 51-96.

[3] *Ibid*, 79-94.

been made and *put behind* us. Would that the teachers of our high and low schools, and with them the progressive element among the clergy of our established churches would forthwith resolve to have done with a battle that once had its time but has now *had* it. The special *content* of this human document, the remarkable *something* with which the writers of these stories and those who stood behind them were concerned, the biblical *object* [*biblische Objekt*]- this is the question that will engage and engross us today.[4]

Whether Barth thought of the "biblical object" here as necessarily eschatological in nature has to be balanced by the fact that, for the most part, the lecture is directed against the view that the essence of the Bible resides in its historical and psychological character.[5] What is left when the history and the psychology, the piety and morality are "put behind us" is "not religion but reality, not history but truth."[6] This truth is its other-worldliness,[7] the Wholly Otherness of God.[8] This, as we shall see, did not necessarily have to be instantiated by the eschatological. Though the eschatological entailed something non-historical (in history but not of history) and non-psychological in character ("Last *things*, as such, are not *last* things, however great and significant they may be"),[9] the converse is not necessarily true: it is not *only* the eschatological which is non-historical and non-psychological. In the *Church Dogmatics*, Barth presents us with a "biblical object", which, while not an endorsement of *stark orthodoxy*, is not exclusively or even mainly eschatological in nature (in the traditional sense), though it is: the *strange new world within the Bible*.

---

[4] *Ibid*, 60-61.

[5] To say that the essence of the Bible does not "reside in its historical character" is to say that it does not reside in its historical character as this term is understood by conventional critical-historical methodology. It should not be taken to mean that Barth rejects the thesis that biblical narrative, for example, is historical. Rather, as regards the strange new world, we are in the realm of *sui generis* historical event. Hence when I refer to the "non-historical" character of this world, this should not be taken to mean that this world itself is "non-historical", only that it is so in the sense in which critical-historical methodology understands it.

[6] Barth, "Biblical Questions, Insights, and Vistas", 66.

[7] *Ibid*, 69.

[8] *Ibid*, 74.

[9] Barth, *The Resurrection of the Dead*, 110.

## 2. "The Strange New World Within" the *Church Dogmatics*

The conclusion that it is not *only* the eschatological which is non-historical
and non-psychological is further substantiated by a lecture Barth had given
some three years before encountering Overbeck. Three years before, Barth
had conceived of a world of God that was, on the one hand, non-historical
and non-psychological, but on the other, *was not necessarily
eschatological*: 'the new world of God' conceived other than in
eschatological terms (other than a *post*-historical event). Barth equates this
world with the kingdom of God: it is the new world *within* the old
'historical' world. The new world of God *was* eschatological in the sense
that it heralded a new, unanticipatable irruption of the old world; but it was
not necessarily restricted to a Barthian construal of the literal eschatological
'last things' of apocalyptic: it was not necessarily *last* things.

Barth's indebtedness to Overbeck extended beyond the *parousia*, beyond
the eschatological *per se*. If the content of the Bible was *not* qualitatively
different from history, psychology, anthropology - non-theology - then
theology was a non-subject; and everything hitherto studied in the theology
faculty or department ought to transferred to the departments of history,
pyschology, anthropology, etc. In other words, if there was no new world
then the metatheological dilemma remained unresolved: do non-theology or
nothing.

Barth gave early notice that his historic task would be to reassert the
reality of a theology that possessed its own *sui generis* identity.[10] As early
as February 1917, even before the publication of the first edition of
*Romans*, Barth had made a theological address to the Church in the village
of Leutwil, in the canton of Aargau in Northern Switzerland. The content of
this address takes on a distinctly prophetic quality when viewed from the

---

[10] In the wake of Overbeck's metatheological dilemma theology was faced with two
equally undesirable alternatives: do non-theology or nothing. To resolve this dilemma
theology as non-theology (history, anthropology, etc.) had to be displaced by a theology
whose (descriptive) rationality was of its own kind, peculiar, unique (*sui generis*).
Though this is in fact what Barth found when he looked into the Bible (finding the
"strange new world within the Bible") it is not *a priori* inconceivable that he might have
been faced everywhere in the Bible with the descriptive rationality of *Historie*; in which
case theology as non-theology would have supplied an exhaustive definition of
theology. Happily for Barth the world of the Bible is a "strange new world" since (i) it is
'inhabited' above all by the resurrection-appearances history and the creation history,
but also by the empty tomb, the virgin birth - and angels; (ii) these 'objects' have their
own peculiar, unique (descriptive) rationality. The reason that (i) on its own is not a
sufficient condition of avoiding the reduction of theology to non-theology is that there is
nothing necessarily *a priori* about these objects which would exclude them from being
historical objects in the ordinary sense.

retrospect of Barth's insistence on the reality of *sui generis* theology. It is another datum to add to the thesis that the objective of Barth's *whole* enterprise is to take up and refute the challenge that theology is a non-subject. The title of the address was "The Strange New World Within the Bible",[11] a title intimating Barth's as yet faint impression that the world or realm therein contained was not to be assimilated to our known and habitual modes of classification. He opened his address with a statement of his theme that day:

> We are to attempt to find an answer to the question, What is there within the Bible? What sort of house is it to which the Bible is the door? What sort of country is spread before our eyes when we throw the Bible open?[12]

But rather than attempt to answer the question straightaway Barth does something else that is the very paradigm of immediacy: he takes the collective imagination of his audience (congregation) on a chronological journey through the history of the Old and New Testament. Barth offers his congregation an inventory or itemisation of the contents of the Bible. One short and sharp yet intensive *in medias res* biblical encounter is enacted after the other, with Barth rekindling the life of each story in not inconsiderable detail once the imagination of the congregation has, so to speak, found its feet in these foreign lands (though the strangeness Barth wants to impress on us is not that *inter alia* it depicts distant, exotic, and even - for Western civilisation - alien lands):

> We are with Abraham in Haran. We hear a voice which commands him
> [13]
> ....

---

[11] Barth "The Strange New World Within the Bible", 28-50. The original title is *Die neue Welt in der Bibel* but to translate this as *The New World Within the Bible* omits the intention of the German to convey the sense in which the world of the Bible is a world we must see in a new light, as different; in which case it is to appear "strange" to us. The historical circumstances surrounding its origins can be found in Busch, *Barth*, 100f. Busch himself writes that the lecture "was the first public account of the results of his new Bible studies." *Ibid*, 101. It unambiguously charted his "gradual awareness of the Bible." *Ibid*, 98. Not unconnected is what Barth himself wrote when writing the first edition of *Romans*: "During the work it was often as though I caught a breath from afar, from Asia Minor or Corinth, something primeval, from the ancient East, indefinably sunny, wild, original that somehow is hidden behind these sentences." *Ibid*, 98-9. In what follows it is not assumed that Barth remained steadfastly committed to everything he said in this address. Nevertheless there is no doubt that in retrospect it can be read as programmatic for what was to follow in *Romans* I and II (especially *Romans* II) and the *Church Dogmatics*.

[12] Barth, "World", 28.

Then:

> We are with Moses in the wilderness. For forty years he has been living among the sheep ....[14]

Then we are no longer with Moses in the wilderness but with Gideon at Ophrah in the land of Canaan:

> It is a time of severe oppression in the land of Canaan. Under the oak at Ophrah stands the farmer's son, Gideon. The "angel of the Lord" appears to him ....[15]

Now at Shiloh with Samuel:

> In the tabernacle at Shiloh lies the young Samuel. Again a call: Samuel, Samuel! ....[16]

Then we hear of Elijah being called by "the Lord" to defy the whole authority of his king, followed by his acquaintance with the same "Lord" in the form of a "still, small voice";[17] we hear of Isaiah's and Jeremiah's divine judgement and divine blessing on a sinful people[18] - all these Barth also brings to life for the benefit of his audience's and ultimately our imagination.

At the end of each story a recognisably similar refrain is uttered in which Barth asks himself and his audience what it is they have encountered, what common factor emerges from the encounters. Thus after having been with Abraham in Haran Barth asks:

> What is the meaning of all this? We can but feel that there is something behind these words and experiences. But what?[19]

And after being with Moses in the wilderness he says:

---

[13] *Ibid*, 28.
[14] *Ibid*, 28.
[15] *Ibid*, 29.
[16] *Ibid*, 29.
[17] *Ibid*, 29-30.
[18] *Ibid*, 30.
[19] *Ibid*, 28.

Here again are words and experiences which seem at first to be nothing but riddles. We do not read the like in the daily papers or in other books. What lies behind?[20]

And again having been given entry to the tabernacle at Shiloh where young Samuel lies:

We read all this, but what do we read behind it? We are aware of something like the ceaseless thunder of ocean waves against thin dykes; but what really is it that beats at the barrier and seeks entrance here?[21]

Yet the answer one might have expected from a theologian who turned out to be as Christocentric as Barth, is not what is submitted on this particular occasion. To be sure, Barth speaks of "the incomprehensible, incomparable days, when all previous time, history, and experience seem to stand still - like the sun at Gibeon - in the presence of a man who was no prophet, no poet, no hero, no thinker, and yet all of these and more!"[22] - the days, that is, of Jesus Christ. But notwithstanding the fact that these days are absolute and everything else relative, and that elsewhere Barth will hold they are the fulfilment of all Old Testament history, when the single utterance - "Then the echo ceases. The Bible is finished." - brings the exercise in imagination to a close,[23] Barth will still exclaim: "And again we ask: What is there within the Bible?"[24] In other words, it is not who or even what the Bible is about that is at stake here but rather: what type of phenomenon, what ('philosophical') kind or character or essence of phenomenon are we confronted with in the Bible? This is the vaguely monistic 'meaning' Barth is at pains to uncover from the *sacra biblica* or even point at in an almost impossible way. This is what still beckons on the horizon. What kind of world is it? A historical world criss-crossed with cause and effect?:

---

[20] *Ibid*, 29

[21] *Ibid*, 29.

[22] *Ibid*, 30.

[23] *Ibid*, 31. It is noteworthy that Barth ends his address by returning his audience once more to the realm of the Bible: "A certain man made a great supper, and bade many; and sent his servant at supper-time to say to them that were bidden, Come, for all things are now ready! ...."

[24] *Ibid*, 31.

What is there within the Bible? *History* [*Gechichte*]*!* The history of a remarkable even, unique, people; the history of powerful, mentally vigorous personalities; the history of Christianity in its beginnings ....[25]

Is history then the answer? Barth considers the possibility carefully before rejecting it:

Now one can content oneself for a time with this answer and find in it many true and beautiful possibilities. The Bible is full of history; religious history, literary history, cultural history, world history, and human history of every sort. [...] But the pleasure is short-lived: the picture, on closer inspection, proves quite incomprehensible and flat, if it is meant only for history .... For when we study history and amuse ourselves with stories, we are always wanting to know: How did it happen? How is it that one event follows another? [...] It is just at the decisive points of its history that the Bible gives us no answer to our Why? .... [The] Bible meets the lover of history with silences quite unparalleled.[26]

History then is not the answer  Or, rather: "religious history, literary history, cultural history, world history, and human history of every sort" is not the answer. It is all doubtless there in the Bible, precisely history susceptible in principle to the methods of the historical critics. But there is another history in the Bible,  a history whose direct subject is God Himself, a  history which is "wholly other" than the history of which the historical critics speak :

... we may not deny or prevent our being led by Bible "history" far out beyond what is elsewhere called history - into a new world, into the world of God.[27]

It is this history  - a history which is identified with '*last* things' in *Romans* II - which points us toward the  *sui generis* historicality of "the world of God." Barth's aim in "The Strange New World Within the Bible" is to recreate a sense of the 'otherness' of the realm spoken of in the Bible, an 'otherness' represented in a "history" that is precisely 'other' than history: "Once more we stand before this "other" new world which begins in the Bible."[28] The  truth with which the Bible was concerned was not history,

---

[25] *Ibid*, 34-35.
[26] *Ibid*, 35-36.
[27] *Ibid*, 37.
[28] *Ibid*, 39.

morality, or religion; the strange new world within the Bible witnessed to a *sui generis* historicality proper to God.[29]

Retrospectively, what makes "The Strange New World Within the Bible" revolutionary is not that it is capable of semiotic incarnation in the revolutionary, crisis-ridden, hyperbolic, and ironic dialectical language of *Romans* II ("otherness" reappears in *Romans* II as the arresting mode of hyperbolic expression *totaliter aliter*); or even that, once the dust of *Romans* II has settled and one is amidst the relative imperturbability, even calm, of the *Church Dogmatics*, "history" and historical methodology remain in the realm of non-theology; it is not even that once the dust settles and one is amidst the ostensible calm of the *Church Dogmatics*, "The Strange New World Within the Bible" plays a not inconsiderable role in deciphering the apparently intractable (because habitually and consistently misinterpreted) code of the Bible; it is rather that in carrying out this not inauspicious task it discloses a latent noumenal 'self' far more radical than hitherto imagined: an affirmation of the *sui generis* historicality of the history found in the Bible, a proclamation that the character of the phenomena of the *sui generis* historical is such that its "otherness" is an otherness that defies and even rebukes realism as the key to the truth of the Bible insofar as the latter is a function of the non-theological and thus its mode of expression an example of non-theology.

---

[29] Speaking of the relation between the Bible and the Christian community George Lindbeck writes: "When the text ... controls communal reading, Scripture can speak for itself and become the self-interpreting guide for believing communities amid the ever-changing vicissitudes of history. It is thus that Christians come to live in the 'The Strange New World Within the Bible' of which Karl Barth spoke in one of the better known of his early addresses delivered seventy years ago at the Swiss church in Leutwil." George Lindbeck, "Barth and Textuality", *Theology Today*, XLIII (3), 1986, 362. It may be true that the relation between the Bible and the community is as Lindbeck describes it, but in conforming to it Christians do not "come to live in 'The Strange New World Within the Bible' of which Karl Barth spoke." One should not be misled into thinking that interpreting our lives in terms of the intratextual world of the Bible is the theme of the lecture. The theme of the address can be made clear by tracing the thematic development of Barth's address to its climax. What is it that is in the Bible? Is it religion? No! Is it morality? No! Is it history? No! What is it then? Barth's answer consisted in essence of a decidedly rhetorical question in which he rejected all proposals which implied the possibility of 'measuring God with our own measures': "Even in these answers, earnest and pious as they may be, have we not measured God with our own measure, conceived of God with our own conceptions, wished ourselves a God according to our own wishes?" Barth "The Strange New World Within the Bible", 47. As will be seen, this theme contains in itself the blueprint for the epistemology of the *Church Dogmatics*.

## 3. Angelology and Overbeck's Dilemma

It is no literary conceit to say that students of Barth can do no better than begin with Barth's angelology. For it is there that what is implicit in "The Strange New World Within the Bible" - the *sui generis* historicality of its history - is made explicit. Indeed what makes this point of departure doubly germane (not to say ironic) is that Barth's doctrine of angels encapsulates not only in quasi-parabolic terms but also in quasi-real terms the point at which he makes contact with the question of the existence or otherwise of autonomous theology. For this question is the very question originating with Hume (implicitly) and Kant (explicitly) (see Chapter 1); and Hume and Kant both represent (the latter to a lesser degree) a historical Enlightenment dedicated to eliminating what it perceives as mythology.[30]

Accordingly, Barth's angelology represents his answer - honed to a fine degree - as to what type of phenomenon, what ('philosophical') kind or essence or character of phenomenon it is we encounter in the sagas of the Bible. The significance of the angels, for Barth, is summed up in a sentence of Adolf Schlatter's: "The mystery is near to us." The theological - *sui generis* historical - identity of the angels is no more (and no less) than this: angels do not exist beyond their bearing of the message of the imminence of God. This is the pattern that exists whenever reference is made to angels in the Bible. This is the 'point of view of the whole', of each and every saga in which angels are mentioned.

I refer to § 51 "The kingdom of Heaven, the Ambassadors of God and their Opponents" of *Church Dogmatics* III/3, completed in the summer of 1949.[31] Approximately thirty years had passed since Overbeck had entered

---

[30] For the history of the progressive elimination of myth  leaving behind a supposed 'essence of Christianity', (a history culminating in von Harnack's *The Essence of Christianity*), see Gay *Enlightenment*, II "The Tension With Christianity", 212-419, esp. Ch 6 'In Dubious Battle' and esp. §III.

[31] Busch relates that Barth turned with special delight to angelology: "In depicting modernist angelology, which he called 'angelology with a shrug of the shoulders', he had almost a carnival night in his class. 'And when I said that these theologians did not allow the angels an entry permit, let alone a permanent visa, the room was filled with shouts of laughter.'" Busch, *Barth*, 365. This laughter is reciprocated by the angels. Barth jokingly acknowledged that they had the last laugh even when it came to him and his *Church Dogmatics*. "The angels laugh at old Karl. They laugh at him because he tries to grasp the truth about God in a book of Dogmatics. They laugh at the fact that volume follows volume and each is thicker than the previous one. As they laugh, they say to one another, 'Look! Here he comes now with his little pushcart full of volumes of the *Dogmatics*!' - and they laugh about the men who write so much about Karl Barth instead of writing about the things he is trying to write about. Truly, the angels laugh."

Barth's consciousness. But like the eschatological itself, angelology became a test-case - in the *Church Dogmatics*, *the* test-case, for the existence of theology 'in and of itself'.

Barth writes that the dogmatic sphere of angelology "is the most remarkable and difficult of all":[32] "the most remarkable" because a sphere subjected to a modern attitude bordering on derision is in fact a key to the resolution of Overbeck's metatheological dilemma (talk about angels is essential otherwise there is no theology); "the most difficult" because all through the history of theology, theologians have allowed their preconceptions about the existence and nature of angels to frustrate what it is the Bible really has to say about them:

> Decisive for all that follows is the emergence and the rapid domination of the assumption that it is possible, legitimate and necessary to seek the existence and nature of angels elsewhere than in their function as God's messengers. Certainly this took place in answer to a natural requirement of logic. But it did not take place in the sense and according to the pattern of the Biblical witness. It was under the sway of an alien interest that there was an increasing desire to know about the nature of the angels and an increasing belief that it was possible to know what these beings are in themselves, and therefore prior to and apart from the fact that they are *angeli*, the messengers of God.[33]

Nowhere is this better exemplified than in the *Summa Theologiae* of St. Thomas Aquinas where the appropriately named *Doctor angelicus* poses no less than 118 individual questions on the matter of angels. There, angels are treated as *essentiae spirituales*, *substantiae separatae*, little more than individual human beings and existences anthropomorphically transposed together with their social existence to the realm of a purely intellectual existence.[34]

In other words, throughout the history of theology theologians have found it impossible to resist assimilating talk of angels to the canons of philosophical realist discourse, generating confusion rather than clarity. Come the Enlightenment the "moderns" wish to speak of God metaphysically, and hence - unable to rid themselves of the traditional

---

Quoted in G McAfee Brown, "Introduction", in G Casalis, *Portrait of Karl Barth* (Garden City: Doubleday and Company, 1963), 3.

[32] Barth *CD* III/3, 369.

[33] *Ibid*, 381. Once again it is the Augustinian legacy that wielded its powerful though ultimately misleading influence: "The basic innovation involved, although not introduced by Augustine, received at his hands its classical formulation." *Ibid*, 381.

[34] *Ibid*, 390-401.

"natural" picture of angels - eschew the language of angels because it is unable to co-exist with the scientific account of the world. Barth quotes D F Strauss on this: "If the modern idea of God and conception of the world are right, there cannot possibly be room for beings of this sort."[35] Yet that the older orthodoxy sided with the existence of "beings of this sort" (the same angels the Enlightenment rejected) was paradoxically a manifestation of the same error later compounded by the Enlightenment. (Thus Barth's reaction to Strauss's sceptical declaration as against the older orthodoxy is [as in the case of Overbeck] one of irony: "Quite so, there can be no room for beings of this sort!"):

> If we are guilty of [imposing our own preconception of what angels are] ... we need not be surprised if we are entangled in all kinds of questions and difficulties which secretly hampered the angelology of older orthodoxy, which were merely increased by the sun of the Enlightenment that lit up so many other things, and which finally brought the whole subject into the disrepute from which it suffers to-day. These do not derive from what is discernible in the Bible as the witness to the work and revelation of God which also includes the existence and work of angels, but from the preconception by means of which it was hoped even in early days to provide rather than to facilitate an understanding of this witness .... They derived from the false translation with which even in the early days, and with the best of intentions, the biblical view and concept of angels were to be made more readily accessible.[36]

Even though the older orthodoxy had the Scripture-principle firmly in its mind as it proceeded with exegesis, it was no less committed to the preconception that the existence of angels was *independent* and *autonomous*, in the sense that the existence of human beings was independent and autonomous. An old-fashioned 'common-sense' realism reigned supreme. That even the tradition of *sola scriptura* could succumb to this error explains Barth's caution when he wishes to learn what Scripture has to teach:

> There is every reason to be particularly strict in our application of the Scripture-principle in this field because tradition has been unhelpful in this respect, not merely preparing the catastrophe which broke later and still affects us to-day, but doing something which was far worse, i.e., binding and obscuring the positive instruction to be gained in the matter.[37]

---

[35] *Ibid*, 413.

[36] *Ibid*, 379.

[37] *Ibid*, 379.

According to Barth "the name and concept of angels denotes a reality [*Wirklichkeit*] which is distinct from both God and man"[38] Yet even this must be carefully qualified: "the doctrine of angels, unlike that of predestination, creation, or man, has in the strict sense no meaning and content of its own. Angels are not independent and autonomous subjects like God and man and Jesus Christ. They cannot therefore be made the theme of an independent discussion. [...] Strictly speaking, every angelological statement can only be an auxiliary or additional statement, an explanation and elucidation of what is not said properly and essentially of angels but ... of the divine action in Jesus Christ."[39] Yet the *theological* identity of angels not only precludes an ancient or modern "mythological" objectification; the name and concept of angels is a necessary component of the vocabulary of *sui generis* theology:

> How are we to steer a way between this Scylla and Charybdis, between the far too interesting mythology of the ancients and the far too uninteresting "demythologisation" of most of the moderns? How are we to advance without becoming rash, exercise discretion without overlooking what has to be said, not saying too much and yet not failing to say what has to be said? How are we to be both open and cautious, critical and naive, perspicuous and modest? There are no spheres of dogmatics where we are not well advised to take note of these questions. But there are reasons why they are particularly dark and oppressive in the doctrine of angels which must now concern us.[40]

*Prima facie*, it appears the biblical writers have also succumbed to the all too natural temptation to objectify the existence of angels. Yet Barth is adamant that one can steer through the "far too interesting mythology of the ancients" to a distinctly theological kernel of truth:

> ... it obviously makes no odds that in the construction of these accounts, the active imagination of the biblical authors, as is only to be expected, lived with images and conceptions which were stamped by the outlook and the mythology of their day and which we can no longer accept, but which it was not the purpose of the texts in question to impart or force on us.[41]

---

[38] *Ibid*, 370.
[39] *Ibid*, 370-1.
[40] *Ibid*, 369.
[41] *Ibid*, 375.

For Barth it is immaterial whether we reject the biblical writers' mythology in favour of the modern scientific account. Whatever mythological objectification the texts may harbour (e.g. an obsolete world view such as the three-decker universe) it is only a contingent means to a *sui generis* historical end. Hence, had the biblical writers' representation of the world coincided with the modern scientific account, this would not have altered one whit the need for the name and concept of angels to appear in the theological vocabulary.

In other words, in diametrical opposition to Bultmann's "modern" demythologisation programme, the narrow course Barth steers is precisely one of theological truth embodied in *sui generis* historical truth. As if riding roughshod over the conscious will of the biblical writers, the intention of the texts is to depict a *sui generis* historical realm peculiar to theology, the *strange new world within the Bible*.

That the Biblical writers used images and conceptions derived from their own world-view and outlook, a world-view and outlook which, from our own, appears obsolete, cannot be gainsaid. Yet if they are mere means to an end then, notwithstanding their derivation from this 'mythological' world-view, their presence in the Bible is not logically irreconcilable with there being, in the holistic sense, ('mythological' elements being the 'parts' of a 'whole') a strange new world within the Bible - *the* strange new world within the Bible. Neither Strauss nor, later, Bultmann, considered this possibility. They took such elements to be a sufficient condition of the phenomenon best characterised (holistically) as *the mythological world within the Bible*. Barth did not; according to him, Strauss and Bultmann had simply reached a false conclusion.

Barth is at his ironic best when he says that, given the phenomenon of the strange new world within the Bible, *it is surprising that angels - as they are delineated in the Bible - are not mentioned more often*. In other words, given the strange new world within the Bible, *the rational attitude would be to have been surprised by less rather than by more reference*:

> ... we are even forced to say that the appearance of angels is always a distinctive sign of the basically continuous proximity of the biblical sphere to this sphere, and of its continual secret tendency in this direction. There is reason for surprise that angels are not more frequently mentioned in the Bible. The whole history of the Bible, while it intends to be and is real spatial-temporal history has a constant bias toward the sphere where it cannot be verified by the ordinary analogies of world history but seen and grasped only imaginatively and represented in the form of poetry. How can it be otherwise when it is the history of the work and revelation of God, which as such, as the history of the action and lordship of the Lord of heaven and earth, although it can also take place in the comparatively

narrow sphere of historically verifiable occurrences, is not confined to the sphere of earthly analogies? To some extent the angels mark this transition, this reaching of the incommensurable into the commensurable, of mystery into the sphere of known possibilities.[42]

To a theologian such as Rudolf Bultmann angels are an uncomfortable embarrassing presence best dealt with by demythologising.[43] To a theologian with such a cast of mind, Barth's assertion that it is surprising angels are not mentioned more in the Bible appears mere dogmatic defiance (as if the more reference were made to angels the better it would be for Barth's case) . Yet to a man in pursuit of a *sui generis* theology the modern insistence that talk of angels be eliminated is synonymous with a tacit endorsement of the consequences of Overbeck's dilemma and the end of "theology in and for itself". It sanctions the historical Enlightenment's assertion of the inevitability of theology as non-theology. To be sure, though angels are "figures of biblical saga and legend [*Sage und Legende*]"[44]

this assertion cannot mean that *fides quaerens intellectum* has to halt at the angels, or that the question of theological truth [*die theologische Wahrheitfrage*] has not to be raised in this matter.[45]

Why not?:

If this were the case, there would be no question of theological truth at all, and therefore no theology, no *fides quaerens intellectum*.[46]

If we halt at angels, if we refuse to countenance their admittance into our vocabulary, the question of theological truth collapses and with it theology; all that is left is mere history (non-theology) with no strange new world within the Bible:

---

[42] *Ibid*, 375.

[43] It is clear that Bultmann's "friendly reception" to the second edition of Romans was based on his belief that Barth had (at least partially) demythologised the eschatological. But as we now know, the reverse was the case: Barth had responded to Overbeck in the realm of the eschatological precisely in order to reclaim the eschatological into the realm of *sui generis* theology and thereby resolve Overbeck's dilemma. That is, he had reclaimed the eschatological for precisely the same reason he was to reclaim the angels: it appeared that it was on these cases that theology was in greatest difficulty (the New Testament had been comprehensively falsified in these instances).

[44] *Ibid*, 375.

[45] *Ibid*, 376.

[46] *Ibid*, 376.

For in some way ... the whole of the biblical history is engaged in that transition to saga or legend, and the angels in particular can only make this clear.[47]

Eliminating talk of angels, eliminating saga and legend, far from purifying theology of its mythological elements, eliminates the vocabulary, and with it the language, of *sui generis* theology. This is why "... the doctrine of angels is to be theological in character ...."[48]

But if this is the case - if there is theology "in and for itself" - then there is theological truth. What is such truth with regard to angels? Barth readily acknowledges that the biblical ciphers concerning angels are "so obscure"; nevertheless the key that apologetics and hermeneutics undoubtedly provide leads to results which are either "artificial or platitudinous."[49] Juxtaposed to the non-theological realms of apologetics and hermeneutics is the theme of the autonomy of theology. If we look to either hermeneutics or apologetics then:

Our philosophy will spoil our theology, and our theology our philosophy. Our present concern is the first point. The knowledge which does not dare to be wholly and exclusively theological and therefore based on the witness of Holy Scripture will as such be a pale and uncertain knowledge and erroneous at the decisive point. As theological knowledge it could be free. Bound to other concepts, even though incidently for hermeneutical or apologetic reasons, it is unfree, and therefore an unfaithful half-knowledge estranged from itself and its object.[50]

Again:

Theology has only to be theology at this point too. It has to be on its guard against unwittingly becoming philosophy. It has to accept the discipline of being wholly and exclusively theology.[51]

How does theology manifest itself as being "wholly and exclusively theology" [*ganz und ausschliesslich Theologie*] in angelology? That the name and concept of angels are among the means of grasping imaginatively what cannot be verified by the ordinary analogies of world history is as it

---

[47] *Ibid*, 376.
[48] *Ibid*, 378
[49] *Ibid*, 404.
[50] *Ibid*, 404.
[51] *Ibid*, 410.

should be since we are dealing with a *sui generis* historical realm. But though angels have no analogy in world history, but are rather represented by saga and legend, it does not follow that they do not possess its own distinctive form, their own *intelligere*. Indeed, it is this *intelligere* to which we should "confine" ourselves - "the *intelligere* which the Bible offers."[52]

Even though the outlook of the biblical writers is stamped by an obsolete mythological world-view, "faith is confident that it will not be left in the lurch either hermeneutically or apologetically if it confines itself to [the biblical] witness."[53] Indeed "we are summoned to think and speak as they did, not without the divination, imagination and poetry which they found necessary in view of the fact that this history is continually engaged in that movement of transition, yet not with any divination, imagination, history and poetry, but like them with the divination, imagination and poetry which are ordered and filled with meaning and disciplined by this particular history. ... we are summoned to think with the true theological knowledge [*in echter theologischer Erkenntnis*]."[54] Though the *intelligere* is no species of common-sense realist rationality (a realism such as this is not a necessary condition of rationality) it is rational. It is a rationality befitting theological truth as embodied in the *sui generis* historicality of angels.

Such a rationality has nothing to say on a whole series of questions prompted by the typical realist mentality. It tells us nothing about "the much ventilated question of the 'nature' of the angels, whether they are persons, or what is their relationship to the physical world and to space, their number and order, their creation, their original unity, their ensuing division into angels and demons, and many other things which later there was both the desire and a supposed ability to know."[55] Such questions may be the standard fare of a *science*, which is to say, a *non-theology* of angels, but they have no place in the realm of theological truth: there it makes no sense to pose the standard questions of origin and cause and effect.

> According to the witness of the Old and New Testaments, to this revelation and work of God there belongs also the character of the kingdom of God as the kingdom of heaven, and the angels as His heavenly messengers. They belong to it in a particular way, not as leading but as subsidiary characters, and these not as autonomous subjects but merging as it were into their function, which is wholly and exemplarily that of

---

[52] *Ibid*, 401.

[53] *Ibid*, 403.

[54] *Ibid*, 377.

[55] *Ibid*, 410-11.

service. It is only in this way that they do belong to it. But in this way they do belong to it.[56]

It is not merely that they disappear when Jesus Christ appears, it is that they do not exist independently of Him.[57] They exist insofar as they do not exist when He is present. They are, so to speak, couriers whose existence is instantiated wholly and exclusively in proclaiming the imminence of the theological realm. That is what makes them *angeli*, messengers of God. Barth's point is that they themselves are no more than this message. Accordingly, that they disappear when Jesus Christ appears is attributable to the fact that once their message is redundant, superfluous, they no longer "exist":

> What angels are is to be understood wholly and exclusively from their function and activity. They are wholly and utterly angels, messengers. They are beings which are as they are engaged in the action thereby denoted. We grope in the void if we speak of a being of angels presupposed in this action and distinguishable from it .... We know them only in their action and service as God's messengers. [...] Naturally, we cannot deny or suppress the fact that angels exist. But we deny that they exist otherwise than in the execution of their office.[58]

That is why they have no independent existence, are not independent characters; that is why their reality is such that they have no independent reality; that is why angelological statements are auxiliary. "There is no independent doctrine ... independent definition, depiction or account of angels .... They cannot be regarded as independent objects, nor constitute an independent theme."[59] Accordingly, empiricism has no role to play in our

---

[56] *Ibid*, 372.

[57] Barth implies that those occasions in which an angel appears in the same frame as Jesus - the temptation in the wilderness (Mk 1.12f, Mt 4.11) and Gethsemane (Lk 22.43) - serve to "emphasise the tempted *humanity* [my italics] of Jesus". As such "we have to think of a special attestation of the presence of God." *Ibid*, 501. Matthew and Mark indicate the presence of God "ministering" to his humanity, not his Godness. Luke indicates the presence of God "strengthening" his humanity in the face of temptation. In other words, according to Barth, in these stories the angels are used as means of indicating the presence of God to the humanity of Jesus, to the man Jesus. The general rule that the angels are messengers of God and have no independent existence beyond this function is not falsified by the citation of these examples. Falsification of course would have occurred had the angels and the *Godness* of Jesus appeared in the same frame, at the resurrection appearances, for example.

[58] *Ibid*, 512.

[59] *Ibid*, 411.

apprehension of them: "There can be no question of any special, autonomous experience of angels in and for themselves. The subjects of this kind of experience could not be the angels of God."[60] Yet nonetheless they are to be apprehended as an "object of knowledge";[61] they display their own *sui generis* rationality: though "the angels cannot conduct themselves in accordance with what may be desired of them for the purposes of an orderly angelology, ... to be genuinely orderly an angelology must keep to the angels as they encounter us in the Bible, whether they fit in easily with our theories or not."[62] Were there no such "inward coherence"[63] - no *intelligere* - there would be no rationality, no place for saga and legend, no logical exclusion of myth or critical-historical truth. The latter perspectives would remain valid; and in their wake would be the concomitant verdicts of non-existence.

### 4. "Quite So! There Are No Beings of that Sort!"

Irony is, at the simplest level, saying the opposite thing with the same sequence of words. Accordingly, the irony in Barth's riposte to Overbeck - "Quite so, Overbeck! Any Christianity that is not absolutely and utterly eschatological has absolutely and utterly nothing to do with Christ" - is no less present in "Quite so, Strauss, Bultmann and all you 'moderns'! There *are* no beings of the sort you postulate!"[64] The wholesale irony that characterises Barth's response to Overbeck (and Feuerbach) - and angels ("Quite so, there is are no beings of that sort in the Bible!") - quietly emerges from the *Church Dogmatics* as a kind of Barthian signature (a signature, it should be said, missing from the orthodox Barthian portrait), nominally encompassing the very things in Christian theology that liberal Protestantism of the nineteenth century felt duty-bound to eradicate: the resurrection, the empty tomb, the virgin birth etc. Again Barth was to reply "Quite so, there is no room for beings of that sort!", meaning the core lexicon of Christian theology as it had been appropriated by non-theology, instantiated in the realm of history as historical criticism conceived it - and

---

[60] *Ibid*, 477.

[61] *Ibid*, 411.

[62] *Ibid*, 411.

[63] Barth, *CD IV/2*, 142.

[64] Here the language of *Romans* II is deliberately evoked. Indeed, insofar as *Romans* II is a blueprint for the future *Church Dogmatics*, we can see that at the locus of the "utterly and absolutely" *sui generis* theological - the resurrection appearances - *Romans* II slowly but surely grows into the *Church Dogmatics* as the other *sui generis* elements of the Christian vocabulary are added - the empty tomb, the virgin birth, the incarnation, etc.

identity dissolved in the process. Instead, for Barth that same classical lexicon became the *sine qua non* of Christian theology - and therefore was to be sharply distinguished from its *doppelgänger* yet twilight zone counterparts in the non-theological critical-historical lexicon subsequently rubbed out from the language of modernity and consigned to myth.

For if the refusal to speak of angels meant a refusal to entertain theological truth, then how much more crisis-ridden became the situation for theology if the other so-called "mythical" elements critical to the Christian story yet couched in the language of saga and legend - the resurrection appearances, the empty tomb, the virgin birth, etc. - were omitted. Refusal to talk about them (not their non-theological historical therefore twilight counterparts) was *ipso facto* to jettison theological truth altogether (there is no theological truth if the whole of biblical history is not engaged in that transition to saga or legend, which means that biblical history must have a constant bias toward this sphere of *sui generis* historicality); indeed it is even more essential that what is true for angels is heeded now: to eliminate such vocabulary, far from purifying and modernising theology, was wholly to eschew the core vocabulary of talk about *God*. In other words, such terms were the *sui generis* theological equivalent of the traditional philosophical theologian's metaphysical vocabulary. To eliminate them was to leave the metatheological dilemma unresolved, and leave us with Overbeck's choice: do non-theology or nothing.

## Concluding Remarks

*Romans* II is not essentially a post-modern theologian's work, nor does the *Church Dogmatics* bear the stamp of "neo-orthodoxy"; rather, in the strictest continuity, both seek to resolve Overbeck's metatheological dilemma with the most ferocious dialectical irony. The ambition of the *Dogmatics* to do this on a grand scale, encompassing *all* the elements of the Christian story, means carrying on where the earlier work left off, taking it, as it were, to its logical conclusion. Nowhere is this irony so telling than when it is brought to bear on the relation between the Bible and historical reality, an issue on which Enlightenment epistemology had rightly much to say. It is to this that I now turn: the nature of the decisive historical truth-claims of the Bible.

# Chapter 5
# Historical Truth-Claiming
# and the Strange New World within the Bible

## 1. Introduction

In the foreword to *Church Dogmatics* VI/1 written in June 1953 Barth wrote:

> The present theological situation and also the particular themes of this book have made it necessary for me throughout to engage in an intensive though, for the most part, implicit conversation with Rudolf Bultmann. His name does not appear often, but his arguments have always been in my mind, even in places where, with his method and his results in view, I have deliberately ignored him.[1]

The present theological situation was no less than that Bultmann's star was in the ascendant and Barth felt duty-bound to combat this state of affairs. In particular, by pointing to the strange new world within the Bible, Barth was intent on redressing Bultmann's perception that history in the critical-historical sense and myth together exhausted the 'ontological' categories applicable to the Bible.

It comes as no surprise then that it was less Bultmann's method of demythologising (Barth was all for demythologising!) and more its result - a theological existentialist philosophy of the human being - to which Barth objected: "What caused my restraint against [Bultmann] was less his 'demythologising' of the New Testament as his 'existentialist interpretation' of its statements".[2] In a letter dated 29 May 1947 to Bishop Wurm of the Council of the Evangelical Church in Germany, predating the debate proper with Bultmann, Barth made an indirect reply to a certain Pastor Brun who had objected to the Marburg theologian's statements on

---

[1] Barth, *CD* IV/1, ix.
[2] Busch, *Barth*, 386.

the 'legend of the empty tomb' and the 'marvel of the resurrection'. Bultmann's statements, Barth said

> ... *could in themselves* be taken *in a good sense.* The term *"legend"* may simply denote the literary genre of the Easter stories of the Gospel (a *necessary* one in virtue of their unique content). The resurrection of the one who is dead and buried, or his existence as the one who is now alive, obviously cannot be reported in the form of a "historical narrative" but only as a "saga" or a "legend". This term says nothing about whether what is reported really happened or not. A legend does not necessarily lack substance. It may relate to real history which took place in space and time but cannot be told "historically" (i.e., in a form which is demonstrable and illuminating for everybody). In this sense I too [like Bultmann] can and must describe the Easter story as a "legend".[3]

Barth continues:

> For myself then, I would have to follow Bultmann's appeal to "most" of his colleagues - if I were not unfortunately aware that by the term "legend" he has in mind the idea that what the "legend" narrates never really took place. It is here that discussion should begin; the mere assertion that Bultmann used the term "legend" does not touch upon the truly serious question that needs to be put to him. The same applies to the derogatory expression "marvel". [...] I must assume that Bultmann meant it differently, i.e., that by means of it he wished to put the fact of the resurrection truly and definitively in the realm of credulous fancy. This and not the mere use of the term is what we need to discuss with him.[4]

Hence, while Barth agreed with Bultmann that the resurrection appearances stories could not be assimilated to 'historical narrative' as Bultmann understood this genre, he disassociated himself from any suggestion that saga or legend, as he understood the terms, should carry the derogatory implication of (necessary) non-existence with which Bultmann charged myth. In other words, saga was not myth; and it was not myth in virtue of the fact that it described theological truth. In a letter to a Herr Herrenbruck dated 15 February 1952 he wrote:

---

[3] B Jaspert (ed), *Karl Barth-Rudolf Bultmann: Letters 1922-1966,* translated and edited by G W Bromiley (Edinburgh: T & T Clark, 1982), 143-144. The characteristic Barthian irony is detectable in the final sentence: Barth agrees with Bultmann's description of the stories as legend. He has no quarrel with this Enlightenment characterisation at all!

[4] *Ibid,* 143-144.

I think that one can only demythologise demythologising by a better explanation of what Bultmann and his followers seem to have understood as no more than "myth" and shudder at with horror again and again.[5]

For Barth's theology the "better explanation" was theological truth. It was the answer to the "truly serious question that needs to be put to Bultmann." But since theological truth for Barth is *sui generis geschichtlichen* truth it followed among other things that, as will be shown, he was no less concerned than the historical critics were with the question of the relation between the Bible and historical reality.

## 2. The Relation Between the Bible and Historical Reality: "Quite so! the *Historie* of the Bible does not Witness to God's Self-Revelation, *Sage* Does!"

For Barth, the Bible was constituted by a number of different kinds of literary genres.[6] Most of these were not of the essential nature of a historical truth-claim about reality. Address, law, epigram, epic and lyric, for example, were not. And even though the genre of doctrine makes a truth-claim about reality, it is not essentially about making a historical truth-claim of the kind that historical narrative makes. Clearly, the relation between the Bible and historical reality depends on those genres that speak historically of events in the real world. The tradition of Reformation exegesis construed all such genres as history in the ordinary sense of the term.[7] The Enlightenment eliminated from this category those narratives that appeared

---

[5] Busch, *Barth*, 337-8.

[6] Barth provides a list of genres in *CD* III/1. Barth, CD III/1, 83.

[7] To be committed to understanding historical narrative as "history in the ordinary sense" means that in principle all the details of the narrative - the events described in the literal sense of the narrative - can be linked up together into one continuous chain satisfying topographical and chronological coherence. I shall have more to say about this later. Suffice to say that Calvin was motivated by such a commitment when he sought to harmonize what appeared to be discrepant historicity on the surface of the literal sense of the text. Historicity is a matter of onticity. Onticity is logically independent of, and prior to, the epistemic procedures employed to justify one's historical (ontic) truth-claims. It is at this point in the analysis that Troeltsch's methodological principles - the most famous being the principle of analogy - may or may not be relevant. As we shall see below, there may well be good reason for refusing to subject Calvin to Troeltsch on the grounds that Calvin affirms the illocutionary stance of historical truth-claiming narrative as one of basic belief.

to be mythological in character: creation history, the resurrection appearances, the virgin birth, the empty tomb, miracles, and angels. Barth's attitude to this history of biblical interpretation is captured in the following passage. Within the words can be detected a characteristic Barthian irony:

> ... the idea that the Bible declares the Word of God only when it speaks historically is one which must be abandoned, especially in the Christian Church. One consequence of this misunderstanding was the great uncertainty of faith which resulted from an inability wholly to escape the impression that many elements in the Bible have the nature of saga, and an ignorance where and how to draw the line which marks off what is finally historical and therefore the true Word of God. But in other cases it led to a rigid affirmation that in the Bible, as the Word of God, we have only "historical" accounts and no saga at all - an affirmation which can be sustained only it we either close our eyes or violently reinterpret what we see. In other cases again it resulted in an attempt to penetrate to a "historical" kernel which is supposed to give us the true, i.e., "historical" word of God - the only trouble being that in the process it was unfortunately found that with the discarding of saga we do lose not only a subsidiary theme but the main point at issue, i.e., the biblical witness. We have to realise that in all three cases the presumed equation of the Word of God with a "historical" record is an inadmissible postulate which does not itself originate in the Bible at all but in the unfortunate habit of Western thought which assumes that the reality of a history stands or falls by whether it is "history." It was when this habit emerged and asserted itself (at the close of the seventeenth century) that developing theological Liberalism began to be preoccupied with the thought of a "historically" purified Bible, and declining theological orthodoxy took its stand on the theory that the Bible contains nothing but "history" and is therefore in its entirety the Word of God. Both Liberalism and orthodoxy are children of the same insipid spirit, and it is useless to follow them. For after all, there seems no good reason why the Bible as the true witness of the Word of God should always have to speak "historically" and not be allowed to speak in the form of saga. On the contrary, we have to recognise that as holy and inspired Scripture, as the true witness of God's true Word, the Bible is forced to speak also in the form of saga precisely because its object and origin [*Gegenstand und Ursprung*] are what they are, i.e., not just "historical" but also frankly "non-historical." It would not be the Bible if it did not do this, and if it did not do it by mingling the two elements - and that in such a way that a dividing line can only be drawn with the greatest difficulty. Undoubtedly it is not by this dividing line that

it can be decided that it is God's revelation and must be believed. The decision about its nature as revelation, the confirmation of its reality as the Word of God, is reached by the fact that in its "historical" parts and also particularly and precisely in its "non-historical" (or sagas) - although always in connexion with the former - it attests the history of the great acts of God as genuine history, and that this witness is received and accepted through the power of the Holy Spirit.[8]

The assumption that the Bible declares the Word of God only when it speaks of history in the ordinary sense is, as Barth puts it, "an unfortunate habit of Western thought". Either it "led to a rigid affirmation  that in the Bible, as the Word of God, we have only 'historical' accounts and no saga at all."  For Barth, such was the error of orthodoxy: it attempted to treat the sagas of the Bible as if they were history in the ordinary sense (all saga is history and there is no distinction between them). This is "an affirmation which can be sustained only  if we either close our eyes or violently reinterpret what we see." Or, in the hands of liberal critics - especially the liberal theologians of the nineteenth and twentieth century - "it resulted in an attempt to penetrate to a 'historical' kernel which is supposed to give us the true, i.e., 'historical' word of God - the only trouble being that in the process it was unfortunately found that with the discarding of saga we do not lose only a subsidiary theme but the main point at issue, i.e., the biblical witness." For Barth, the error of theological liberalism was that it dealt with saga as if it were myth and consequently eliminated it (contrary to the pre-critical exegetes there *is* a distinction but: all saga is myth, and the categories 'myth' and 'history' are exhaustive ones). However, in eliminating saga the liberal critics had eliminated the biblical *witness*. Barth agreed with the Enlightenment that the relation between the Bible and reality, and therefore the historical problem of the Bible, depended crucially on witness. But since the Enlightenment critics had eliminated saga - failing to distinguish it from myth - these critics had, in fact, eliminated that which was crucial for evaluating the relation between the Bible and historical reality.

Implicit in  the passage quoted from *CD* III/1,  it is submitted, is Barthian irony reaching its highest heights. Eliminate saga - decipher it as either *Historie* - history in the ordinary sense - or as *mythos*, and the Enlightenment eliminates the very thing whose truth it should wish to evaluate were it were serious about asking the critical question about the relation between the Bible and historical reality. That is to say, according to Barth, "with the discarding of saga we do not lose only a subsidiary theme

---

[8] Barth, *CD* III/1, 82.

but the main point at issue, i.e., the biblical witness" to God's revelation, the "attestation to the history of the great acts of God". Conversely, to quote a remark from Barth's essay "The Christian Understanding of Revelation": "The more clearly the biblical witnesses of Jesus Christ speak, the more what they say gets lost in what we should today call the realm of pure legend."[9] That is to say, contrary to our preconceptions, the clearest statement in the realm of *witness* to Jesus Christ is "lost" in the realm of saga and legend, "lost", that is, in the realm of *sui generis Geschichte*. To eliminate saga was, repeat, to eliminate the very thing whose truth the Enlightenment should wish to evaluate were it were serious about asking the critical question about the relation between the Bible and historical reality. This is Barth's greatest subversion of the historical Enlightenment: "Quite so, Strauss, Overbeck, and Bultmann! The *Historie* in the Bible does not claim *witness* to those acts of God that are constitutive of His self-revelation!" *Sage* does.

Let us assume that the Enlightenment, on reflecting on the high seriousness of its duty, decides to reinstate that *whose truth it should wish to evaluate if it were serious about evaluating the question of the relation between the Bible and historical reality.* That is, it decides to reinstate saga. What had it reinstated? Clearly, saga had to bear directly on this question, viz., the relation between the Bible and historical reality. Therefore it was reinstating 1) a *historical truth-claiming* genre.[10] The Enlightenment had

---

[9] Barth, "The Christian Understanding of Revelation", Against the Stream. Shorter Post-War Writings, 1946-52, edited by R G Smith, (London: SCM press, 1954), 222.

[10] Meir Sternberg and Nicholas Wolterstorff have recently made the criticism that Hans Frei's omission of the category of historical truth-telling (or -claiming) - opting instead for the category of historicity - makes him unable to distinguish between history-telling and fiction-telling. Meir Sternberg, *The Poetics of Biblical Narrative* (Bloomington: Indiana University Press, 1987), 81-82; Nicholas Wolterstorff, *Divine Discourse: Philosophical Reflections on the Claim that God Speaks* (Cambridge: CUP, 1995), 242-243. According to them, Frei uses the categories of history-likeness (which can be assimilated to literal sense) and historicity, when he ought to have substituted history-telling for the latter. As Sternberg points out, historicity, or more broadly, historical truth-value, has little to do with meaning and hermeneutics. Sternberg, *Poetics*, 82. As Wolterstorff observes, whether something "counts as fiction is not determined by the truth or falsehood of the designative content of that discourse." Wolterstorff, *Divine Discourse*, 243. However, in my view, not even historical truth-claiming and literal sense collectively suffice for an adequate conceptual framework as regards the transition from pre-critical to critical interpretation of biblical narrative (as Frei describes it in *The Eclipse of Biblical Narrative*). One also needs the final form of the text (as opposed to a reduced narrative form). This is the fundamental rationale behind my choice of: historical truth-claiming, literal sense, and the final form of the text. Historically, allied

eliminated, for example, the resurrection appearances stories because, according to the *Religionsgeschichtliche* formulation of myth as evaluated by the Enlightenment, the question of factuality need not arise. As Hans Frei put it: "it is frequently (and doubtless rightly) asserted that, if the meaning of an account can be discovered by mythological interpretation, the question of its factuality need not arise. The explanation of its origin is enough. Myth thus becomes the unconscious poetizing of a folk consciousness."[11] Frei could be speaking of Strauss or Bultmann here.[12] According to Albert Schweitzer, however, a historic personality could be detected from "behind the mist of myth" - the historical Jesus understood "as a Jewish claimant of the Messiahship, whose world of thought is purely eschatological."[13] Or, in other words, apocalyptic. Strauss had not entirely disagreed with this since he too believed that there were real historical foundations for major parts of the synoptic Gospels' accounts of Jesus' public ministry and his death, (potentially inclusive of an apocalyptic dimension to Jesus' belief about himself).[14] The crucial fact of the matter is that both affirmed an understanding of the Gospel story in which the

---

to final form is the concept of basic (as opposed to non-basic) belief as understood by Reformed epistemologists such as Wolterstorff. See this chapter, 99-104.

[11] Frei, *The Identity of Jesus Christ* (Philadelphia: Fortress Press, 1975), 139.

[12] As Roger A Johnson has cogently argued, Bultmann's concept of myth is "an eclectic construct consisting of three elements logically and historically independent of each other." Roger A Johnson, *The Origins of Demythologising: Philosophy and Historiography in the Theology of Rudolf Bultmann* (Leiden: E J Brill, 1974), 30. These three elements are: the *Religionsgeschichtliche* formulation of myth; the Enlightenment formulation of myth; the existentialist formulation of myth. *Ibid*, 30. It is the Enlightenment formulation of myth which is of most relevance with regard to Barth. Bultmann judges myth to be a pre-scientific form of objectification. *Ibid*, 253. It is in virtue of this dimension of objectification that it is continuous with science. But it is *discontinuous* with science in the sense that, unlike science, it is not objectification according to law [*Gesetz*]. *Ibid*, 54. It is objectification in a random, arbitrary pattern, determined by inner subjective needs and not by the structure of reason. *Ibid*, 253. The objectification that myth provides is the projection on to reality by a primitive mentality unrestrained by scientific norms. Barth clearly agrees with Bultmann's definition of myth; what he disagrees with is Bultmann's assertion that the biblical account belongs to this genre. Moreover, he denies that science provides the appropriate norm against which to measure the truth of the biblical account. He argues that one can discern in the strange new world within the Bible a norm which accords with a determinate *sui generis* rational form, a form all of its own.

[13] Albert Schweitzer, *The Quest of the Historical Jesus: a Critical Study of Its Progress from Reimarus to Wrede*, introduction by F C Burkitt, translated by W Montgomery (Baltimore: John Hopkins University Press, 1998), 95.

[14] See David Friedrich Strauss, *The Life of Jesus Critically Examined*, translated by George Eliot, edited with an introduction by Peter C Hodgson (London: SCM, 1973).

historical figure of Jesus emerging from "the mist of myth" was
constrained within a mythological framework decreeing what could, and
could not, have happened. Now, the same stories had to be taken as
making a truth-claim relating to historical reality - *a historical truth-claim.*
Therefore the Enlightenment was reinstating a second thing closely allied to
the first. It was 2) evaluating the historical truth of the *literal sense* of the
narratives.

   In this respect, what the Enlightenment was being asked to do in its
reinstatement of saga was to set aside for the moment its thesis that such
stories - the resurrection appearances stories or the creation stories - were
*expressive of something other than the literal sense of the stories construed
as historical truth-claiming.*[15] No matter that it thought that the truth of
myth was religious rather than historical or factual,[16] it was not to seek the
use to which such stories were put (precisely historical truth-claiming) *other
than in the stories themselves*; not, therefore, 'off the page' as it were, as in
expressive of an archaic myth-making mentality, for example. (As an aid to
suspending such a firmly-held belief about primitive expressivism, the
Enlightenment at this point could learn from Erich Auerbach's *Mimesis*

---

[15] I am aware that there is more than one view as to what literal sense means within the
context of the Bible. One position that has been brought to prominence is that of
Thomas Aquinas who argued that, rather than limiting our readings of the Bible to one
single sense, literal sense allows for, and indeed maintains - is inclusive of - a plurality
of readings. See Eugene F Rogers , Jr, "How the Virtues of the Interpreter Presuppose
and Perfect Hermeneutics: The Case of Thomas Aquinas", *Journal of Religion* 76
(1996), 64-81. Stephen Fowl claims this Thomistic notion informs those contemporary
advocates of the literal sense of scripture such as George Lindbeck, the later Frei, and
Kathryn Tanner who treat the literal sense as the meaning established within the
community who take the Bible to be their scripture. Stephen E Fowl, *Engaging
Scripture* (Oxford: Blackwell, 1998), 37-40. But the literal sense of narrative *construed
solely within the context of historical truth-claiming* seems to impose constraints on a
similar kind of plurality as regards truth-claims on historical reality. Not all historical
truth-claims are compatible: in the strictly logical sense, some are contraries of each
other (though both may be false, both cannot be true). *Inter alia*, I implicitly argue in
this book that Barth's view of the historical truth-claims of the biblical narratives,
relating as they do to real historical space and time cannot, for example, be reconciled
with Calvin's view as regards the historical truth-claims of the same narratives
(especially the resurrection-appearances narratives). Notwithstanding this, Calvin, like
Barth, affirms that the biblical narratives are making determinate claims on historical
reality. It is this emphasis that most probably explains Brevard Childs' preference for
the Reformers' position on literal sense. Brevard Childs, "The Sensus Literalis of
Scripture: An Ancient and Modern Problem" in H Donner et al, *Beiträge zur
alttestamentlichen Theologie: Festschrift für Walter Zimmerli* (Gottingen:
Vandenhoeck and Ruprecht, 1977), 80-94.
[16] Frei, *The Identity of Jesus Christ*, 140.

what Frei himself had learned, namely that - as one lesson of comparative antique literature - it was not implausible that the Gospels be understood as a species of *realistic* narrative.)[17]

Now, in reinstating that which it had previously eliminated as myth the Enlightenment reinstates *all* of the narratives, in particular, the *four* Gospel accounts of the resurrection appearances and the *two* accounts of creation in Genesis. It therefore reinstated 3), *the final form of the text.* To reinstate the sagas of the Bible entailed reinstating the final form of the text. The identity of saga demanded this. Otherwise it could not be saga that was being reinstated.[18] That the Enlightenment would resist this particular reinstatement most of all cannot be gainsaid. But was it right in its judgement that Barth was seeking to bring back Calvin and Augustine and all the great exegetes of the Bible in their full and complete glory?

To recapitulate: in reinstating saga the Enlightenment was reinstating *historical truth-claiming, literal sense,* and *the final form of the text.* Accordingly, it could not be blamed for assuming that Barth was asking it to reinstate a pre-critical approach to the Bible. But was this really what it was being asked to do? To be sure, affirming the final form of the biblical text had been a defining characteristic of the pre-critical approach. And, moreover, one of the great merits of this tradition was that it provided an interpretation of scripture that *in itself* was sufficient for evaluating the relation between the Bible and historical reality. (Among other things, this meant that when a minister of the Word preached the Gospel, he did not have to go outside the text itself in order to vouchsafe the truth of the biblical narrative; he did so on the basis of the text alone.) How so?

To reiterate: not only had the pre-critical tradition attempted to maintain simultaneously historical truth-claiming, literal sense, and the final form of the text, the tradition had presumed that - given the first two, the last was

---

[17] See Erich Auerbach, *Mimesis: The Representation of Reality in Western Literature,* translated by William R Trask (Princeton: Princeton university Press, 1953). The history of ideas which Auerbach, Frei, and Barth represent is a historical reaction to the conclusions reached about the Bible in the nineteenth century - and beyond - in the wake of the thesis that the historical consciousness of first-century Palestine was crucial to the interpretation of the Gospel narratives, and indeed, the Bible as a whole. The three do not deny the historical, (broadly mythological) consciousness but they reject the inference that it is necessary to the interpretation of the Gospel narratives. This is, broadly speaking, because all three view the narratives as *realistic* narratives. See Frei, *Identity of Jesus Christ,* 12-13 for a definition of this genre,

[18] The reason this is the case will be seen later. The basic rationale is to do with Barth's definition of saga. Barth defines saga "in the sense of an intuitive and poetic picture of a pre-historical reality of history which is enacted once and for all within the confines of time and space." Barth, *CD* III/1, 81. It is this that Barth is asking the Enlightenment to reinstate.

*sufficient* for evaluating the question of the relation between the Bible and historical reality. This was an exceptionally bold claim but it was one that, with hindsight, could be seen to have been made with some justification. In a famous sentence in *The Eclipse of Biblical Narrative*, Hans Frei wrote that "... if it seemed clear that a biblical story was to be read literally, it followed automatically that it referred to and described actual historical occurrences." It is reasonable to surmise that, for both Augustine and Calvin, the belief that the biblical narratives described true historical occurrences (as ordinarily understood) was - to use the language of Reformed epistemology - a *basic belief*, and therefore not a belief based on any other beliefs or evidence. A pre-critical exegete such as Calvin did not doubt for a moment that the world in which he breathed, ate and slept was the very same world which God had created, the very same world in which Jesus Christ had been crucified dead and buried and had risen again on the third day, the very same world in which Jesus Christ would come again in glory to judge the living and the dead. Not for a second did Calvin doubt any of these articles of faith. Since the biblical world was the source of Calvin's understanding of the world in which he lived - it was after all the world he experienced in every waking second as *God's* world - it followed that the earth on which he stood with his two feet was to be interpreted in terms of the "one real world detailed and made accessible in the biblical story." This is the sense in which Calvin's belief that the biblical narratives described true historical occurrences was a basic belief.

Accordingly, when Calvin came to interpret the Gospels in his *A Harmony of the Gospels* he understood the mind-set of the Evangelists in a similar way. As Calvin put it:

We will not say that the diversity which we perceive in the three Evangelists was the object of express arrangement, but as they intended to give an honest narrative *of what they knew to be certain and undoubted* [my italics], each followed that method which he reckoned best.[19]

---

[19] Calvin, *A Harmony of the Gospels, Matthew, Mark, Luke*, vol I, translated by A W Morrison, edited by David F Torrance and Thomas F Torrance, (Edinburgh: St Andrew Press, 1972) xiii. Clearly, to say that the Evangelists gave an "honest" narrative - or intended to give one - of what they knew to be "certain and undoubted" does not entail that they gave an *identical* narrative. Later, Calvin writes: "Indeed, God's spirit, who appointed the Evangelists as recorders, deliberately controlled their pen, so that all should write in complete agreement, but in different ways. It gave more certainty and light to God's truth when it was established His witnesses did not tell a pre-arranged tale, but that each of them without respect of the others, wrote simply and freely what the Spirit dictated." *Ibid.*, 82.

What Calvin appears to be saying is that, though it was *the same thing in substance* that each Evangelist "knew to be certain and undoubted" - and which was therefore expressive of a basic belief on the basis of the *inward testimony of the Holy Spirit* - each followed the method or manner of writing  which each thought most appropriate for its subject-matter: the *same* subject-matter.[20] It was from this stand-point that Calvin attempted to affirm the historical truth-claims of each Gospel, simultaneously as it were. In this he was representative of the pre-critical tradition as a whole. That is to say: it is within the context of the concept of basic belief that the pre-critical approach to the Bible is best understood.

The pre-critical tradition had attempted to hold to the three parameters of historical truth-claiming, literal sense, and the final form of the text, simultaneously and consistently, precisely by means *of narrative harmonisation.*[21] It had attempted to answer the question: in view of the *variation* in details - two different accounts of creation and four different accounts of the resurrection appearances - what is, in each case, the correct explanation of such variations? Variations on the surface of the text that exhibited apparent chronological and topographical disparity and inconsistency were to be harmonised and  seamlessly sewn into a larger garment of  chronological and topographical coherence and continuity, the histories arranged "in one unbroken chain, or in a single picture", to use Calvin's description. That is to say, pre-critical harmonisation sought to keep 'on the score' all notes of each Gospel or of each creation narrative - all respective truth-claims - and make of all a harmonious unity.[22]

---

[20] This is the fundamental rationale behind affirming the historical truth-claiming of biblical narratives as expressive of a basic belief. One knows the *truth* of the narratives on the basis of the inward testimony of  the Holy Spirit. There is no conception of  faith requiring justification, of seeking to go outside the text to see if it matched up to historical reality.

[21] The title of one of the most important harmonies in the sixteenth century, written by the Lutheran theologian Andreas Osiander, epitomises the aim of such harmonisations. Its title was *Greek and Latin Harmony in Four Books, in which the Gospel Story is Combined According to the Four Evangelists in Such a Way that No Word of Any One of Them Is Omitted, No Foreign Word Added, the Order of None of Them is Disturbed, and Nothing is Displaced, in which, However, the Whole is Marked by Letters and Signs Which Permit One To See at a First Glance the Points Peculiar to Each Evangelist, Those He Has in Common with the Others, and with Which of Them.*

[22] When I said that the concept of final narrative form versus reduced narrative form was integral to explaining the transition from pre-critical to critical interpretation, I had in mind the kind of analysis one finds in Brevard Childs' *The New Testament as Canon: an Introduction*: "The basic error of the traditional harmony", writes Childs, "was that the

For example: the pre-critical theological tradition made the assumption that the creation history and the resurrection-appearances history, respectively, satisfied chronological and topographical coherence and continuity. Hence, not only did the pre-critical tradition as embodied, for example, in Calvin and Augustine affirm literal sense - Augustine wrote a commentary on Genesis entitled *The Literal Meaning of Genesis*; Calvin too emphasised in his commentary on Genesis the literal sense of the two accounts of creation - both affirmed the final form of the text. The biblical witness *in toto* was to be taken to be speaking literally in the assertoric mode of a historical happening in the ordinary sense.

In the case of creation this meant that the assertion "God created cattle, wild animals and reptiles before man" was true in the sense in which "William Pitt was born before Winston Churchill" was true. However, in Genesis 1, cattle, wild animals and reptiles are made before man. But in Genesis 2 all the wild animals and all birds of heaven are made after God had formed man. In *The Literal Meaning of Genesis*, Augustine introduces the distinction between actual and potential existence to account for the apparent discrepancy between Genesis 1 and 2 concerning the order in which created things were created. As John Hammond Taylor puts it of Augustine's apologetic: "God had 'again formed' the birds and beasts in the sense that after the sixth day His creative power at work in the seminal reasons brought forth the birds and the beasts which he had created potentially in their causes (*potentialiter atque causaliter*) on the fifth and sixth days."[23]

Another apparent inconsistency: in the resurrection accounts of Mark and Matthew, for example, there is one angel, but in Luke and John there

---

canonical assumption had been deficient in leaving the Gospel form in their plural form rather than completing the process by fusing them into a fixed authoritative interpretation." Brevard Childs, *New Testament Canon: an Introduction* (London: SCM, 1985), 156. Such a fusion involved the "*addition* [my italics] of the parts into a complete harmony ...." *Ibid*, 154. It is clear from passages such as this that Childs' canonical position on Gospel harmony is quite different from the approach taken by the pre-critical harmonists on behalf of Gospel harmony, for example, Augustine and Calvin. Barth's is too!

[23] Augustine, *The Literal Meaning of Genesis*, vol I, translated by John Hammond Taylor, SJ, (New York: Newman Press, 1982), 262; see also 182-184, 252-254. Taylor explains the seminal or causal reasons as follows: "These causal reasons implanted by God in the original creation are not seeds in the sense of visible, tangible substances out of which organisms grow ... but they are seed-like powers in the created world, causing the seeds to develop according to God's plan." *Ibid*, 253. Augustine believed in the simultaneous creation of all things, "but that living things made in that original creative act were not made in actuality in their own proper substances but only potentially in their causal reasons placed in the earth by the Creator." *Ibid*, 253-254.

are two. In response, Calvin says in his *A Harmony of the Gospels* that "this kind of contradiction is easily resolved, as we know that instances of synecdoche are frequently to be found in Scripture. Two angels were seen, first by Mary, then by the others with her."[24]

Whatever one thought of the adequacy of such harmonisation, it did *not* follow that failure to provide a successful reconciliation of   apparent historical discrepancies *was of itself crucial to the belief that these biblical narratives described true historical occurrences*. To be sure, Calvin may well have been  deeply convinced of the success of his harmonisation of the synoptic Gospels. However, even were his arguments to fail because they proved to lack the force of demonstration*, the failure would imply nothing whatsoever as to the rationality of his belief that the biblical narratives describe true historical occurrences so long as this belief is a properly basic belief.*[25] True, there had to be   an account that dealt with the

---

[24]Calvin,  *A Harmony of the Gospels*, vol III, 224. John Wenham writes: "It should be said once and for all that the mention by one evangelist of two angels and by another of one does not constitute a contradiction or discrepancy. If there was two there was one." John Wenham, *Easter Enigma: Do the Resurrection Stories Contradict One Another?* (Exeter: Paternoster Press, 1984), 87. I find neither Calvin's nor Wenham's respective accounts convincing. Certainly there is no contradiction or discrepancy if Wenham is correct about the illocutionary stance of the witness. But the stance he attributes is, to my mind, improbable. In the absence of some additional reason as to why the witness would only speak of one angel when he experienced two - we are speaking of angels after all! - one cannot take this apologetic as seriously as one might wish. The interesting question as regards Calvin's attempted harmonisation is whether it is compatible with his view that the Holy Spirit "deliberately controlled their pen, so that all should write in complete agreement, but in different ways." Calvin,  *A Harmony of the Gospels*, vol I, 82. Calvin might well have said that the Holy Spirit was behind the evangelists' employment of synecdoche.

[25] The rationale behind this is Nicholas Wolterstorff's seminal article "The Migration of the Theistic Arguments: From Natural Theology to Evidentialist Apologetics", R Audi and W J Wainwright (ed), *Rationality, Religious Belief, and Moral Commitment: New Essays in the Philosophy of Religion* (Ithaca: Cornell University Press), 38-81. The emergence of evidential apologetics during the seventeenth and eighteenth century testified to a fundamental shift in epistemic stance from a 'faith seeking understanding' paradigm  to what may be termed a 'faith requiring justification' one. The 'faith seeking understanding' paradigm constituted the fundamental rationale behind the respective theological epistemologies of Augustine, Anselm, and Aquinas. And it was no less central to Calvin's basic epistemic stance. As Wolterstorff puts it, on the matter of epistemic stance, Calvin is closer to Aquinas than to Locke. Pre-Enlightenment theologians such as Augustine, Anselm, Aquinas and Calvin did not attach foundationalist conditions to theistic beliefs. *Ibid*, 80. Wolterstorff contrasts this epistemic stance with that of a Enlightenment thinker such as Locke: for Locke "the

discrepancies successfully, but it did not follow that one's belief was
irrational in the absence of providing one.[26] Crucially then: though such
harmonisations as Augustine and Calvin had proposed might well be
sufficient conditions of proving the rationality of the belief that the biblical
narratives of the four Gospels described true historical occurrences, they
did not constitute necessary conditions. Notwithstanding any of this, the
essential point was that the pre-critical tradition had provided an argument
whose motivated conclusion was precisely that *the final form of the text*
was *sufficient* for evaluating the relation between the Bible and historical
reality. The tradition had provided grounds on which it could validly claim
that *one did not require to go outside the text itself in order to answer this*
*question, and answer it positively.*

   Historically, the Enlightenment response to the pre-critical tradition went
like this. Critical interpretation had sought to answer the question: in view
of the variation in the *order* of events as narrated by the different
evangelists, what is the more *probable* chronological order?[27] It took up a
vantage-point outside the biblical world depicted in the final form and sought
to uncover 'the Gospel behind the Gospels.'[28] If the consequence of such an
attempt resulted in the discarding of a great number of 'notes' - discarding the
final form of the text in effect - then so be it. Harmony was understood in
terms of historical reference to a unitary external historical referent, the truth
of which logically ruled out the possibility that all Gospel accounts could, so
to speak, be true simultaneously, and moreover precluded - on the grounds of
critical-historical methodological principles such as those of Troeltsch -[29] the

---

failure of evidentialist apologetics implies that the believer must surrender his faith."
*Ibid*, 80.

[26] Nicholas Wolterstorff has suggested an illocutionary stance compatible with Calvin's
understanding of the Evangelists' epistemic stance: the Evangelists are telling of 'the way
it might well have been'. Clearly, '*what* might well have been this way' coincides with the
material substance of what each Evangelist "knew to be certain and undoubted."
Wolterstorff, *Divine Discourse*, 258-260.

[27] M B Riddle conceives of the relationship between pre-critical and critical interpretation
in terms of the questions it poses to Scripture. M B Riddle, Introductory Essay to
Augustine's *De Consensu Evangelistarum*, vol vi *Augustine* The Nicene and Post-Nicene
Fathers, First Series (Grand Rapids: Eerdmans, 1956), 67-70.

[28] Stephen Neill and Tom Wright, *The Interpretation of the New Testament 1861-1986* 2nd
ed. (Oxford: Oxford University Press, 1988), 252-312.

[29] See Ernst Troeltsch's classic paper, "Historical and Dogmatic Method in Theology",
in Ernst Troeltsch, "Historical and Dogmatic Method in Theology", *Religion in History*,
translated by J Luther Adams and W F Bense, introduction by James Luther Adams,
(Edinburgh: T & T Clark, 1991), 11-32. Whenever I refer to Troeltsch in this book this
paper should be taken as the focus.

possibility that intrinsic to this unitary figure was that He had revealed Himself as God in his resurrection-appearances history.[30] *In other words, the critical tradition did not accept that historical events could properly be the object of a basic belief.* All rational historical beliefs (and perhaps all rational beliefs) were necessarily non-basic beliefs, beliefs based on other beliefs in turn founded on evidence.[31]

Nevertheless, the question the Enlightenment now asked was: was it possible to hold to historical truth-telling, literal sense, and the final form of the text simultaneously and consistently *without* affirming the pre-critical approach toward the final form of the text? It was clear that one could avoid the pre-critical approach were one's commitment to historical truth-telling and literal sense only: having reinstated what had been previously eliminated as myth, the Enlightenment was duly committed to historical truth-telling and literal sense. But it might well demur from taking the additional step of affirming the final form of the text - no matter that such refusal was incompatible with the identity of saga - were it to believe pre-critical harmonisation to be the only option available. In other words, *when the final form of the text was added* - in this case four apparently inconsistent resurrection appearance narratives, two apparently discrepant creation narratives - it appeared that one could only satisfy topographical and chronological coherence and consistency if one retraced the direction of the history of biblical interpretation toward the past, toward pre-critical harmonisation, toward what Strauss considered to be nothing more than "a tissue of historical conjectures or worse"? Did the

---

[30]According to Childs, the critical-historical school of interpretation cannot but be unfaithful to the Gospel witness, in its search for a reconstructed historical reference, a 'historical Gospel behind the Gospels': the "basic error of the historical critical position was the assumption that the canonical shape was of no exegetical significance and that valid interpretation depended on a critical reconstruction which re-aligned the Gospels in their original historical sequence." Childs, *New Testament Canon*, 156. Such critical reconstruction - of the life of Jesus, for example - involved "the *subtraction* [my italics] and critical sifting of the evidence in order to discover the real Jesus behind the levels of accretion." *Ibid*, 154. Hence, when Childs charges the critical-historical school of unfaithfulness to the Gospel witness, he should be taken to mean that the school subtracts from the testimony those truth-claims which are irreconcilable with the underlying unitary historical referent whose reality is conceived in terms of principles such as Troeltsch's.

[31] I am not going to enter into the debate of who is right between the historical Enlightenment and Reformed epistemology. I will simply note that a book such as Austin van Harvey's *The Historian and the Believer* did not consider the possibility that such a position could be rational. See Austin van Harvey's *The Historian and the Believer: the Morality of Historical Knowledge and Christian Belief* (London: SCM, 1966).

Enlightenment have to reinstate pre-critical harmonisation when it reinstated saga?

The answer is, no! *Though the three parameters were a necessary condition of pre-critical harmonisation they were not sufficient.* In other words, though the pre-critical tradition affirmed the parameters of historical truth-claiming, literal sense and final form, it construed the narratives as claiming historicity in the ordinary sense of history - a "rigid affirmation of history", to quote Barth. *It did not treat the creation or resurrection appearances stories as saga.* And to the Enlightenment question, 'Could one affirm historical truth-telling, literal sense, and the final form of the text as *sufficient in itself* for evaluating the truth of the relation between the Bible and historical reality *without* affirming pre-critical harmonisation in the context of basic belief?', Barth's answer was a decided 'yes'. There is no doubt that he is in fundamental continuity with the pre-critical tradition of Augustine and Calvin on the question of sufficiency. And indeed with Hans Frei.[32] *But the means by which he affirmed sufficiency in this sense is qualitatively different from both.*

---

[32] It is one of the seminal achievements of Hans Frei's *The Identity of Jesus Christ* that it appeared to be able to emulate the pre-critical achievement in respect of providing an interpretation of the Gospel that was sufficient in itself for evaluating the relation between the Bible and historical reality. Had Frei's ingenious interpretation of the Gospel narrative been valid, he had in fact cited grounds for making the claim that the final form of the text was sufficient for evaluating the truth of the relation between the Bible and historical reality, that is, *without going outside the text, and without employing the concept of basic belief.* The premise behind Frei's argument was that the final form of the text - the final form of the Gospel narratives - narrated the identity of Jesus Christ as 'he who cannot not exist." It can argued that, without the category of historical truth-claiming, Frei's position on the Gospel narrative is open to Kant's 'hundred thalers' criticism which correctly objected to the validity of deriving existence from essence: a narrative identity in itself cannot move the conclusion that there exists *in reality* the person Jesus Christ who cannot not exist. This latter point was well made by Garrett Green. Garrett Green, "Fictional Narrative and Scriptural Truth", Garrett Green (ed), *Scriptural Authority and Narrative Interpretation* (Philadelphia: Fortress Press, 1987), 79-96. One can see that the apparent strength of Frei's position in *The Identity of Jesus Christ* was illusory. Frei's implicit point was: if Jesus' identity as rendered by the biblical narrative was as he said it was, in what sense could historical research discover that Jesus Christ had not or did not exist or - more germanely - no longer existed after his death on the cross? But of course, as Wolterstorff has implicitly shown, the truth of Frei's claim about the narrative itself (independently of other factors such as inspiration of the Holy Spirit) has no logical bearing on the relevance of historical investigation. Fiction-telling was compatible with the narrative identity of 'He who cannot not exist.' Frei seemed to concur with the rationale behind these critiques. In an essay subsequent to *The Identity of Jesus Christ* he expressed the misgiving that

### 3. The Final Form of the Text:
### *Sui Generis* Historicality, *Sage*, and Overbeck's Dilemma

Paradoxically, Barth could not but agree with the Enlightenment's demurral at taking a retrograde step back toward the past, toward the traditional harmonisation of, for example, the Gospels. The reason is that *given the resolution of the metatheological dilemma*, it was not *open* to Barth to render the literal sense of the final form of these key narratives of the Bible - the creation history, the resurrection-appearances history - *as history in the ordinary sense.* In other words, *it was not open to Barth to approach these narratives in their respective totalities - as respective wholes - in the manner in which pre-critical exegetes such as Calvin had. It was not open to Barth to resolve the apparent discrepancies and contradictions that appeared on the surface of the literal sense of these narratives - the four Gospel accounts of the resurrection appearances and the two accounts of creation in* Genesis *- by harmonising them as history in the ordinary sense.*

It is not that the subject-matter of the parameters of historical truth-claiming, literal sense, and final form was non-historical truth (*ungeschichtliche* truth). Far from it: it had to be, and it was, historical. It is precisely *geschichtliche* truth. But it was *geschichtliche* truth "of a

---

he had, as the Anglo-American "New Critics" had done before him, advocated a self-referential 'meaning' world the truth of which subsisted *in the text* independently of the real historical world. Frei, "The Literal Reading of the Biblical narrative: Does It Stretch or Will It Break?", in F D O'Connell (ed), *The Bible and the Narrative Tradition* (Oxford: Oxford University Press, 1986), 63-64. However, the question remains: can Frei's position be rescued if one adds the illocutionary stance of truth-claiming to history-like narrative? One could then say that the Gospels employed a truth-telling genre which narrated the history of 'He who cannot not exist.' Therein lies the rub: it may be that in claiming that there was *in reality* a person Jesus Christ who cannot not exist one is still faced with the ontological and epistemological problem of the *events* - the historical events of crucifixion and most especially resurrection appearances - in which this identity is constituted (in reality). How did one ground or justify one's belief in them? The strength of the pre-critical epistemic stance lay in the fact that it had an answer to this question (at least implicitly) in the form of the concept of basic belief. Frei could have gone in this direction (preferring it to affirming the events in question as the object of non-basic belief). Barth gave another answer: *sui generis* historicality as the epistemic point of departure for one's evaluation of the relation between the Bible and historical reality. I would argue that it is the most cogent of all the answers offered since the Enlightenment. But in this book I am more content to state what Barth's position is.

different kind":[33] *sui generis geschichtliche* truth (hence, when Barth speaks of *theological truth* as regards the biblical witness to angels, for example, he has in mind the *sui generis* historicality of this history). The resolution of Overbeck's dilemma implied *sui generis* historicality.

In other words, in order to answer the question of the Bible and historical reality, Barth's exegesis of the Bible shares many important features in common with a tradition that can be said to stretch back to Calvin and beyond. Barth's exegesis affirms historical truth-claiming, the primacy of the *sensus literalis*, and the final form of the text. However, given Overbeck's dilemma, Barth affirms a   final textual form other than in the 'one-dimensional' historical sense found in Augustine and Calvin. All of this, it had to be said followed, utterly ironically, from Barth's attempt to answer the question of the relation between the Bible and historical reality in the context of Overbeck's dilemma. "Quite so!" Barth said to the Enlightenment, "given Overbeck's dilemma, the final form of the text cannot be   reconciled and harmonised as   history in the ordinary sense." The creation and the resurrection appearances narratives are, respectively, speaking of a *sui generis* historicality.

Barth's approach to the final form of the text is qualitatively different from both pre-critical and critical interpretation. Though he shares pre-critical hermeneutics' - and especially Calvin's - concern for a literal reading of the Gospels, he does not derive a synthesis that incorporated all the details of each Gospel in such a way that the synthesis refers to *a unity of actual historical occurrences in the ordinary sense*.

Nevertheless, Barth's hermeneutics is closer in spirit to pre-critical than to critical-historical hermeneutics. In continuity with the underlying principles of pre-critical interpretation, Barth retains a literal reading that incorporates all the details of each Gospel - the final form of the text. Hence, unlike critical interpretation, he does not eliminate literal detail that does not conform to the most probable course of events - 'the Gospel behind the Gospels' for example. Indeed, he does not eliminate literal detail at all. But he does not 'keep all the notes on the score of the harmony' by synthesising the literal detail at the level of ordinary historical occurrence.

The harmony Barth discovers in the Bible, and in the strange new world within the Bible in particular, is, precisely, a synthesis - *Aufhebung* - at the level of a specific theological identity, *sui generis* historicality. Hence though Barth's epistemological 'centre of gravity' is always the Bible rather than an unitary historical reference governed by principles such as those proposed by Troeltsch, this centre of gravity is not the Bible as Calvin and pre-critical hermeneutics had envisaged it. Barth's vision is not synthesis at the simplest

---

[33] Barth, *CD* IV/1, 334.

one-dimensional historical level; it is synthesis - resolution of discrepancy and disharmony - at a *sui generis* historical dimension qualitatively different from, if not higher than, the ordinary historical dimension.[34] In practice, this will mean a rejection of the pre-critical attempt to harmonise and arrange the resurrection appearances stories into "one unbroken sequence or in a single picture" as in a continuous historical framework. Though each resurrection appearance story is historically continuous with the passion story, they are historically discontinuous one with the other, being of the nature of a discrete event with other. As we shall see: the historical event is that Jesus Christ revealed Himself as the Crucified One.

That the realm of historicality be enlarged (or extended as in a continuum) to include the possibility of such an event is all that Barth asks. That it be conceded that such an event be logically or 'metaphysically' possible in historical space and time is all Barth asks that the Enlightenment grant. He will want to add the point in a manner similar to Anselm's *Cur Deus Homo* that, were *God to reveal Himself as God*, reveal Himself as *Himself* in historical space and time, such a self-revelation would have to be in the form of such an event. Otherwise, it would not be the 'God who is *God*'. In point of fact, he will ask the Enlightenment - and Kant in particular - to consider his book on Anselm, *Anselm: Fides Quaerens Intellectum*. In this book he thinks that he - or Anselm - has proved the possibility of the coherence of such an event - an event whose only means of measurement is it itself - in God revealing Himself as 'that than which a greater cannot be conceived'. *Anselm: Fides Quaerens Intellectum* is absolutely pivotal to the rationality of *sui generis*

---

[34]According to Barth, pre-critical interpretation offered "a rigid affirmation that in the Bible, as the Word of God, we have only "historical" accounts and no saga at all - an affirmation which can be sustained only if we either close our eyes or violently reinterpret what we see." Barth, *CD* III/1, 82. Critical interpretation "resulted in an attempt to penetrate to a 'historical' kernel which is supposed to give us the true, i.e., 'historical' word of God - the only trouble being that in the process it was unfortunately found that with the discarding of saga we do not lose only a subsidiary theme but the main point at issue, i.e., the biblical witness." *Ibid*, 82. In other words, to construe all saga as history in the ordinary sense, as pre-critical interpreters had, meant having to make the kind of assumptions Calvin and Augustine did to achieve harmony. This followed from the desire to hold on to a literal reading of each Gospel simultaneously - hold on to a literal reading of all the details of each Gospel simultaneously, as it were. Similarly, to eliminate what was, in fact, saga, on the grounds that it was the product of a primitive 'myth-making' mentality, entailed that one achieved harmony with a unitary external historical referent in such a way that one lost not "only a subsidiary theme but the main point at issue, i.e., the biblical witness."

historicality and therefore fundamental to Barth's answer to the question of the relation between the Bible and historical reality.[35]

Thus when the Enlightenment reinstates saga, all that Barth asks of it is that it in fact consider the possibility - no more than this - that there could be such a historicality. That the sagas in question - the resurrection appearances and the creation stories - do in fact tell of such a historicality, do in fact make such a historical truth-claim - is a matter of the content or meaning (for want of a better word) of the final form of the text, and therefore a matter for exegesis. All that Barth asks of the Enlightenment is that it resist from damning *sui generis* historicality as impossible or as incoherent from the outset.

## 4. *Sui Generis* Historicality Contra *Sui Generis* Historicity

In this book I have used the phrase '*sui generis* historicality' as opposed to the conceptually simpler '*sui generis* historicity.' The reason is that I do not think Barth thought there was such a thing as *sui generis* historicity. He thought that the concept of historicity, like the concept of truth, was same the world over, so to speak: to say of Jesus Christ's resurrection-appearances history that it was a historical event was to say that it was a historical event in exactly the same sense in which the history of the death of Nelson was a historical event. The historicity of the former - if true - was not a *sui generis* historicity, it was historicity pure and simple. Historicity is do to with the sheer 'that it happened' of the event and this is the same in both cases. Hence when Barth spoke of the "historical character" of the resurrection appearances [their *Geschichtlichkeit*] he merely meant that they were real objective historical events and therefore not to be re-interpreted as subjective mythological projection.[36] He was speaking of 'historicity.'

But does Barth use the concept of historicality? If one were to ask Barth *what it is* that had happened, his most articulate answer would have been "a historical sphere of a different kind [*ein Geschichtsbereich anderer, eigener*

---

[35] 'That than which a greater cannot be conceived' is pivotal for Barth because it allowed him to state the sense in which Jesus Christ's resurrection appearances history could be a historical event in space and time and yet not be susceptible to the critical-historical method. A *sui generis* historical event is, for Barth, 'that which nothing analogous can be conceived' rather than 'that than which nothing greater can be conceived.' But the same logic applies, as will be seen in Chapter 6 section 2 and Chapter 8.

[36] Barth, *CD* IV/1, 388.

*Art*]"[37] or even "history of a different kind" (what Barth refers to somewhat awkwardly as a "pre-historical" happening or event).[38] Such historical events are ultimately what Barth characterises as a historical event whose only means of measurement is it itself: God revealing Himself as creator and God revealing Himself as reconciler. Such events are in this sense history "of a different kind."

The concept of historicality is presupposed in making such a distinction. The *essence* of the history of the death of Nelson and of the event of Jesus Christ's resurrection-appearances history  is that they are historical events or, to put it another way, historicality is an essential property of these events: if they are historical events then it is difficult to conceive in what sense they could be *other* than historical events (say chemical events) and remain the *same* event. Just as 'existence' is not a predicate of the concept of  God (Kant is right about this), 'historicity' is not a predicate of the concept of event. But 'historicality' is a predicate - a necessary predicate - of the concept of historical event. Herein lies the fundamental distinction between the two concepts. Historicity is to do with the *existence* of the event, historicality with the *essence* of the event. Hence the need for a distinction between historicity and historicality.

But to say that the death of Nelson is history of one kind and Jesus' resurrection-appearances history is history of another, different kind is to say that what is *different* between the two kinds of historical events is their respective *historicalities*. In other words, given that the events in question are historical, one would want to say that the reason one is a *sui generis* event and the other not is because of the *nature* (as opposed to the sheer *thatness*) of their historicity - *the way in which each is historical.*[39] *Sui generis* is a predicate of historicality, not of historicity.  Hence, though to say something is a *sui generis* historical event is not to imply a *sui generis*

---

[37] *Ibid*, 334.

[38] See Barth, *CD* III/1, 80-82; *CD* IV/1, 336.

[39] It may be said that the death of Nelson is also a *sui generis* historical event; that his death is a unique event because every individual's death (and, indeed, every individual's life for that matter) is unique in a philosophical sense. However, the fundamental rationale behind Barth's employment of this concept in the context of biblical narrative is that it is a 'once-and-for-all' event which "differs absolutely" from every other 'once'." Barth, *CD* III/2, 454. This is the sense in which such events are events whose only means of measurement is itself. Hence, though there is no conceptual difficulty in speaking of the historical event of the death of Nelson as a *sui generis* historical event, such an event is not an event whose only means of measurement is it itself. Given that the latter designates Barth's concept of a *sui generis* historical event in the context of biblical narrative, the historical event of Nelson's death - or any such like event - cannot be *sui generis* in Barth's  sense.

historicity, it is - if it is an event whose only means of measurement is itself - to imply a *sui generis* historicality.

## Concluding Remarks

To conclude: The question of the relation between the Bible and historical reality was of no less importance to Barth than it was to the Enlightenment. Barth concurred with the conclusions drawn by historical critics as regards the intrinsic connection between literal sense and historical truth. The resolution of Overbeck's dilemma had to provide an answer to the question of the relation between the Bible and historical reality  since it was precisely because of  Overbeck's failure to answer  this  question that he had lost faith in the Bible. Barth agreed that one was in the realm of historical truth *per se* and likewise affirmed the literal sense of the narrative passages that the Enlightenment had previously eliminated but had now reinstated.

The resolution of the metatheological dilemma demanded this from him: the literal sense of the Bible is crucial to the resolution of Overbeck's dilemma. (To be sure, not all parts of the Bible which are to be understood in a literal sense bear  on the relation between the Bible and historical reality. Many of the ethical imperatives (or commands) found in the Bible, for example, are to be understood literally but have no obvious bearing on this question. Nevertheless, the parts which do bear on this relation - the *narrative* parts - do have  be understood thus.)  The resolution of the metatheological dilemma also demanded that  the answer to the question must be based on  the final form of the *sensus literalis*. Clearly, Barth was not unduly perturbed by this. Indeed, that he affirms the significance of the final form of the text is clear from many passages in the  *Church Dogmatics*; for example in *CD* IV/2 Barth states that "... we allow the New Testament texts to say what they themselves say and do actually say."[40] This dictum he applies most emphatically to the Old Testament, to Genesis 1.1-2.4a and 2.4b-2.25, and to the New Testament, to the resurrection appearances stories. I take this story up in Chapters 7-9. What I want to do in the next chapter is to provide the philosophical context in which Barth's exegesis and understanding of these narratives is to be situated. The context is that of Kant and the Enlightenment. It is to this that I now turn.

---

[40] Barth, *CD* IV/2, 150.

# PART III

## The Enlightenment's Final Epistemological Reckoning With the Bible:

## Kant's 'Measure of the Divine' *Versus* Barth's Conception of the Reformers' *Analogia Fidei*

# Chapter 6
# The Strange New World Within the Bible Against Kant's 'Measure of God': *Sui Generis* Historicality and the Reformers' Conception of the *Analogia Fidei*

## 1. Introduction

According to Barth, the basic epistemological theme behind the *sui generis* historicality of the resurrection-appearances history, and of the creation history, repudiates the historical Enlightenment's immanent 'measure of the divine' - the Enlightenment's conception of the problem of God that Barth argues is exemplified in Kant's *Religion Within the Limits of Reason Alone*. What is this theme? Barth's understanding of the resurrection-appearances history and the creation history coincides with the Reformed tradition's understanding of the *analogia fidei* as a norm or criterion operative as a means of measurement. The concept of norm or criterion is central to Barth's conception of the *analogia fidei*; more so than the concept of analogical correspondence. The fundamental difference between Barth's and the Reformed tradition's 'measure of faith' (in the sense of a genitive of apposition) resides in the fact that the latter's measure was essentially an immanent measure against which to measure truth and meaning. Barth's was not. The reason it was not was because of the strange new world within the Bible. This world constituted a 'an object of measurement' whose only means of measurement was it itself. The strange new world within the Bible was constitutive of a conceptual foundationalism: central to Barth's *analogia fidei* - and his position on epistemology in the *Church Dogmatics* - arc the concepts of *Ursprung, Quelle* and *Norm*.

The epistemological rationale behind the strange new world within the Bible was precisely that there was no immanent measure of God's revelation in Jesus Christ. Hence, any such measure had to *originate* in revelation. Consequently, there was no sense in which one could measure truth or falsehood as regards revelation - set up an immanent conceptual measure - independently of revelation itself. As will be seen in Chapter 10, God's self-revelation is itself the (non-Kantian) transcendental condition of such a measurement. According to Barth, this position on epistemology is sufficient to repudiate the Kantian conception of the problem of knowledge of God.


## 2. Kant's 'Immanent (Conceptual) Measure of God'

The one epistemological problem with which Barth's position on epistemology in the *Church Dogmatics* is concerned above all else is the Enlightenment's conception of the problem of God as exemplified in Kant's *Religion Within the Limits of Reason Alone*. The first signs that Kant's conception of the problem of God, as stated in *Religion Within the Limits of Reason Alone* is Barth's fundamental problem, surface in his treatment of Kant in *Protestant Theology in the Nineteenth Century*. The book was published in its original German form in 1946. But, as Barth said in the foreword, it was not a new book. What one has in the book is a course Barth gave during the winter semester of 1932-33 and the summer semester of 1933 at Bonn on the 'background' and then the 'history' of Protestant theology from the time of Schleiermacher.[1] However, the chapter on Kant originated even earlier, in a set of lectures Barth gave at Munster in the winter of 1929-30.[2]

The crux of the matter for Barth is Kant's affirmation of the logical prevenience of reason over revelation. It is no exaggeration to say that, of the theologians who came after Kant, only Barth recognised that Kant had got to the heart of the issue. Refuting Kant's derivation of God from moral concepts was, Barth realised, not a sufficient condition of refuting the logical prevenience of reason over *God's* revelation. According to Kant, revelation is logically compatible with reason taking priority over revelation. This is because the measure of the object of faith originates in us, as an ideal of reason. Against this, Barth had to move the conclusion that setting up a measure of God's revelation was impossible precisely because it was *God's* revelation with which one was dealing. Barth's conclusion did not imply that revelation was opposed to reason, or that revelation was contrary to reason; rather, reason as it pertained to revelation originated in revelation. It is clear to Barth that Kant's conception of the problem is the fundamental rationale behind the Enlightenment's conception of the question of the relation between the Bible and reality. That is to say, when the Enlightenment seeks to evaluate the relation between the sagas of the Bible - the biblical witness - it sets up a pre-

---

[1] Barth, *PT*, 11.

[2] In the 1929-30 set of lectures 'Protestant Theology in the Nineteenth Century' Barth gave at Munster, he prefaced his discussion of Schleiermacher with studies of Lessing, Kant, Herder, Novalis and Hegel. Busch, *Barth*, 197. Rousseau was added later on, at Bonn in the winter of 1932-3.

existing means of comparison - as in Troeltsch's principle of analogy - against which to measure the historical truth-claim. Indeed, no less an authority than Kant said that it had no alternative but to do so. In one of the supplementary notes Kant added at the foot of the text in the second edition of *Religion Within the Limits of Reason Alone* published in 1794 he wrote the following:[3]

> ... in whatever manner a being has been known to him by another and described as God, yea, even if such a being had appeared to him (if this is possible), he must first of all compare [*vergleichen*] this representation with his ideal in order to judge whether he is entitled to regard it and to honor it as a divinity.[4]

For Barth, the essence of the case against Kant's position takes its point of departure from precisely this supplementary note:

> Kant expressly declared that while indeed it had a dubious sound it was 'by no means reprehensible to say that every man makes a God for himself, and indeed, according to moral concepts, ... one must make a God for himself, in order to worship in him the One who made him.' He has to be in a position to measure the God who is, perhaps, proclaimed to him, or who, perhaps, even reveals himself to him, against an ideal conception of God which he has set up for himself [*zu messen an einem von ihm selbst aufgerichteten Gottesideal*], in order (it is surely only thus that it is possible!) to recognise the former as God.[5]

He continues:

---

[3] Kant, *Religion Within the Limits of Reason Alone*, translated with an Introduction and Notes by Theodore M Greene and Hoyt H Hudson, (New York: Harper Torchbooks, 1960), 157. Kant published the first edition in 1793.

[4] Kant, *Religion Within the Limits of Reason Alone*, 157.

[5] Barth, *PT*, 282. The latter half of this quotation is undoubtedly a paraphrase of Kant's assertion here. For Kant, it follows that the concept takes logical priority over revelation: "Hence there can be no religion springing from revelation alone, i.e., without *first* positing that concept, in its purity, as a touchstone." *Ibid*, 157. And he adds: "Without this all reverence for God would be *idolatry*." *Ibid*, 157. As Emil Fackenheim puts it: "... if religious experience were cognitive, it could not be autonomously cognitive." Emil Fackenheim, "Immanuel Kant", N Smart et al, *Nineteenth Century Religious Thought in the West*, vol 1 (Cambridge: CUP, 1985), 32. He quotes a passage from Kant to substantiate this claim: "'If such an immediate intuition happened to me ... I would still have to use a concept of God as a standard by which to decide whether the phenomenon in question agreed with the necessary characteristics of a Deity.'" *Ibid*, 32.

He must therefore have already perceived God directly and in himself before any act of revelation has taken place. Kant finds himself in agreement with Augustine's teaching that the knowledge of God is a recollection of a notion of God which has already dwelt within our reason beforehand, because it has always been within us from the very beginning.[6]

As Emil Fackenheim points out, even if religious experience were cognitive, it could not be *known* to be so. But if it *could* be known to be so, it could only be known by reason since one would still require a concept of ideal reason against which to measure this immediate intuition.[7] According to Barth, Kant believed that the choice between a criterion of God derived from experience and a criterion of God derived from pure reason - practical reason - was not only mutually exclusive; it was also exhaustive. Since Kant affirms the latter conception, he rejects the former conception as false. Barth paraphrases Kant's position as follows, interposing Kant's own words when necessary:

We shall certainly not find any criterion [*Kriterium*] in the sphere of our experience [*Erfahrung*] by means of which a revelation which is thus encountered, as experience, might be distinguished from other experiences, and which might be perceived as revelation as distinct from these. 'For if God really spoke to man, he would never be able to know that it was in fact God speaking to him. It is an utterly impossible demand that man should grasp the Infinite One by means of his senses, distinguish him from sensory beings, and perceive him thereby.' But neither is it permissible to characterise such experience, difficult and impossible as it seems to us to exalt it to the level of empirical knowledge on account of its incomprehensibility, as divine revelation, since in order to do this we would already have to have some prior knowledge of what revelation is, and of what God is. 'It might at most be allowed, that man had some inner experience of a change which he was at a loss to account for other than by a miracle, an experience, therefore, of something supernatural. But an experience concerning which he cannot even be certain whether it was an experience because (being supernatural) it cannot be reduced to any rule partaking of the nature of our understanding, and thus substantiated, is an interpretation of certain sensations we do not know what to make of, and concerning which we do not know whether, as something belonging to knowledge, they have a real object, or whether they are mere fantasy. The wish to feel the direct influence of the Deity as such is a self-contradictory

---

[6] *Ibid*, 282.
[7] Fackenheim, "Kant", 31-32.

piece of presumption, since the idea of the Deity has its seat in reason alone.'[8]

Barth then re-introduces Kant's conclusion in the following manner:

If then there is no empirical criterion [*erfahrungsmäßiges Kriterium*], and therefore no empirical knowledge [*Erfahrungserkenntnis*] either, of true revelation of the true God, this criterion can only ever be perceived by its 'correspondence with that which reason declares to be proper for God', and it should now be made clear where in fact we must look - judging always from the standpoint of the religion of reason - for the true, original revelation ....[9]

Barth summarises Kant's religion of reason as follows:

Since it is reason itself which has alone been able to perform the critique of reason and has thus supplied those results of the critique of reason which have now become criteria, it has already been taken for granted by the very starting-point of this philosophy of religion, and by the conception of the problem it is supposed to involve, that it is the agent of reason, man, that is, who, just as he is the measure of all things, is here thought of and provided for as the measure of religion too: of its practical and theoretical possibilities, and also, and in particular, as God's measure [*Maß Gottes*].[10]

According to Barth, Kant's position that all measures of God had to originate in *a priori* human reason implies that man possesses a native and original capacity operative as an immanent norm or standard against which to compare the revelation which encounters us in Jesus Christ. The position Barth defines in the following passage, taken from *CD* II/1, is easily reconcilable with Kant's:

Any native and original capacity which is ascribed to our viewing and conceiving of God or to our human language must mean that on the strength of this capacity we have a second source and norm of the revelation within ourselves. We will always apply this to the revelation which encounters us in Jesus Christ. We will use it to *measure and judge* [*my italics*] [*messen und burteilen*] this revelation at least by way of

---

[8] *Ibid*, 282-283. The two passages Barth quotes are from Kant's *Disputation of the Faculties*, published in 1798.

[9] *Ibid*, 283. The passage quoted is from *Disputation of the Faculties*.

[10] *Ibid*, 304.

comparison [*Vergleich*]. And because it lies so much closer to us, there is no doubt that secretly, and very soon openly, we will subordinate the revelation to it, so that in what seems to be an irresistible development it finally turns out to be the real and unique source of what we regard as revelation.[11]

To be sure, where Kant argues that there is no logical alternative to that of using an immanent 'measure of the divine', Barth's talk of a "second source and norm of the revelation" that is "within ourselves" implies just the opposite. Since such a measure does not, and, in fact, cannot, constitute *Maß Gottes*, its very existence poses a temptation to which man will succumb all too easily. (And, indeed, that the great Kant argued for its necessity on logical grounds might well have been for Barth testimony that the urge to use an immanent measure of faith was universally overwhelming.) Further, though Kant's 'conception of the problem of the divine' was not universally acceptable in all its details to theologians of the nineteenth century, Barth argues that, at bottom, all adhered to the principle of an immanent measure. This is what Barth proceeds to explain in remainder of the chapter on Kant in *Protestant Theology*.

According to Barth, Kant's "conception of the problem ... consists in a great 'if ... then' statement: *if* the reality of religion is confined to that which, as religion within the limits of reason alone, is subjected to the self-critique of reason, *then* religion is that which is fitting to the ideally practical nature of pure reason, and that only."[12] Barth perceives that, historically, there have been three responses to Kant's position. First, there have been those who have accepted the Kantian premise just as it is as its stand-point, even though they may have executed the Kantian programme in a way different from the way in which Kant did. Barth cites Ritschl and Herrmann, among others, as having made this response.[13]

The second group did not accept the Kantian premise as it stood. It undertook to

broaden and enrich the conception of reason which forms the premise by pointing out that there is yet another capacity *a priori* which is part of the necessities of human reason, apart from the theoretical and practical ones: the capacity of feeling, as Schleiermacher put it, or that of 'presentiment', as de Wette preferred to express it .... It is this second possibility, that of correcting Kant's conception of the problem ... which became characteristic of the stamp of theology in the nineteenth century.[14]

---

[11] Barth, *CD* II/1,196.
[12] *Ibid*, 305.
[13] *Ibid*, 306.
[14] *Ibid*, 306.

In other words, it was not that the concept of an immanent measure *per se* was jettisoned; the issue was rather *what* constituted the immanent measure.

There was, however, a third possibility which broke rather more radically with Kant on the above matter. This third possibility Barth describes as not having been taken "seriously into account throughout the whole of the nineteenth century.[15] It questioned "not only the application of the Kantian conception of the problem, but the conception itself, and therefore the autocracy and its competence to judge human reason in relation to the religious problem."[16] It clear that Barth is speaking of his own theology here. His theology is the third possibility.[17] He characterises the third possibility as follows:

It might be possible to object that with the problem conceived as 'religion within the limits of reason alone' only the one side of the problem, namely religion as human function, is seen, and not the other side, the significant point to which this function is related and whence it springs, the dealings, namely, of a God who is not identical with the quintessence of human reason, with the 'God in ourselves' ....[18]

In other words, what if the measure of God were "not identical" with the concept derived from "the quintessence of human reason, with the 'God in ourselves'"? What then? The fundamental distinction between the first two responses and Barth's response lies in this point, and this point alone. Whether in accord with Kant's original definition or an augmented definition of reason, the first two responses affirm the thesis that human immanent reason must constitute the measure or standard against which God is measured. Both responses affirm an immanent measure of the

---

[15] *Ibid*, 306.

[16] *Ibid*, 306-307.

[17] The first two possibilities Barth cites are two of the four possibilities Claude Welch mentions in his account of nineteenth-century theology in the wake of Kant. But one of Welch's four possibilities is, in fact, Barth's theology. Welch sees in Barth's theology an expression of "the turn to the role of the subject, a turn which had its epistemological expression in Kant's analysis in the *Critique of Pure Reason*." Claude Welch, *Protestant Thought*, vol i, 47-48. But Barth did not accept the Kantian premise. *Contra* Welch, Barth's denial of reason's right to establish the point of departure of theology did not follow from an acceptance of reason's criticism of itself. *Ibid*, 47-48. Barth's denial issues from revelation's right to establish *what is it* reason is but in a way that does not contradict the limits of reason.

[18] *Ibid*, 307.

divine. To be sure, Barth concurred with Schleiermacher that Kant was right to reject a (positivistic) empirical criterion. And he agreed with Schleiermacher that one had to jettison Kant's moral standard or measure. But this was not because he thought the latter ought to be replaced with another human standard, another *a priori* standard. It was because he thought that one had to jettison *every* immanent measure of God. Indeed, Barth almost certainly thought that Schleiermacher's 'capacity of feeling' remained subject to the quintessentially Kantian criticism that concept was logically prevenient to 'capacity of feeling'. According to Barth, one had to deal with the logical status *per se* of Kant's position on the logical prevenience of concept over revelation. In this respect, Barth gleaned from Kant himself how this might be done. Kant had pondered the possibility of a theology which would be *different* from the philosophical theology which he himself was propounding. Indeed, according to Barth, Kant explicitly called this other theology, which limits philosophical theology, '*biblical* theology'. What constituted the material possibility of such a biblical theology? Barth quotes part of a letter written by Kant in 1793, in which Kant mentions the possibility of a conclusion other than the one he reaches in *Religion Within the Limits of Reason Alone*. According to Barth, in this letter Kant acknowledges that

> reason, after it has established in religion those things which it is fitted to establish as such, 'must wait the arrival of everything else, which must be added beyond its capacity, *without reason being permitted to know in what it consists* [my italics], from the supernatural helping hand of heaven [*alles Übrige, was über ihr Vermögen noch hinzukommen muß, ohne daß sie wissen darf, worin es bestehe, von dem übernatüralichen Beistand des Himmels erwarten muß*].'[19]

What is it that constitutes the material possibility of a biblical theology? The chapter on Kant in *Protestant Theology* ends with one of Barth's more famous sentences: '*The biblical theologian proves that God exists by means of the fact that he has spoken in the Bible.*'[20] It is plausible to suggest that what Barth had in mind was the idea that the Bible refers to an event which adds beyond reason's capacity - precisely without reason being permitted to know in what it consists. The Bible speaks of the revelation of a God who is not identical with the quintessence of human reason, not identical with the 'God in ourselves'. Whether Kant really thought such a state of affairs was a logical possibility - 'without reason being permitted to know in what it consists' - is subject to debate. But Barth thought it was possible, and indeed actual. He did so with regard to *God's* self-revelation: '*without*

---

[19] *Ibid*, 309.
[20] *Ibid*, 314.

*reason being permitted to know in what revelation consists' is a central theme of Barth's position on epistemology.*

Barth took from Kant the thought: what if the measure of God were given by 'the helping-hand of heaven' and not by immanent reason? In the *Church Dogmatics* this question became: what if the Bible told us that the 'measure of God' necessarily ultimately originated in *God's* revelation? Is this what the Bible told us? Barth's answer was, yes. He discovered this answer in the strange new world within the Bible, which is to say, in the *sui generis* historicality of God's self-revelation in the creation history and in the resurrection-appearances history.

At about the same time Barth was to discover in Anselm's *Proslogion* the claim that God had revealed Himself as 'that than which a greater cannot be conceived.' It is crucial to Barth's interpretation of Anselm that 'that than which a greater cannot be conceived' be construed as a noetic conception and not an ontic conception. 'That than which a greater cannot be conceived' does not describe the ontic nature of God but functions as a noetic designator. When Barth asserts "we are dealing with a concept of strict noetic content which Anselm describes here as a concept of God",[21] he means that it expresses nothing about - and therefore tells us nothing about - the nature of God. 'That than which a greater cannot be conceived' in itself tells us nothing about any of God's real properties. 'That than which a greater cannot be conceived':

> ... does not say that God is, or what he is, but rather, in the form of a prohibition that man can understand, who he is. It is *une définition purement conceptuelle*. It contains nothing in the way of statements about the existence or about the nature of the object described.[22]

*Yet it designates God and, in particular, God's self-revelation.* The importance of Anselm's noetic conception of God's self-revelation - of God revealing Himself as 'That than which a greater cannot be conceived' - is that it *occurs* 'without reason being permitted to know in what revelation consists', in particular, in what God's self-revelation consists. The significance of Anselm for Barth is that he proved such an event is an entirely coherent conception, involving no contradiction. In particular, there is no contradiction is saying, on the one hand, that God's self-revelation is an event in historical time, and, on the other, saying that it takes place 'without reason knowing in what it consists.' Indeed, it is in this sense that, as an ontic event designated by a noetic conception, the event is 'added' on

---

[21] Barth, *FQI*, 75.

[22] *Ibid*, 75. The logical consequence of this claim is dealt with in greater detail in Chapter 9.

to the world, as it were, beyond reason's capacity. Does Barth mean a miracle? No. Barth is not *juxtaposing miracle to Troeltsch's principle*. Supernaturalist interpreters of Barth, note well! 'That than which a greater cannot be conceived' - and by extension, 'that which nothing analogous can be conceived' - says nothing at all about miracle. It is not inconsistent with the concept but neither does it entail it. Or, in other words: to say that an event is designated by 'that than which a greater cannot be conceived' does not commit one to the view that the event is a miracle.

Something else of great import follows from the event being 'that which nothing analogous can be conceived': there is no conceptual measure - neither of theoretical reason nor of practical reason - against which to measure the event for reality prior to, or independently of, the event itself. It is an *event prior to which and side by side with which* there are no other events "of the same basic type with which it can be compared and integrated."[23] Within the context of the concept of *sui generis* historicality as Barth understands it in the *Church Dogmatics*, 'that than which a greater cannot be conceived" can be recast as 'that which nothing analogous can be conceived.' A *sui generis* historical event is precisely an event which corresponds to the definition of 'that which nothing analogous can be conceived.' An event 'which nothing analogous can be conceived' entails that no one can possess a measure of this event prior to, independently of, the event itself.

One can put this point another way: God's self-revelation to Anselm as 'that than which a greater cannot be conceived' can itself be conceived as a historical event, in particular, a *sui generis* historical event.[24] Hence it - just like 'that which nothing analogous can be conceived' - is *entirely consistent with Troeltsch's principle of analogy* (a principle which is subsumed under Kant's more general immanent measure). It does not contradict it. Therefore, *Barth did not have to repudiate Troeltsch's principle at this point.* This is crucial to note for those who think Barth essentially critical of Enlightenment epistemology. Barth did not have to reject Enlightenment epistemology, and in particular, historical epistemology in the form of Troeltsch in order to make his case. This is why Barth could well say to Troeltsch with characteristic irony, "Quite so, I too might question any

---

[23] This quotation is part of a larger very important passage found in *CD* III/1, 78. The full passage will be given in Chapter 7 and its logical consequences will be examined in detail in Chapter 8.

[24] That Barth understands God's self-revelation to Anselm as 'that than which a greater cannot be conceived' as an *objective event* seems to me fatally to undermine the thesis of Barth as idealist. He is a thorough-going theological realist. That he would understand it as a *historical* event - as he does the creation history and the resurrection-appearances history - seems to me incontrovertible proof that Barth's theological realism coincides with historical realism.

historical event which was not a *sui generis* one and which did not measure up to your principle of analogy!"[25]

One can therefore put Barth's reaction to Kant by means of another question: What if the means of measurement of God's self-revelation were only given in, or by, the very object of measurement that Kant insisted must be measured by a pre-existing means of measurement? For an event to be measured at all - and in this sense be an object of measurement - there must be a means or unit of measurement of some kind. Kant assumed that revelation had necessarily to be measured by a pre-existing means of measurement ('it is thus only that it is possible!'). Barth argued that the witness of the Bible to God as *God* (where God reveals Himself as *God*) - the resurrection-appearances history and the creation history - witnesses to an event or events each whose only means of measurement is it itself. To say that God's self-revelation is an event whose only measure is it itself is to say that God's self-revelation is an event whose only means of measurement is it itself. If one designates the event of God's self-revelation as the object of measurement then it follows that the only means of measurement of the object of measurement is the object of measurement itself. In other words, the means of measurement cannot be had independently of the object of measurement itself. This is the fundamental feature of *sui generis* historicality. But this feature is also central to Barth's conception of the *analogia fidei*; God's self-revelation is a *sui generis* historical event, an event therefore whose only means of measurement is it itself. Therefore Barth's conception of the *analogia fidei* is central to his understanding of *sui generis* historicality. Where does one find antecedents for Barth's conception of the *analogia fidei*?

A theological precedent to Barth's conception of the *analogia fidei* can be found in the Reformed tradition's conception of the *analogia fidei* (Barth's affinity with the Reformed tradition is not only visible in his adherence to the significance of literal sense and final form of the text). The

---

[25] One could say of Troeltsch with his principle of analogy that he had not conceived of such an event. He might well have said that such historical events could not exist. But then he would have had to have argued for the impossibility, indeed incoherence, of such a conception. What Anselm had shown according to Barth was that such a conception *was* coherent. One might have doubted that God had revealed Himself to Anselm as "That than which a greater cannot be conceived" but this was a quite different logical matter from assuming that the formula itself was contradictory. And the whole history of critical thought inclusive of the Enlightenment and Kant (especially Kant) had not doubted the validity of Anselm's argument on the grounds that it thought 'that than which a greater cannot be conceived' logically incoherent. Barth knew that the Enlightenment and Kant in particular had acknowledged the premise of Anselm's argument if not his conclusions. And it is coherence only that Barth has to assume.

rationale behind Barth's conception of the *analogia fidei* implies the conceptual pairing of 'means of measurement' and 'object of measurement'. Barth's conception stands in the closest relation to the Reformed tradition's conception of the *analogia fidei*. For, as we will see in the following section, the Reformed tradition understood the *analogia fidei* as means of measurement, a 'measure of faith' in the sense of a genitive of apposition.

### 3. Barth and the Reformed Tradition: The *Analogia Fidei* Conceived as a Norm or 'Measure of Faith'

According to Barth, Jesus Christ, and, in particular, *Jesus Christ's* self-revelation (*God's* self-revelation), is the norm against which talk about God is measured:

> Talk about God has true content when it conforms to the being of the Church, i.e., when it conforms to Jesus Christ [*wenn sie Jesus Christ gemäß*] ... *eite prophetitian, kata ten analogian tes pisteos* (Rom. 12.6). It is in terms of such conformity [*Gemäßheit*] that dogmatics investigates Christian utterance. Hence it does not have to begin by finding or inventing the standard by which it measures [*das Maß, an dem sie mißt*]. It sees and recognises that this is given with the Church. It is given in its own peculiar [*eigenen*] way, as Jesus Christ is given, as God in His revelation gives Himself in faith. But it is given. It is complete in itself. It stands by its claim without discussion. It has the certainty which a true standard or criterion [*ein Kriterium, ein Maß*] must have to be the means of serious measurement [*an dem erstlich gemessen*].[26]

This passage is a very important one since it intimates at the outset of the *Church Dogmatics* a fundamental sense in which Barth is to be assimilated to the Reformed tradition. It is submitted that it sets forth the fundamental conceptual parameters within which Barth's conception of the 'analogy of faith' - and his position on epistemology - operates. 'Analogy of faith' here is interpreted as a standard of measurement, a "means of measurement" - a 'measure of faith'. It is in this sense that Jesus Christ, and in particular, his self-revelation, is the *analogia fidei*.[27] His self-revelation is the 'measure of faith'. That it is a measure of faith in its "own peculiar way" coincides with the fact that the measure is the strange new world within the Bible.

The essential properties of Barth's position on epistemology in the *Church Dogmatics* coincide with the essential properties of the Reformed

---

[26] Barth, *CD* I/1, 12.

[27] *Ibid*, 12. See also Barth, *CD* II/1, 320.

hermeneutical doctrine derived from Paul's phrase *analogian tes pisteos* in Romans 12.6. The Reformed conception is one of a 'measure of faith' construed as a norm of criterion of faith against which meaning and truth are *measured*. This conception implies in turn the distinction between, on the one hand, *the means of measurement*, and, on the other, *the object of measurement*. This is a crucial distinction for Barth's exegesis of the resurrection appearances stories, as will be seen.

What is the Reformers' conception of the *analogia fidei*? The Vulgate translation of the *koine* Greek rendered *analogian tes pisteos* as *ratio fidei*, paralleling its translation of *metron pisteos* as *regula fidei* at 12.3. According to Graham Ward, in the Vulgate the concept of *analogian tes pisteos* connotes *regula fidei*, a theological norm (*quae creditur*) in the form of a rational proposition. *Ratio fidei* is imbued with the sense of 'account' or 'computation'.[28] The phrase 'measure of faith' is, in fact, the standard English rendition of Paul's phrase *metron pisteos* in Romans 12.3. As C E B Cranfield notes, "there has been very widespread agreement" that *metron* here means *measured quantity*.[29] But he himself concludes that *metron* is to be translated as *a means of measurement*.[30] According to Cranfield, *means of measurement* can mean: "(a) literally, a *measuring-rod or -line, vessel for measuring capacity* ...; (b) metaphorically, *a standard, norm* ...."[31] Though it is more probable that Paul *did* mean 'measured quantity', Cranfield's interpretation of *metron pisteos* as *means of measurement* provides an accurate representation of the Reformers' conception of the 'analogy of faith'. As will become evident, the Reformers' conception measures meaning and truth in Cranfield's second sense, the metaphorical sense.

To be sure, the Reformers, and Calvin in particular, did not interpret 12.6 in terms of their interpretation of 12.3. Calvin interprets *metron pisteos* as *a measured quantity of faith*.[32] For Calvin, the measured quantity of faith

---

[28] Graham Ward, *Barth, Derrida and the Language of Theology* (Cambridge: Cambridge University Press, 1995), 97.

[29] C. E. B. Cranfield, "*Metron Pisteos* in Romans XII.3", *Journal of New Testament Studies* 8, 345-351. See also Cranfield, *The Epistle to the Romans*, vol ii, (Edinburgh: T and T Clark Ltd, 1979), 613-616.

[30] Cranfield, "*Metron Pisteos* in Romans XII.3", 351.

[31] *Ibid.*, 346.

[32] The passages in question are: "For by the grace of God given to me I bid every one among you not to think of himself more highly than he ought to think, but to think with sober judgement, each according to the measure of faith [*metron pisteos*] God has assigned him" (12.3); "Having gifts that differ according to the grace given to us, let us use them: if prophecy then in proportion to our faith [*analogian tes pisteos*]", (12.6). Both passages are taken from the RSV.

each man receives constitutes the limits within which he is to keep his own opinions and beliefs.[33] (The question whether the measured quantity of faith could itself be construed as a standard or criterion is irrelevant.)[34] Yet though the Reformers, and Calvin in particular, did not interpret 12.6 in terms of their interpretation of 12.3., they interpreted 'analogy of faith' not essentially in terms of 'analogy' or 'simile';[35] they interpreted it essentially in terms of 'measure of faith' construed as a criterion, norm or means of measurement of meaning. In the address to King Francis I of France prefacing the 1536 *Institutes*, Calvin wrote:

> When Paul wished all prophecy to be to accord with the analogy of faith (*ad fidei analogiam, Rom 12.6*) he set forth a very clear rule to test all interpretation of the Scripture. Now, if our interpretation be measured by this rule of faith (*ad hac fidei regulam*), victory is in our hands.[36]

In his *Commentary on Romans* Calvin interpreted 12.6 in a similar way. Calvin takes *prophetian* to mean "the peculiar gift of revelation by which a man performs the office of interpreter with skill and dexterity in expounding the will of God. In the Christian Church, therefore, prophecy at the present day is simply the right understanding of Scripture and the particular gift of expounding it, since all the ancient prophecies and all the oracles of God have been concluded in Christ and His Gospel."[37] Indeed, Paul is to be understood as "admonishing those who prophesy in the Church to conform their prophecies to the rule of faith, lest at any point they deviate from the straight line. By the word *faith* he means the first principles of religion, and any doctrine that has been found not to

---

[33] J Calvin, *The Epistle of Paul the Apostle to the Romans and to the Thessalonians*, trans. Ross MacKenzie, eds. David W. Torrance and Thomas F. Torrance (Edinburgh: Oliver and Boyd, 1961), 266-67.

[34] It was not, of course, only the Reformers who interpreted *metron pisteos* in this way. Luther interprets the phrase to mean "the measure of the gifts of faith, that is, in faith there are many gifts, and though believers live in the same faith, yet they have a different measure of the gifts of faith." Martin Luther, *Lectures on Romans*, Vol. 45, ed. Hilton C. Oswald (Saint Louis: Concordia Publishing House, 1972), 444. Luther goes on to use the following analogy to make his point: "Just as if you were to say: the prince has divided to each citizen a measure of the city or a measure of the household, that is, the things which are in the household or the city." Ibid., 444. Clearly, he too understands the phrase *metron pisteos* in the genitive partitive sense.

[35] Unlike Calvin, Luther's emphasis is on likeness or analogy in his exegesis of Rom 12.6. See Luther, *Romans*, 444.

[36] Calvin, *Institutes of the Christian Religion*, vol 1, ed. John T. McNeill, trans. Ford Lewis Battle (Philadelphia: Westminster Press, 1961), 12-13.

[37] Calvin, *Romans*, 269.

correspond with these is condemned as false."[38] In other words, intrinsic to Calvin's interpretation of *analogian tes pisteos* is the concept of a standard or criterion of faith - a measure of faith. Calvin does not specify the identity of these first principles of religion (one of them surely is that expressed in Romans 8.32: God not sparing His own Son but giving Him up for us all).[39] But he is clear about one of properties of these principles: they constitute a norm or criterion *against which all doctrines and interpretations are measured* for truth or falsehood.

Insofar as the first principles of religion coincided with those passages of the Bible whose meaning was manifest or clear, these first principles constituted the 'measure of faith' against which the meaning of obscure or ambiguous passages was measured. William Tyndale's advice from the epilogue to the Worms New Testament in English (1526) exemplifies the way in which the Reformers understood the principle of *analogia fidei* in practice: "Marke the playne and manyfest places of the scriptures, and in doubtfull places, see thou adde no interpretation contrary to them; but (as Paul saith) let all be conformable and agreynge to the faythe."[40] Heinrich Heppe's *Reformed Dogmatics* - a book which greatly influenced Barth - provides three examples of the Reformed conception of the *analogia fidei*. Wilhelm Bucanus understood the *analogia fidei* as "namely, the constant and unchanging sense of Scripture expounded in the opening passages of Scripture and agreeing with the Apostles' Creed, the Decalogue and the Lord's Prayer."[41] Charmier asserts: "The analogy of faith is the argument from general dogmas which contain the norm of all that is taught in the Church."[42] The Second Helvetian Confession describes it as "the comparison of the more obscure with the more manifest."[43]

If one accepts this sample of statements as representative of the Reformed tradition's position on the *analogia fidei*, one is led to conclude that the Reformed tradition can be defined according to this conception of

---

[38] *Ibid.*, 269.

[39] See Calvin, *Institutes*, 13.

[40] Quoted in Rivkah Zim, "The Reformation: the Trial of God's Word", in Stephen Prickett (ed.), *Reading the Text. Biblical Criticism and Literary Theory* (Oxford: Basil Blackwell, 1991), 121-122.

[41] Quoted in Heinrich Heppe, *Reformed Dogmatics*, ed. Ernst Bizer, trans. G. T. Thompson (London: Allen and Unwin, 1950), 35. Again, the Anglican Church argued "that no sense bee received contrary to the ten commandments, Lords prayer, and the Articles of our beliefe." Zim, "The Reformation: the Trial of God's Word",74. As Zim puts it, these three elements "provided the basic 'analogie of faith' in plain, straightforward statements." *Ibid.*, 74.

[42] Quoted in Heppe, *Reformed Dogmatics*, 35.

[43] *Ibid.*, 39.

the *analogia fidei*. Common to all of them is the concept of 'measure of faith' construed as a norm of criterion of faith against which meaning and truth are *measured*. This conception implies in turn the distinction between, on the one hand, the means of measurement, and, on the other, the object of measurement. The former determines the nature - the dimensions, as it were, of the latter. In Calvin, for example, the first principles of religion constitute the means of measurement; doctrine, and interpretations of Scripture, define the object of measurement. The latter is measured against the former and its nature, or dimensions, or identity, established. In Tyndale, the meaning of obscure or ambiguous passages is measured against the manifestly clear passages of Scripture. The latter constitute the means of measurement, and the former, the object of measurement. It is clear that both these passages accord with Cranfield's metaphorical definition of *metron*, rather than his literal definition. Though the concept of measurement is either explicit, as in Calvin, or strongly implicit, as in the others, it is not used in Cranfield's literal sense.

From the vantage-point of the *Church Dogmatics*, Barth's rejection in *Protestant Theology* of Kant's position that all measures of God had to originate in *a priori* human reason - a native or original capacity - is unequivocal confirmation that the concept of 'measure of faith' will be invoked in an epistemological context. But the epistemological context retains the concept's identity as a criterion against which interpretation is measured. In other words, central to Barth's account and critique of the Kantian 'conception of the problem' is the concept of measure or comparison, derivable from the Reformers' hermeneutical use of the concept of *analogia fidei*.

### Concluding Remarks

In the 1917 lecture "The Strange New World Within the Bible" Barth had asked the question: What is there in the Bible? His answer, as will be recalled from Chapter 4, essentially consisted of a decidedly rhetorical question in which he rejected all proposals that implied the possibility of 'measuring God with our own measures':

> Even in these answers, earnest and pious as they may be, have we not measured God with our own measure, conceived of God with our own conceptions, wished ourselves a God according to our own wishes?[44]

The strange new world within the Bible coincides with an event whose only means of measurement is it itself. Hence, insofar as the event of God's

---

[44] Barth, "The Strange New World Within the Bible", 47

self-revelation is treated as an object of measurement, it can of necessity only be measured in terms of itself. This, in essence, is Barth's biblical answer to Kant. It is also then his answer to those who seek to evaluate the relation between the Bible and historical reality at those points where the Bible claims witness: the creation history and the resurrection-appearances history. In his book *The New Testament as Canon* Brevard Childs criticized the 'New Yale Theology', and George Lindbeck's *The Nature of Doctrine* in particular, for, among other things, gravely underestimating, if not eliminating, the relationship between the Bible and reality. While acknowledging that the emphasis "on the 'intratextuality' of meaning provided a much needed service in checking the abuses of a crude theory of historical referentiality", he wrote that

> the concept [of intratextuality] is not without serious problems when used as a positive formulation of the Bible's relation to the external world. Above all, the New Testament bears witness to realities outside itself. The prophets and apostles spoke of things which they saw and events which they experienced as testimonies to what God was doing in the world. It is far too limiting to restrict the function of the Bible to that of rendering an agent or an identity. ... To recognise that the Bible offers a faith-construal is not to deny that it bears witness to realities outside the text. Christians have always understood that we are saved, not by the biblical text, but by the life, death, and resurrection of Jesus Christ who entered into the world of space and time.[45]

---

[45] Childs, *The New Testament as Canon: an Introduction*, 545. It is true, as Stephen Fowl has pointed out, that Lindbeck nowhere in *The Nature of Doctrine* denies the existence of 'extra-textual reality.' Stephen Fowl, *Engaging Scripture* (Oxford: Blackwell, 1998), 24. But I believe Childs' concern is legitimate if his fundamental criticism is that witness to historical reality has become secondary rather than primary. As an account of Barth's biblical project I think Lindbeck's understanding of Barth inadequate. In a recent essay Lindbeck does not disagree with the view that "it is better to describe Barth's practice (though not his theory) as that of interpreting Scripture for the symbolic world or worlds that it projects rather than for its witness." Lindbeck, "Postcritical Canonical Interpretation: Three Modes of Retrieval", C Seitz and K Greene-McCreight (ed), *Theological Exegesis: Essays in Honour of Brevard Childs* (Grand Rapids: Eerdmans, 1998), 33. He then asserts: "Everything depends, not on whether interpreters construe their task as that of describing a symbolic world from the inside, but on what they find once they have entered, and on whether that world is the most comprehensive of outlooks, *which alone has within it the criteria for determining what is ultimately right or wrong, real or unreal [my italics].*" *Ibid*, 35. If this is an interpretation of Barth as regards the issue of "real or unreal", then it seems to commit him to a view that I do not think he held, namely that the epistemic and ontological criteria and, in particular, the concept of truth operative in the biblical world is different from, even

On the one hand, then, the 'New Yale School' was to be praised for checking the abuses of a crude theory of historical referentiality; but, on the other, 'intratextuality' was to be criticized insofar as it was used as a positive answer to the question of the Bible's relation to the external world. It is clear that what Childs desires is an account of the Bible's "historical referentiality - an account of the relation between the Bible and historical reality - which does not commit one to "a crude theory of historical referentiality." I am going to argue in what follows that Barth gives the most logically coherent and most cogent account of this relation, precisely an account of the relation between the Bible and reality which does not commit one to "a crude theory of historical referentiality". What Barth gives us is an explanation of how the Bible could 'bear witness to external realities outside itself' *and those external realities not be susceptible in principle to Kant's immanent measure of God or Troeltsch's principles of historical evaluation.*

---

incommensurate with, the concept of truth with which we are all acquainted - even those who have never entered the biblical world. I do not think this was Calvin's view and I don't think it was Barth's view. Calvin believed as a matter of basic belief that the world in which he breathed, ate and slept was the very same world which God had created, the very same world in which Jesus Christ had been crucified dead and buried and had risen again on the third day. *Mutatis mutandis*, Barth thought the same. The point is that their concept of truth, what it means to say something is true - inclusive of what it means to say something is historically true - is in essence no different from that held by someone who rejects their truth-claims. As I say in Chapter 12, Lindbeck's view closely resembles that of D Z Phillips' interpretation of the later Wittgenstein. This interpretation, as will be seen in the same chapter, is flawed in much the same way.

# PART IV

## Barth Against the Enlightenment's Final Reckoning:

## The Creation History, the Resurrection-Appearances History, and the Pre-Easter Gospel Narrative

# Chapter 7
# The *Sui Generis* Historicality of the Creation History:
# God Reveals Himself as Creator

## 1. Introduction

For Barth to refer to the creation narratives in Genesis 1.1-2.4a and 2.4b-2.25 as creation *history* was not without precedent: Calvin wrote of the "history of the creation of the world" in his commentary on Genesis. What seemed more problematic precisely because it *was* without precedent was the inference that this meant that the narratives were *historical truth-claiming* narratives and, as such, to be treated in exactly the same way that the Enlightenment would deal with any other biblical truth-claim and its relation to historical reality. The Enlightenment was to reinstate literal sense, the final form of the text, and historical truth-claiming. And, crucially, with respect to the latter it was to go about its duty as it would in evaluating any another biblical truth-claim: measure its correspondence to historical reality. However, historically, the methodological tools for this particular task were those defined by Troeltsch, most especially the principle of analogy. Was Barth really asking the Enlightenment to employ Troeltsch in the realm of creation, in the domain of the beginning of the world as it were? Was this really feasible? It was one thing to understand the creation narratives as a creation history, but it was quite another to understand them as historical truth-claiming narratives if this meant, as Barth appeared to mean, that the application of Troeltsch's historical methodology was to be permitted in principle. Did this not from the outset demonstrate the folly of understanding the creation narratives in this manner? To add that in Kant Troeltsch had an ally in philosophy, a subject historically and apparently conceptually more suited to the question of Creator and creation only appeared to harden the apparent incongruity. For the presence of Kant was not the Kant of the famous critique of the classical proofs of the existence of God, and in particular of those proofs that attempted to move the existence of God the creator on the basis of the content or form (structure) of the world. No. The Kant who was cited by Barth as relevant to God the creator was the Kant of *Religion Within the Limits of Reason Alone*, the Kant who affirmed the necessity of an immanent 'measure of the divine.' This particular Kant implicitly endorsed the fundamental rationale behind the application of Troeltsch's methodology, namely a pre-existent means of measurement.

Yet it can be argued that, ultimately, there was a certain sublime method and rationale to Barth's apparent folly of treating the creation narratives as historical truth-claiming narratives, and asking of the Enlightenment that it treat them as it would any other. It can be argued that Barth was not wrong to insist on the final relevance of Kant and Troeltsch. His endorsement of Kant's critique of the classical proofs of the existence of God in *The Critique of Pure Reason* somewhat ironically was finally based on his rejection of Kant's pre-existent 'measure of God' *in Religion Within the Limits of Reason Alone.*[1] That is to say, in the realm of the doctrine of creation it could finally be traced back his understanding of the creation history.

Barth's affirmation of the creation narratives as historical truth-claiming narratives allows us better to understand his famous "Nein!" to natural theology. It is not that Barth disagreed with Calvin's description of the world as *theatrum gloriae Dei*, the theatre of His glory. What he did disagree with was Calvin's claim that God "reveals and daily discloses himself in the whole workmanship of the universe."[2] The fundamental rationale behind Barth's rejection of natural theology as he understood it is that God emphatically does not reveal Himself in creation (the creation). He reveals Himself as the reconciler in the creation (in the resurrection-appearances history, as we shall see in subsequent chapters) but not as creator in the creation. To repeat: God reveals Himself as Creator of this creation. He does not reveal Himself as Creator in creation. Rather, He reveals Himself as Reconciler in creation. This is an ineradicable difference between Calvin and Barth.

To be sure, late in life Barth made the claim that "nature does objectively offer a proof of God, though the human being overlooks or misunderstands it."[3] There is no doubt that in this assertion Barth concurs

---

[1] Barth's endorsement of Kant's rejection of the classical modes of proving God's existence - the cosmological, the teleological, the ontological - can be found in volume 1 of *The Göttingen Dogmatics*. Barth, *The Göttingen Dogmatics: Instruction in the Christian Religion*, ed. Hannelote Reiffen, trans. G W Bromiley (Grand Rapids: Eerdmans, 1991), 350. It was an ironic endorsement because what Barth was really saying was 'Quite so! There can be no proof of God based upon human concepts. After all: God is *God*!'

[2] Calvin, *Institutes of the Christian Religion*, vol I, 52.

[3] Barth, *A Late Friendship: The Letters of Karl Barth and Carl Zuckmayer*, trans. G W Bromiley and T F Torrance, (Grand Rapids: Eerdmans, 1982), 42. As will be seen, I

with Aquinas' view that the *telos* of creation is God in the sense that for Barth the creation is the "external basis of the covenant between God and man", the covenant the "internal basis of the creation."[4] In this sense Barth and Aquinas are agreed. But this does not mean that Barth's understanding of nature is to be assimilated to Aquinas' understanding of his 'Five Ways'- even if the latter construed them as taking place within a 'faith seeking understanding' paradigm rather than a 'faith seeking justification' paradigm. In a seminal essay on the history of ideas of the rationality of religious belief entitled "The Migration of the Theistic Arguments: From Natural Theology to Evidentialist Apologetics", one of Nicholas Wolterstorff's objectives is to show that the evidential apologetics of the Enlightenment was "fundamentally different" from the mediaeval and, indeed, early modern project of natural theology. In this respect the emergence of evidential apologetics during the seventeenth and eighteenth century testified to a fundamental shift in epistemic stance from a 'faith seeking understanding' paradigm to what may be termed a 'faith requiring justification' one. The 'faith seeking understanding' paradigm constituted the fundamental rationale behind the respective theological epistemologies of Augustine, Anselm, and Aquinas. But it was no less central to Calvin's basic epistemic stance. As Wolterstorff argues, on the matter of epistemic stance, Calvin is closer to Aquinas than to Locke. Pre-Enlightenment theologians such as Aquinas and Calvin did not attach foundationalist conditions to theistic beliefs. Both Aquinas and Calvin are "deeply convinced of the success of natural theology as polemic (and apologetic)." However, "even if the polemic of belief with unbelief should fail because the arguments all prove to lack the force of demonstration, the failure would imply nothing whatsoever as to the acceptability of the believer's faith."[5] Wolterstorff contrasts this epistemic stance with that of an Enlightenment thinker such as Locke:  for Locke "the failure of evidentialist apologetics implies that the believer must surrender his faith."[6] In other words, the fundamental difference between natural theology and evidentialist apologetics resides in the fact that, whereas the former occurs in the context where theistic belief is construed as a basic belief - one not

---

take Barth's assertion to mean that this is because God *reveals* Himself as having created it! In this sense nature offers "objective proof."

[4] These assertions, as is well known, are fundamental themes in Barth's interpretation of, respectively, the first and second creation narratives, Genesis 1.1-2.4a and Genesis 2.4b-25.

[5] Wolterstorff, "The Migration of the Theistic Arguments: From Natural Theology to Evidentialist Apologetics", 80.

[6] *Ibid*, 80.

based on any other belief - the latter occurs in a context where theistic belief is construed as a non-basic belief.[7]

The crucial crux of comparison between Aquinas and Barth is that, for the latter, the proof that resides in nature cannot ever be a matter of transmuting what is believed into what is known. (For Aquinas it is.) Hence the Reformed-epistemological conclusion that one does not have to give up what is believed even if the "arguments all prove to lack the force of demonstration" (for the believer and the unbeliever) is not, for Barth, a sufficient condition for endorsing the existence of natural theology in Aquinas' sense. To put it another way: if the mediaeval epistemological project is one of the transmutation of faith into knowledge by means of nature then the fact that it is done in a 'faith seeking understanding' context is not, for Barth, a sufficient reason for endorsing the existence of natural theology as Aquinas understood it.

The charge that Barth erroneously excluded the mediaeval project of natural theology as found in such as Thomas Aquinas when he ought only to have ruled out evidential apologetic as practised by such as the eighteenth-century deists - this charge is mistaken.[8] Insofar as one can speak of the 'transmutation of faith into knowledge' in the context of speaking of

---

[7] Natural theology occurs in the context where theistic belief is construed as a basic belief, a basic belief being one that is believed not on the basis of any other belief, that is, as a foundational belief itself. Therefore there is no need to justify the belief in terms of some further belief(s). In contrast, evidentialist apologetics occurs in a context where theistic belief is construed as a non-basic belief, a non-basic belief being a belief that *is* based on some further belief(s). Alvin Plantinga provides an introduction to the concept of basic belief in his "Is Belief in God Properly Basic?", C D Delaney (ed), *Rationality and Religious Belief* (Notre Dame: University of Notre Dame, 1979), 41-42.

[8] I am referring to Eugene Rogers , Jr, "Thomas and Barth in Convergence on Romans I?" *Modern Theology* 12:1, 1996, 57-83. See also his *Thomas and Karl Barth: Sacred Doctrine and the Natural Knowledge of God* (Indiana: Notre Dame Press, 1998). Notwithstanding the fine work that Rogers has carried out in his comparison of Barth with Aquinas, the conclusions he reaches must be tempered with Barth's understanding of the historicality of the creation history in *CD* III/1. Rogers devotes little of his otherwise brilliant analytical skills to this understanding. The original criticism of Barth's logic in ruling out natural theology - as opposed to Enlightenment apologetics - came from Wolterstorff's seminal paper. Notwithstanding the brilliance of this paper I believe it was at fault in judging Barth's logic to have been invalid. Barth knew what he was doing! To be sure, that knowledge of the creation history is a necessary and sufficient condition of knowledge of God as creator does not, by itself, exclude the possibility that the creation itself could be a sufficient condition. But the latter is excluded by Barth on the grounds that the creation history is an event (or events) whose only means of measurement is it itself. Since the creation is precisely the realm where Kant's and Troeltsch's principles of, respectively, 'pre-existing measure' and 'analogy' are justifiably operative, this must mean for Barth that arguments from creation can never constitute sufficient grounds for knowledge of God as creator.

God the creator in the first article of the creed, one is confined completely and exclusively to the creation history. So Barth. But since one can only know this on the basis of the self-revelation of God as creator there is no sense in which knowledge of the creation history can be other than a necessary and sufficient condition of knowledge of God as creator. Hence, if Barth is a 'faith seeking understanding' theologian in the realm of creation it is only with respect to the creation history as attested in Genesis 1-2.4a, not with respect to the creation. For Aquinas, as for Calvin, it may be the case that belief (faith) in God the creator can be transmuted into understanding through "the whole workmanship of the universe." Not so Barth. It is not only the 'faith' part of 'faith seeking understanding' that is confined to God's self-revelation in the creation history, it is also the 'understanding' part. A large part of what Barth has to say on matters hermeneutical and epistemological in *Church Dogmatics* III/1 underlines this point.

There is another aspect of Barth's rejection of natural theology which needs to be emphasised before I proceed to the body of this chapter. Barth's rejection is in fact absolutely central to the fundamental feature of his doctrine of creation: the significance of what it means to say that God reveals Himself *as creator*. It is not often realised - if at all - that it is precisely because of this rejection of natural theology, and the concomitant emphasis on revelation as the key to creation, that he is able, at least *prima facie*, to have a free, indeed positive, attitude to the discoveries of natural science and, in particular, to those of biology. I touch on these matters toward the end of the following section.

## 2. The Literal Sense and the Final Form
## on the Plane of *Sui Generis* Historicality:
## the *One* Creation History

Barth's most systematic hermeneutical and epistemological 'commentary' on the historical witness to God's self-revelation focuses on the Old Testament and the Genesis creation narratives in particular.[9] I say this because in the next chapter I will argue that this commentary is also the hermeneutical context of the resurrection-appearances history. Barth is keenly aware of the critical tradition of Pentateuchal criticism culminating in the source-critical hypotheses of Julius Wellhausen. And he has no axe to grind against the validity of such hypotheses; indeed in his affirmation of the final form of the text as historical truth-claiming narrative he employs its presence somewhat ironically to move the historical truth-claim of *sui generis* historicality. But the starting point for Barth must be the literal

---

[9] See Barth, *CD* III/1 §41.1 'Creation, History and Creation History.'

sense of the final form of the text. It may, he thinks, be unnecessary to stray from the final form in order to reach source-critical conclusions. The literal sense of the text may be all that one needs. Nevertheless, Barth's understanding of the *sensus literalis* (and the final form of the text) goes beyond that of Calvin or Augustine on creation. Speaking of the creation narratives of Genesis 1 and 2, Barth says:

> All their utterances should be taken literally; not in a shallow but a deep sense; not in a narrow but in an inclusive sense; yet in such a way that the obvious meaning of the direct narration should always be given its proper weight; in such a way, too, that the account does not give rise to a picture of all kinds of timeless connexions and relationships which cannot be recounted; but in such a way that the narrative has also and primarily to be taken in all seriousness; in such a way that even the deeper and more inclusive literal sense is sought only on the plane of the historical and therefore of that which can be recounted and is in fact recounted.[10]

And Barth adds:

> What the biblical accounts offer is creation saga. But this means creation history and not creation myth.[11]

As against the Enlightenment critique and dismissal of these passages as myth, Barth concurs with the pre-critical view that the literal sense of the final form has to be embraced ('*all* their utterances should be taken literally in an inclusive not in an exclusive sense' such that, to borrow Hans Frei's famous phrase used earlier, there was "no gap between the representation and the represented": the narrative passages meant what they said). Moreover, it had to be affirmed "in such a way that even the deeper and more inclusive literal sense is sought only on the plane of the historical". To be sure the "shallow" and "narrow" sense of the *sensus literalis* is no less affirmative of "the plane of the historical." But what the "more inclusive, deeper, literal sense" attests to "on the plane of the historical" is precisely *sui generis* historicality. We are firmly in the realm of Overbeck's dilemma and the strange new world within the Bible. The historical truth-claiming of the creation narratives is an attestation to the *sui generis* historicality of its history. This becomes clear in Barth's attitude to both in comments he makes on Genesis 1.1-2.4a and 2.4b-25:

> ... on the first pages of the Bible we do not have only one but two different accounts of creation .... When we come to the exegetical appraisal of these

---

[10] *Ibid*, 84.
[11] *Ibid*, 84.

passages, and the attempt to understand them in the setting in which they confront us in Genesis, it is to be noted that they not only describe the events with greatly varying interests but also in very different ways. *Seen from the point of view of the other, each of these accounts reveals painful omissions and irreconcilable contradictions.* [my italics] The suspicion becomes strong that they derive from different sources, originating at different times against different backgrounds, and from a different intellectual approach. A thoughtful consideration will certainly hold itself aloof from the evaluation and disparagement (Gunkel) often associated with the familiar hypothesis of different sources, because they really have nothing to do with exposition. Yet even if that is done, even if we do not fail to see the common denominator of both narratives, even if we establish that the common denominator is undoubtedly the decisive element in both, we cannot fail to see again that what might be considered "historical" in either - if not contradicted on other grounds - does not come under this common denominator, so that even if it were intrinsically possible to construct a "historical" picture from the narratives we cannot actually do so without doing violence to one or the other or both. The older expositors who attempted a "historical" harmonisation of the two accounts did not adhere too closely to what is actually written. What is written - and this may be said independently of all source-hypotheses - is ill-adapted in its juxtaposition of two different accounts to mediate a "historical" sub-stratum. We can only do violence to it if we read and interpret it in this way.[12]

Barth acknowledges that, among the narratives that the historical critics have reinstated in order to evaluate the question of the Bible and historical reality, there are "two different accounts of creation," even if their contents overlap. Moreover, he agrees that, on the basis of the accounts themselves, the likelihood is that they "derive from different sources, originating at different times against different backgrounds, and from a different intellectual approach." Nevertheless, the "evaluation and disparagement" often associated with the *Quellenscheidungshypothese* - with 'difference', in fact - such as one finds in Hermann Gunkel,[13] has nothing to do with exposition *per se*. For Barth, disassociating oneself from such "disparagement" coincides with establishing, not only that there is a "common denominator" [*Gemeinsame*] in the two creation narratives, but that this common denominator is the decisive element in both. But,

---

[12] *Ibid*, 80.

[13] See Herman Gunkel, *Genesis*, translated by Mark E Biddle, foreword by Ernest W Nicholson (Macon: The Mercer University Press, 1987). Gunkel's commentary on Genesis was published in 1901. It provides the context in which - and against which - Barth's own understanding of *Sage* is worked out.

crucially, the decisive element - constituted by the common denominator - cannot, without distortion, deliver one unbroken chain or single picture of history in the  sense meant by pre-critical interpreters such as Augustine and Calvin. And it is precisely because of this - not in virtue of the validity of the *Quellenscheidungshypothese* - that "older expositors"  such as Augustine and Calvin are wrong about the nature of the relation between the creation narratives and historical reality. In other words, that the older harmonicists such as Augustine and Calvin were unable to render the creation narratives as one unbroken chain or single picture of history without doing violence to the text  is not to be explained by the hypothesis of different sources; it is to be explained at the level of the final form of the text itself.

To reiterate: Barth agrees with Augustine and Calvin that the final form of the creation narratives is sufficient to answer the question of the relation between the Bible at this point and historical reality.[14] But he argues that it is making a historical truth-claim of a different kind. The pre-critical mode of interpretation distorts the use to which the meaning of the final form is put. In particular, it fails to reflect on the fact that the juxtaposition of two different accounts is ill-adapted if it is in fact intended by the redactor of the final form to tell of history in the sense meant by Augustine and Calvin. One might say that the two accounts would *not* have been juxtaposed one to the other had each been meant to be  read as history in the sense satisfying the criteria of *chronological and 'topographical' continuity* (though it doesn't follow that, had they *not* been juxtaposed in this way, they *would* be most adequately rendered as history in Augustine's and Calvin's sense).[15] It is this that leads Barth to conclude that they speak of *a sui generis* historicality.[16] This is essential if Overbeck's dilemma is to be resolved. What is the *sui generis* historicality of which the narratives speak?

---

[14] One can say this of Augustine on the grounds that he wished to give "a faithful record of what actually happened" as an account of the literal sense of the creation narratives. Augustine, *The Literal Meaning of Genesis*, vol 1, 19. Later, he speaks of "the plain meaning of the historical facts", motivating him to provide a 'historical' harmonisation of certain tensions in the narratives. *Ibid*, 39. And even where he speaks of creation as an act or event outside time, as a happening "all at once" (*Ibid*, 143),  he is also inclined to speak of the same acts as happening "in sequence." *Ibid*, 143.

[15] Robert Alter makes a similar point in *The Art of Biblical Narrative*. Robert Alter, *The Art of Biblical Narrative* (London: Allen and Unwin, 1981), 141-147.

[16] Childs is essentially correct when he writes of Barth's understanding of the creation history: "Barth interpreted the genre of the Genesis story  as a particular literary and theological vehicle which was neither mythical nor historical in terms of critical verification, but arose truthfully to testify to the unique beginning of God's redemption and to point forward to an eschatological confirmation in the resurrection of Jesus Christ of a new creation. [...] ... the witness to God the creator in all its remaining mystery and hiddenness was of a different order from all general epistemological and ontological

First and foremost one has to say that the narratives speak of events each of which is an event whose only means of measurement is it itself. For Barth, as for Gerhard von Rad, both *Sage* and *Historie* are historical truth-claiming *genres* whose respective referents are historical  events in space and time: events of the realm of *Geschichte*.[17] But the kind of history referred to by the genre of *Historie* is to be comprehended as

> creaturely history in the content of other creaturely history, as an *event prior to which and side by side with which* [*vor dem und neben dem*] there are other events  of *the same basic type* [*prinzipiell gelechartiges*] with which it can be compared  and integrated    [*mit dem sich jenes vergleichen, mit dem es sich zu einem Bilde zusammenordnem la*].[18]

This is what Barth refers to as *historische Geschichte*.[19] In contrast,  Sage *depicts  an event which absolutely lacks these properties*.[20] The history-

---

categories." Brevard Childs, *Biblical Theology of the Old and New Testaments*, (London: SCM, 1992), 405.

[17] See Gerhard von Rad, *Genesis*, translated by  John H Marks, (London: SCM, 1963), 30-35. It is clear from von Rad's comments that he understands *Historie*, like *Sage*, as a literary genre. Whether this particular distinction is to be taken as the dominant understanding of these terms cannot be taken for granted, though Bromiley's observation should be noted: Barth understands *Geschichte* and *Historie* "more in their ordinary senses - history as event and history as record." G W Bromiley, *Introduction to the Theology of Karl Barth* (Edinburgh: T & T Clark, 1979), 112.  This, I submit, is more or less, the distinction that one finds in both Barth and von Rad. McGrath notes two other important English translations of the terms *Historie* and *Geschichte*. The first is: *historisch* translated as 'objective-historical'  and *geschichtlich* as 'existential-historical.' The second is: *historisch* translated as 'historical' and *geschichtlich* as 'historic.' The first, attributed to Bultmann, "brings out the distinction between the objective facts of history, and their perceived significance for the individual." The second "emphasises the distinction between an event *in* history, and an event *making* history." Alister McGrath, *The Making of Modern German Christology* (Oxford: London, 1986), 76-77.

[18] Barth, *CD* III/1, 78

[19] *Ibid*, 84

[20] Barth defines saga "in the sense of an intuitive and poetic picture of a pre-historical reality of history which is enacted once and for all within the confines of time and space." *Ibid*, 81. In *Church Dogmatics* I/1, he defined myth as follows: "Myth uses narrative form to expound what purports to be always and everywhere true. It is an exposition of certain basic relationships of human existence, found in every time and place, in their connexions to their own origins and conditions in the natural or historical cosmos, or in the Deity. Barth, *CD* I/1, 327-328. In *CD* III/1 he defined it as: "... the essential principles of the general realities and relationships of the natural and spiritual cosmos, which, in distinction from concrete history, are not confined to definite times and places." CD III/1, 84. It is clear that the point of contrast Barth wishes to draw is one between, one the one hand, a

telling narratives of the creation narratives   and (as we shall see) the resurrection appearance stories are defined as saga precisely because they depict events "prior to which and  side by side which" there are *no* other events - no other event - "of the same basic type with which it can be compared and integrated": each event is *sui generis. Each event is an event whose only means of measurement is it itself* in this sense.[21] Each possesses

---

'once and for all' *sui generis*  historical event in space and time, and, on the other, a phenomenon which is of the nature of a general truth, always and everywhere true and therefore not confined to a definite time and place. The question is whether the narratives he affirms and exegetes as saga, in particular, the creation and resurrection-appearances history, can bear the weight of his  definition; that they do speak of historical truth rather than a general eternal truth about the man or the cosmos. Pannenberg agrees with Barth that the genre of saga ought to be distinguished from myth: "sagas ... [are] not seen, as in the case of myth, as something happening in the primal age as the basis of the present world order, but as historical events distinguished by their extraordinary nature, yet lacking the general validity of myth which derives from its function of providing a basis for the present order of things." Wolhart Pannenberg, "The Later Dimensions of Myth in Biblical and Christian Tradition" in Pannenberg, *Basic Questions in Theology* (London: SCM Press, 1973), 4. The whole essay is to be highly recommended.

[21] Barth was no stranger to the thesis that antiquity's methodological perspective on history was quite different from that of modernity's. In particular, he accepted and even endorsed the thesis that antique historical truth-telling was not motivated by the scientific empirical mode of historical truth-claiming that was later to inform modernity's wish meticulously to *record* the facts as they had actually happened. Antique historical truth-telling had "no knowledge of a historical question" in the modern sense. Barth, *CD* I/1, 325-326 *But this fact does not of itself explain the presence of saga  in the Bible.* The reason is that the Bible does not only contain saga, it also contains history: "In the Bible we usually have to reckon with both history and saga [*mit Historie und mit Sage*]." Barth, *CD* III/1, 82.  Hence the fact that saga is present requires an additional explanation. That explanation is that it attempts to speak of events each whose only means of measurement is it itself, of *sui generis geschichtlichen* events in this sense. Barth, *CD* I/1, 326. The point is: notwithstanding that the *Historie* in the Bible is permeated by the characteristic predisposition of antique history-claiming as outlined above, its referent is to events  "prior to which and side by side with which there are other events  of the same basic type with which it can be compared  and integrated." Hence, for example, notwithstanding the difference in details found in the four Gospels pertaining to the crucifixion of Jesus, the four Gospels are (in one sense) speaking of a historical event which can be compared with other events of the same basic type. The creation history and the resurrection-appearances history speak of a *sui generis* historicality. Nicholas Wolterstorff has characterised the antique historical mentality as one which wishes to say how it *might well have been*, not how things *actually were*. Nicholas Wolterstorff, *Divine Discourse*, 258-260. Nevertheless, notwithstanding Wolterstorff's insight,  the fundamental rationale behind the presence of both *Sage* and *Historie* in the Bible is that biblical narrative speaks of *two* kinds of historical event: a general and a *sui generis* theological historicality.

a *sui generis* historicality.[22] Hence though Barth affirms *unhistorische Geschichte* - which he also calls *praehistorische Geschichte -*[23] this should not be taken to mean that he is speaking of timeless metaphysical truths in the sense of a "true description of the timeless relationship between God and His creature."[24] Rather, these events are: "once-and-for-all words and acts" in space and time.[25]

But are they? Or more pertinently: can they be? In both the *Confessions* and *The City of God* Augustine took the view that there was *no time* before the creation. Hence, according to him, the creation of the world could not be said to have occurred *in* time. It could not properly therefore be called a creation *history* since a history presupposed events occurring in time. In order therefore to affirm the creation history as a real history Barth has to argue against Augustine's position. This is what he does. He argues that there is no contradiction in saying, on the one hand, that the creation history is a history in time, and, on the other, that the history of creation includes among its created 'objects' the creation of time.[26] The fundamental rationale behind this is the assertion that God's

> creation is simultaneous with the emergence of that which He creates, and therefore, simultaneous with the time which begins with it, and therefore not outwith but in this time.[27]

The reason this assertion is fundamental is as follows. Were creation *prior* or *antecedent* to "the emergence of that which [God] creates", then of course it would follow that there could be no such thing as a creation *history*. Augustine would be right. Creation would include the creation of time but creation itself could not be in time since it would be antecedent to, not simultaneous with, "the emergence of that which [God] creates." The critical tradition might be inclined to think that Augustine is right in what he

---

[22] Barth, *CD* III/1, 84.

[23] *Ibid*, 80, 81.

[24] *Ibid*, 64.

[25] *Ibid*, 64. "… that is precisely what the first creation narrative expressly says when it describes creation as an articulated sequence of individual words and acts of God and a consequent emergence of the creature, and when it makes the completion of each divine work and the essence of each creaturely being coincide with the passage of a day, and the completion of the whole with that of a week. According to this account time undoubtedly begins with the first divine 'Let there be' and the first creaturely 'It was'." *Ibid*, 71.

[26] I do not wish to venture into the question what kind of ontology time has in Barth's doctrine of creation. It is a difficult question beyond the scope this book. What is unequivocally clear is that the creation of time is itself an event, a *sui generis* historical event.

[27] *Ibid*, 71.

claims. If one thinks of human creation one tends to think of the creative act preceding the emergence of the creation, as in a painting or a symphony for example. But Barth would say that human creative acts are poor analogies for divine creation. According to Barth, God's act of creation is simultaneous with the emergence of the object of creation. Therefore when God says in the priestly narrative 'Let there be light!' the creation of light is simultaneous with the emergence or coming into being of light. The emergence or coming into being of light is an event in time. God's creating of it is simultaneous with it. Therefore the creation of it - the creating of it - takes place in time. This observation is of the order of a general conceptual point. Whatever God creates is "the emergence of that" or 'the coming into being of that' which is created. The "emergence of that" which is created is for Barth an event in time, a *sui generis* historical event in time. But since God's act of creation is simultaneous with this event, it follows that creation is too a history, a creation history in time.

The distinction between, on the one hand, the *coming into being* of created reality and, on the other, *created reality* itself constitutes the rationale behind Barth's response to his eight-year old grand-niece's specific question about evolution. In a letter to his grand-niece he wrote that there is as little question of harmony as of contradiction between, on the one hand, the biblical creation story and, on the other, a scientific theory like that of evolution:

> The creation story deals only with the becoming of all things, and therefore with the revelation of God, which is inaccessible to science as such. The theory of evolution deals with what has become ....[28]

Barth's response to his grand-niece contains an essential plank of his doctrine of creation: that in dealing with "the becoming of all things" the creation history is dealing with "the revelation of God." The coming into being of reality coincides in a temporal sense with God revealing Himself as creator. It is this fact that makes it almost - though not quite - a subordinate or secondary by-product of God revealing Himself as creator.[29] *The creation is not the primary focus of the creation history.* It is the

---

[28] Barth, *Letters 1961-68*, translated by G W Bromiley, (Edinburgh: T & T Clark, 1981), 86. In his preface to *CD* III/1 Barth wrote that "there is free scope for natural science beyond what theology describes as the work of the Creator." And, interestingly, he added: "I am ... of the opinion that future workers in the field of the Christian doctrine of creation will find many problems worth pondering in defining the point and manner of this twofold boundary." Barth, *CD* III/1, x.

[29] What makes it not quite a secondary by-product is, of course, precisely the seventh day of creation in which God reveals Himself as the God who has time for his creation, and in particular, his human creature.

secondary focus. The primary focus is God's self-revelation.[30] Moreover, that the coming into being coincides with *God's revealing Himself as creator* means that the *coming into being* of reality is precisely an event whose only means of measurement is it itself. The reason is that God *revealing* Himself as God the creator is such an event (God is *God*).[31] In other words, a sufficient condition of it being the case that man was created by God (and, indeed, a necessary condition since Barth would say it is *God* of whom we speak) is that *God reveals Himself* as the creator of man, as creating man. *And this remains the case no matter what science discovers.* In other words, a truth *solely* about God the creator is *sufficient* to entail that God created man. In *Dogmatics in Outline* Barth summed up his doctrine of creation in the following way. Speaking of God the creator in the context of the apostles' creed he wrote:

> … the confession does not speak of the world, or all events it does so incidentally, when it speaks of [God the creator] of heaven and earth. It does not say, I believe in the created world, nor I believe, in the work of creation. But it says, I believe in God the Creator. And everything that is said about creation depends absolutely upon this Subject. The same rule holds always, that all the predicates are determined by Him. This holds also for creation. Fundamentally, what is involved here is the knowledge of the Creator; and after that and from that viewpoint, His Work must be understood.[32]

---

[30] This seems to me to be one implication of the analysis Jüngel gives in his seminal *The Doctrine of the Trinity: God's Being is in Becoming*, though his trinitarian-revelatory analysis does not explicitly develop Barth's doctrine of creation in this way when he examines the traditional doctrine of appropriation. See Jüngel, *The Doctrine of the Trinity: God's Being is in Becoming*, 36-41.

[31] That the creation history is *in toto* an event whose only means of measurement is it itself - and in this sense a historical event - enables Barth to deal with the following epistemological question: "From what source and in what way can man know this history and be able to recount it?" As he acknowledges: "The obvious difficulty of this question has often led to a denial of the historicity and temporality of creation and the reinterpretation of the biblical witness as a declaration which really aims at an unhistorical and timeless relationship between the Creator and the creature." Barth, *CD* III/1, 77. For if the history of God's self-revelation as creator is *in toto* an event whose only means of measurement is it itself then there can be no pre-existing means of measurement independently of the object of measurement itself. Hence, it is not because there were no human witnesses to the 'foundation of the world' that there exists no independent verification; it is because the history of creation - *in toto* an event whose only means of measurement is it itself - can have no historical or empirical ratification in this sense.

[32] Barth, *Dogmatics in Outline*, 50. The brilliance, originality and the potential of Barth's doctrine of creation is contained in this assertion (an assertion mostly under-

"All the predicates are determined by Him" - an absolutely pivotal sentence in this passage. It means: it is God *revealing Himself as the creator* of heaven and earth, or of man, that determines whether He is the creator of these realities. That and that *alone!* It is this position that Barth juxtaposes to Kant, Troeltsch and the Enlightenment conception of God the creator. This is the testimony of the strange new world within the Bible: God *reveals* Himself as creator, and this event is an event whose only means of measurement is itself.[33]

### 3. The History and Goal of the First Creation Narrative: *God* Reveals Himself *Through Himself* With the Result That He Reveals *Himself* as Creator

That the history of creation is *in toto* a *sui generis* historical event whose only means of measurement is it itself is corroborated by the fundamental content of the history. The fundamental content is God, and in particular, God's self-revelation. To reiterate a point made in Chapter 5: were *God to reveal Himself as God*, reveal Himself as *Himself* in historical space and

---

appreciated, if at all, in the Barthian literature). Is the assertion logically coherent? What Barth is saying is that, if God reveals Himself as the creator of man then - no matter what science turns up - it is true that God created man. It is true because this is what God says in his self-revelation. Assume, for example, that the genetical theory of evolution via natural selection is true, and that, as a consequence, man evolved from lower life forms. Nevertheless, God's self-revelation as creator tells you that God created man, or more precisely, that God *revealed Himself* as the creator of man. As Barth might have put it in his letter to his grand-niece: in dealing with the coming into being of man one is dealing with God revealing Himself as the creator of man. The question of course will be asked: if the genetical theory of evolution via natural selection is true, how could it be the case that God revealed Himself as the creator of man is true? Aren't the two propositions logical contraries - if one is true the other must be false? (They are not contradictories since both of course may be false.) It is beyond the scope of this book to examine this question. I will simply say that it is not a simple question. Logical contrariness is not as easy to deduce as is thought - even in this case. Does it make a difference if one rejects Barth's distinction between 'coming into being' and 'created being'? Possibly - except that it seems that this distinction was introduced to allow for the possibility of the creation history being a real history. There are genuinely difficult problems involved in a logical appraisal of Barth's doctrine of creation and it seems prudent to leave this appraisal to another time. Nevertheless the brilliance of Barth's insight here - at the very centre of his doctrine of creation - cannot be doubted.

[33] As Barth puts it in *CD* III/1: "Only if God is in fact its Creator, if it is in fact His creature, and if we have in fact to reckon with this because *He Himself has told us* [my italics], is this statement of dogma [God the Creator of heaven and earth] certain, demonstrable and indisputable ...." Barth, *CD* III/1, 8-9.

time, such a self-revelation would have to be in the form of such an event.[34] Otherwise, it would not be the 'God who is *God*'. In *Church Dogmatics* I/1 Barth proposed three famous theses as the answer component of a simple question-answer dialectic:

> Who reveals Himself? How does it come about, how is it actual, that this God reveals Himself? What is the result? (What does this event do to them to whom it happens?)

The answer Barth gave was:

> *God* reveals Himself. He reveals Himself *through Himself*. He reveals *Himself*.[35]

The three theses combine in one sentence to read: *God* reveals Himself *through Himself* with the result that God reveals *Himself*. This is a very important statement for Barth. It is intrinsic both to the theological identity of the creation narratives and (as we shall see in the following chapter) the resurrection appearances narratives. In the resurrection-appearances history the end result of each event of this history is that in Jesus Christ revealing Himself as the one whom the disciples had encountered in His pre-Easter history - culminating in His identity as the Crucified One - God reveals Himself as *Reconciler*. Moreover, if it constitutes valid exegesis, it reinforces the historicality of the creation history since it describes an event, an act of God, the God who is *God*.

In the creation history God reveals Himself as the *Creator* (not simply *a* creator but *the* creator: the creator of the heavens and the earth!). But He reveals Himself as the Creator who wills to be with, and for, man. For Barth what is decisive in this respect is the seventh day of creation, the day of the event of God's Sabbath freedom - the 'seventh day of the week':

---

[34] Barth speaks of saga as referring to 'once-and-for-all' events in space and time, historical space and time, in effect. One can understand his reference to creation history taking place in time. The idea of this same history occurring in historical space is perhaps more problematic. But it may be that spatiality here is simply a *conceptual* consequence of the creation history being an *event*. That is, if something is an event, and a historical event at that, then it must by definition occur in space; otherwise it is not an event. And this conceptual commitment may be all Barth is committed to when he speaks of the event as a 'pre-historical' historical event occurring in space and time.

[35] Barth, *CD* I/1, 295-6. For a clear-headed exposition of the three-fold nature of revelation as the root of the Barth's doctrine of the Trinity, see Jenson, *God After God: the God of the Past and the God of the Future, seen in the work of Karl Barth* (Indianapolis and New York: Bobbs-Merrill, 1969), 95-122.

"God blessed the seventh day and made it holy."[36] This event - the covenant of grace of God - constitutes "the supreme starting-point for all that follows." Crucially: "the history of the covenant was really established in the event of the seventh day."[37] Moreover: "Everything that precedes is the road to this supreme point. The connexion and sequence of the individual events in the history of creation, and these individual events themselves - each in its own place and manner - all point to this last event ...."[38] Hence even though God reveals Himself as creator in the preceding sequence there is a sense in which precisely because of the seventh day, the end or result of the creation history is that God reveals *Himself* as creator. One might go as far as saying that insofar as the event of the creation history is *God* revealing Himself *through Himself* with the result that He reveals *Himself*, the point of creation is not merely or mainly the creation; the point is God revealing Himself as creator - creator of creation, and, in particular, creator of man. Or more accurately: God reveals Himself as the creator who, literally, has time for man. This is whom God reveals Himself to be.

In other words, it is only within the context of the final day of the history of creation that one can understand the goal of creation. As Barth puts it: "Creation is finished but the history of creation is not yet concluded."[39] The Church fathers who understood the history of creation as the *hexaemeron*, rather than the *heptaemeron* missed this point and in doing so missed the meaning and purpose of creation intrinsic to the creation history itself.[40] God's resting on the seventh day has no less the character of a *sui generis* historical event than the other (preceding) *sui generis* historical events of creation. God's resting on the seventh day is posited as itself a (positive) event in the history of creation. Indeed, it is the supremely positive event of the history of creation. In this event God is there as *Himself*. He reveals *Himself* in the history of creation: "He has made this last day and act of the history of creation an element in His own History."[41] (In contrast, it could be said that the previous historical events of creation were exclusively elements of the history of creation, although one would not wish to draw too rigid a

---

[36] Von Rad writes: "It is significant that God 'completed' his work on the seventh day (and not, as seems more logical, on the sixth - so the LXX!). This 'completion' and this rest must be considered as a matter in itself. One should be careful about speaking of the 'institution of the Sabbath', as is often done. Of that nothing at all is said here. The Sabbath as a cultic institution is quite outside the purview. The text speaks, rather, of a rest that existed before man and still exists without man's perceiving it." *Genesis*, 60-61.
[37] Barth, *CD* III/1, 217.
[38] *Ibid*, 98.
[39] *Ibid*, 213.
[40] *Ibid*, 220.
[41] *Ibid*, 217.

distinction.)[42] It is in virtue of the seventh day that the history of creation is a history in which *God* reveals *Himself through Himself* with the result that He reveals *Himself*. It too - like the other events of creation history - is an event whose only means of measurement is it itself in which God reveals Himself as the One who has given Himself to belong to creation, has united Himself with creation, though without becoming other than Himself:

> the content of this event of the seventh day was the revelation of the true deity, the genuine freedom and love, of the Creator.[43]

The event of the seventh day constituted the beginning of the *history* of God's covenant with man - the history of God's election of man - of God willing to be with man in history, though without becoming other than Himself.[44] The seventh day is the event of God's Sabbath freedom for man to be at rest with God. It is in this sense that creation itself is the external basis of the covenant, and the seventh day in particular the beginning of the history of the covenant. But even this history, even the covenant God makes with Noah (Gen.9:8-17), Abram (Gen. 15; 17), and later with Abraham's descendants, the Israelites of the Exodus (Exod. 19-24), is subordinate to the covenant that God has made with man from eternity in Jesus Christ. The election of grace in Jesus Christ which encompasses man even in his fall and sin constitutes the fundamental covenant between God and man. God reveals Himself in the history of Jesus Christ as who He is in eternity, as Reconciler, as the God who wills to elect man even though he will choose to sin.[45]

---

[42] Perhaps it would be better to say, as Barth does, when he asks rhetorically: "When is He God more truly, or more perfectly Himself, in the whole course of His work of creation, than in this rest on the seventh day?" He continues: "Here it is revealed unequivocally that His work cannot have any claim on Him or violate Him; that as the Creator He is always His own Lord, the One who is free and the one who loves, and in both cases God; that precisely as the Creator He has confirmed and revealed Himself as His own Lord, as the One who is free and the One who loves, as God. Here God is quite alone, no less but just as much as He was and is prior to His creation in the aseity of His inner glory - the only difference being that He now willed to be and was this truly as the One who works *ad extra* and in relation to His work." *Ibid*, 215-216.

[43] *Ibid*, 216.

[44] The fact of God positing Himself - revealing Himself - as the positive completion of the history of creation is the historical repetition of what God has willed in eternity: "Speaking of God's rest on the seventh day the biblical witness actually tells us that what God was in Himself, and had done in eternity, He had now in some sense repeated in time, in the form of a historical event, in His relationship with His creation, the world and man; and that the completion of all creation consisted in the historical event of this repetition." *Ibid*, 216.

[45] Barth, *CD* II/2, 167.

This is why Barth claims that "an exposition of the first creation narrative can be concluded without reference to the Christological content of the passage only if the truth and faithfulness of God" toward man and creation is left "an open question."[46] But since the latter has not been left an open question, one must make reference to Christological content. The answer has already been decided in God's self-revelation on the seventh day. It has already been decided in Jesus Christ in the will of God from eternity that, notwithstanding man's fall into sin, God will be faithful to His eternal will to elect man. The truth and faithfulness of God in the blessing and sanctification of the seventh day are confirmed in the resurrection - and resurrection appearances - of Jesus Christ. That is how we know: through reconciliation, through the self-revelation of God the reconciler.

### 4. The Second Creation Narrative Culminates in the Fall (But Not Outside the Context of the First Creation Narrative)

The first creation narrative, Genesis 1.1-2.4a, culminates in the blessing and sanctification of seventh day. The seventh day - and the sanctification of creation and of man - is the goal of creation, inclusive of reconciliation. The trajectory of the second creation narrative, Genesis 2.4b-25, is quite different. It culminates, according to Barth, in the fall:

> If we ask what the story is really leading up to, a general answer is given by its direct connexion with the ensuing account of the fall. It is palpable that it aims immediately at the commencement of the history of covenant between God and man which takes place when the man created by God becomes disobedient and has to bear the consequences of this disobedience, but God for His part does not really cease but continues to be his God and faithful to him in this modification of the relationship between the Creator and the creature ....[47]

It is as if the creation history has two different endings: one sanctified by God and one where man chooses his own death apart from God. The first creation narrative ends with God revealing *Himself* as the good creator; the second creation narrative ends with the fall.[48] Is there a contradiction here?

---

[46] Barth, *CD* III/1, 228.

[47] *Ibid*, 233.

[48] According to Childs, Barth would seem to be on rational ground in this assertion: "The structure of chapter 2 makes it abundantly clear that it is only a part of a larger story which continues in ch. 3. [...] In the light of the structure of the story it is very unlikely that the J creation account ever had an independent existence apart from its role as an introduction to chapter 3." Childs, *Biblical Theology of the Old and New*

No. What Barth appears to be saying is that the second creation narrative constitutes the link between man in the first creation narrative and the fallen man - who is a sinner from the outset - in Genesis 3. Genesis 2 is related to Genesis 1 through identity: Genesis 2.4b-25 has "the same pre-historical historical event in mind but takes its own individual line *vis-à-vis* the first."[49] But the reason it takes its own individual line, Barth would say, is precisely because of its relation to Genesis 3:

> There can be no doubt that we are again in the sphere of beginning and the becoming of all things; it is again a question of historically explaining their being, and therefore the history of the covenant, by what has taken place prior to this history as the divine foundation of the creature. [50]

But Barth continues:

> ... in this case the explanation is limited to the narrowest possible sphere. And this sphere is as near as possible to the history which follows. What takes place is depicted wholly in the manner and with the colours of this later history. Only the fact that it has to do with a divine activity, and indeed a basic divine activity, shows us unmistakably that we are in fact dealing with creation history.[51]

In other words, Genesis 2.4b-25 deals with an aspect of the same creation history narrated by Genesis 1.1-2.4a. The reason it manifests itself in the way that it does - its mode of presentation (its "manner and colours") - is because it is brought into as close a proximity as is possible to Genesis 3 - the account of the fall of man. It is brought into as close a proximity with as possible with Genesis 3 *without compromising its identity as creation history*. Both Genesis 1 and Genesis 2 deal with the same creation history but "the smallness of the sphere, the narrowness of the selection made, and the immediate proximity of the later history" all "involve an essential foreshortening" in Genesis 2 of the "teleology" of the history of creation as narrated in Genesis 1.[52] The first is an all-encompassing

---

*Testaments*, 113. However, earlier, Childs remarks: "It is ... an unresolved question whether one can really speak of the Yahwist tradition of ch. 2 as a creation tradition since it is very possible that it originally functioned along with ch. 3 to describe divine order and human life." *Ibid* , 108. Barth would agree with the latter part of Childs' comment entirely, though he would not take it to imply that ch. 2 is not a creation narrative. The two assertions, for Barth, are not mutually exclusive, and chapter 2 is, in fact, the means by which Genesis 1 is linked to Genesis 3.

[49] Barth, *CD* III/1, 229.
[50] *Ibid*, 232.
[51] *Ibid*, 232-233.
[52] *Ibid*, 233.

perspective on the whole, the second a short-distance perspective on a particular aspect of the whole leading into the focus on the terrestrial history of man in relation to God and vice-versa: "a history of creation from inside."[53] In particular, "the history of creation in Genesis 2 is the immediate presupposition" of the event of the fall - the event of man in his created being being from the first a sinner.[54] The history of creation in Genesis 2:

> describes the coming into being of the world, and supremely of man as that of the being in whose nature and mode of existence is prefigured in the history which follows, and particularly this first event in this history, for all that it is so new and incomprehensible in relation to creation.[55]

In effect, Genesis 2 tells us that man created in the image of God as narrated in the first creation narrative is *revealed by God* to be identical with man who was from the first a sinner as narrated in Genesis 3. Genesis 2 narrates the coming into being of man who, in his created being, is from the first a sinner. In Genesis 1, man is described as *coming into being* in an event coincidental with God's self-revelation (and therefore an event whose only means of measurement is it itself). In Genesis 3 we have an account which says that *the created being of man* is from the first a sinner: the first man - "the man who owes his existence directly to the creative will and Word and act of God without any human intervention, the man who is to that extent the first man" -[56] was from the first a sinner. As he puts it: "There never was a golden age. There is no point in looking back to one. The first man was immediately the first sinner."[57]

According to Barth, it is as if Genesis 1-3 were saying: without Genesis 3, Genesis 2 and Genesis 1 would have been identical "in manner and colour" as regards its narration of the coming into being of man (Genesis 2 would have been the identical to Genesis 1 on this matter). Perhaps more paradoxically, it is as if they were saying: Genesis 2 *is* the same as 1 as regards the coming into being of man - if one removes the presence of Genesis 3 and the fall.[58] It is the fact that Genesis 2 is narrated from the

---

[53] *Ibid*, 232.

[54] *Ibid*, 233.

[55] *Ibid*, 233.

[56] Barth, *CD* IV/1, 508.

[57] *Ibid*, 508.

[58] The creation of the first man (in Barth's sense) is the coming into being of the first man coinciding with God's self-revelation as creator. God's act of creation of the first man is simultaneous with the emergence or *coming* into being of this man. Therefore the emergence of this man is an event whose only means of measurement is it itself, the coming into being of man created good in the image of God, indeed created, as has been said above, in the image of Jesus Christ.

perspective of the fall that introduces the difference. It is primarily in this
sense that "the second saga - particularly with reference to the creation of
man - provides an elucidation of the first."[59]

Moreover, it is the fact that Genesis 2 is narrated from this perspective
that the coming into being of man in Genesis 1 is revealed to be identical
with the same man who falls of his own free choice in Genesis 3. What is
revealed in God's self-revelation in Genesis 2 is that the fallen man in
Genesis 2 - man who from is the first a sinner - is identical with man who
was created in the image of God in Genesis 1.[60] That this fact also coincides
with God's self-revelation means that there is no question of a natural
theology at this point.   The coming into being of man - God's self-
revelation - is brought into closest proximity with the created being of man
who is from the first a sinner as narrated in Genesis 3. This is what God's
self-revelation as creator in Genesis 2 tells us. As Barth puts it: "... the
biblical witness to ... God's self-revelation tells us that there is a history of
creation, the history of the creation of unfallen man and his world."[61]
Otherwise, we cannot know anything about "unfallen man and his world."
But in telling us this, God's self-revelation tells us precisely that this man is
no other than the man who was from the first a sinner - even though this
latter event is nowise a part of God revealing Himself as creator.

To reiterate: God revealing Himself as creator in Genesis 2 - particularly
the creator of man - reveals the coming into being of man as identical with
the man in Genesis 3 who is the beginning of world history, history, one
might say, in the empirical sense (history that is capable of being recorded).
This beginning of world history - Adamic history - is "the structure of the
whole history of Yahweh and Israel. And that history is a type of the
historical existence of all nations and the will and achievements of all men
and all groups of men ...."[62] God's self-revelation as creator in Genesis 2

---

[59] Barth, *CD* III/1, 229.

[60] As Barth puts it: "The Bible gives to this history and to all men in this sense  the
general title of Adam. Adam is mentioned relatively seldom both in the Old Testament
and the New. There are only two passages which treat of him explicitly: Gen. 2-3 and
Rom. 5.12-21 (to which we might add 1 Cor. 15.22 and 45). The meaning of Adam is
simply man, as the bearer of this name which denotes the being and essence of all other
men. Adam appears in the Genesis story as the man who owes his existence directly to
the creative will and Word and act of God without any human intervention, the man who
to that extent is the first man." Barth, *CD* IV/1, 507-508.

[61] Barth, *CD* III/1, 73.

[62] Barth *CD* IV/1, 509. As Barth puts it: "The biblical tradition undoubtedly means that
[Adam' successors] were the physical descendants of  Adam .... But while they are
connected to him in a creaturely order" there is no physical connection as regards the
transmission of sin. *Ibid*, 510. The relation between, on the one hand, the first sinner as the
first sinner and, on the other hand, our existence today as sinners is the same one as the
relation between us and fallen man in Jesus Christ, the Word made flesh, the Word made

tells us that man who comes into being in Genesis 1 (coinciding with God's self-revelation itself) is identical with the man who is from the first a sinner. It is God's self-revelation that tells us this. Otherwise, we do not know the truth about ourselves.[63]

---

fallen man, *homo lapsus. It is revealed to us in the history of reconciliation of Jesus Christ.* "We are known by God in Adam, i.e., as those who are subject to the law revealed in him. In him, therefore, we have simply to recognise ourselves and mankind and the whole history of man. Adam is not a fate which God has suspended over us. Adam is the truth concerning us as it is known to God and told to us." *Ibid,* 510. Our sin is not therefore something we can determine for ourselves, it is not something that we can know independently. Nor is it something which Adam bequeaths to us as in the traducian understanding of the transmission of original sin: "The relationship between him and us, and us and him, is not therefore one which is pragmatically grounded and demonstrable, nor is it one which can be explained in terms of a transmission between him and us." *Ibid,* 510. Natural theology has no more place in the context of the doctrine of sin than it has in the doctrine of creation. Rather, it God who establishes - in the sense of *reveals* - the relation between Adam and us: "It is God who establishes it. It is the Word of God which gives this name and title to mankind and the history of man. It is God's Word which fuses all men into unity with this man as *primus inter pares* [first among equals]." *Ibid,* 510. It cannot go unnoticed that what we have here is, once again, a truth solely and wholly dependent on what God *reveals Himself* to be. Once again, Barth's brilliance is unmistakable.

[63] This is why Barth says: "We miss the unprecedented and incomparable thing which the Genesis passages tell us of the coming into being and existence of Adam if we try read and understand it as history, relating it either favourably or unfavourably to scientific paleontology, or to what we know with some historical certainty concerning the oldest and most primitive forms of human life." *Ibid,* 508. We might say God's *revelation of Himself as creator* in Genesis 2 *tells us* that this man - the man who is connected with "what we know with some historical certainty concerning the oldest and most primitive forms of human life" - is identical both with man who was from the first a sinner, and with man whose coming into being is narrated in Genesis 1. To reiterate: this is what God's revealing Himself as creator tells us. In other words, as Barth has it in his letter to his eight year-old grand-niece: "The creation story deals only with the becoming of all things, and therefore with the revelation of God, which is inaccessible to science as such. The theory of evolution deals with what has become ...." Barth, *Letters 1961-1968,* 68. Therefore, as was said, there is as little question of harmony as there is of contradiction between science and Barth's doctrine of creation. Notwithstanding scientific truth, and in particular biological or evolutionary truth, it is God's self-revelation in the creation history which tells us the essential truth about ourselves in relation to God's revealing of Himself as creator, and in particular revealing Himself to be creator of us. It is this revealing which we cannot gainsaid no matter what we know through science. We cannot defy what is revealed in God's self-revelation - an event whose only means of measurement is it itself - no matter what else is scientifically true. It is a necessary and sufficient condition of our divine createdness that God reveals Himself in the creation history to be our creator. It is God *revealing* Himself as our creator which is crucial in this regard - nothing else.

To be sure, the context of the coming into being of man - man created good - is the creation history. The context to the creation history - and therefore the creation of man - is the history of election fulfilled on the seventh day of creation. The context of the coming into being of man is '*God* reveals Himself *through Himself* with the result that He reveals *Himself*.' In contrast, the context of the fall of man is not the creation history. It is not part of the God who reveals Himself in the history of creation. The fall is not part of the creation history - which is confined to the *emergence* of man simultaneous with God's self-revelation - but something that occurs immediately with man's createdness. To reiterate: for Barth, man is from the first a sinner. However, the context of the fall, like creation history, is the history of election fulfilled on the seventh day. The fall shares this property with creation. One might say that the context of the history of fallen man is the seventh day. This explains why Barth treats the fall primarily within the context of the doctrine of reconciliation in IV/1, the history of reconciliation (though of course this means treating it within the context of the history of election) and not within the context of the doctrine of creation in III/1.

The act of sinful man is also *a sui generis* historical event. Though the fall of man as narrated in Genesis 3 is not part of the history of creation in which man is created good, in the sense of created for fellowship with God - but is rather the freely chosen act of sin - it too, for Barth, is cast in the genre of biblical saga. It too therefore is an event whose only means of measurement is it itself. Man is from the first a sinner. But this lost man - man immediately in his existence a sinner - and therefore this lost time, is an event also narrated by saga. It too is a *sui generis* historical event. Hence this fall, encapsulated in man's disobedience to God, and therefore the event narrated in Genesis 3, is itself an event whose only means of measurement is it itself. It itself is such an event freely brought into existence by the sinful act of man himself. The narrative of Genesis 3 itself speaks of a *sui generis* event of *Geschichte*. Barth is quite clear about this in *CD* IV/1. Not only man created good, but man as he freely chooses to sin is a *sui generis* historical event. It was this sphere of history "where there can be no historical proof"[64] that "Adam came into being and existed"[65] and likewise:

> It was this sphere of existence - again by virtue of the prophetically attested Word and judgement of God - that there took place the fall, the fall of the first man.[66]

---

[64] Barth, *CD* IV/1, 508.

[65] *Ibid*, 508.

[66] There is another rationale behind this claim. This is that Genesis 2 and 3 are one continuous narrative. Hence if Genesis 2 is narrated saga, Genesis 3 must be too. Hence

The rationale behind the claim that the fall of man is a *sui generis* historical event is precisely because the emergence of lost time is itself an event which occurs within the context of God's gracious election of man in Jesus Christ. It is not an event that can occur outside this particular temporal, historical realm. Otherwise the emergence of lost time *would be* eternally lost time.[67] Lost time is already bounded within the domain of the original time coinciding with - in the sense of simultaneous - the emergence of the creature created good. The emergence of the creature created good gives way immediately to the freely-chosen creaturely act of sin. The crucial point is that not only the first event but also the second event take place within the context of the "prophetically attested Word and judgement of God." In other words, as has been said, "an exposition of the first creation narrative can be concluded without reference to the Christological content of the passage only if the truth and faithfulness of God" toward the creature is left "an open question."[68] But it is not. It is already answered in Jesus Christ. It is already answered in what occurs on the seventh day of creation. As Barth puts it in his doctrine of election: "We cannot hold it against God that He did not prevent but permitted the fall of man, i.e., in his succumbing to temptation of the devil and his incurring of actual guilt."[69] Why not?

In God's decree these things did not involve any injustice to the creature, for by this same decree God decided that the risk which He allowed to

---

according to Barth's definition of saga, Genesis 3 must be brought under the epistemological remit of being an event whose only means of measurement is it itself.

[67] How then does Barth explain the relation between, on the one hand, time as it applies in the case of the history of creation, and, on the other, time as it unfolds in the history of the world itself, and in particular in the human realm? Are we to understand the relation as a *transition* between the time in which the creation history takes place as *sui generis* historical event to the "subsequent history" (Barth, *CD* III/1, 72) of the world as our human conceptions of time conceive it? No. For Barth it would be conceptual folly to think in this way. Barth does not explain the relation in terms of a relation between time *per se*. Rather, 'subsequent time' is to be explained *entirely in terms of* the sin of man. It is defined in terms of the sin of man. It follows as a logical consequence of fallen man. This time Barth refers to as "lost time" - "the time of man as isolated from God and fallen into sin." *Ibid*, 72. In other words, "as the time of lost man it can only be lost time." *Ibid*, 72. And since the first man is only 'first among equals' as regards sin, lost time continually comes into existence with the existence of each sinful man.

[68] Barth, *Ibid*, 228.

[69] Barth, *CD* II/2, 165. The devil for Barth is precisely one supreme expression of the reality of nothingness, *das Nichtige*. Barth's comment on Mephistopheles in Goethe's *Faust* is apt here. He refers to him as the "great negator." Barth, *Dogmatics in Outline*, 22.

threaten the creature and the plight into which He allowed it to plunge itself should be His own risk and His own plight.[70]

This means that the fall of man as an event is an integrative sub-history of reconciliation. God is already the God who wills to go into the far country as Barth has it in his doctrine of reconciliation. The man who falls is already the man who in Jesus Christ comes home to God (the 'Homecoming of the Son of Man').[71] In other words, the covenant that God makes with man on the seventh day of creation in Jesus Christ already has reconciliation built into it should man break with the covenant in his freely chosen acts of disobedience. Though Barth distinguished between, on the one hand, the coming into being of man created good, and, on the other, the immediate sinfulness of created man, he notes "that in the Yahwistic account (Gen. 2.4-3.24) the story of creation and the subsequent story of the fall almost merge into one another without transition. That in and with his existence, man is already the object of the electing grace of God is shown by the context of both accounts ..."[72]

---

[70] Barth, *CD* II/2, 165-166. The purpose of creation history is precisely creation itself. But creation itself is the external basis of the covenant between man and God and therefore subordinate to the covenant. It is a means to this divine end. Man is elected to be with God. Therefore God did not will man for his fall into sin in act. But he willed him - and indeed created him - as *homo labilis*, man who in his divinely ordained freedom is liable to sin. The object of election is not *homo lapsus* - fallen man - but rather *homo labilis*. Barth is a supralapsarian rather than infralapsarian. See Barth CD II/2, 137-145. Is God then culpable for the fact of human sin? No. As has been said, God takes the risk of man's fall on to Himself. *This means that God's self-revelation as reconciler is part of the history of God's revelation of Himself as the electing God who from eternity willed not to be thwarted by man succumbing to temptation and sin.* Man is the one whom God loved from all eternity in Jesus Christ, who is himself electing God and elected man, elected man from all eternity. That God was in Christ reconciling the world to Himself is part of this particular history of eternity willed from eternity. Jesus Christ is also *homo labilis* (*Ibid*, 143). This is a crucial point for Barth for two reasons. First, man is made in the image of Jesus Christ who is elected *homo labilis* because He is to take on the risk of the fall of *homo labilis*. Otherwise, Jesus Christ would not be true man. The second point pertains to the history of reconciliation fulfilled on the cross. Though Jesus Christ is the elected *homo labilis*, made flesh, and therefore made sin - made in fact *homo lapsus* - He does not fall. Though He is subject to temptation as *homo labilis*, He is obedient *homo labilis* even unto death on the cross. And because He is *homo labilis* made *homo lapsus* who yet does not sin, *homo lapsus* - the fallen creature -.is brought home to God. This is the essence of the Way of the Son of God into the far country which is also the Homecoming of sinful man - *homo lapsus*. I deal with these matters in more detail in Chapter 11.

[71] I discuss Barth's doctrine of reconciliation in Chapter 11.

[72] Barth, *CD* III/1, 63. Barth's view of the relation between theology and science is decisively determined by his understanding of creation and the fall. Both the creation narratives and the narrative of the fall of man speak of *sui generis* historical events:

The two accounts of creation - the final form of the text as regards the creation history - are inwardly coherent in that, though possessed of formally (and materially) different patterns, taken together they constitute a rational whole, a *sui generis* theological identity; they pertain to the one creation history. The "common denominator", then, is the internal and external relationship between the covenant and the creation. This is the 'higher harmony' [*höreren Harmonie*] discernible in, because intrinsically motivated by, the creation narratives themselves. Moreover, as has been said, the second creation narrative, as a foreshortening and historical close-up of an aspect of the first narrative, occurs within the historical bounds of the latter, not outwith it. To repeat: one creation history.

"*Seen from the point of view of the other, each of these accounts reveals painful omissions and irreconcilable contradictions.*"[73] But seen from a point of view other than the point of view of the other - a point of view that sees both, as it were (though not without first seeing the point of view of each individually) - the problem of painful omissions and irreconcilable contradictions is resolved. The point of view that sees both is one that identifies the common denominator of the two accounts without suppressing the individual theological content of each account. As Barth puts it, in seeking the meaning of the whole - the one creation history - our

best course is to accept that each has its own harmony, and then to be content with the higher harmony which is achieved when we allow the one to speak after the other. Hence the second of the accounts must be read as if it is the only one. And superfluous though it must seem after reading the first account, the whole problem must be reconsidered from new angle.[74]

---

events whose only means of measurement is each one itself. It is because of this that the history of the creation of the creature and the history of man's fall into sin cannot be apologetically harmonised with "the fullness of our own natural science" (as one finds in Aquinas for example as regards the science of his day). Barth *CD* III/1, 64. Science - be it the genetical theory of evolution via natural selection, relativity, or quantum mechanics - speaks of events which (however rare as in quantum mechanics) "prior to which and side by side with which there are other events of the same basic type with which [they] can be compared and integrated." Though the history creation itself - and the history of the fall of man - has as such a historical character and are historical events in time, this historical character is precisely that of a *sui generis* historicality. In the creation history God reveals *Himself* as Creator, creator of the creature, God who has graciously given time to the creature. This means that the history of the first sinner - and, indeed, the history of all sinners - is included in the history narrated on the seventh day of creation history. And since this latter event is an event in time, so then is the fall of man. It too is a *sui generis* historical event.

[73] *Ibid*, 80.
[74] *Ibid*, 229.

The two accounts of creation - the final form of the text as regards the creation history - are inwardly coherent in that, though possessed of formally (and materially) different patterns, taken together they constitute a rational whole, a *sui generis* theological identity; they pertain to the *one creation history*. The "common denominator", then, is the internal and external relationship between the covenant and the creation. This is the 'higher harmony' [*höreren Harmonie*] discernible in, because intrinsically motivated by, the creation narratives themselves. Moreover, as has been said, the second creation narrative, as a foreshortening and historical close-up of an aspect of the first narrative, occurs within the historical bounds of the latter, not outwith it. To repeat: one creation history.

The rest of Genesis and indeed the rest of the Old Testament provide a context in which the two creation narratives are to be understood. As Barth puts it: "The decisive commentary on the biblical histories of creation is the rest of the Old Testament. ... The details of the biblical creation histories call for this commentary."[75] Why is this? Barth's answer is: "The connexion between creation and history as it emerges in the fact that the history of creation and the rest of the Pentateuch and therefore the rest of the Old Testament belong together, illuminates on the one hand the meaning and purpose of creation, and therefore of the existence of man and the universe."[76] Modern critical biblical hermeneutics takes the view that authorial intentionality is crucial to the interpretation of texts. Therefore the rest of the Pentateuch and the rest of the Old Testament could only constitute a commentary on the creation history if it was so intended. Barth's answer might well be to say that, even though the creation history was not one of the things that was intended by the rest of the Pentateuch and by the rest of the Old Testament, this is what they were speaking of. In other words, what constitutes it being a commentary on the creation history is the historicity of the creation history as attested in scripture and the similarity or coincidence of the fundamental pattern of this history with the fundamental pattern of the history of Israel as attested in scripture. In this way Barth can defend the rational status of his position on Pentateuch and the Old Testament as commentary.

## Concluding Remarks

Notwithstanding the fact then that there are two different accounts of creation, according to Barth *there is only one creation history*. But there is one creation history only insofar as Genesis 1 and 2-3 possess a *sui generis* theological identity - the "common denominator" as Barth puts it. This

---

[75] *Ibid*, 65.
[76] *Ibid,* 63.

"common denominator" involved a "point of view" other than the "point of view of the other". It involved a kind of Hegelian *Aufhebung* of the various and sometimes diverse (even apparently contradictory) parts germane to an item or article of faith - the 'point of view of the final form of the text' reconciled on the plane *of sui generis* historicality. It is this sense that one could say that "The Strange New World Within the Bible was prophetic in a dimension other than the one indicated in Chapter 4. In the midst of a series of questions - and subsequent to the question, "What is there within the Bible?", Barth asked: "What is the one truth that these voices evidently all desire to announce, each in its own tone, each in its own way?"[77] In other words, there could be *more than one voice* announcing the *same* truth, *each with its own tone, each in its own way* - a truth that was neither history, nor morality, nor religion but, rather, the strange new world within the Bible.

Barth's understanding of creation history as quintessentially God revealing Himself as creator - in an event whose only means of measurement is it itself - is the fundamental rationale behind his epistemological answer to Kant and Troeltsch, and in particular to Kant's exposition of the Enlightenment's conception of the epistemological problem of God as exemplified in his *Religion Within the Limits of Reason Alone*. This means that Barth's account of the creation history is a more subtle - and dare I say it - a more modern understanding than the traditional 'faith seeking understanding' paradigm as found in Aquinas and Calvin. Barth offers what George Lindbeck has called a "post-critical retrieval" of a pre-critical mode of interpretation.[78] Barth accepts and affirms the final form of the text as in Genesis 1-3 but in such a way that he is able to provide a cogent response to the Enlightenment conceptions of Kant and Troeltsch.

I have used the phrase, 'an event whose only means of measurement is it itself' a number of times both in this chapter and in the previous one. It is fundamental to Barth's historical ontology. What I have not done yet is explain in detail the epistemological consequences of such an event, though I have the particular history of ideas from which Barth takes his point of departure vis-à-vis the Enlightenment, and indeed vis-à-vis Reformed theology. I turn to this in the following chapter. There I examine the epistemological consequences of Barth's understanding of the resurrection-appearances history. What I will have to say about the consequences applies no less to the creation history but my focus will be entirely on the event whose only means of measurement is it itself in which Jesus Christ revealed Himself "in His identity with the One previously followed and who had died on the cross and been buried."

[77] Barth, "The Strange New World Within the Bible", 47.
[78] Lindbeck, "Postcritical Canonical Interpretation: Three Modes of Retrieval", 26.

# Chapter 8
# The *Sui Generis* Historicality
## of the Resurrection-Appearances History

## 1. Introduction

At the beginning of the previous chapter I said that Barth spoke of the creation narratives as creation history, and that this had a precedent in, for example Calvin's commentary on *Genesis*. What was without precedent was his assertion that the creation narratives were historical truth-claiming narratives and, as such, to be treated by the Enlightenment in exactly the same way as it would any other historical truth-claim. When one compares Barth's treatment of the resurrection-appearances history the air of paradox is less heady. To speak of the resurrection appearances as *history* and the resurrection-appearances stories as *historical truth-claiming narratives* is less likely to conflict with our preconceptions about the truth-claims of the Bible. Yet the fact that Barth insists that the resurrection-appearances history and the creation history share a common *sui generis* historicality, a theological historicality, if you will, should be sufficient to warn us off from thinking that the former is ordinary history susceptible to the critical-historical method in the sense in which the latter is not.

In *Romans* II Barth understood the resurrection, and by implication the resurrection appearances, as a historical event. Eschatology - the eschatological event - was in essence a post-historical event which though not *of* history was *in* history. The resurrection as *the* eschatological event was then also a historical event in this sense.[1] It was this that led Barth to argue that revelation could only be affirmed indirectly, by statement and counter-statement, by dialectical language.

In the *Church Dogmatics* Barth no longer understood the resurrection - and here I wish to put the emphasis on Barth's understanding of the resurrection-appearances history - as a historical event accessible only through the medium of dialectical speech. The resurrection-appearances history are directly (even non-dialectically) affirmed as history

---

[1] See Chapter 3.

[*Geschichte*]. The appearances stories are unambiguously affirmed as historical truth-claiming narratives. Eschatology remains on board but, as will be shown in chapter 11, is fulfilled on the cross rather than in the resurrection appearances (as against a position such as the one held by Pannenberg in his book *Jesus - God and Man*).[2]

A historical event? Yes. Did this mean that Barth affirmed a pre-critical understanding of the resurrection-appearances history? No. In truth Barth was doing something else. To be sure, the Enlightenment was to reinstate the resurrection appearances narratives as the biblical canon has them: to reinstate, in effect, historical truth-claiming, literal sense and the final form of the text. But, from this point on, the question was one of epistemological evaluation, verification even, in the characteristic Enlightenment manner. How was the Enlightenment to measure the truth of the historical truth-claim? Answer: it was to set up, in the manner of Troeltsch, a pre-existing means of measurement against which to measure the historical truth-claim of the resurrection appearances narratives. It did this in the case of any other historical event; it was not to be denied doing the same in the case of the resurrection-appearances history.

However, though the consequences of such a methodological approach - the critical-historical method, and in particular the principle of analogy - were unproblematic in the case of historical events other than *sui generis* historical events, when the principle of analogy encountered 'that which nothing analogous can be conceived' - when it encountered a historical event whose historicality was a *sui generis* historicality - a radically different epistemological outcome ensued. For the principle of analogy was encountering a historical event whose only means of measurement was it itself. And in this case the question became: how did one measure - verify - an object of measurement whose only means of measurement was it itself? For in order to measure the *realität* of such an object - in this case a historical event - one had to have the means of measurement of *what it is* God's self-revelation was. But since this means of measurement could only be had with the event itself, one did not know *what it is* God's self-revelation was prior to the event itself (nor indeed subsequently). It was not at all like evaluating the historicity of historical events whose historicality fell within the remit of Troeltsch's principle of analogy. In the case of such events one *did* have a pre-existing means of measurement. One did know *what it is* they were prior to meeting them, in the flesh so to speak. One did have a concept of what would be the case if this or that historical event had or had not happened. This was not the case when one was dealing with historical events in which God revealed Himself as *God*.

---

[2] Pannenberg, *Jesus - God and Man*, translated by L Wilkins and D Priebe (London: SCM, 1968).

## 2. The Resurrection-Appearances History: Saga Depicts an Event Whose Only Means of Measurement is It Itself

In Chapter 7 Barth summarised his position on the creation history in the following way:

> The biblical history of creation is pure saga, and as such it is distinguished from "history" on the one side and myth on the other. Precisely in this form it is constituent form of the biblical witness and therefore itself a witness to God's self-revelation.[3]

*Mutatis mutandis*, such a claim is no less true as regards the resurrection-appearances history. According to Barth, the history of the forty days and pre-Easter history of the Gospel narratives "differ formally in the way in which they take place in the human sphere and human time, and therefore in the way in which they have to be understood as history."[4] Accordingly:

> ... in common with the creation story and many others, indeed the decisive elements in biblical history, the history of the resurrection has to be regarded  and described - in the thought-forms and terminology of modern scholarship - as "saga" and "legend."[5]

This means that, like the creation history, the resurrection-appearances history is other than the kind of history referred to by the genre of *Historie*.[6] The latter is  understood as

> creaturely history in the content of other creaturely history, as an event prior to which and side by side with which there are other events  of the same basic type with which it can be compared  and integrated.[7]

---

[3]  Barth, *CD* III/1, 90.

[4] *Ibid*, 334.

[5] Barth, *CD* IV/1, 335-336.

[6] *Ibid*, 80. Many of the most important things Barth has to say about saga - how he defines the term, how it relates to source-criticism, how it relates to history and myth, etc. - are said explicitly about the creation stories, and as such appear in *CD* III/1. But in *CD* III/2 Barth explicitly assimilates the resurrection narratives to the creation narratives: "The creation narratives in Gen. 1-2 ... are history in this higher sense; and so too is the Easter story." Barth, *CD* III/2, 446. In other words, the resurrection appearances are also saga "except for a tiny 'historical' margin", *Ibid*, 446, (the "margin" being the empty tomb though even the empty tomb is historical only in a certain specialised sense. See the following chapter for a more detailed discussion of this issue.

[7] Barth, *CD* III/1, 78.

This is what Barth refers to as *historische Geschichte*.[8] In contrast, as was said in Chapter 7, *Sage depicts an event which absolutely lacks these properties*. This means that the history-telling narratives pertaining to the resurrection appearance stories are defined as saga precisely because they depict events "prior to which and side by side which" there are *no* other events - no other event - "of the same basic type with which it can be compared and integrated": each event is *sui generis. Each event is an event whose only means of measurement is it itself* in this sense. This is precisely the sense in which the resurrection-appearances history is a *sui generis* historical event, possessing *sui generis* historicality.

That Jesus appears as who He was in his pre-Easter history - God - is not expressed as a paradox in the resurrection stories.[9] Who He is is now completely unveiled and manifest in the appearances. He is not both veiled and unveiled; He is completely unveiled.[10] Yet the simple descriptive realism one might have expected to emerge at this point fails to materialise. It is precisely because *God* reveals Himself and this God reveals *Himself* in historical space and time that, in a manner characteristic of Anselm's *Cur Deus Homo?*, Barth will say that God must of necessity reveal Himself in an event whose only means of measurement is it itself. Otherwise, it cannot be the 'Wholly Other' *wholly* revealing Himself. As Barth puts it in *CD* I/1:

> A result of the uniqueness of this object of knowledge might well be that the concept of its knowledge cannot be definitively measured by the concept of the knowledge of other objects or by a general concept of knowledge but that it can be defined at all only in terms of its own object.[11]

Though Jesus' self-revelation "finds a way of becoming the content of our experience and our thought", though "it gives itself to be apprehended by our contemplation and our categories", it "does that beyond the range of what we regard as possible for our contemplation and perception, beyond the confines of our experience and our thought."[12] One should note that Barth uses the phrase 'beyond what *we regard* [my italics] as possible', or, in particular, beyond what Kant had regarded as possible - not that it was beyond what *was possible*. The *strange new world* within the Bible was such that it was absolutely without precedent. The ancients, according to Barth, were just as unprepared for it as the moderns: nothing in one's prior

---

[8] *Ibid*, 84
[9] Barth, III/2, 449.
[10] *Ibid*, 449.
[11] Barth, *CD* I/1, 190.
[12] Barth, *CD* I/2, 172.

experience equipped one by way of analogy as if in anticipation of what it was like. For what it was was absolutely *sui generis*; therefore in answer to the question what it was like, it could and had to be said with utter earnestness that what it was like was nothing else. One would never be in a position to predict what it would be like a *priori* (and, indeed, as we shall see, what it is like a *posteriori*). That is, *even though the Evangelists had used the concepts and images of their own time, that their written record was cast in the form of saga and legend, rather than myth, indicated that that to which they pointed - the strange new world within the Bible - was not only: i) enacted once and for all within the confines of time and space; but was also ii) absolutely different from every other 'once'.*[13] God's self-revelation

---

[13] Barth, *CD* III/2, 454. In other words, it was qualitatively different from miracle. A miracle is measurable in principle by an immanent measure. It is by such an argument that Barth is able to subvert Hume's ironic 'endorsement' that theology's "best and most solid foundation is *faith* and divine revelation", which, in Hume's sense of these terms, categorised theology merely in terms of (supernatural) miracle. To know whether something is a miracle presupposes having the criterion of miracle against which to judge and evaluate whether something is a miracle or not; such knowledge entailed a position or point of comparison against which to judge whether a miracle had taken place. If *sui generis* historicality, and Jesus' self-revelation in particular, is assimilated to the concept of miracle, it would follow one had an independent conception of what it was for something to be revelation. But then one would not be talking about *sui generis* historicality. Hence *sui generis* historicality, and Jesus' self-revelation, cannot be assimilated to the concept of miracle. (The historicality of miracle is in fact no different from the historicality of ordinary historical events. Hume makes no distinction in terms of historicality.) Barth's position on epistemology is as uncompromising with the concept of miracle as it was with concept of the critical-historical method - and for exactly for the same reason. Troeltsch's "Historical and Dogmatic Method in Theology" set out three principles which he thought governed all historical inquiry. E Troeltsch, "Historical and Dogmatic Method in Theology", *Religion in History*, translated by J Luther Adams and W F Bense, (Edinburgh: T & T Clark, 1991), 11-32. The historical arena of the New Testament could not be exempted except on pain of *sacrificium intellectus*. These principles were respectively: the habituation on principle to historical criticism; analogy; and the mutual interrelation of all historical developments (correlation). Troeltsch's principle of analogy is a particular example of the concept of analogical reasoning Hume affirms as the basis for all experimental reasoning. According to Hume, theology had a basis in experience in so far as it had a basis in analogical reasoning, that is, in so far as it had a basis in replicable experience (ideally approximating to constant conjunction). Yet it is clear that Hume did not think this was true of theology; which is why he concluded that theology's "best and most solid foundation is faith and *divine* revelation" (i.e., a miracle, which by definition contradicts extremely well-established laws of constant conjunction). It may be thought that Barth took Hume's advice and founded his theology on faith and revelation in the sense of miracle *outside* the domain of Hume's "fork". But this is not what Barth did. Though he accepted Hume's view that, had the resurrection appearances been merely and (therefore) necessarily a nature-miracle,

comes to us as a *Novum* which, when it becomes an object for us, we cannot incorporate in the series of our other objects, cannot compare with them, cannot deduce from their context, cannot regard as analogous to them. It comes to us as a datum with no point of connexion with any other previous datum.[14]

Such a description of God's self-revelation constituted, for Barth, the essence of the strange new world within the Bible. God's self-revelation excluded the possibility of 'measuring God with our own measures, conceiving of God with our own conceptions, wishing of ourselves a God according to our own wishes'. The resurrection stories told their own detailed story in this respect. As Barth put it in *CD* IV/2, Jesus "can be perceived only as He comes [*Nur indem er kommt, wird er ihnen wahrnehmbar*]": God "can only be perceived as He comes."[15]

---

they would have belonged to the category Hume defines by the terms 'faith' and 'divine revelation', Barth is clear that miracle does not make *sui generis* historicality what it is. Barth, *CD* III/2, 451. It is not only that "the 'once' of this event differed absolutely" from our own history, it differed absolutely from "every other 'once'." *Ibid*, 454. This is why Barth asserts that a *sui generis* historical event is such that it is "beyond the reach of general polemics against the concept of miracle [such as Hume's] and indeed of general apologetics in favour of this concept", (*Ibid*, 451) even though a *sui generis* historical event would not be what it is in absence of miracle (*Ibid*, 451). To repeat: it is defined as a 'once' event that "differs absolutely" from every other 'once'. *Sui generis* historicality *is* outside the scope of analogical reasoning but this in itself does not entail that it takes the form of a miracle. Otherwise, this would be to define it negatively, in terms of the (suspension of the) laws of nature, and not positively, in terms of *sui generis* historicality. Hence, as was said in Chapter 6, Barth is not juxtaposing miracle to Troeltsch's principles. An event which is 'that which nothing analogous can be conceived' says nothing at all about miracle. It is not inconsistent with the concept but neither does it entail it. As was said before, to say that an event is designated by 'that than which a greater cannot be conceived' is not necessarily to say the event is a miracle. Barth is thus free to say it is not, for the reasons given above.

[14] *Ibid*, 172.

[15] Barth, *CD* IV/2, 144. As we will see, what Barth means is that we have no conception of *what it is* a perception of Jesus *revealing Himself as the crucified one* would be independently of the event itself. And this means that we have no conception of *what it is* Jesus *revealing Himself* as the crucified one would be independently of the event itself.

## 3. Literal Sense and *Sui Generis* Historicality:
## The *One* Resurrection Appearances-History

Was *sui generis* historicality what the historical truth-claiming narratives had claimed *contra* the Enlightenment and *contra* even the pre-critical tradition? Barth's exposition of the resurrection narratives is formally identical to his exposition of the creation narratives. Like the creation narratives, these narratives involve historical truth-claiming, literal sense and the final from of the text. And, to be sure, as in the creation narratives, Barth notes discrepancies and inconsistencies. Even within the confines of *each individual Gospel account of the resurrection-appearances history*, it is impossible, as Barth says, to isolate even a nucleus of history in the modern sense:

> It is clearly impossible to extract from the various accounts a nucleus of genuine history, quite apart from the intelligibility or otherwise of the resurrection itself. The statement in Acts. 1.3 to the effect that the appearances extended over forty days is obviously connected with the forty days of the flood (Gen. 7.4; cf. also Ez. 4.6; Jonah 3.4) and with the forty days of the temptation at the beginning of Jesus' ministry (Mt. 4.2; Lk. 4.2). [...] These parallels are sufficient to show that the forty days are not meant to be taken literally but typically. *They do not offer precise chronological information as to the duration of the appearances. The topography is just as vague. There is no clear dividing line between one scene and another, as a comparison of the various episodes will show* [my italics]. Nor do we have independent sources from which to check the evidence. Hence the harmonisations to which the older commentators resorted in an attempt to supply the deficiencies and clear up the obscurities, are almost amusingly incongruous. The narratives are not meant to be taken as "history" in our sense of the word. Even 1 Cor 14, 3-8 is treated in a strangely abstract way if it is regarded as a citation of witnesses for the purpose of historical proof. True, these accounts read very differently from myths. The Easter story is differentiated from myth, both formally and materially, by the fact that it is all about a real man of flesh and blood.[16]

To be sure, if one attempts to reconcile the apparent discrepancies and contradictions on the level of history in the ordinary sense the results are - as in the case of the creation narratives - "amusingly incongruous". Calvin's employment of synecdoche to reconcile what he took to be conflicting historical truth-claims as regards the number of angels present at the empty tomb, is one such example. Barth does not attempt to affirm the

---

[16] Barth, *CD* III/2, 452.

narratives as historical truth-claiming in the ordinary sense; therefore he does not feel obliged to "attempt to supply the deficiencies and clear up the obscurities." He affirmed the final form of the resurrection appearances narratives - as the canon has it in the four Gospels. He affirmed the literal sense of each pericope of each resurrection narrative; but he affirmed what he termed in his exegesis of the creation history the 'deep' literal sense of each pericope (not necessarily giving the same weight to each pericope). As a 'form-critic' of a more sophisticated kind, he took each pericope at literal face-value and rejected any attempt to arrange the stories "in one unbroken chain, or in a single picture" as in historical truth-claiming in the ordinary sense (hence, he rejected Calvin and Augustine). To sew the literal sense of each pericope into a larger garment of chronological and topographical coherence and continuity was at odds with the hermeneutics of the pericopes. They pointed toward what Barth understood as the 'deep' literal sense.

Barth's approach - undergirded by the motivation to resolve Overbeck's dilemma - was to affirm the final form of the literal sense at the level of *sui generis* historicality.[17] The "inwardly coherent" *sui generis* theological identity, the "higher harmony", the "common denominator" of the resurrection appearance stories coincides with the one resurrection-appearances history: *God* reveals Himself *through Himself* with the result that He reveals *Himself*, reveals *Himself* in this case, as was said in the previous chapter, as the Crucified One.[18] In *CD* IV/2 Barth observes of the resurrection stories that:

---

[17] In *The New Testament as Canon: An Introduction*, Brevard Childs prefaces his canonical solution to the problem of the harmony of the Gospels, with separate sections allocated respectively to pre-critical (e.g., Augustine, Calvin) and critical-historical (e.g., Weiss, C H Dodd) approaches to the question of harmonisation. Childs, *The New Testament as Canon: An Introduction*, 155-209. Indeed, on the specific question of harmonisation of the resurrection narratives, Childs allocates an additional section to the individual contribution Barth made to exegesis of the resurrection stories. *Ibid*, 199-209. Though Childs' analysis of Barth's exegesis does not coincide with (though it does not contradict) my analysis of Barth on this matter, I too have found it useful to compare Barth's exegesis with the other two approaches.

[18] The *sui generis* theological identity '*God* reveals Himself *through Himself* with the result that He reveals *Himself*' was central to Barth's position on epistemology. Not only did it mean corroborating the decision to read the resurrection stories for what they were saying in themselves; it confirmed that they were to be taken exactly as they were written, `gaps and all': imprecise "chronological information as to the duration of the appearances"; "topography" which is "just as vague"; "no clear dividing-line between one scene and another". What is from one perspective - the critical-historical perspective - a disjointed disjunctive corpus of stories, is, from another perspective - that of *sui generis* historicality - an entirely rational form.

The event [the resurrection and ascension] of Jesus Christ consisted in a series of concrete encounters and short conversations between the risen Jesus and his disciples. In the tradition these encounters are always described as self-manifestations of Jesus in the strictest sense of the term. In this context self-manifestation means (1) that the execution and termination as well as the initiative lie entirely in His own hands and not in theirs. Their reaction is a normal one but it is to an action in whose origination and accomplishment they have no part at all. They have really encountered their Lord. He controls them but they do not control Him. Self-manifestation means (2) that the meaning and purpose of these encounters consists simply and exhaustively in the fact that the risen Christ declares Himself to them in His identity with the One previously followed and who had died on the cross and been buried.[19]

Note that, in spite of the contradictions, discrepancies and inconsistencies Barth says that these encounters are "*always* [my italics] described as self-manifestations of Jesus in the strict sense of the term." That is, in spite of the difference in details the same theme occurs in each of the stories, each resurrection appearances pericope. The one historical event that is the resurrection-appearances history is a *sui generis* historical event. Barth identifies its content as '*God* reveals Himself *through Himself* with the result that He reveals *Himself*.' But whereas in the creation history *God* reveals Himself *through Himself* with the result that He reveals *Himself* as Creator, in the resurrection-appearances history, *God* reveals Himself *through Himself* with the result that He reveals *Himself* as Reconciler (in revealing Himself as the Crucified One). How so? In the remainder of this chapter I will focus on (1) alone. (2) will be the subject of Chapter 9. I do not mean to suggest that that (1) and (2) constitute separate events. They do not. '*God* reveals Himself *through Himself* with the result that He reveals *Himself*' is one event. There is no *God* revealing Himself *through Himself* that is not also God revealing *Himself*. There is no God revealing *Himself* that is not also *God* revealing Himself *through Himself*.

---

[19] Barth, *CD* IV/2, 143-144.

## 4. *God* Reveals Himself *Through Himself* with the Result that He Reveals *Himself*: *God* Reveals Himself *through Himself*

Self-manifestation means that the "execution and termination as well as the initiative lie entirely in His own hands and not in theirs. Their reaction is a normal one but it is to an action in whose origination and accomplishment they have no part at all." How does Barth justify this reading? He observes that:

> ... It is to be noted that we are nowhere told that the disciples sought, found, or even expected Jesus. But "Jesus came" (John 20.24). "Jesus Himself drew near and went with them" (Luke 24.15). He "met" the women (Matthew 28.9). He "stood in the midst of his disciples" (Luke 24.36; John 20.19,26). He "stood on the shore of the sea of Tiberias"(John 21.4). It is never explained where He came from or how He came (a point which is underlined by the mention of the closed doors in John 20.19, 26). He is always uninvited and unexpected. He really comes as a "thief in the night" (Matthew 24.43; 1 Thessalonians 5.2) .... The word ... used three times in 1 Corinthians 15.5f (and also in Luke 24.34) definitely means sensual perception. That is why we read in John 20.14 that Mary Magdalene "turned herself back and saw Jesus standing"; or in Matthew 28.17 that "they saw him". But again, his perception is not as simple as all that. He can be perceived only as He comes. And whether or not they see him effectively is not under their own control .... Jesus was certainly seen and heard by those who went to Emmaus, but at first he was not recognised as Jesus .... Even Mary Magdalene saw and heard Him without realising that it was Jesus (John 20.14). And the disciples by the sea-shore "knew not that it was Jesus" (John 21.4). [...] When their eyes are open, when there is the seeing and hearing of recognition ... (Luke 24.31); "We have seen the Lord" (John 20.25); "It is the Lord" (John 21.7) - the possibility and freedom for this always seemed to be given them by Jesus himself. Everywhere and especially in 1 Corinthians 15.5f it is finally presupposed that there is no longer any question of a continuous companionship of Jesus with his disciples, but always of individual encounters with them which he himself both began and terminated. In Luke 24.31 we are told that ... "He vanished out of their sight" and the ascension itself has this character of a termination of one of these encounters, the final one, and therefore of the whole event ... (Luke 24.51).[20]

Though Barth did not say it explicitly in IV/2, there is no doubt that the "inwardly coherent" *sui generis* theological identity of these particular

---

[20] *Ibid*, 144.

stories is: '*God* reveals Himself *through Himself*'. In particular, *origination* tells us that '*God* reveals Himself' (revealer) and *accomplishment* tells us that 'God reveals Himself *through Himself*' (revelation). No one else or other thing reveals God except Himself (e.g., not nature nor human beings) and it is through Himself that the act of revelation occurs.

As regards '*God* reveals Himself', we are "nowhere told that the disciples sought, found, or even expected Jesus" but rather that "Jesus came" (John 20.24). "Jesus Himself drew near and went with them" (Luke 24.15). He "met" the women (Matthew 28.9). He "stood in the midst of his disciples" (Luke 24.36; John 20.19,26). He "stood on the shore of the sea of Tiberias" (John 21.4). Yet though the narrative speaks of seeing *Jesus* - that Mary, for example, "turned round and saw Jesus standing" - perception of Jesus is never merely "as simple as" that obtained under the ordinary conditions of sense-perception. Jesus "can be perceived only as He comes. And whether or not they see him effectively is not under their own control": ".... Jesus was certainly seen and heard by those who went to Emmaus, but at first he was not recognised as Jesus .... Even Mary Magdalene saw and heard Him without realising that it was Jesus (John 20.14). And the disciples by the sea-shore "knew not that it was Jesus" (John 21.4) ... when their eyes are open, when there is the seeing and hearing of recognition ... (Luke 24.31); "We have seen the Lord" (John 20.25); "It is the Lord" (John 21.7)." In other words, the "possibility and freedom" for seeing Jesus as Jesus "always seemed to be given them by Jesus himself" - it is as if Mary would not recognise Jesus as Jesus unless he reveals himself - even were he standing there as himself for a substantial duration of time (and even though Mary is given the freedom to go to the limits of what is humanly possible in order to ascertain his identity). In other words, one seriously undermined the deep sense of the narrative details of the sense-perception of Jesus if one did not understand that their context must be one in which "the execution and termination as well as the initiative lie entirely in [Jesus'] own hands and not in theirs." '*God* reveals Himself' is the deep literal sense of these historical truth-claims. As regards God revealing Himself '*through Himself*' the deep literal sense corresponding to this historical truth-claim is that it is "never explained where He came from or how He came (a point which is underlined by the mention of the closed doors in John 20.19, 26).

But in what precise sense do such narrative details correspond to *sui generis* historicality, to the concept of an event whose only means of measurement is it itself? The first moment of '*God* revealing Himself *through Himself*' with the result that He reveals *Himself* - God revealing Himself *through Himself* - is crucial to the *sui generis* historicality of the resurrection-appearances history. It is because of this that the distinction between on the one hand *the means of measurement* and on the other *the object of measurement* plays a crucial explanatory role in elucidating the *sui generis* historicality of the resurrection-appearances stories, and, in particular, his resolution of the meaning and significance of two paradigmatic resurrection appearances stories, Luke 24.15-31 and John 20.14-16. As in the Reformed tradition, Barth's conception of the means of measurement is a metaphorical one. But there is a vital difference between his and the Reformed tradition's 'measure of faith'. It resides in the fact that the latter's 'measure of faith' was essentially a pre-existing means of measurement against which to measure meaning or truth. Barth's was not; and the reason it was not was because the strange new world within the Bible constituted 'an object of measurement' whose only means of measurement was it itself. In other words, according to Barth, *the means of measurement for measuring Jesus Christ's self-revelation could not be had independently of the object of measurement itself, could not be had without the object of measurement itself, without Jesus Christ's self-revelation itself.* This was not true of the earlier Reformed tradition, and of Calvin's exegesis of the resurrection narratives in particular: as will be seen, the latter's exegesis assumed the existence of a prior means of measurement as regards Jesus' self-revelation. It is in this sense that one can say that the position of Calvin and the Reformed tradition in general did not suffice to repudiate Kant's in *Religion Within the Limits of Reason Alone.*

The position on epistemology Barth derived from the resurrection stories implied the following features. First, excepting a "tiny historical margin" - the reference to the empty tomb - the resurrection appearances stories *do not describe actual historical occurrences.*[21] Barth broke with the pre-

---

[21] I do not think there is any doubt about this. See, for example, Barth, *CD* I/1, 327-329. See, in particular, Barth, *CD* III/2, 452: "... the evidence for the resurrection can only be fragmentary and contradictory, as is actually the case in the New Testament. Compare, for example, the Matthean and Lukan accounts or the Synoptic accounts as a whole, with that of John; or again, all the Gospel accounts with that of 1 Cor. 15. It is clearly impossible to extract from the various accounts a nucleus of genuine history, quite apart from the intelligibility or otherwise of the resurrection itself. The statement in Ac. 1.3 to the effect that the appearances extended over forty days is obviously connected with the forty days of the flood (Gen. 7.4; cf. also Ez. 4.6; Jonah 3.4) and with the forty days of the temptation at the beginning of Jesus' ministry (Mt. 4.2; Lk. 4.2). [...] These parallels are sufficient to show that the forty days are not meant to be taken literally but typically." Nevertheless, Barth concludes that: "There can be no doubt that all these [resurrection] narratives are about the same event, and that they are agreed in substance, intention and interpretation. [...] Each is a specific witness to the decisive things God said and did in this event. And we can be glad that there is the possibility of adducing one [biblical passage] in explanation of the others. `*Egenomen nekros kai idou zon*` (Rev 1.18) - it is here that all these very saga-like accounts have their common ground. This, and this alone, is what they tell us." *Ibid.,* 452. In other words, notwithstanding the discrepancies, the details of the stories - all of them - say something specific that adds to the *substance* of the stories, which is one and the same.

critical tradition of interpretation in this sense. Second, the stories are *a product of imagination and intuition* - except for the "tiny historical margin".[22] But that they are a product of imagination and intuition, rather than a description of actual historical occurrences, is precisely because their subject-matter is *an event whose only means of measurement is it itself*.[23] Third, according to Barth, such a *theological realism* emerges from the narratives when the literal details of each Gospel are synthesised at a level other than a simple historical one; when the literal details are synthesised at a higher 'theological' level. Such a synthesis or *Aufhebung* - coinciding with the "common denominator" of the stories - enabled Barth to side with

---

[22] The details of the stories themselves do not describe actual historical occurrences. What then is their rationale? The details of the stories serve a distinctive theological realism. But the details themselves are the product of *imagination and intuition*. See *CD* III/1, 82-83, 91-92; *CD* III/3, 374-377. The ultimate measure of the truth of the Bible is not at the mercy of reliable historical report - as the practitioners of the critical-historical method maintained; rather, it is in the hands of the 'faculty' of imagination and intuition (except, as was said, the tiny historical margin that is the empty tomb). This was not the great tragedy that it might seem to the modern mind. First, Barth distinguished, as Kant and Coleridge had before him, between imagination and fancy, or fantasy. The products of the latter were essentially substitute objects for old emotions, compliant to our emotional demands. Fantasy posited what one wished to believe; some sceptics would claim that such wishful thinking was the motivation behind the stories of Jesus' appearances after his death. Barth did not understand the Evangelists' stories as the product of fantasy or wishful thinking; rather, the form and content of the products of imagination and intuition are guided by and therefore originate in an 'object' whose only criterion is it itself (the theological realism peculiar to the strange new world within the Bible). *That, according to Barth, is why the stories originate in the 'faculty' of intuition and imagination, and not in historical description.*

[23] Ultimately, what Barth discovered in the resurrection-appearances history exemplified that which he had asserted of the creation history, namely that its "standpoint, presentation and depiction rests on a very different possibility from the account which rests on perception and concept [*Anschauung und Begriff*], and which in the region of perception and concept deduces, compares, co-ordinates, and in this way demonstrates. This other possibility, in virtue of which 'non-historical' and 'pre-historical' history can also be recognised and presented, is that of ... poetical historical saga." Barth, *CD* III/1, 82. Kant - against whom this passage is obviously directed and whose language it uses - presumed that all areas of (theoretical) rational enquiry involved comparison with an already pre-existing immanent measure of *what it is* one was measuring for truth or falsity. But, according to Barth, the depiction of the strange new world within the Bible was not based on an immanent measure. Its depiction had originated in an event whose only comparison could be with it itself. Hence, one had no concept against which to measure what had occurred, for example, in Jesus Christ's resurrection-appearances history. What the New Testament writers had spoken of in their intuitive, poetic and imaginative depiction of Jesus Christ's resurrection appearances was a resurrection-appearances history whose key property was that it constituted an event of which the only measure was it itself.

pre-critical interpretation in its attempt to maintain all the details of the resurrection stories in 'one harmonious story' - but without affirming them as actual historical occurrences in the ordinary sense. These three characteristics, as we will see, are in evidence in Barth's treatment of Luke 24.15-31 and John 20.14-16.

The paradigm-cases of Barth's understanding of the resurrection-appearances history are: Luke 24.15-31 (the Emmaus story); John 20.14-16 (Mary Magdalene's encounter with Jesus); and John 21.4-14 (the disciples' encounter with Jesus on the shore of Galilee). For the purposes of my exposition I will discuss the first two examples only.

In Luke 24.15 we are told "Jesus Himself drew near and went with them." As Barth puts it: "Jesus was certainly seen and heard by those who went to Emmaus, but at first he was not recognised as Jesus."[24] Subsequently, recognition comes when Jesus breaks bread. Barth describes the words of 24.30 - "as he sat at with them, he took bread, and blessed it, and brake, and gave to them" (Luke 24.30) as follows: "But even to the very words and order this is exactly what had happened at the last supper and the earlier feeding of the five and four thousand."[25]

In John 20.14-16 we are told that Mary Magdalene "turned herself back and saw Jesus standing, but she did not know that it was Jesus." As Barth puts it: "Even Mary Magdalene saw and heard Him without realising that it was Jesus."[26] We are then told that Jesus said to her: "Woman, why are you weeping?" Whom do you seek?" Mary, supposing him to be the gardener said to him: "Sir, if you have carried him away, tell me where you have laid him, and I will take him away." Jesus said to her: "Mary." Mary turns and says to him: "Rabboni!" Barth's comment is: "Mary Magdalene recognises him simply by the fact - obviously not for the first time - He calls her by her name (John 20.16)."[27]

---

[24] Barth, *CD* IV/2, 144.

[25] *Ibid*, 145.

[26] *Ibid*, 144.

[27] *Ibid*, 145. What in fact Barth discerns in Luke 24.13-31 and John 20.14-16 is a particular, though undoubtedly the prototypical, instantiation of the *terminus a quo* of '*God reveals Himself through Himself* with the result that He reveals *Himself*', that is, the instantiation of God as revealer. Barth discerns, as was said, the same in John 21.4-14. But there are, according to Barth, other less paradigmatic instantiations of this *terminus a quo*, for example, in Luke 24.36-42, John 20.24-29, and Matthew 28.17. In these passages the irreducible thematic relation between Jesus initiating recognition and initial non-recognition is replaced by the irreducible thematic relation between, on the one hand, Jesus being exclusively responsible for recognition, and, on the other, this recognition being preceded by "doubt in the seeing and hearing". That is to say, according to Barth, the literary *raison d'etre* of "doubt even in the seeing and hearing" lies again in the fact that only Jesus himself can bring around recognition. Barth, *CD* IV/2, 144. This irreducible relation is the "common denominator" of all the stories.

What Barth discerns in these stories is this. It is not merely that the witnesses do not recognise Jesus; it is that the witnesses do not recognise Jesus when Jesus first presents himself as *himself*, that is, when he presents himself, not in disguise or in the form of someone else, but as himself. Jesus is as objectively in front of the witnesses as Himself (both visually and aurally) before recognition as he is at the moment of his recognition. The strange yet (Barth would say) systematic phenomenon emerges that *Jesus' initial appearances do not coincide with his self-revelation.*

To be sure, though the most straight-forward historical narrative would have been an account in which Jesus is recognised immediately whenever he is present (a hundred per cent correlation) and therefore when he is first present, it would not necessarily follow that one in which he is not so recognised could not be a historical account in the ordinary sense. The aim of Calvin's exegesis, for example, is to show that the story - even with this characteristic - be understood as narrating actual historical occurrences. Since Calvin's purpose is to ensure that all of the Gospels is history in the ordinary sense, he is determined to explain this phenomenon in terms of a causal interaction of natural and supernatural history. Accordingly, he explained the failure of both the Emmaus disciples and of Mary to recognise Jesus in terms of a failure of normal sensory capacity. Since Calvin believed that normal sensory capacity originated at all times in God himself, he explained the witnesses' failure to recognise Jesus in terms of God's temporary suspension of normal sensory capacity.[28] To be sure, though the later perspective of Ernst Troeltsch's three principles governing historical methodology (analogy, correlation, habituation) ruled out the supernatural component of Calvin's extra-literary supernatural apologetic (though not natural apologetic of this kind), it remained the case that the meaning of the narratives was such that the Evangelists are to be taken as relating history in the ordinary sense of the term.

Taking them to be formally descriptive of history in the ordinary sense, Calvin attempted, as Augustine had before him, to reconcile the discrepancies existing in the Gospels: if one could have the reality only under the description provided by each Gospel, it followed that the Gospels *in toto* described a harmonious reality. Consequently, one had to find a way of showing that this was true *without eliminating the truth of any sentence of any Gospel*. Such was the aim of Calvin's harmonisation. Yet, clearly, Calvin's attempt was entirely compatible with seeking to explain the facts of the Bible in causal terms; indeed, that the attempt was itself a consequence of the

---

[28] See: Calvin, *A Harmony of the Gospels: Matthew, Mark and Luke*, vol III, translated by A W Morrison, edited by David W Torrance and Thomas F Torrance, (Edinburgh: St Andrews Press, 1972), 232-233; Calvin, *The Gospel According to St John, 11-21*, translated by T H L Parker, edited by David W Torrance and Thomas F Torrance, (Edinburgh: Oliver and Boyd, 1961), 197-198.

primacy of the biblical world over any other world made this inevitable. Though Calvin can ask, 'Why did the Evangelist tell us that 'Mary did not recognise Jesus?', he does not consider for a moment that the answer is not 'This is what happened.' For Calvin, what remains a matter for explanation is the indisputable facts to which the biblical statements refer. He is motivated to answer the question, 'Why did Mary not recognise Jesus?'; hence, his answer is in terms of impaired sensory capacity.

Now, as we have seen, Barth's approach was qualitatively different from both pre-critical and critical interpretation. Though Barth shared pre-critical hermeneutics' - and especially Calvin's - concern for a literal reading of the Gospels, he did not derive a synthesis that incorporated all the details of each Gospel in such a way that the synthesis referred to *a unity of actual historical occurrences in the ordinary sense*. To be sure, he retained a literal reading that incorporated all the details of each Gospel. But he did not 'keep all the notes on board the harmony' by synthesising the literal detail at the level of ordinary historical occurrence. The harmony Barth discovered in the Bible, and in the Gospel narratives in particular, was, as was said in Chapter 5, a synthesis - *Aufhebung* - at the level of *sui generis* historicality. Though Barth shares with Calvin the objective of synthesis without discarding literal detail, he does not share with the latter the objective of synthesis at the level of history in the ordinary sense; he seeks synthesis at a different, higher, *sui generis* theological level. *This fact is of great significance in explaining Barth's account of the Easter pericopes in question.*

Like Calvin, Barth discerns, and is motivated to explain, the fact of the Evangelist telling us that Jesus is as objectively there as Himself during or at the time of non-recognition as he is at the moment of recognition, between before and after, as it were (Jesus' resurrection appearances prior to recognition are identical to Jesus' resurrection appearances at the moment of recognition). But though Barth, like Calvin, rejected the explanation of an alteration in Jesus' form (either visually or aurally),[29] his rationale was not that there was another causal explanation superior to this particular one. Barth rejected the very rationale behind the concept of a causal explanation. This rationale was precisely the presumption that the details of the story described actual historical occurrences. For Barth, the details of these pericopes do not testify to historical fact; rather, they attest to the fact that, as was said, Jesus Christ's self-revelation 'can be defined only in terms of its own object.' There is only a "tiny 'historical' margin" in the stories *in toto*, namely the empty tomb, and that "margin" is 'historical' only in the sense described in the next chapter: the empty tomb is a historical event only insofar as it is a logical corollary of - follows from - Jesus Christ's self-revelation itself. It has no 'empirical' status in its own right.

---

[29] Calvin, *A Harmony of the Gospels*, vol III, 232; *The Gospel According to St John, 11-21*, 197.

Like Calvin, Barth affirmed that the Evangelists intended the stories to be read in the literal sense; unlike Calvin, he did not draw the conclusion that the details of the stories described actual historical occurrences. It is precisely because the stories accord with the *sui generis* theological identity, '*God* reveals Himself *through Himself* with the result that He reveals *Himself*', that they originate in imagination and intuition. Such an identity cannot be instantiated in history in the ordinary sense. For Barth, the theological realism of the resurrection narratives is not to be identified with actual historical occurrences as depicted in the details of the resurrection stories. To reiterate: theological realism as regards the resurrection narratives is to be identified with the *one* resurrection-appearances history, '*God* reveals Himself *through Himself* with the result that He reveals *Himself*'. Where, for Calvin, the object of explanation is the indisputable 'first-order' fact, for Barth the object of explanation is the so-called 'second-order' textual object itself. But since he explains this object in terms of *a theological realism peculiar to the strange new world within the Bible*, Barth is not in any sense an adherent to the twentieth-century movement of post-modern 'textuality.'[30]

In Calvin's exegesis, the 'norm' against which the actual story is measured is the historical occurrence in which Jesus is recognised immediately as the one he had been in his pre-Easter history. Accordingly, the change from non-recognition to recognition has to be accounted for in terms of, and therefore accompanied by, a parallel change or adjustment in the causal chain: something had to have changed somewhere. For Barth the solution of the problem lies elsewhere. The synthesis - *Aufhebung* - of the story lies at a different, higher, level. According to Calvin, Mary had a 'measure of Jesus' originating in the pre-Easter Jesus, in the one historical pre-Easter Jesus described in the four Gospels. Hence, the question he implicitly asked is: Why did Mary not recognise Jesus when she first encountered Him? Calvin answered in terms of a divine intervention, a deviation from the normal course of events. For Barth, on the other hand, *the initial failure of recognition is part of 'the normal course of events'*.[31] It is only to be understood within the context of a self-revelation whose only means of measurement is it itself; hence it only occurs in Luke and John (and Barth would say, *can* only occur) as part of an irreducible thematic relation.

---

[30] See Chapter 10 for further objections to a post-modern interpretation of Barth.

[31] For Calvin, and pre-critical interpretation in general, the event of Jesus Christ's self-revelation is within the reach of immanent reason: that the witnesses do not recognise Jesus because of impaired sensory capacity implies that, had they been in possession of normal capacity, they *would* have recognised Jesus. For Barth, the story is not meant to 'work' on the plane of immanent reason at all. The point of the story is that Jesus' self-revelation as God is beyond the measure of immanent reason; hence it is not appropriate to invoke causal (immanent) factors in explanation. For Barth, Calvin's 'naturalistic' assumptions are irrelevant to exegesis.

That Jesus is not recognised as himself when he is, to all intents and purposes, in front of the witnesses as himself serves to show that, *even, or more accurately, precisely, in the limiting case where Jesus is there as himself* - even then - *unless Jesus takes the initiative* - reveals Himself - there is no *possibility* of recognition.[32] This is the deep literal sense of the stories. To reiterate: it is not merely that Jesus is not recognised; it is that he is not recognised when he is there as *himself*. Not only is it "never explained where He came from or how He came"; it is never explained *how he reveals Himself*. The answer is of course that, in the revealed being of God, He reveals Himself *through Himself*.

To repeat: even, or more accurately, precisely, *in the limiting case where Jesus is there are himself* - even then - unless Jesus takes the initiative - reveals Himself - there is no possibility of recognition. Hence, to imagine the non-recognition detail outside the context of Jesus' self-revelation is to miss the real historical point at stake. To conceive the thematic relation as reducible to two logically independent historical truth-claims was *ipso facto* to deny that one was dealing with an event whose only means of measurement is it itself. More importantly, it was to affirm two historical truth-claims each of which corresponded to a pre-existent measure.[33] In effect,

---

[32] What Barth has to say of the empty tomb may be of some relevance to this point: "The Easter story is not for nothing the story whose most illuminating moment according to the account of Mark's Gospel consists in the inconceivable fact of an empty sepulchre, a fact which ... lays hold of the three woman disciples and reduces them to complete silence; for they told no one about it ... (Mk. 16.8). Everything else related by this story can be heard and believed in the very literalness in which it stands, but can really only be believed, because it drops out of all categories and so out of all conceivability." Barth, *CD* I/2, 115. Barth continues later: "The difficulty of grasping how [the recollection of the New Testament witnesses] was created, a difficulty which manifestly goes back to the fact that the New Testament witnesses themselves scarcely found language (and did not find it at all at the critical point) to transmit this recollection - this difficulty relates to the uniqueness of that to which their recollection is related, that which they manifestly had to say, and which manifestly had to be said." *Ibid*, 115.

[33] One might say that, had the Evangelists used imagination and intuition to depict the recognition of Jesus in terms of a scene in which Jesus' initial appearance corresponded to simple immediate recognition, *it would naturally have been assumed that the witnesses of the resurrection appearances had possessed the means of measurement prior to their encounter with Jesus' revelation of Himself*. It was crucial that it be inferred from the story that the witnesses did not - could not - have had the means of measurement for measuring Jesus Christ's self-revelation independently of Jesus' self-revelation itself. This might well have been the inference had the reader encountered an immediate recognition scene: to the reader the witnesses would have appeared to have had a means of measurement prior to Jesus' self-revelation. In the event of such an interpretation, the one resurrection-appearances history would be construed as a unique, implicitly miraculous, historical event; it would not be construed as an "absolutely different from every other 'once'" event, which

Barth's claim of *sui generis* historicality committed him to a particular position on the history of Gospel tradition, *namely, that the motif of initial non-recognition had never at any time existed outside the context of the theme of Jesus initiating recognition.* Instead, the former had received its literary *raison d'être* from the latter. *That is to say, the two 'elements' not only constituted an independent unit, complete in itself, as form-critics held, they also stood in an irreducible thematic relation, one to the other.* Such literary dependence would not have been the case had both details described actual historical occurrences; for in that case an 'atomic' one-to-one mapping would have prevailed between description and reality such that one could conceive of one event (non-recognition) happening but not the other (recognition). The rationale behind Barth's partial approval of form-criticism was that, in contradistinction to cruder forms of historical criticism, the former was sensitive to the heterogeneous literary forms within the text itself, in particular, within the Gospels themselves. That is to say, it took the "objectivity of the New Testament seriously .... the *form* [my italics] of the witness corresponding to that objectivity."[34] In particular, unlike historical criticism, form-criticism did not necessarily insist that the Gospel narratives affirmed a 'one-to-one' mapping between 'atomic' historical assertions and reality; unlike historical criticism, it was open to the possibility of irreducible thematic relations; finally, unlike historical criticism, it avoided the assumption that the form of the witness should be treated homogeneously, as

---

is to say, it would not be construed as an event whose only means of measurement is it itself. Jesus Christ's self- revelation would not be understood as being 'definable only in terms of its own object.' Accordingly, instead of Jesus' Easter recognition being in terms of immediate recognition, it is characterised in terms of an *irreducible thematic relation*, an irreducible thematic 'compound' relation between two 'elemental' details.[33] I am not necessarily claiming that the evangelists explicitly thought in this way. I am simply stating their position counterfactually - what would have been the case had the resurrection stories been speaking of a historical event assimilable to the critical-historical method. For evidence that it is not an implausible deduction to make, I refer you to Erhardt Güttgemanns, *Candid Questions Concerning Gospel Form Criticism: A Methodological Sketch of the Fundamental Problematics of Form and Redaction Criticism*, translated by William G Doty (Pittsburgh: Pickwick Press, 1979), chs. 7 and 8. In these chapters Güttgemanns refers to Johann Gottfried Herder's and Wilhelm von Humboldt's insight that the conversion of an earlier oral tradition into a written form brought in its wake two connected phenomena. The first was that the naturalness and spontaneity intrinsic to the oral 'folk' form was lost. The second was that this loss was compensated for by the imposition of reason on, and hence the emergence of the true rational form from, the earlier oral tradition. Moreover, if Meir Sternberg is right, one lesson to be derived from his book is not to underestimate - or second-guess - the sophistication of the evangelists' employment of literary devices as regards the historical truth-claim they wish to make. See Meir Sternberg, *The Poetics of Biblical Narrative*.
[34] Barth, *CD* I/2, 493-494.

historical reference. Though it is easier to conceive the Emmaus story than the Jesus-Mary Magdalene story as a 'one-to-one' mapping between detail and reality, the form-critical studies of Rudolf Bultmann and Martin Dibelius had concluded that the Emmaus story had never existed in any form other than as the story it is. Martin Dibelius argued that we have the Emmaus story in its "pure [i.e., original] form."[35] Bultmann, under the influence of Gunkel, took the view that the story "had the character of a true legend." The implication is that the story was conceived according to its present form.[36] And even V Taylor's judgement that Luke did "not leave the Emmaus story as he found it" is not inconsistent with the existence of the irreducible relation in question since the part of the story that Luke did "not leave alone" is not this relation.[37]

*Nevertheless, though Barth would have agreed with those form-critics who argued that the stories did not originate in actual historical occurrences, he would have disagreed with the conclusion that their origin was exclusively to be sought in a particular faith-determined* sitz im leben; *rather, the rationale behind the irreducible thematic relation - indicative of the fact that the non-recognition motif had never at any time existed outside the context of the theme of Jesus initiating recognition - was to affirm that Jesus' self-revelation was a 'measure of faith' whose only measure was it itself. That such a theme - pattern - can be discerned across the Gospels provided, for Barth, reinforcement for the following position: notwithstanding the emphasis that each individual redactor would give to each detail of their respective stories, in terms of topography and personnel, etc., a 'point of view of the whole' emerges from the stories. This 'point of view of the whole' is precisely that indicated above: an event whose only means of measurement is it itself corresponding to* sui generis *historicality,* 'that which nothing analogous can be conceived.'

The crucial import of such *sui generis* historicality is this: *one cannot have the means of measurement for measuring Jesus Christ's self-revelation independently of the object of measurement itself, without Jesus Christ's self-revelation itself. This is because there is no criterion of measurement other than the object of measurement itself. This in turn implies that there is no human capacity for knowledge of what it is Jesus' self-revelation is independently of the event itself.* The conceptual point of comparison against which to measure the truth of God's self-revelation originates in God's self-revelation and nowhere else, not, therefore, in an immanent 'measure of the divine', which latter Calvin's exegesis implicitly affirms. The norm - the *analogia fidei* - against which the truth of the story is to be measured is

[35] Martin Dibelius, *From Tradition to Gospel*, trans. Bertram Lee Woolf (London: Ivor Nicholson and Watson, 1934), 56.
[36] Bultmann, *History of the Synoptic Tradition*, trans. John Marsh (Oxford: Blackwell, 1968), 89-93.
[37] Vincent Taylor, *The Formation of the Gospel Tradition* (London: MacMillan, 1933), 71.

precisely an 'object of knowledge' which 'can be defined only in terms of itself', a 'measure of faith' whose only measure is it itself.[38] To repeat: the

---

[38] For Barth, the *one* resurrection-appearances history - *God* reveals Himself *through Himself* with the result that He reveals *Himself* - constitutes the means of measurement, the 'measure of faith', not merely of the truth of the Christian story, but also of *what it is* God's revelation is. The concept of a 'measure of faith' (in the genitive appositive sense) is uniquely suited to reconciling the differences between, on the one hand, those interpretations which utilise the concept of 'narrative' realism as the key to Barth, and, on the other, those interpretations which insist on Scripture as witness to "the absolute act of God's self-manifestation in free grace", or as Bruce McCormack calls it, "an absolute act of divine self-positing." McCormack, Review of *Barth's Ethics of Reconciliation* by John Webster", *The Scottish Journal of Theology* (49) 4, 274. Hans Frei claimed that though "there was no break, no sharp rupture, or later retraction between the methodological introduction and the subsequent content of the *Church Dogmatics*: "... Barth's vision and statement of the world of discourse of which he was rendering an account became increasingly and self-consciously temporal rather than cognitivist. It was a world in which time elapsed, and that was of its very essence, so that he had both to proceed diachronically in describing it and take temporality into account in articulating the most appropriate and least distorting methods. He no longer saw the whole range of divine human commerce, as it is described in the language of the Church, simply under the auspices of an 'act' of divine self-projection together with its fit apprehension ('revelation')." Frei, *Types of Christian Theology*, edited by G Hunsinger (New Haven: Yale University Press, 1992), 159-160. For McCormack, for example, this "act" is obviously crucial; yet, according to Frei, Barth shifted his attention toward 'narrative' time and, in the process, became less preoccupied with a *Realdialektik* of veiling and unveiling. But, in fact, Barth's exegesis of the resurrection narratives incorporates a crucial reference to the earlier 'cognitivist' concerns of I/1 and II/1. The literary fact of, for example, Jesus revealing who He is to the Emmaus witnesses after some time in their company, *then* disappearing immediately from their midst - that, on the one hand, the witnesses do not recognise Him during all the time He is with them, and, on the other, that as soon as they do He withdraws Himself from them - this narrative fact is of great importance in defining the 'cognitivist' dimension of the 'measure of faith.' In incorporating the valid concerns of the 'cognitivist' interpretation, the narrative or 'story' approach is able to provide a valid conceptual bridge between the two schools of thought. Nevertheless, it is the discovery of the strange new world within the Bible and not merely the discovery of narrative *per se* that ultimately drives Barth's theology. Indeed, it is a mistake to speak of Barth's 'narrative' realism. Barth's endorsement of the literal sense of the narrative does not entail that he located realism at the level of the details of the narrative, that he affirmed a one-to-one correspondence between detail and reality. Although the *sui generis* theological identity of each 'inhabitant' of the strange new world within the Bible is discovered in the details of the narrative, that identity is not identical with the literal sense of the details themselves. The means of measurement, the measure of faith, is not to be found in the details themselves; rather it is to be found in the theological realism posited by the strange new world within the Bible, pre-eminently in the *one* resurrection appearances story: '*God* reveals Himself *through Himself* with the result that He reveals *Himself*.' It is this 'measure of faith' that Barth juxtaposes to Kant's 'immanent measure.'

biblical witness avoided positing an immediate recognition scene because it would have been inferred by its readers to mean that the witnesses possessed the means of measurement for measuring Jesus' self-revelation prior to the event itself. Such ownership *would* have been the norm in an account professing to be a simple historical report. In the case of such an account the means of measurement would exist independently of the object of measurement. But in the case of the resurrection-appearances history - in the case of '*God* reveals Himself *through Himself* with the result that he reveals *Himself* - it does not. It is in this sense that the distinction between on the one hand *the means of measurement* and on the other *the object of measurement* plays a crucial explanatory role in Barth's epistemology. It explains the implications of an event whose only means of measurement is it itself.

If Jesus Christ's self-revelation is an event whose only means of measurement is it itself then it follows that *the possibility of recognition must originate in Jesus alone*: "When their eyes are opened, when there is the seeing and hearing of recognition - 'We have seen the Lord' (Jn 20.25); 'It is the Lord' (Jn 21.7) - the possibility and freedom for this always seem to be given them by Jesus himself."[39] If Jesus Christ's self-revelation is an event whose only means of measurement is it itself then it follows that: "He can be perceived only as He comes."[40] That is to say, *contra* Kant's position that an immanent measure constituted a necessary condition of recognition, reason "must wait the arrival of" Jesus Christ's self-revelation, "which must be added beyond its capacity, without reason being permitted to know in what it consists, from the supernatural helping hand of heaven". Barth did not, I think, understand the phrase "supernatural helping hand of heaven" literally (as Calvin, I think, would have); for him it meant precisely that any possibility on our part for knowledge of God had to originate in God. Hence, for Barth, a rational *sui generis* theological identity can be attributed to the fact that Jesus is as objectively in front of the witnesses (as the person they had encountered in the previous history of his passion and crucifixion) at the moment of non-recognition as he is at the moment of recognition without, and indeed *in virtue of not, invoking external naturalistic or supernaturalistic causal apologetic.* That is to say, the story as saga is complete in itself; it does not require to be supplemented by causal apologetic; to add to an already complete story is act of 'literary violation'. The rationale behind the literary fact of non-recognition is that Jesus' revelation of *Himself* (as God) can be measured only in terms of itself. Neither we nor the original witnesses have the means of measurement of *what it is* God revealing *Himself* is, independently of *God* revealing Himself *through Himself*, independently of the object of measurement itself - Jesus Christ's self-revelation. That is to say, the Church past, present and future does not have, nor did the original witnesses have, a measure of *what it*

---

[39] *Ibid*, 144.
[40] Barth, *CD* IV/2, 144.

*is* God revealing *Himself* is, independently of *God* revealing Himself *through Himself*. To repeat: the latter can be measured only in terms of itself.

*The theological realism peculiar to the strange new world within the Bible is a realism whose cardinal defining property is that it constitutes a criterion or measure whose only criterion or measure is it itself. It can, as it were, only be measured against itself.* Hence, one cannot have the means of measurement for measuring Jesus Christ's self-revelation independently of the object of measurement, Jesus Christ's self-revelation itself. In order to conceive of the possibility of not(*God's* revelation) there had to be a criterion of *what it is God's* revelation is against which to measure *what it is* one conceived was not the case. But this could be given only by Jesus' self-revelation, God's self-revelation.[41]

*Implicit in Barth's theological realism is an argument of rational philosophical status.* If revelation is the unique source and norm of knowledge of God, any such valid conceptual measure must originate in God's self-revelation itself. Consequently, if there is any valid conceptual point of comparison at all - any conceptual measure at all - it must of necessity *originate* in the resurrection-appearances history itself. Judgement and reality had to fit one another for the simple reason that the means of making the judgement - the *Maß Gottes* - had originated in God's self-revelation. One could never occupy a position where one could decide for or against, or even remain agnostic about, *God's* revelation independently of, and hence prior to, *God's* revelation itself. How could one ever be in a position where one decided whether *God's* revelation took place? For against which measure was one measuring *God's* revelation? There was no measure

---

[41] That knowledge of God must be bound to revelation if it is to be at all possible, that it cannot take place outside of revelation explains why Barth introduces a subtle nuance into an assertion he makes at the end of *CD* II/1, 25.1: "It is quite essential to this human position of the knowledge of God bound to the Word of God [Jesus Christ] that it cannot let its reality or possibility be questioned from without, that it can reply only by a reference to its fulfilment [*nur mit dem Hinweis auf ihren Vollzug*] or rather only by the fulfilment itself, allowing the actuality to speak for itself [*oder vielmehr nur mit ihrem Vollzug selbst antworten, das sie nach aussen nur ihre eigene Tatsachlichkeit fur sich selber sprechen lassen kann*]." Barth, *CD* II/1, 30. Not only can we not allow revelation to be questioned from without, even from within we cannot "refer to its fulfilment". To assert that one can "reply only by such a reference" would insinuate a pre-existing knowledge of *what it is God's* revelation is, is an immanent measure. Hence Barth revises his position, preferring to speak only of the fulfilment itself, allowing the actuality speak for itself. This is the fundamental rationale behind Barth's description of John the Baptist "pointing in an almost impossible way" to Jesus Christ in Grünewald's Isenheim altar-piece painting. To repeat: since to "refer to its fulfilment" implied an immanent measure, Barth asserts that we can only really "allow the actuality to speak for itself." The latter is consistent with the view that the measure of faith originates in revelation alone.

against which one could establish (justify) or criticise *God's* revelation, other than that which had originated in *God's* self-revelation itself. To reiterate: in order to conceive of the possibility of not(*God's* self-revelation) there had to be a criterion of *what it is God's* self-revelation is against which to measure *what it is* one conceived was not the case. That is the position in which the Bible, and the strange new world within the Bible, puts us. In such a position, our critical-historical cognitive powers are, for an entirely rational reason, to no avail. Barth's position on epistemology was truly inspired by a 'Reformed Reformation' vision in that it transposed the principle of 'justification by faith alone' to the realm of epistemology.

Let me recapitulate briefly Kant's position in *Religion Within the Limits of the Reason alone*. Kant objects to the possibility of theoretical knowledge of God's revelation for the same reason he objects to the classical proofs for the existence of God in the *Critique of Pure Reason*. In *Religion Within the Limits of Reason Alone* Kant asserts that there can be no empirical criterion against which to measure God's revelation. But the reason that there is no such measure is precisely because no measure originating in the *a priori* theoretical categories of the understanding can constitute a measure of *what it is* God is. Hence, given that any rational measure of God's revelation must be an immanent measure of the divine, such a measure must originate in an ideal of pure reason 'within ourselves'. As Barth puts Kant's position: man "has to be in a position to measure the God who is, perhaps, proclaimed to him, or who, perhaps, even reveals himself to him, against an ideal construction which he has set up for himself, in order (it is surely only thus that it is possible!) to recognise the former as God."[42]

The rationale behind Barth's reaction to Kant's insistence on an 'immanent measure of the divine' is as follows. Barth agrees with Kant that the synthetic *a priori* categories are unable to recognise God as God. But his response to Kant on this matter is ironic. Of course the synthetic *a priori* categories are unable to recognise God's self-revelation as God's self-revelation.[43] *This is what is to be expected given that God's self-revelation is precisely an event whose only means of measurement is it itself, a 'measure of faith' (in the genitive appositive sense) whose only measure is it itself.* Such an event cannot be apprehended or perceived within the 'epistemic' boundary set by the synthetic *a priori* categories. But neither can it be apprehended or perceived by - measured against - an ideal of pure reason. In other words, according to Barth, an ideal of pure reason fares no better than the *a priori* categories as a measure of God's self-revelation. For

---

[42] Barth, *PT*, 282.

[43] It is perhaps anachronistic to speak of Kant measuring God's self-revelation since the concept of self-revelation is a later development. See McCormack, *Karl Barth's Critically Realistic Dialectical Theology*, 359. But the point I make remains valid.

if God's self-revelation is an event whose only criterion is it itself then *no* immanent measure can provide a valid measure of *what it is* God's self-revelation is. Therefore, it followed that any such perception [*Erkennen*] and indeed, measure of God [*Maß Gottes*], must originate in God's self-revelation itself. It had to be added on beyond immanent reason's capacity.[44] Barth writes in *Church Dogmatics* IV/2:

---

[44] As was pointed out in Chapter 1, McCormack argues that Barth's theological epistemology and the philosophical conceptuality he employed to explicate it remained basically unchanged from *Romans* II through *Anselm: Fides Quaerens Intellectum* to the *Church Dogmatics*. McCormack, *Karl Barth's Critically Realist Dialectical Theology*. As was also pointed out, he argues that Barth's epistemological position can be expressed in an unambiguously Kantian conceptuality: "... God is the one noumenal reality which - precisely because He is the omnipotent divine Subject who created all things and is therefore Lord even over the subject-object split - is capable of grasping us through the phenomena from the other side. Without setting aside or altering the cognitive apparatus as it is given in the human knower, God makes Himself the object of our knowledge by giving Himself to be known in and through a creaturely veil and granting to us the eyes of faith to see what there is to see in this veil." McCormack, "Review Article: Graham Ward's *Barth, Derrida and the Language of Theology*" *The Scottish Journal of Theology* 49 1 (1996): 105-106. It is not difficult to see how this understanding of Kant's concept of noumenal reality could be applied to Barth's exegesis of the resurrection appearances stories in *Church Dogmatics* IV/2. As *the* noumenal reality, Jesus can become the object of knowledge - even though He is to all intents and purposes there as Himself - *only* if He reveals Himself to us. Otherwise, unless he 'breaks through the epistemological veil' in this sense, He is 'beyond immanent reason's capacity.' I have preferred to state Barth's position on the resurrection-appearances history in terms of the more obviously historical concepts of *sui generis* historicality and theological historicality. And on the matter of attempting to state the strength of Barth's argument as regards this history, I have preferred to use the conceptual apparatus of means and object of measurement, though there is no doubt that the concept of noumenal reality could be reconciled with this apparatus and therefore substituted into Barth's argument as I have it here. One obvious advantage of stating Barth's argument in my terms is that one does not have to assume that those who think about it accept Kant's noumenon-phenomenon divide. Since many modern philosophers, mainly of the analytical mould, reject the divide, discussing Barth's position on epistemology in terms of the alternative conceptuality does, I submit, have the advantage of emphasising Barth's genuine 'apologetic' credentials outwith Kantian apparatus. In this respect, the concept of an event whose only means of measurement is it itself coincides with a particular *historical realism* which avoids Pannenberg's charge of subjectivism (or idealism) without falling prey to revelational positivism. (See McCormack's reference to this problem. *Ibid*, 496-497.) Perhaps more importantly: the alternative conceptuality provides a more appropriate conceptuality in which to elucidate the *historical* consequences of the presence of the strange new world within the Bible for his position on epistemology. As was noted in the introduction to the present book, in response to a recent review of his book, McCormack posed the important question whether Barth needed Kantian epistemology to describe his understanding of God's self-revelation. "To that question", McCormack replied, "I would

Taking place in the series of all other events, [Jesus Christ's self-revelation] is not controlled by that series, nor does it have its basis in their nexus. And in the same way, although the perception [*Erkennen*] which it meets takes place within the order of all human perception, it is conditioned by the newness of the subject which confronts it, and it is not, therefore, limited by the limits imposed by other subjects. The actuality of this new being and occurrence, grounded in the divine act of majesty, creates the possibility of a special perception to meet it, a perception which is controlled and mastered by it, attaching itself to it, following and accompanying it, imitating and repeating it. Like all other objects, but as this particular one, it establishes itself in the knowing subject. It does not allow itself to be halted by the normal and customary limitation and contingency of the latter's ability to know. Both *de facto* and *de iure* it makes a place for itself in human cognition [*menschlichen Erkennen*], claiming respect and consideration. It accepts all responsibility for the fact that this cognition may not be equal to it in view of the fact that it is so new and strange. But it also deprives it of the pride of a self-complacent repetition and reflection of other objects, and therefore the insistence of its usual contingency and limitation. It gives it this capacity, and therefore summons it to see and think and interpret it as a reality, as this being and occurrence, repeating and reflecting it, both in thought and word, in all its singularity.[45]

This special perception is not one that "in the region of perception and concept deduces, compares, co-ordinates, and in this way demonstrates" -[46] in contrast to those perceptions operating under the control of the *a priori* categories. It is singularly unable to do this, though that this is so is entirely logical since the perception *originates* in God's self-revelation. (Hence, to perceive an event whose only means of measurement is itself entails that the measure of God cannot ever pass over to human control. It cannot ever become an *immanent* measure of the divine.) To repeat: we have no conception of *what it is* a perception of Jesus *revealing* Himself as the crucified one would be independently of the event itself, which is to say, we

---

say, it may indeed prove possible to improve on Kant; to retain Barth's theological epistemology while making adjustments in the philosophical conceptuality he employed to explicate it." McCormack, "Barth in Context: A Response to Professor Gunton", *The Scottish Journal of Theology* 49 4 (1996): 498. My interpretation of Barth implicitly takes up McCormack's line of thought on the possibility of an improved translation of Barth's theological epistemology in the realm of *Geschichte*.

[45] Barth, *CD* IV/2, 119-120.

[46] Barth, *CD* III/1, 82.

have no conception of *what it is* Jesus *revealing* Himself as the crucified one would be independently of the event itself.[47]

## Concluding Remarks

One should not underestimate the significance of Kant's conception of the problem. Not only was his conception implicit, in some form or another, in the work of the major theologians of the nineteenth century, it was also implicit in some famous attacks on Barth's epistemological position from twentieth-century theologians. Bonhoeffer wrote in *Letters and Papers from Prison* that Barth's theology offered no more than a 'positivism of revelation' [*Offenbarungpositivismus*]. In 1956 Barth wrote:

> [I] just did not know how to make sense of this criticism. Simply put forward dogmas - "take it or leave it" - where do I do that in the *Church Dogmatics*?[48]

That positivism is to be equated with a dogmatic 'take it or leave it' position tantamount to accepting the givenness of revelation (theological positivism), is, for Barth, the very reason it ought to be opposed. *Positivism is no less subject to the criticism that it presupposes a norm or criterion of what it is revelation is, independently of revelation itself.* Indeed, Barth had already criticised Schleiermacher for holding to positivism as early as 1927. According to Simon Fisher, "it was Barth's considered opinion that Schleiermacher's theology was ... fundamentally defective because of its alien and naturalizing methodology. The sheer actualism of divine revelation when expounded in categories perilously close to cause and effect, together with the assumption that some revelation in religious experience forms the datum for both philosophical and theological investigation yielded sufficient evidence to call Schleiermacher a positivist."[49]   As Fisher points out, the critique Barth directed at Schleiermacher is only applicable to his own theological journey at its earliest stage. Only then could it have been said that Barth was a theological positivist.[50]

Like Bonhoeffer, Pannenberg criticised Barth for advocating a 'positivism of revelation':

---

[47] The logical coherence of this claim is taken up in Chapter 9.

[48] Quoted in Busch, *Barth*, 381.

[49] Simon Fisher, *Revelatory Positivism? Barth's Earliest Theology and the Marburg School* (Oxford: Oxford University Press,1988), 318.

[50] *Ibid*, 318.

The radical nature of Barth's position brings out very clearly a truth of more general relevance. The Enlightenment questioned anything on authority which was not subject to proof by reason and experience. If we accept this as a valid stance, a 'positive' theology of revelation which does not depend on rational argument can rely only on a subjective act of will or an irrational venture of faith. For Barth's word of God - the church's preaching? scripture? Jesus himself? - demanding the obedience of faith cannot be unambiguous because it remains at least problematical whether it *is* God and divine revelation and not merely human convictions. If proof through rational enquiry is ruled out in advance, but for some reason or other we still want to hold the Christian tradition, nothing remains but the whole uninsured venture of faith.[51]

Barth would have agreed with Pannenberg's assertion that the Enlightenment questioned everything which was not subject to proof by reason. Nevertheless, Barth's theology of revelation *is* based on rational argument. Pannenberg's critique presupposes an immanent measure of *God's* self-revelation independently of *God's* self-revelation itself. It presupposes a norm, a criterion, which Barth would say Pannenberg cannot have independently of *God's* revelation. In other words: in order to conceive of the possibility of not(*God's* self-revelation) - the vantage-point in terms of which one criticises *God's* self-revelation - one has to have a criterion of *what it is God's* self-revelation is against which to measure what it is one is conceiving is not the case. Barth's argument is that one cannot have this criterion independently of *God's* self-revelation itself because it does not exist independently of the latter.[52] Were such independence the case, it would be possible to take up a position in terms of which to criticise *God's* self-revelation independently of, and hence prior to, *God's* self-revelation. It is not at all like criticising the existence of unicorns because in that case one knows *what it is* a unicorn is independently of the existence of unicorns. In this particular case one *does* have a criterion against which to measure what it is one is conceiving is not the case.[53] This is not true of the resurrection-appearances history: it tells

---

[51] Pannenberg, *Theology and the Philosophy of Science*, 273.

[52] To put the point in terms of Jesus Christ: in order to conceive of the possibility of *what it is* not(Jesus Christ's self-revelation) is - this is essential to the position of the historical critic - there had to be a means of measurement of *what it is* Jesus Christ's self-revelation is against which to measure *what it is* one conceived was not the case. But since the means of measurement could not be had independently of Jesus Christ's self-revelation itself, one could only conceive of the possibility of not(Jesus Christ's self-revelation) against Jesus Christ's self-revelation itself.

[53] Barth's particular form of theological realism - derived from the 'narrative' facts of the resurrection narratives - is a swingeing double-edged sword. Philosophical realism

us we do *not* have - and *never* can have - an independent measure of *Jesus Christ* revealing *Himself.*

Kant's point was: even were revelation the unique source and norm of knowledge of God, it would have to be measured by an immanent measure if it were to be defined as knowledge. Barth's reply was: it is precisely *because* God's self-revelation is the unique source and norm of knowledge of God that there can be no such immanent measure. It can originate only in, and with, God's self-revelation. This was what was entailed by the epistemological theme behind the resurrection-appearances history, *God* reveals Himself *through Himself* with the result that He reveals *Himself.* When the Enlightenment went about its business of evaluating the truth of the Bible at those points where the Bible claims *witness* to divine historical reality, it set up, in the manner of Troeltsch's principle of analogy, a pre-existing means of comparison against which to measure the historical reality. Indeed, as we saw, on the matter of God's self-revelation in history, no less an authority than Kant said that it had no alternative but to do so.

---

presupposes an immanent 'measure of faith' meaning. Hence, it is to be rejected because it entails that one can have an independent conception of what it is one is judging to be true or false. Empiricism, positivism, historicism, idealism, philosophical realism - all assume this is possible (the 'Kantian conception of the problem' of God is the fundamental rationale behind all the major philosophical conceptions of the possibility of knowledge of God). The anti-realist is subject to the same strictures. Making an *a priori* argument presupposes that one knows *what it is* one is making the argument for. The (rationalist) *a priori* argument also presupposes an immanent conceptual measure. Barth rejected an immanent conceptual measure for one reason and one reason only: it presupposed that one could know *what it is God's revelation is independently of God's revelation itself.* The series of lectures Barth delivered in 1929 under the title "Schicksal und Idee in der Theologie" ("Fate and Idea in Theology") bears witness to the fact that this argument is the fundamental rationale behind Barth's case against the *analogia entis,* (which concept was discussed there in print for the first time). For the rationale behind Barth's rejection of both realism and idealism, as he defined them in these lectures, is that both assume that they know *what it is* God's revelation is independently of God's revelation. Though realism is right to assert that God is real, it errs assuming that the created order - the world - provides a criterion against which to measure the reality of God. It posits a *similitudo Dei* on behalf of the world. It affirms an *analogia entis.* As McCormack puts it: "From Barth's point of view the possibility of the knowledge of God in an analogy which is built into the world *as such,* renders revelation superfluous. Revelation can at most be a confirmation and strengthening of what is already known in another way. But that is to misunderstand revelation. Revelation tells us something new, something we could not have told ourselves without it." McCormack, *Karl Barth's Critically Realistic Dialectical Theology,* 386. That is, we have no criterion for the *Wirklichkeit* of revelation independently of revelation. Similarly, though idealism has a valid concern in that it questions the identification of God with the given, it "must be remembered that it too has no criterion at its disposal by means of which it can lay its hands on the truth. The criterion of truth has to be given with revelation - again and again and again." *Ibid,* 388.

Kant's constraint had not reckoned with an event whose only means of measurement is it itself. The Enlightenment insisted that one had to have a measure of God's self-revelation as historical reality against which to measure this history for truth or falsity. But an event whose only means of measurement is it itself can only be measured in terms of itself. It is, after all, God's self-revelation with which Kant's measure is confronted.

One could have imagined Barth dreaming up a repudiation of Kant's `measure of the divine' from his armchair, so to speak. Consequently, that he discovered the Bible converged to just such a precise position in the form of the strange new world within the Bible, was, for him, no fantastic coincidence; rather, it was  additional corroboration of, and therefore, testimony to, the essential truthfulness therein contained.

# Chapter 9
# The *Telos* of the Resurrection-Appearances History: God Reveals *Himself* as the Crucified One

## 1. Introduction

In *CD* IV/2, as was noted in the previous chapter, Barth observes that:

> The event [the resurrection and ascension] of Jesus Christ consisted in a series of concrete encounters and short conversations between the risen Jesus and his disciples. In the tradition these encounters are always described as self-manifestations of Jesus in the strictest sense of the term. In this context self-manifestation means (1) that the execution and termination as well as the initiative lie entirely in His own hands and not in theirs. Their reaction is a normal one but it is to an action in whose origination and accomplishment they have no part at all. They have really encountered their Lord. He controls them but they do not control Him. Self-manifestation means (2) that the meaning and purpose of these encounters consists simply and exhaustively in the fact that the risen Christ declares Himself to them in His identity with the One previously followed and who had died on the cross and been buried.[1]

The previous chapter provided, among other things, an exposition of Barth's exegesis of (1). I argued that (1) is in essence an exposition of the first part of the one event of '*God* reveals Himself *through Himself* with the result that He reveals *Himself*', that is, '*God* reveals Himself *through Himself*'.

In this chapter the first and main thing I do is to complete the exposition of this historical truth-claim. (2) is in reality exposition of the second part, 'with the result that He reveals *Himself*': God reveals *Himself* as the crucified one. While (1) constitutes the rationale behind what kind of event it is, namely, 'an event whose only means of measurement is it itself', (2) provides the rationale behind the identity of the event: what the event

---

[1] Barth, *CD* IV/2, 143-144.

consists of (God revealing Himself as the crucified one or God revealing Himself as creator).

Subsequently, I discuss three potential objections to Barth's understanding of the resurrection-appearances history and of the creation history. The first follows from the premise that two events each of which is an event whose only means of measurement is it itself cannot but be the same event (differing only in time and place). Hence, so the argument might go, to speak of events in which God reveals Himself as creator and reconciler respectively - two different events - is unjustifiable. At best, all one can do is speak of God's self-revelation, but not God's self-revelation *as reconciler or as creator.* Barth's concept of 'noetic conception' in *Anselm: Fides Quaerens Intellectum* is the rationale behind his answer to this objection. The second is more serious. While accepting both the validity of the concept of 'noetic conception' and the claim that it resolves the first objection, this objection argues that whatever noetic conception designates the events of God revealing Himself as the crucified one, or as the creator, it cannot be 'an event whose only means of measurement is it itself.' Rather, the only applicable noetic conception is one that Troeltsch would have argued is intrinsic to the concept of a historical event: 'an event whose means of measurement is *not only* itself' - "an event prior to which and side by side with which there are other events of the same basic type with which it can be compared and integrated."[2] If this argument is valid Barth faces the following dilemma. Either he resolves Overbeck's *metadilemma but at the cost of not being able to say more of an event whose only means of measurement is it itself that it is such an event;* or the events in question are conceivable but *theology remains non-theology and Overbeck's dilemma remains unresolved.* Barth argues that this conclusion is unwarranted.

Third, I examine a potential objection to Barth's resolution of the metatheological dilemma involving the empty tomb motif in the resurrection appearances pericopes. Barth's understanding of this historical truth-claim - the *historischen* element that is the empty tomb - appears qualitatively to *distinguish* the historicality of the resurrection-appearances history from that of the creation history in a manner that makes the former history a measurable one in Troeltsch's sense. But, as in the case of the second objection, I show that this understanding does not conflict with *sui generis* historicality and therefore does not constitute an obstacle to Barth's resolution of Overbeck's dilemma.

---

[2] Barth, *CD* III/1, 78.

## 2. 'God Reveals *Himself*'

What constitutes Barth's exegetical discernment of (2)? Again as in (1) (see Chapter 8) it is a question of the deep literal sense of the individual pericopes. The resurrection-appearances history is constitutive of only one historical event: '*God* reveals Himself *through Himself*' is not one event and 'God reveals *Himself*' another. They are the same event. To reiterate: there is no event in which *God* reveals Himself *through Himself* but does not reveal *Himself*; there is no event in which God reveals *Himself* that is not also *God* revealing Himself *through Himself*. Nevertheless, one can point to the details of the deep literal sense corresponding to the *telos* of God's self-revelation, Jesus Christ's self-revelation:

> ... the question  how [the disciples and followers of Jesus] came to recognise Him when they saw and heard Him is rather strangely answered - although not with equal definiteness - by the  radical assertion that He was known as the One who had been among them before and was then crucified dead and buried. [...] What the Evangelists really know and say is simply that the disciples saw and heard Jesus after his death, and that as they saw and heard Him, they recognised Him, and that they recognised Him on the basis of his identity with the One whom they had known before. *And they say this because it seems to be their particular intention to say it.* [my italics] The disciples who went to Emmaus say that He was known by them ... ["in the breaking of the bread"] (*Luke 24.35*). And Luke tells us that "as he sat at with them, he took bread, and blessed it, and brake, and gave to them" (*Luke 24.30*). But even to the very words and order this is exactly what had happened at the last supper and the earlier feeding of the five and four thousand. In the ensuing appearance to the eleven recognition comes when he allows them to see and touch his hands and feet (*Luke 24.29*). In *John 20.20, 25, 27*, where there is also a reference to the touching of His side, this is rightly to mean that He gave himself to be known by them as the Crucified. Mary Magdalene recognises him simply by the fact - obviously not for the first time - He calls her by her name (*John 20.16*).[3]

Again, even in the presence of imprecise "chronological information as to the duration of the appearances", "vague topography", and "no clear dividing line between one scene and another" - even in the presence of features which appear discrepant and inconsistent at the 'atomic' literal level - the same definite theological identity is manifest in Luke and John: 'God reveals *Himself*' is intrinsic to the nature of the appearances themselves. Even in the case of an apparently "legendary" story like that of

---

[3] *Ibid*, 144-145.

Jesus at Emmaus, the same definite theological purpose is evident in the *intention* of the evangelist: to tell us that the Christ who revealed *Himself* revealed Himself as the One who had been crucified, dead, and buried. The 'canonical' "meaning and purpose of the encounters narrated by the evangelists consists simply and exhaustively in the fact that the risen Christ declares Himself to them in His identity with the One previously followed and who had died on the cross and been buried."

It was noted in Chapter 8 that the ascension appearance story is included among those stories taken as indicative of the origination and accomplishment of revelation. But it is also taken as indicative of 'God reveals *Himself*':

> [what] is revealed in the ascension is again a hidden thing that was true and actual before, in his whole history and existence as son of God and Son of Man as it found fulfilment in his crucifixion. As the Gospel of John has it, his exaltation on the cross was also his exaltation to the Father.[4]

In order to ward off any charge of inconsistency, it should be noted that Barth focuses on two different aspects of the story. As regards (1) - '*God* reveals Himself *through Himself* - he focuses on the fact that the termination property of the ascension is always in Jesus' own hands. In 'God reveals *Himself*', he focuses on the ascension property *per se*, relating it to Jesus' being lifted up on to the cross, and therefore to Jesus' pre-Easter history.

This then is Barth's account of the result of the resurrection-appearances history: Jesus Christ reveals *Himself* as the crucified one and, as we will see in Chapter 11, in doing so reveals *Himself* as God the Reconciler. Putting (1) and (2) together again gives us the following: *Jesus Christ's resurrection-appearances history is an event whose only means of measurement is it itself in which Jesus Christ reveals Himself as the crucified one.* In the following two sections I wish to address three potential difficulties for this way of putting things. Since Barth's account of the creation history follows the same pattern - 'God reveals Himself as creator' breaks down into, on the one hand, *God* reveals Himself *through Himself* and, on the other, 'God reveals *Himself* as creator' - it is clear that the first two objections, if valid, strike at the very heart of Barth's theological epistemology. The third objection, based on the empty-tomb motif, is specific to the appearances history.

---

[4] *Ibid*, 154.

### 3. Barth's *Anselm: Fides Quaerens Intellectum* has the Answer!

The first goes like this. Two events each of which is an event whose only means of measurement is it itself cannot but be the same event. Allowing for the fact that the two events 'can differ in time and place, it would be the same event occurring at a different time or in a different place. Hence, to speak of events in which God reveals Himself as creator and reconciler respectively - two different events - is unjustifiable. Each is an event whose only means of measurement is it itself. This makes each the same event, notwithstanding difference in time and place.

If one reads Barth's book on Anselm closely, one can see that Barth was not unaware of this objection. As was said in Chapter 5, it is crucial to Barth's interpretation of Anselm that 'that than which a greater cannot be conceived' be construed as a noetic conception and not an ontic conception. 'That than which a greater cannot be conceived' does not describe the ontic nature of God; it functions as a noetic designator. When Barth asserts "we are dealing with a concept of strict noetic content which Anselm describes here as a concept of God",[5] he means that it *expresses nothing about - and therefore tells us nothing about - the nature of God*. Noetic conceptions tell us nothing about any of God's *real* properties. 'That than which a greater cannot be conceived':

> ... does not say that God is, or what he is, but rather, in the form of a prohibition that man can understand, who he is. It is *une définition purement conceptuelle*. It contains nothing in the way of statements about the existence or about the nature of the object described.[6]

---

[5] Barth, *FQI*, 75.

[6] *Ibid*, 75. When Barth says he interprets 'that than which a greater cannot be conceived' noetically, rather than ontically, he means that he interprets it as a name in the strict sense of the word - as a name designating [*bezeichneten*] God in the sense of *significatio*, and not as a name designating an accidental or essential property of God's nature. That the name of God is a name in the strict sense of the term follows from the fact that Barth stresses, as against Bonaventura and Thomas Aquinas, that 'that than which a greater cannot be conceived' is not the *nomen essentiale Dei* but plays the role of a *nomen personae*. Though the two Scholastics had perceived that 'that than which a greater cannot be conceived' was the *nomen Dei*, they proceeded to construe this as the *nomen essentiale Dei*. This, according to Barth, is a mistake. *Ibid*, 77. The person Karl Barth's name is "Karl Barth"; in a related sense the Name of God is 'that than which a greater cannot be conceived.' "That than which a greater cannot be conceived', like the name 'Karl Barth', does not describe the person Karl Barth (and in this sense has no ontic content) but simply *names* him. This is what "strict noetic content" means. Notwithstanding the differences between persons and events, the same logic applies in the case of the latter.

As *une définition purement conceptuelle* - as a noetic conception - 'that than which a greater cannot be conceived' tells us nothing about any of God's real properties.[7] Analogously, to say that an event is an event whose

---

[7] It is not often realised how important Barth conceives the concept of noetic conception to be in the context of Anselm's proof of the existence of God. Were 'that than which a greater cannot be conceived' to imply "something in the way of statements about the existence or about the nature of the object described", it would function as a *description* and, accordingly, as an *ontic conception of God*. According to Barth, Anselm believed that an ontic conception of God could not move anything other than invalid proof. Hence, in the guise of Anselm, Barth lambasts Gaunilo for transliterating Anselm's noetic terminology back into ontic terminology - for transliterating the noetic designation 'that than which a greater cannot be conceived' into the ontic *quod est maius omnibus* (which formula Gaunilo had inferred from Anselm's *Monologion*). This latter is not "in the narrow, strict sense a designation or Name of God like *quo maius cogitari nequit*, but in itself is a brief paraphrase of the nature of God. As such, therefore as far as the proof is concerned alike both of the Existence and Nature of God as these are held by faith, it is insufficient. It is no accident that though in various passages in the *Monologion* Anselm asserts the Existence of God as held by faith, he did not try to prove it. The insight that such proof is impossible on the basis of the conception of God assumed in the *Monologion*, is perhaps a later achievement. it comes to formal expression in the answer to Gaunilo and is based on the fact that *quod est maius omnibus* might also be conceived of as not-existing. [...] As long, however, as the conception that is presupposed does not in itself rule out that possibility and as long, therefore, as the non-existence of God is conceivable without the presupposed conception of God being destroyed, this conception is not amenable to proof .... [In] the same context Anselm also declares ... that that conception would not be sufficient to prove what faith holds to be the Nature of God and for the reason that once again *quod est maius omnibus* does not preclude the possibility that a *maius eo (etiam si non sit)* could at least be conceived. [...] Obviously Gaunilo could not have attempted anything more devastating than his ill-considered re-transliteration into ontic terms of the new formula that Anselm introduced in the *Proslogion*. The very thing that Anselm intended should make it valid as a proof, its austere character as a rule for thinking about God, was thereby taken away from it and it is hardly surprising that, on the basis of this presupposition, Gaunilo was not able to appreciate Anselm's actual proof. Again, he is just beating the air when he thinks it necessary to inform Anselm that by means of this conception the Proof is not valid." *Ibid*, 86. However, it is not merely this particular ontic conception of God which issues in invalid proof. It is not only *quod est maius omnibus* which issues in invalid proof. Barth makes a much stronger claim. He claims that *all* ontic conceptions are consistent with the conceivability of the non-existence or imperfection of God. All ontic conceptions of God are logically defective in this sense. He writes: "with *quo maius cogitari nequit* the enemy (denial or doubt) is sought out on his own ground, in thought itself, on which ground this enemy is repeatedly calling in question the assumption of an ontic conception, and is placed under the sign of the Name of God and is thereby challenged to necessary knowledge of God. *Quo maius cogitari nequit* is designed to exclude just this conceivability of the non-existence or imperfection of God which lurks in the background of *every* [*my italics*] ontic conception of God ...." *Ibid*, 89. This is why he thought that Kant's famous 'hundred thalers' criticism repudiated the ontic version of Anselm's proof.

only means of measurement is it itself - 'that which nothing analogous can be conceived' - does not, in itself, inform us of any of the real properties of the event.[8] Hence, there is no reason why one event which is an event whose only means of measurement is it itself has *different real* properties from another event which is also an event whose only means of measurement is it itself. And Barth would say that this is the case as regards God revealing Himself as the crucified one and God revealing Himself as creator.

To recapitulate: Barth's careful conceptual analysis in his book on Anselm leads to the following conclusion. An event whose only means of measurement is it itself does not, in itself, inform us of any of the real properties of the event. *Yet, without contradiction*, it leaves it open for the event to have real properties. Not only can there be more than one of such of an event, there can be many *different* events each of which is an event whose only means of measurement is it itself. The event in which Jesus Christ revealed Himself "as the One who had been among the disciples before, and then was crucified dead and buried" is one event whose only means of measurement is it itself. The events in which God revealed Himself as creator of the heavens and the earth, and the contents thereof, are other, *different* events; each one is an event whose only means of measurement is it itself. And this can be so because an event whose only means of measurement is it itself tells us nothing about the ontic nature of the event, *which is left open*.

I do not think the Enlightenment would have any great problem with Barth's response. It is the second objection which is potentially more damaging to Barth's characterisation of the resurrection-appearances history and the creation history as historical, and therefore conceivable events, yet not susceptible to Troeltsch's principle of analogy. As was said in the introduction, while accepting both the validity of the concept of 'noetic conception' and the claim that it resolves the first objection, this

---

Kant's criticism was directed at Descartes' and Leibniz's version of Anselm's proof, both which took existence to be a perfection and, therefore, a predicate of God. This is why Barth ends his book with the warning not to confuse Anselm's proof with the teachings of Descartes and Leibniz. He was keenly aware that *any* description, or ontic conception, of God was always open to Kant's objection that what it described might not exist in reality; that there might be nothing in reality that corresponded to the description.

[8] It might be said that 'an event whose only means of measurement is it itself' *does* tell us about *one* of the real properties of the event, namely that it possesses *sui generis* historicality (just as 'an event whose means of measurement is not only itself' tells us that it possesses the historicality found in historical events measurable by Troeltsch's principle of analogy). Barth did not get into this kind of philosophical deep-water. But were this claim true (and I think it likely), it would not alter the coherence of Barth's case. For it would merely be a case of speaking of different events, each possessing *sui generis* historicality.

objection argues that whatever noetic conception designates the events of God revealing Himself as the crucified one, or as the creator, it cannot be 'an event whose only means of measurement is it itself.' If the events of God revealing Himself as creator - and especially as the crucified one - are to be  objects of human knowledge, each must be  conceivable. But if each is an event whose only means of measurement is it itself then conceivability is ruled out. The Enlightenment sees nothing unusual or extraordinary about noetic conceptions *per se*. It is simply that conceivability entails the noetic conception 'an event whose means of measurement is *not only* itself' - "an event prior to which and side by side with which there are other events  of the same basic type with which it can be  compared   and integrated."[9] Hence, if God revealing Himself as the crucified one or as the creator is conceivable, it follows, according to the Enlightenment, that each event is measurable by a pre-existing means of measurement.

Barth's answer to this is to demonstrate that an event whose only means of measurement is it itself does not preclude it from being conceivable. Such an event is not in logical conflict with the fact that the events of God revealing Himself as the crucified one, or as the creator, are conceivable. Hence, there is no contradiction in saying, on the one hand, that the latter events are  events whose only means of measurement are, respectively, them themselves, and, on the other, that they are conceivable, and hence can become objects of human knowledge. Barth writes:

> The first thing that has to be noticed is what ['that than which a greater cannot be conceived'] does not say: it does not say – God is the highest that man has in fact conceived, beyond which he can conceive nothing higher. Nor does it say – God is the highest that man could conceive. *Thus it denies neither the former reality nor the latter possibility, but leaves the question of the givenness of them both [my italics].*[10]

Later he writes:

> The designation of God as the *quo maius cogitari nequit* does not assume the existence or nature of any creature, certainly not of God Himself, neither as actually conceived nor as being conceivable. It simply says that if God should or could be conceived – that both these are in fact so is obviously the other assumption, the substance of the proof – then *nothing else* [my italics] may be conceived  of as greater than God.[11]

---

[9] Barth, *CD* III/1, 78.
[10] *FQI*, 74.
[11] *FQI*, 88.

Here Barth pays close attention to the logical properties of the noetic conception 'that than which a greater cannot be conceived.' The gist of what he says is that 'that than which a greater cannot be conceived' does not entail that the 'that' in the formula is what 'cannot be conceived.' In other words, to say that God reveals Himself to Anselm as 'that than which a greater cannot be conceived' does not entail that God is 'that which cannot be conceived.' To be sure, it does not entail that God is 'that which can be conceived' or 'that which is conceivable.' But it does not deny it. *It leaves it open.* To put it another way: the subject of the predicate 'cannot be conceived' is not the demonstrative pronoun 'that', it is the noun phrase 'a greater.' The predicate 'cannot be conceived' is not a predicate of God since it is not a predicate of 'that.' Therefore, the formula does not say that God is inconceivable; as Barth says, it leaves it open.

The moral of the logic is clear. To say that an event is 'that which nothing analogous can be conceived' does not entail that the event itself is inconceivable. Analogously, to say that an event is an event whose only means of measurement is it itself does not entail that it is inconceivable. Hence, there is no inconsistency in saying that the event in which Jesus revealed Himself "as the One who had been among the disciples before, and then was crucified dead and buried" *was an event whose only means of measurement is it itself.* There is no inconsistency in saying that *the sui generis* historical event in which *Jesus revealed Himself as the one who was crucified* is a conceivable event whose only means of measurement is it itself.

In reply, it might be said that, though this is well and good, it remains the case that the historical event in which Jesus revealed Himself as the one who was crucified was *as a matter of fact* a conceivable event whose means of measurement was not only itself, that, *as a matter of fact*, it was an event for which the witnesses had a pre-existing measure. '*God* Reveals Himself *Through Himself* with the result that He reveals *Himself*' breaks down to, on the one hand, '*God* reveals Himself *through Himself*' (corresponding to the exegesis of [1]) and, on the other, the result of this: 'with the result that He reveals *Himself*' (corresponding to the exegesis of [2]). As was said, (1) is the fundamental rationale behind Barth's conception *of sui generis* historicality, of his conception of an event whose only means of measurement is it itself. On its own it is perfectly consistent. The problem arises once it is coupled to (2). Once this is done we seem no longer able to have (in any consistent sense) a historical event whose only means of measurement is it itself. And the reason is that any event with the content described by (2) – an event in which the risen Christ declares Himself to them in His identity with the one previously followed and who had died on the cross and been buried - seems not to be an event whose only means of measurement is it itself. It seems to be an event whose means of measurement exists independently of and (crucially) prior to the event itself

– precisely the measure constituted by "the One who had been among the disciples before, and then was crucified dead and buried." Given that Barth wants to say that Jesus reveals Himself in His resurrection-appearances history as this specific pre-Easter identity he cannot affirm that it is a *sui generis* historical event in his sense without contradiction (the same event is both an event whose only means of measurement is it itself and an event whose means of measurement is not only it itself).

Barth does not deny that Jesus as the crucified one is obviously conceivable and could in fact be conceived independently of the event of Jesus' crucifixion. The fact that I can do the latter, for example, is simple testimony to this. I do have a pre-existing measure of the crucified Jesus. But what one does not have, Barth says, is a pre-existing measure of *what it is* the event is of Jesus *revealing* Himself as the one who had been crucified, dead and buried. And this is why Barth can say that we have no conception of *what it is* a perception of Jesus *revealing Himself as the crucified one* would be independently of the event itself.[12]  Put more simply: we have no conception of *what it is* Jesus *revealing Himself as the crucified one* would be independently of the event itself.  He "can be perceived only as He comes."

Had the second objection been valid Barth would have had to choose between, on the one hand, giving up his claim of *sui generis* historicality and, on the other, either: getting in line with Calvin and Augustine and the pre-critical tradition (historical events as the object of basic belief); or accepting that the resurrection appearances are susceptible to Troeltsch's principle of analogy in the critical-historical sense. In other words, as was said in the introduction: either he resolves Overbeck's *metadilemma but at the cost of not being able to say more of an event whose only means of measurement is it itself that it is such an event*; or the events in question are conceivable but *theology remains non-theology and Overbeck's dilemma remains unresolved*. Barth's position is that the second objection is not valid. Therefore these fateful consequences do not follow.

---

[12] To repeat: though Jesus Christ's self-revelation in this history "takes place within the order of all human perception [*Erkennen*], it is conditioned by the newness which confronts it .... The actuality of this new being and occurrence ... creates the possibility of a special perception to meet it, a perception which is controlled and mastered by it, attaching it to itself, following and accompanying it, imitating and repeating it. [...] Both *de facto* and *de iure* it makes a place for itself within human cognition [*menschlichen Erkennen*] .... It gives it this capacity, and therefore summons it to see and think and interpret it as a reality, as this being and occurrence, repeating and reflecting it, both in thought and word, in all its singularity." Barth, *CD* IV/2, 120.

## 4. The Empty Tomb

There is no doubt but that Barth asserts there to be an element of *Historie* in the resurrection-appearances stories. This is one feature which differentiates his understanding of these stories from his understanding of the creation stories. The *historische* element he has in mind is the empty tomb.[13] But in what sense is the reference in scripture to an empty tomb a historical element? Is it a historical truth-claim of the kind measurable by Troeltsch's principle of analogy? Were this the case Barth's case for understanding the resurrection-appearances history as an event whose only means of measurement is it itself would be fatally weakened. If the empty tomb were a measurable event in the sense of Troeltsch it would follow that the appearances history could not be an event whose only means of measurement is it itself. And since this kind of event - this kind of theological historicality - is the means by which Barth ultimately resolves the metatheological dilemma, it follows that resolution of the dilemma is beyond Barth's reach.

The resurrection-appearances history is the instantiation of the "living Jesus" (the living God);[14] as a necessary ancillary accompaniment there is the "legend" of the empty tomb:

> The "legend" of the finding of the empty tomb is not of itself and as such the attestation of Jesus Christ as He showed Himself alive after His death. It is ancillary to this attestation. The one can be as little verified "historically" as the other. Certainly the empty tomb cannot serve as an "historical" proof. It cannot be proclaimed and believed for itself but only in the context [*Zusammenhang*] of the attestation.[15]

The "context" referred to here is the resurrection-appearances history. The empty tomb cannot be affirmed as an independent object of faith outside of this context. This is why the "legend" is not "of itself and as such the attestation of" the risen Christ. There is no one-to-one 'atomic' correspondence between literal detail and historical reality. Hence, if the empty tomb is a historical concept, it is one without empirical content. It is in fact an irreducibly holistic historical concept: from the vantage-point of the resurrection-appearances history there is no tomb in the *sui generis* historical realm that is not an empty tomb. Hence to speak of an empirically verifiable or falsifiable empty tomb is not to speak of the empty tomb referred to in the stories. outside the *sui generis* historical realm - living a *doppelgänger* twilight zone existence in the non-theological (critical-

---

[13] Barth, *CD* I/1, 325.

[14] Barth, *CD* IV/1, 301.

[15] Barth, *CD* IV/1, 341.

historical) lexicon subsequently consigned to myth by modernity! (Contrary
to an apparent 'empirical' propensity, the empty tomb is no less *sui generis*
theological than the virgin birth; contrary to appearance, the former belongs
to exactly the same conceptual category [saga] as the latter).[16] To say that

---

[16] Barth treats the virgin birth in the exactly same way as the empty tomb. The grounds on
which Barth affirms the virgin birth  testify how simplistic it is to characterise him as a
theologian whose justification of the articles of faith of the classical creeds is based on
an appeal to a crude empirical understanding of *sola scriptura*. For Barth's reasons for
affirming this doctrine are not the passages of scripture - Mt 1. 18-25 and Lk 1.26-35 -
one might have expected a biblical theologian to cite as evidence. Nowhere does the
uni-directional epistemological architectonic of logic from the resurrection-appearances
history to the incarnation, the virgin birth, and the empty tomb apply more than in the
case of the virgin birth. Indeed it is on the basis of such a logic that Barth will ride
roughshod  over the paucity of scriptural (literary) evidence to enter the virgin birth into
the vocabulary of *sui generis* theology. For Barth the virgin birth is to be subsumed
under what he calls the *quaestio facti*, which cannot be answered either by literary or by
dogmatic investigation. Barth, *CD I/2*, 177. Indeed Barth goes as far as to claim that such
literary or dogmatic investigation should be undertaken *sub conditione facti*. This is why
Barth acknowledges that: "As regards the necessity of the dogma, we must begin with the
admission that both in extent and form the grounds for the dogma in the statements of Holy
Scripture are not at first sight so strong or so clear  as one might wish for such a dogma in
the strict sense of the term." *Ibid*, 174. But no matter. It is logic which leads us unerringly
to the virgin birth - not historical investigation (historical proof), nor scriptural exegesis
of the passages pertaining to this article of faith - it is logic which intervenes between
the incarnation and the virgin birth. Like the question of the incarnation, the virgin birth
is a *quaestio facti*, though where the former is ontologically derived the latter is
noetically derived. Indeed, the virgin birth is a *quaestio facti* answered on the basis of
the actuality of the incarnation. The virgin birth is a corollary of the incarnation and
therefore indirectly a corollary of the resurrection appearances (where the legend of the
empty tomb is a direct corollary of the latter). The virgin birth, like the empty tomb, is
noetic rather than ontic. Barth, *CD IV/1*, 207. Just as the empty tomb stands as a sign in
relation to the resurrection appearances, so the virgin birth stands as a sign in relation to
the incarnation. Barth, *CD I/2*, 182. The resurrection-appearances history only implies the
empty tomb. The incarnation only implies the virgin birth. The concept of the empty
tomb is an analytic one; the concept of the virgin birth is an analytic one. There is no
birth of Jesus that could have been other than a virgin birth. It is an analytic truth though
one that can only be attested in the context of attestation of the incarnation. In fact,
everything Barth has to say about the relationship between the resurrection appearances
and the empty tomb applies to the relationship between the incarnation and the virgin
birth. In other words, The virgin birth is not a "critical-historical" concept, it is a *sui
generis* historical concept,  necessary to the *sui generis* historical realm. It is an
irreducible holistic concept. In other words, there is no birth of Jesus Christ in the *sui
generis* theological realm that is not a virgin birth. Conversely, the only factual virgin
birth is outside the *sui generis* theological realm in the non-theological (critical-
historical) lexicon subsequently consigned to myth by modernity. Again, as for the

the context of the attestation of Jesus' resurrection-appearances history implies an empty tomb is not to say that a factual empty tomb is a necessary condition of the former. Were this the case it could be "proclaimed and believed in itself" outside "of the context of the attestation" of the resurrection-appearances history. This means that, in the context of the attestation of this history, the concept of the empty tomb is an *analytic* concept.[17] Epistemologically this means that

> The statement that Christ is risen necessarily implies [*impliziert*] the assertion that a dead man is alive again and that his grave is empty. *But it only implies it* [*my italics*]. If we abstract the latter assertions from the former we may accept them or we may deny or demythologise them, but either way they are irrelevant for an understanding of the texts and their witness. They cannot be considered as a basis of the knowledge of Jesus Christ - not even if we affirm them "historically."[18]

Barth interprets the tradition as an inevitable deduction made in the context of Jesus' self-revelation in the resurrection-appearances history. The tradition of the empty tomb did not exist prior to this history.[19] The resurrection-appearances history only implies an empty tomb: one might say that an *implied empty tomb* or *implied empty grave* is the historical reality – the referent - to which reference is made.[20] Hence, affirming that the concept of

---

empty tomb, that the context of the attestation of the incarnation implies a virgin birth is not to say that a factual virgin birth is a necessary condition of the incarnation.

[17] D Fergusson takes the view that historical "criticism therefore cannot verify the resurrection although it could conceivably falsify it. On such a view the empty tomb and the appearances are necessary but insufficient conditions for knowledge of the resurrection. This position ... is not without its advocates (it seems to be the position of Karl Barth in the *Church Dogmatics*) ...." D Fergusson, Review Article, *the Scottish Journal of Theology* 42 (1989), 454. But if the concept of the empty tomb is an analytic concept, there is no question of a factually non-empty tomb falsifying the appearances. Hence the position attributed to Barth by Fergusson must be false. The fundamental objection to Fergusson's interpretation is that Barth would not be able to make sense of saying that an event whose only means of measurement is falsifiable - for reasons apparent in the concluding remarks in Chapter 8 on Pannenberg.

[18] Barth, *CD* IV/2, 149. Barth makes this observation in the midst of a passage designed to show that miracle is always *post facto*. As he himself puts it: "Always, however, it is the Lord Himself who is the centre of the picture, and not the miracle of His appearing (although this is emphasised too)." *Ibid*, 148.

[19] *Ibid*, 132.

[20] This may well be what Hunsinger means when he writes that the "extratextual referent of the tomb is not therefore a factual empty tomb, as hermeneutical literalism would suppose, but rather the risen Christ himself." G Hunsinger, "Beyond Literalism and Expressivism: Karl Barth's Hermeneutical Realism", *Modern Theology* 3: 3 (1987), 211. He continues: "However, since the risen Christ did not, according to Barth's

the empty tomb has empirical (verifiable or falsifiable) content is no less irrelevant than denying it has empirical content. One can never reverse the logical dependence of the empty tomb on Jesus' self-revelation in the appearances history. To make the truth of the latter depend in some empirical sense on the former is *ipso facto* to be speaking of other than that which the texts speak. The question "Was the tomb empty?" makes no sense outside the context of Jesus' self-revelation. But inside the context the question is redundant since the tomb could not but be empty. This is the rationale behind characterising it as an analytic concept. "Empty tomb" has no normal referential status: the story of the empty tomb is not part of the *biblical witness* – the implied empty tomb or grave is. As Barth puts it:

> Christians do not believe in the empty tomb, but in the living Christ. This does not mean, however, that we can believe in the living Christ without believing in the empty tomb. Is it just a "legend"? What matter? *It still refers to the phenomenon ensuing the resurrection, to the presupposition of the appearance of Jesus.* [*my italics*] Nevertheless rejection of the legend of the empty tomb has always been accompanied by rejection of the saga of the living Jesus, and necessarily so. Far better to admit that the empty tomb belongs to the Easter event as a sign.[21]

In other words, the *witness* of the resurrection appearances stories is not to the empty tomb, but to the resurrection-appearances history, and therefore only to an implied empty tomb. To understand the reference to the empty tomb as a claim to witness is to misunderstand the reference: the reference is *logically* dependent on the historical truth-claim pertaining to the resurrection-appearances history. One cannot believe in the living Christ and not believe in an empty tomb as an implication - a sign - of the resurrection-appearances history.[22] ●

---

interpretation, rise without his body, it would appear that as if some further, though secondary, extratextual referent were implied. For although Barth did not develop the point, would not his interpretation seem to entail a referent, if not a factual empty tomb (whose story might well be legend), at least something analogous to it, in effect its virtual equivalent?" *Ibid*, 211.

[21] Barth *CD* III/2, 453. The legend of the empty tomb "is, in fact, an indispensable accompaniment of the attestation. It safeguards its content from misunderstanding in terms of a being of the Resurrected which is purely beyond or inward." Barth, *CD* IV/1, 341. In other words, Jesus' self-revelation as the crucified one - the one dead and buried - is safeguarded against a docetic (idealist and non-theological) interpretation.

[22] It might be said that Barth's reading of the empty tomb is contrary to the most natural reading of the motif, namely, taking it as the epistemic point of departure and proceeding thence to the appearances. But given that Barth holds that the historical thematic of each resurrection appearances pericope is essentially the same (especially those of Luke and John) he would argue that a pericope such as the Mary Magdalene

## Concluding Remarks

This completes my analysis of Barth's understanding of the resurrection-appearances history begun in Chapter 8, an analysis which, in formal terms, is no less relevant to his understanding of the creation history. We have followed the direction of self-revelation from *Jesus* revealing Himself to Jesus revealing *Himself.* And this means that *sui generis* historicality is the epistemic point of departure for knowledge of the risen Jesus as He was in His pre-Easter existence and history precisely because in the resurrection-appearances history Jesus reveals Himself as the One who had been crucified dead and buried. This person is identical with the person identified in the first and second parts of the pre-Easter narrative, Jesus proclaiming the kingdom of God in Galilee followed by His execution on the cross on Golgotha. Since, as will be seen in Chapter 11, the pre-Easter narrative is the history of God as reconciler, this means that the *sui generis* historicality of the resurrection-appearances history is also the epistemic point of departure of knowledge of God as reconciler.

To recapitulate: the logical coherence of the direction of self-revelation toward Jesus' pre-Easter history, even given *sui generis* historicality, is guaranteed by the conceptual analysis of an event whose only means of measurement is it itself. First, It might have been thought that if one said of the resurrection-appearances history that it was an event whose only means of measurement itself, one could not say anything more about it. And, in particular, one could not say what distinguished it from any other event - say, the creation history - if the latter was also to be categorised as such an event. I have shown this conclusion to be unwarranted. To say that an event is such an event is only to speak noetically about the event. It is not to say anything about the ontic content of the event. Second, since an event whose only means of measurement is it itself does not say that it cannot be conceived, one is perfectly warranted to say of such an event that it is one in which God reveals Himself as the crucified one, or the reconciler, or the creator. In other words, it is perfectly coherent to speak of the content of this event, content which makes it a different event from another event which is also an event whose only means of measurement is it itself. Finally, the hermeneutic Barth accords to the empty-tomb motif means that it does not impinge on the *sui generis* historicality of the resurrection-appearances history.

---

pericope in John, which includes the motif of the empty tomb, is no more fundamental a witness than the Emmaus pericope, which does not include the motif. To affirm the empty tomb as the primary theme - the superordinate rather than the subordinate motif - would be to undermine Barth's fundamental 'canonical' principle derived from his exegesis.

# Chapter 10
# Barth's Non-Kantian Transcendental Argument and the Strange New World Within the Bible

## 1. Introduction

Barth's conception of the *analogia fidei* is precisely that no feature of our language can constitute a criterion against which to measure *what it is God's* self-revelation is. To repeat, *God's* self-revelation:

> comes to us as a *Novum* which, when it becomes an object for us, we cannot incorporate in the series of our other objects, cannot compare with them, cannot deduce from their context, cannot regard as analogous to them. It comes to us as a datum with no point of connexion with any other previous datum.[1]

This is the basic property of Barth's *analogia fidei*. It is a 'measure of faith' whose only criterion is it itself. Though Barth disagreed in principle with Calvin's exegesis of the resurrection narratives he did not break with, and indeed, embraced a large part of, the Reformed tradition's conception of the *analogia fidei* as defined by Paul in Romans 12.6. The strange new world within the Bible, as the norm of measurement of the truth of the Bible, coincided with the *analogia fidei* as Barth understood this latter conception. But that same world confronted Kant's immanent 'measure of the divine'. In other words, though Barth profoundly disagreed with the Reformed tradition's assumption that all biblical narrative was history in the ordinary sense, Barth was able to tackle the Enlightenment's conception of the problem of God, as exemplified in Kant's *Religion Within the Limits of Reason Alone*, by combining the consequences of the presence of the strange new world within the Bible with the Reformed tradition's conception of the *analogia fidei*.

As was said, the fundamental difference between Barth's and the Reformed tradition's 'measure of faith' resided in the fact that the latter's

---

[1] *Ibid*, 172.

measure was essentially an immanent measure against which to measure historical truth-claims. Barth's was not; and the reason it was not was because the strange new world within the Bible - and *sui generis* historicality in particular - constituted a criterion of measurement whose only criterion of measurement was it itself. Though Barth's position on epistemology in the *Church Dogmatics* owes something to Kant's transcendental argument, the form it took in Barth was not found in Kant. Barth tied the Reformers' doctrine of the *analogia fidei* to Kant's transcendental argument in his own unique way. In so doing he came up with something very similar to the central strategy of the later Wittgenstein who himself, as we will see in Chapter 12, advanced his own unique variation of the transcendental argument.

## 2. Barth's Position on Epistemology: The 'Measure of Faith' the Rationale Behind his (Non-Kantian) Transcendental Argument

The resurrection-appearances history is *in toto* an event whose only means of measurement is it itself; likewise, the creation history. Since the *only* means of measurement of such an event cannot be had independently of the event itself, the event itself constitutes a transcendental condition of the possibility of knowledge of it. In this sense, both the resurrection-appearances history and the creation history entail an epistemological dimension of philosophical significance: a transcendental condition of possibility is derived from both histories. I requote a passage quoted in Chapters 8 and 9. Although the perception [*Erkennen*] which meets Jesus Christ's self-revelation in the resurrection-appearances history

> takes place within the order of all human perception [*Erkennen*], it is conditioned by the newness which confronts it .... The actuality of this new being and occurrence ... creates the possibility of a special perception to meet it, a perception which is controlled and mastered by it, attaching it to itself, following and accompanying it, imitating and repeating it. [...] Both *de facto* and *de iure* it makes a place for itself within human cognition [*menschlichen Erkennen*] .... It gives it this capacity, and therefore summons it to see and think and interpret it as a reality, as this being and occurrence, repeating and reflecting it, both in thought and word, in all its singularity.[2]

This means that our "knowledge ... encloses a renunciation of all prior knowledge of the disclosure of this fact or our openness for it. Our

---

[2] Barth, *CD* IV/2, 120.

knowledge can only be an event."[3] The resurrection-appearances history and the creation history respectively create this openness, create *the possibility of faith* within their own respective historical spheres.[4] We can only start from God's self-revelation "in fact, not in theory."[5] Why? The historical event of God's self-revelation in both the resurrection-appearances history and the creation history is a 'measure of faith' whose only measure is it itself. This is why we:

> can never control our knowledge of this fact and therefore our authority to speak about it. It is not our own product, but the work of that fact in its character as revelation. It does not become our possession. We cannot put it in our pocket and carry it round with us. We can only use it at once as its work takes place in its character as revelation.[6]

In other words, God's self-revelation itself - and only itself - creates the very possibility of the means of measuring it. The presence of such a means of measurement - one which cannot be had independently of the event itself - invokes a transcendental argument of a distinctly non-Kantian kind. Though Barth's position on epistemology in the *Church Dogmatics* owes something to Kant's transcendental argument, the form it takes in Barth is not found in Kant. And though Barth's problems are the problems of the Enlightenment rather than the problems of Calvin's own era,[7] Barth does not break with the legacy of Calvin. Barth ties the Reformed tradition's conception of the *analogia fidei* to Kant's transcendental argument in his own unique way.

Although, as Rüdiger Bubner points out, Kant was not the first to use the term 'transcendental argument', he was the first to give it its modern meaning.[8] Hence it is only since Kant that theologians have made recourse to the transcendental argument when attempting to construct proofs for the existence of God. This means that insofar as Barth makes use of a species of transcendental argument he is unambiguously on our side of the Enlightenment and not Calvin's (historical event as Calvin understands it is

---

[3] *Ibid*, 124.

[4] Barth, *CD* III/2, 451.

[5] Barth *CD* IV/1, 123.

[6] *Ibid*, 124.

[7] See: Nicholas Wolterstorff, "The Migration of the Theistic Arguments: From Natural Theology to Evidentialist Apologetics", in Robert Audi and William J Wainwright, *Rationality, Religious Belief, and Moral Commitment* (Cornell University, Ithaca, 1986), 38-81; Kenneth Konyndyk, Kenneth, "Faith and Evidentialism", in Audi, Robert, and William J Wainwright, *Rationality, Religious Belief, and Moral Commitment* (Cornell University, Ithaca, 1986), 82-108, esp. 97.

[8] Rüdiger Bubner, "Kant, Transcendental Arguments and the Problem of Deduction", *Review of Metaphysics (28)* 1975, 453-467.

not a transcendental condition of possibility). Kant's transcendental argument has to show that, without the *a priori* synthetic categories, the experience of objects, of a unity or series of representations, ordered in time, would be impossible. For the Roman Catholic theologian Karl Rahner the existence of God is a transcendental deduction implicit in the experience of the transcendental ego. Rahner attempts to combine the epistemic status of the transcendental argument with Kant's endeavours in rational theology, which not so much tried to prove the existence of God as to show that belief in God is implicit in finite moral consciousness.[9]

That a transcendental argument is intrinsic to Barth's position on epistemology does not, as it does in Rahner, entail an innate or *a priori* disposition for the possibility of experience of God. Quite the reverse. As George Hendry puts it, the theme of the fulfilment of the knowledge of God in *Church Dogmatics* II/1 is "introduced in unmistakably Kantian terms as an inquiry into the condition of the possibility of our knowledge of God."[10] He cites Barth's statement that "where the actuality exists, there is also the corresponding possibility".[11] For Barth, and, as we shall see, for Wittgenstein too, it is the given or what is actual that is the condition of possibility:

> We cannot ask how [God's revelation] happens, but only, assuming that it does, how it can happen .... Now this very question has led us back again, and for the first time in full truth, to the event itself. We have found that the possibility of the knowledge of God is absolutely grounded, implied and included in the event of its actualisation, and our Yes to this possibility is one long reference to this event. We cannot produce this event and so we cannot give a basis for this reference; we could do so only by producing the event to which it points and letting it speak for itself. Hence, we can only ask - and we certainly must ask - what reference means in this context, how far in what sense, with what special necessity we refer to that event as the place where the question of the knowability of God is decided. [...] Faith ... is the making possible of knowledge of God's Word that takes place in the actual knowledge of it.[12]

Again:

> ... what this reality is in so far as the knowability is included ....[13]

[9] Emil L Fackenheim, "Immanuel Kant", 23.
[10] George Hendry, "Transcendental Method in Barth", *Scottish Journal of Theology (37)* 1984 213-277.
[11] Barth, *CD* II/1, 5.
[12] Barth, *CD* I/1, 227-228.
[13] *Ibid*, 228.

And, perhaps most Kantian of all:

God is the substance of the possibility, presuppositions and conditions of this event.[14]

It is not only that Barth makes no reference to a (synthetic) *a priori* condition of the possibility of experience of God; it is that the species of transcendental argument he employs repudiates not only the possibility of the transcendental deduction such as that employed by Karl Rahner, but also repudiates *any* argument that makes our experience the premise of theological construction. It does this on the grounds that, as we shall see, we have no criterion, outside of God, to tell us what we should be looking for were we looking for something to satisfy the concept expressed by "an innate disposition for the possibility of experience of God." Barth's argument also jettisons the possibility of more traditional 'pre-Kantian' empirical proofs/disproofs in so far as they make use of the concept expressed by "experience of God".

Thus, although Barth says there can be no "objection in principle to describing" the event of revelation as "'experience' and even as 'religious experience'" he is forced to make a crucial objection: "But the term is burdened - this is why we avoid it - with the underlying idea that man generally is capable of religious experience or that this capability has the critical significance of a norm."[15] Note the term norm [*Norm*]. It is the term Barth uses in expounding the concept of *analogia fidei* in a way that reinforces the Reformers' sense of *regula fidei*, a theological norm, a "measure of faith" as Barth has it in *CD* I/1. Barth's objection returns to the impossibility of a criterion independent of revelation. The concept of religious experience implies that we know what it is revelation is, that we possess the power to arbitrate on the issue.

The question of whether we have innate knowledge of God cannot be settled by 'looking inside us', as it were, for we have no idea for what it is we would be looking. Barth can go so far as to say that it is not the religious *a priori per se* to which he objects:

Even the concept of the religious *a priori*, which played such a big part in religious philosophy around 1910, would not have to be rejected so absolutely or intrinsically if it were not for the unfortunate fact that on the basis of a right or wrong understanding of Kant it is understood as a

---

[14] Barth, *CD* II/1, 67.
[15] Barth, *CD* I/1, 193.

capability or property grounded in man as such and as the corresponding freedom of control.[16]

Here Barth appears to want to absolve Kant from responsibility for the theological tradition whose most important and influential figure was Schleiermacher (a tradition cited by Welch and quoted in Chapter 1). Here Barth appears to entertain the possibility of a religious *a priori* insofar as it did not entail capability or control in the above sense. It is any suggestion of the latter that Barth rejected. To proceed as if this rejection were not in force was tantamount to speaking a private language. For Barth the "development of anthropological speculation by way of Descartes and Kant to Schelling and Hegel and finally and logically Feuerbach"[17] is a error of historic proportions. Feuerbach's idea of God as man's own projection of himself - God the *imago humanitas* (*imago Dei*) reversed - is the *reductio ad absurdum* of the delusion that we have a capacity to conceive of God of ourselves. *Not only do we believe we have such a capacity - and therefore possess a criterion - we believe that we ourselves are the criterion.* It is in this context that Barth understands the significance of the cry of the Second Commandment, "thou shalt not make unto thee any likeness." It is in this sense that it is a central theological proposition in Barth's position on epistemology in the *Church Dogmatics*.

The power of Barth's transcendental argument is demonstrated not only by its repudiation of any kind of anthropological *a priori* proof. Natural theology is conceptually impossible precisely because we have no idea what it is we want to prove and neither we in ourselves nor the universe can give even the smallest clue. This precludes any form of cosmological argument. That we have no idea what it is we want to prove is the reason the cosmological argument is impossible in principle. Barth's transcendental argument is designed to undermine the possibility that one knows what one is looking for and can subsequently decide whether it is the case or not. (There is no correlation between God as creator and creation that is not completely determined by God's self-revelation. This is why the emphasis in Barth's doctrine of creation is on faith in God as Creator and not on the creation itself providing grounds for believing it to be God's creation.)[18]

To say that we have no original capacity [*Machtigkeit*] for knowledge of God is, for Barth, to say that we have no means of measurement of *what it is* God's self-revelation is independently of revelation. Accordingly, it is on the basis of the 'criterial' argument that Barth repudiates the possibility of an 'innate religious *a priori*'. The aim of Kant's critical philosophy to make a space not only for itself, but for faith - "I have found it necessary to deny

[16] *Ibid*, 193.
[17] *Ibid*, 343.
[18] See Chapter 7.

knowledge, in order to make room for faith" - allowed for an *a priori* vantage-point in terms of which reason could proceed.[19] For Kant, faith is located firmly in the moral sphere, a consequence of the moral postulate of practical reason, the product of the will of a rational being.[20] In other words the limits imposed by the dictates of reason on theoretical reason create a space for faith whose rational justification, whose theology, so to speak, is provided by practical reason.[21]

As Welch indicates, the majority of nineteenth-century theologians affirmed an alternative *a priori* point of departure. Schleiermacher's turn to *Gefühl* [*feeling*] was the most widely followed.[22] Schleiermacher agreed with Kant that "God cannot appear in a concept (*Begriff*) or judgement (*Urteil*). That sort of objectification is epistemologically inaccurate."[23] But he rejected Kant's deduction that faith in God and immortality was, if rational, necessarily moral. Instead of treating God in abstract moral terms, Schleiermacher located religion in the realm of feeling or immediate self-consciousness converging on a consciousness of "ourselves as utterly dependent [*schlechthin abhängig*] or which is to say the same thing, as being in relation to God."[24] Indeed, insofar as he opposed the translation of religion and theology into the intellectualistic or moralistic categories favoured by the Enlightenment and contraposed to them the Romantic categories of feeling and intuition,[25] Schleiermacher may be said to have

---

[19] Kant, *The Critique of Pure Reason*, 29.

[20] Wood, *Kant's Rational Theology*, 15-24.

[21] Hence Kant's *Religion Within the Limits of Reason Alone* refers to religion within the limits of practical reason.

[22] Sources for my analysis of Schleiermacher are: F Schleiermacher, *On Religion: Speeches for the Cultured Despisers of Religion* (Cambridge: CUP, 1988); Schleiermacher, *The Christian Faith* (Edinburgh: T & T Clark, 1928); C Welch, *Protestant Thought in the Nineteenth Century*, vol i; B Gerrish, *A Prince of the Church: Schleiermacher and the Beginnings of Modern Theology* (London: SCM, 1984); Gerrish, *Tradition and the Modern World: Reformed Theology in the Nineteenth Century* (Chicago: University of Chicago Press, 1978); K Clement, *Schleiermacher, Pioneer of Modern Theology* (London: Collins, 1987).

[23] Welch, *Protestant Thought*, 77. Schleiermacher, taking his lead from Kant, denies the possibility of the epistemological project embodied in the classical proofs of the existence of God. However, this does not make Schleiermacher any less a realist than it does Kant. Gerrish raises objections to the thesis that Schleiermacher was a panentheist. See Gerrish, *A Prince of the Church*, 52.

[24] Schleiermacher, *The Christian Faith*, 12.

[25] For Schleiermacher's relation to the Romantic spirit of the first decade of the nineteenth century see R F Streetman, "Romanticism and the *Sensus Numinus* in Schleiermacher", in D Jasper (ed.) *The Interpretation of Belief: Coleridge, Schleiermacher and Romanticism*, (London: MacMillan, 1986), 104-125.

attempted to reassert the *sui generis* identity of religion. Claude Welch comments:

> It is frequently said that the great achievement of Schleiermacher, his creative breakthrough was his fresh interpretation of religion in its own integrity, according it fundamental institution and its locus in feeling or in the immediacy of human existence, whereby the traditionalist-orthodox debate was wholly undercut and a new possibility for understanding religion was opened. This is correct.[26]

Barth's criticism of Kant and Schleiermacher extended to the nineteenth century as a whole (this was not unexpected since the two were the greatest influences on theology in this century). The whole nineteenth-century tradition, derived from Kant's turn to the subject (and indeed Descartes' rationalist approach to God implicit in the *cogito*),[27] was based on a fundamental misconception. The failure of this tradition - Kant's "rational will", Schleiermacher's "feeling of absolute dependence", Hegel's "absolute idealism", the left-wing Hegelians Marx and Feuerbach, Bultmann's "pre-understanding", Brunner's "point of contact" - was that they had succumbed to the illusion that they knew *what it is* they spoke of, independently of God' self-revelation itself. Barth absolutely denied what Schleiermacher's theology, and its legatees assumed, namely the possibility of a religious *a priori* disposition for the possibility of experience of God; and he denied this on the basis of his own species of a non-Kantian transcendental argument traceable back to *sui generis* historical truth, traceable back to the strange new world within the Bible, traceable to the resolution of the metatheological dilemma. Indeed, it is now clear that the resolution of the metatheological dilemma lay in discerning in the Bible a 'measure of faith' whose only measure was it itself.

The question I wish to pursue at this point is the following. The established view is that the relation of 'analogical correspondence' is the fundamental principle behind Barth's conception of the *analogia fidei*. But is there evidence in the *Church Dogmatics* to support the view that the fundamental rationale behind Barth's conception is 'means of measurement' rather than 'analogical relation'?

## 3. The Fundamental Rationale Behind Barth's Analogy of Faith: Norm rather than Analogy

If the strange new world within the Bible is central to Barth's position on

---

[26] Welch, *Protestant Thought*, vol i, 68.
[27] See Barth, *CD* III/1, 350ff, esp. 360.

epistemology in the above way, an important adjustment must be made to the traditional view as regards where the emphasis lies in Barth's conception of the 'analogy of faith'. The effect of this adjustment is an emphasis which coincides with what Barth himself explicitly said about the phrase 'analogy of faith' as used by Paul in Romans 12.6. The emphasis also coincides with the Reformers' interpretation of 12.6., and the use to which they put it in both hermeneutics and doctrine. That the fundamental rationale behind the Reformers' interpretation of *analogian tes pisteos* constitutes the essential properties of Barth's position on epistemology (and indeed, his position on hermeneutics) is, as we have seen, testimony to Barth's loyalty to the Reformed tradition at a fundamental level.

It is not, I think, contentious to say that fundamental to the received view of Barth's 'analogy of faith' today is the concept of analogy or simile. According to Bruce McCormack, for Barth, the *analogia fidei*

> refers most fundamentally to a relation of correspondence between an *act* of God and an *act* of a human subject; the act of divine self-revelation and the human act of faith in which that revelation is acknowledged. More specifically, the analogy which is established in a revelation event is an analogy between God's knowledge of Himself and human knowledge of Him through human concepts and words.[28]

For McCormack there are "three aspects to this analogy":[29]

> First, the analogy in question is not posited with creation. It is not an analogy between the *being* of the Creator and the *being* of the creature - which Barth refers to as an *analogia entis* in contrast to an *analogia fidei*. Second, there is nothing in the being or knowing of the human subject which helps to bring this event about - no capacity or pre-understanding which might be seen as a necessary precondition to its occurrence. The only capacity needed for the analogy is one which God graciously provides in the event itself as a gift, namely faith. In the event of revelation, human knowledge is made by grace to conform to its divine object. Thus (the reader will forgive an overused metaphor, but it is good Barthian language), the direction in which the analogy works is always 'above to below'. That is to say, God's self-knowledge does not become analogically related to a prior human knowledge of Him in revelation; rather, human knowledge is conformed to His. [...] Third, the analogy of faith is to be understood 'actualistically', that is, strictly as an event. The relation of correspondence does not become a predicated of the human subject. [...] The analogy endures only so long as the revelation-event

---

[28] Bruce McCormack, *Karl Barth's Critically Realist Dialectical Theology*, 17.
[29] *Ibid*, 17.

endures. Thus, the 'analogy of faith', once realized, does not pass over to human control.

McCormack continues:

The central area of theological reflection to which this understanding of analogy was applied by Barth is that of the relation of the content of revelation to human language (concepts and words). Barth's view is that human language in itself has no capacity for bearing adequate witness to God. If human language is nevertheless able to bear witness, it will only be because a capacity not intrinsic to it has been brought to it from without. [...] ... God takes up the language of human witness and makes it conform to Himself.[30]

To be sure, Barth's concept of 'analogy of faith' *does* refer to "a relation of correspondence" as set out in the first quotation. It is also true to say that Barth's concept coincides with the properties set out in the second quotation. But it is to put the emphasis in the wrong place to say that, for Barth, the concept of 'analogy of faith' "refers *most fundamentally* [my italics]" to an analogical "relation of correspondence". And it would be making the same mistake were one to say that Barth's analogy of faith "refers most fundamentally" to the "three aspects" of analogy as McCormack defines them. Consequently, though it is true that the "central area of theological reflection to which this understanding of analogy was applied by Barth is that of the relation of the content of revelation to human language (concepts and words)", it is not true that this understanding is the fundamental concept at work in *Barth's understanding* of "the relation of the content of revelation to human language (concepts and words)." *The reason is that Barth's concept of 'analogy of faith' "refers most fundamentally" to the concept of 'measure of faith' construed as a criterion, norm or means of measurement.* It is this conception that constitutes the rationale behind the presence of an analogical "relation of correspondence" and not vice versa. It is this conception that constitutes the rationale behind the presence of the three aspects of analogy affirmed above.

To be fair, there is no doubt that, for McCormack, the concept of criterion is present in Barth's *analogia fidei*. For example, as we have seen, when discussing Barth's Dortmund lecture of 1930, "Fate and Idea in Theology", McCormack interprets Barth's criticism of idealism with the following words: "it ... has no criterion at its disposal by means of which it can lay hands on the truth. The criterion of truth has to be given with

---

[30] *Ibid*, 17-18.

revelation - again and again and again."[31] Moreover, in the essay "Historical Criticism and Dogmatic Interest in Karl Barth's Theological Exegesis of the New Testament", McCormack cites what is undoubtedly a, if not the, central feature of Barth's concept of criterion, namely, that the criterion of *what it is* God's revelation is cannot be anticipated independently of revelation.[32] However, it is my opinion that McCormack never anywhere makes it clear that explanation of Barth's *analogia fidei* does not come to an end with the observation that the analogy "endures only so long as the revelation-event endures", does not "pass over to human control". That is, it is never anywhere made clear that there is a *further* reason why the analogy "endures only so long as the revelation-event endures", does not "pass over to human control". This further reason is, precisely, Barth's concept of analogy of faith construed as a criterion of measurement.

The passage most often cited as central to Barth's conception of the *analogia fidei* goes as follows:

> We say ... that the analogy in question is not an *analogia entis* but according to Rom. 12.6 the *analogia tes pisteos*, the likeness [*die Entsprechung*] of the known in the knowing, [the likeness] of the object in thought, [the likeness] of the Word of God in the word that is thought and spoken by God, *as this differentiates true Christian prophecy in faith from all false prophecy* [my italics].[33]

There is no doubt that the concept of likeness or correspondence looms large in this quotation. But my attention is drawn to the clause, "as this differentiates true Christian prophecy in faith from all false prophecy [*wie sie die wahre, im Glauben stattfindende, christliche Prophetie von aller unwahren unterscheidet*]." Clearly, the likeness that Barth speaks of is made *subject to the condition* that it "differentiates" in the above sense. A likeness that did not differentiate true Christian prophecy in faith from all false prophecy would not be a likeness defined in accordance with the analogy of faith. Such a likeness would be a likeness conforming to some other category (the category *analogia entis* if *analogia fidei* and *analogia entis* are not only mutually exclusive but also exhaustive categories). In

---

[31] *Ibid*, 388.

[32] McCormack actually writes: "Since the shape of the analogy is determined from above, and not on the basis of ordinary usage, we cannot anticipate what it will look like." McCormack, "Historical Criticism and Dogmatic Interest in Karl Barth's Theological Exegesis of the New Testament", in Mark S Burrows and Paul Rorem (eds.), *Hermeneutics from a Historical Perspective: Essays in Honour of Karl Froehlich* (Eerdmans: Grand Rapids, 1991), 332.

[33] Barth, *CD* I/1, 243-244.

other words, without the final clause, one would have no way of knowing (from the passage itself) whether such a likeness conformed to the *analogia entis* rather than to the *analogia fidei*; and identical indeterminacy would ensue were there no reference to *faith* in the final clause.

Clearly, the final clause is essential to Barth's definition of the *analogia fidei*. The question is: does the passage enable one to derive the conclusion that the concept of analogy or likeness is subordinate to the concept of norm or criterion? The passage would enable one to do this if one could logically infer that the likeness differentiated the true from the false only insofar as the likeness itself presupposed a norm or criterion against which it was measured. But one cannot make this inference: for, equally, the passage could be taken to mean that the likeness itself is the norm or criterion which differentiates the true from the false. *One has to conclude that the passage by itself does not enable one to derive the conclusion that the concept of analogy or likeness is subordinate to the concept of norm or criterion.* But, clearly, the passage is not logically irreconcilable with this conclusion. It is a plausible interpretation.

There is, in fact, another passage in the *Church Dogmatics* in which this meaning is unambiguously present. This less well-known (and consequently less quoted) passage occurs in *CD* IV/1, chapter XIV, § 61, 'The Justification of Man', sub-section 4, 'Justification by Faith Alone'. In it Barth is discussing the *imitatio Christi*:

> the *analogian tes pisteos* is the norm [*Norm*] which true prophecy must observe and which distinguishes [*unterscheidet*] between the true and the false. To whom faith and prophecy are analogous - not identical, but corresponding, similar in all their dissimilarity - there can, of course, be no question as far as Paul is concerned.[34]

It should be noted that the same verb *unterscheiden* is used. But in this passage Barth is explicit that the *analogian tes pisteos* is described as "the norm which true prophecy must observe and which distinguishes between the true and the false." The norm, clearly, is Jesus Christ ("Phil. 2.5 speaks of a definite *phronein*, which primarily, originally, and properly is in Jesus Christ ....");[35] and it is to Jesus Christ to "whom faith and prophecy are analogous - not identical, but corresponding, similar in all their dissimilarity." In other words, the clear implication is that the concept of likeness is logically subordinate to the concept of norm. The concept of analogy or similarity functions under the conceptual jurisdiction of the concept of norm.

[34] Barth, *CD* IV/1, 634-5.
[35] *Ibid*, 635.

What is the implication of this conclusion for the interpretation of I/1? Does it allow us infer that I/1 also means that the concept of analogy or similarity is logically subordinate to the concept of norm? Is this what Barth meant by I/1? The most plausible inference to make is that it was. Immediately before the passage from IV/1 - in the same paragraph - Barth asks that: "In this connexion may I recall what I wrote in CD I/1, 242f, concerning the 'divine' conformity of faith."[36] The most obvious implication is that he understood I/1 as expressing a similar, if not identical, point to the one he was explicitly making in IV/1.

The divine conformity of faith is a conformity constituted by analogy or simile to a norm, Jesus Christ. *But that it is conformity in this sense is measured by that same norm.* In other words, as has been said, Jesus Christ is the norm against which talk about God is measured. The key passage has already been quoted but, for convenience, I quote it again:

> Talk about God has true content when it conforms to the being of the Church, i.e., when it conforms to Jesus Christ ... *eite prophetitian, kata ten analogian tes pisteos* (Rom. 12.6). It is in terms of such conformity that dogmatics investigates Christian utterance. Hence it does not have to begin by finding or inventing the standard by which it measures. It sees and recognises that this is given with the Church. It is given in its own peculiar way, as Jesus Christ is given, as God in His revelation gives Himself in faith. But it is given. It is complete in itself. It stands by its claim without discussion. It has the certainty which a true standard or criterion must have to be the means of serious measurement.[37]

It is evident that insofar as the concept of analogical correspondence surfaces in this passage it does so only implicitly, under the aegis of the concept of conformity. Here, the central concept Barth attributes to Romans 12.6 - and the phrase *analogian tes pisteos* - is a criterion, a means of measurement, against which one measures one's statements for truth, falsity, and, indeed, meaning itself.

#### 4. Barth's *Analogia Fidei* Not Essentially a Rhetorical Technique

Though Barth's conception of the *analogia fidei* can be assimilated to the Reformed tradition, this does not imply that the essential nature of Barth's conception coincides with that of a rhetorical technique. Indeed, it can be demonstrated that the Reformers' conception was *not* essentially a rhetorical technique. I therefore take issue with the position advocated by

---

[36] *Ibid*, 634.
[37] Barth, *CD* I/1, 12.

Graham Ward in his book, *Barth, Derrida, and the Language of Theology.* Ward argues that the Reformers interpreted the *analogia fidei* as a rhetorical device. He asserts that: "... 'analogy' is a rhetorical technique for the presentation of an argument, synonymous with 'simile'." He concludes: "... it is this conception of the word that lies behind the Reformer's use of the term '*analogia fidei*'."[38] If what I have said thus far is correct, the Reformers' *analogia fidei* cannot be a rhetorical device synonymous with simile - for the simple reason that simile is not central to the Reformers' conception of the *analogia fidei*. Barth's position on epistemology in the *Church Dogmatics* is not an ontological and epistemological extension of a rhetorical technique the essence of which is 'simile'; it is an ontological and epistemological extension of the concept of 'measure of faith' as delineated above.

However, the latter conclusion does not exclude the possibility that, construed as a measure of faith, the Reformers' *analogia fidei* is itself essentially a rhetorical technique. The mistake this position makes is, I believe, the following. From the fact that the analogy of faith *can* be used as a rhetorical device - *can* be used rhetorically - it mistakenly moves the conclusion that the *analogia fidei* is in its essential nature a rhetorical technique. Ward assimilates the Reformers' use of *analogia fidei* to sixteenth-century humanist rhetoric. Humanist rhetoric supersedes scholastic logic: "logic gives way to rhetoric and ... the point of argumentation was no longer to ascertain the truth, to prove it, but to persuade, to render probable."[39] The source for Ward's argument is Lisa Jardine's contribution to *The Cambridge History of Late Mediaeval Philosophy*, "Humanism and the Teaching of Logic".[40] But in Jardine's account no mention is made of simile or analogy, far less of the Reformers' *analogia fidei*. This fact, of itself, is not fatal to Ward's argument if it could be shown that the Reformers' conception coincided with Jardine's definition of the aims of sixteenth-century humanist rhetoric. But, for Jardine, humanist rhetoric is designed to persuade one's opponent to a desired conclusion regardless of whether one's argument is actually valid. As Jardine puts it of Agricola's *De inventione dialectia*: "The object of the text is unashamedly to enable the student to make the appropriate debating moves: the only criterion for preferring one strategy to another is its effectiveness in polemic."[41]

---

[38] Ward, *Barth, Derrida, and the Language of Theology*, 98.

[39] *Ibid*, 98.

[40] Lisa Jardine, "Humanism and the Teaching of Logic", in N Kretzman, A Kenny, and J Pinborg (ed), *The Cambridge History of Late Mediaeval Philosophy* (Cambridge: CUP, 1982), 797-807.

[41] *Ibid*, 805.

It is submitted that there is nothing in any of the Reformed conceptions of the *analogia fidei* cited above that would necessarily entail adherence to Agricola's criterion. It is not disputed that the *analogia fidei could* be employed as a strategy to persuade an opponent to a desired conclusion regardless of the validity of the argument; but such employment is not essential to the identity of the *analogia fidei*. Calvin's reference to 'the first principles of religion' may be used to differentiate the true from the false and the probable from the improbable; but neither course of action necessarily reduces to a rhetorical strategy. To assert that the fundamental rationale of the Reformers' use of the *analogia fidei* was "no longer to ascertain the truth, to prove it, but to persuade, to render probable" - or that the Reformers' "only criterion for preferring one strategy to another" was its "effectiveness in polemic" - is to attribute a degree of 'worldliness' (perhaps even cynicism) to Calvin and other Reformers not borne out by their concern for the truth. To "render probable" did not exclude the possibility that the Reformed objective was precisely to ascertain the truth (and, indeed, it should be noted that the *analogia fidei* allowed one to derive non-probablistically that which was false, i.e., anything "contrary" to, for example, the Apostles Creed*)*. The simple fact that the *analogia fidei* can be, and was, used non-rhetorically, as a means of logical argument, is sufficient to repudiate Ward's 'post-modern' re-reading of sixteenth-century Reformed theology. To say the *analogia fidei* is, contingently at least, a literary (non-ontological) technique does not entail it is a rhetorical technique.

According to Ward, Barth's *Die christliche Dogmatik im Entwurf* testifies to an epistemological and ontological extension of the Reformed 'hermeneutical' notion of *analogia fidei* construed essentially as rhetorical technique.[42] But even there Barth implements the *analogia fidei* in such a way that a standard or criterion is non-rhetorically invoked against which rival interpretations of Scripture are measured. The particular case at issue is Romans 5.1 and whether the text should read 'Therefore, since we are justified through faith, we have peace with God through our Lord Jesus Christ' or 'Therefore, since we are justified by faith, may we have peace with God through our Lord Jesus Christ'. Though it does not logically follow from what has been accomplished in Jesus Christ that Paul could not have meant the latter, the probability, for Barth, is that the former is the correct reading since what Jesus Christ has accomplished for us is, in fact, peace with God rather than the mere possibility of such peace. In other words, Jesus Christ's atoning death on the cross is invoked as the criterion against which the meaning of Romans 5.1 is measured. As Ward himself notes, Barth ends this particular discussion with the acknowledgement that all that can be decided is "the form of testimony to revelation most likely in

[42] Ward, *Barth, Derrida, and the Language of Theology*, 100.

the text."[43] But such acknowledgement implies that Barth's argument is not reducible to rhetoric (otherwise he would not have added his acknowledgement); the acknowledgement is testimony simply to an honest man pointing out the limitations of logical argument in this particular case!

As Ward points out, Barth's use of the term *analogia fidei* in *Die christliche Dogmatik im Entwurf* "reflects his preoccupation throughout the 1920s with Reformation theology."[44] In particular, his use of it developed out of his adherence to the Scripture-principle. In his 1922 lectures on Calvin he refers to the objective of Reformed Reformation as being "the establishment of the Word of God contained in the Bible as the norm of faith and life."[45] In 1923 he delivered a lecture entitled "Reformed Doctrine: Its Essence and Task" in which he said that "every doctrine must be measured against an unchangeable and impassable standard": the Word of God, "discoverable in the Scriptures."[46] In the *Gottingen Dogmatics*, the theme is continued: the Bible is a "norm" of faith, a "ruler or plumb line or rule".[47]

## Concluding Remarks

Though Barth's position on epistemology in the *Church Dogmatics* owes something to Kant's transcendental argument, the form it takes in Barth is not found in Kant. Barth ties the Reformers' doctrine of the *analogia fidei* to Kant's transcendental argument in his own unique way. In so doing he comes up with something very similar to the central strategy of the later Wittgenstein who himself, as was said, advances his own unique variation of the transcendental argument. That is, it is in the later Wittgenstein that we find a parallel development: an ingenious fusion of transcendental argument and language. Central to Barth's position on epistemology is a species of *conceptual foundationalism* similar to that which one finds in the later Wittgenstein. Concepts such as *Quelle, Norm* and *Ursprung* are central to the argument Barth proposes in the *Church Dogmatics*. They are also central to the later philosophy. It is the later philosophy that I will examine in Chapter 12. Now I turn to Barth's exposition of the pre-Easter Gospel narrative.

---

[43] *Ibid*, 99-100.

[44] *Ibid*, 97.

[45] Barth, *Die Theologie Calvins, 1922*, edited by Hans Scholl, (Zurich: TVZ, 1993), 2.

[46] Barth, "Reformed Doctrine: Its Essence and Task", Barth, *The Word of God and the Word of Man*, 240-241.

[47] Barth, *Gottingen Dogmatics*, 216; *ibid*, 212.

# Chapter 11
# Barth on the Historical Truth-Claims of the Pre-Easter Gospel Narrative: God as Reconciler

## 1. Introduction

In the preceding three chapters I have sought to delineate Barth's understanding of the historical truth-claims of the Gospel narratives as regards the resurrection-appearances history. But, no matter what the Enlightenment might make of this history in the light of Barth's understanding, there was still the matter of the historical truth-claims of the pre-Easter narrative. The eighteenth and nineteenth centuries (and indeed the twentieth) in the form of, on the one hand, Kant and Troeltsch, and, on the other, the tradition of Strauss through Weiss to Schweitzer had provided respectively, the epistemological and the hermeneutical context to Barth's understanding of the Easter history. I now want to argue that the latter, hermeneutical (or perhaps more accurately, notwithstanding Strauss, critical-historical) tradition is no less relevant to Barth on the historical truth-claims of the pre-Easter narrative. To be sure, Barth had a decided preference for pre-critical Reformed Christological categories over the critical Christological orientation of the nineteenth century.[1] But what he saw in the pre-critical categories was precisely a way of countering conclusions reached by such as Schweitzer in *The Quest of the Historical Jesus*, conclusions perhaps reached with no great pleasure, (at the very least Schweitzer claimed one should write a biography of Jesus only in hate) but with no little intellectual integrity. For Barth the value of the Reformed christological categories - the threefold work of Christ as prophet, priest and king - was that they could be suitably adapted to reflect the emphasis actually found in the historical truth-claiming Gospel narrative. In other words, the value of these unashamedly pre-critical categories was that they were intrinsically better suited to countering the historical analysis of the nineteenth

---

[1] See McGrath, *The Making of Modern Christology*, 113.

century than, say, metaphysical or philosophical conceptualities. Speaking of them in his commentary on Calvin's 1545 Catechism Barth wrote that:

> If we study what Calvin tells us of Christ we shall notice that he does not give us any abstract definition of his manhood and his Godhead, nor of their relations. But he shows us a succession of the FACTS: the fact that Jesus Christ is not only a man, or the fact that his Godhead is hidden under his manhood, or the fact that he glorifies his manhood by his Godhead.[2]

According to Barth, Calvin does not give us a static 'system-orientated' picture of Christ. Instead:

> He bids us to enter into the history of Christ. The same holds for Christ as it does for a full bird in flight. No picture will convey that flight, except a moving picture. [...] You must ... view the whole, not as if it were a system, but as a history.[3]

Of course, to say that such categories are intrinsically better suited to counter the historical analysis of the nineteenth century than philosophically-orientated ones does not of itself entail that this was in fact the way in which they *were* used in Barth. What I think *does* entail this conclusion is the curious twist in the tale that Barth tells of the threefold office of the work of Christ, a twist to do with his treatment of the priestly office in particular. In conjunction with this adaptation of the threefold office, a close reading of both *CD* IV/1 (the section entitled "The Judge Judged in Our Place") and *CD* IV/2 (the section entitled "The Royal Man")[4] reveals that, throughout these pages, what is crucial for Barth is that – as against the reversal, conflict, and ultimate division claimed by such as Schweitzer between (crucially) Jesus' proclamation of the kingdom of God in Galilee and his death on the cross outside of the gates of Jerusalem[5] - there is utter continuity and absolute harmony. If there is not – if the

---

[2] Barth, *The Faith of the Church: A Commentary on the Apostles' Creed According to Calvin*, edited by Jean-Louis Leuba, translated by Gabriel Vahanian, (New York: Meridian, 1958), 56.

[3] *Ibid*, 56. There is an excellent summary of Barth's employment of the 1545 and the Heidelberg Catechism in Philip Putin, "Two Early Reformed Catechisms, the Threefold Office and the Shape of Karl Barth's Christology" *The Scottish Journal of Theology* (44) 1991, 195-214. Unfortunately it fails to note that Barth subordinates the priestly office to the judicial work of Christ.

[4] Barth, *CD* IV/1, 211-283; *CD* IV/2, 154-264

[5] Schweitzer, *The Quest of the Historical Jesus*, 370-371, 386-397.

tradition culminating in Schweitzer is right - then Christological doctrine is fatally undermined, and the substance of what Barth has said in the earlier respective sections of IV/1 and IV/2 - 'The Way of the Son of God into the Far Country' and 'The Homecoming of the Son of Man' - is without a basis in reality. (Barth would have heartily agreed with the absence of Christology [in the orthodox sense] from Schweitzer's book: as we shall see below, Barth would have insisted that Schweitzer's historical analysis *obliged* him to omit it.)

The tradition beginning with Strauss through Weiss and culminating in Schweitzer insisted that the first half of the pre-Easter narrative – Jesus in Galilee proclaiming the imminence of kingdom of God - had to be taken seriously in any historical analysis. Barth concurred with this view, and the pages of IV/1 and IV/2 show this. They also show, notwithstanding the modifications Barth instituted for reasons of historical truth-claiming more radical than those of Calvin, that he employed the Reformed Christological categories in a manner which stood in stark opposition to the conclusions reached by the nineteenth century on the historical Jesus.

Allied to Barth's affirmation of historical truth-claiming, literal sense, and the final form of the text is his affirmation of a theological interpretation of Scripture. But what is theological interpretation for Barth? Is it inimical to historical interpretation? Such a judgement would be a mistake. A theological interpretation for Barth is one that affirms *a historical truth-claiming narrative* that, among other things, narrates the history of God in Christ going to the cross in order to reconcile the world to Himself. As Barth puts it: "The atonement is noetically the history about Jesus Christ, and ontically, Jesus Christ's own history."[6]The latter claim is crucial to Barth because it is clear that he wishes to understand this history as *one unitary* event. Jesus' "death on the cross was and is the fulfilment of the incarnation of the Word and therefore the humiliation of the Son of God and exaltation of the Son of Man."[7] But it is not merely a question of *fulfilment*, it is also one of *completion*: "In the earlier sequence He was moving towards this fulfilment – but only moving towards it. How could that which *had not yet been completed* [my italics] be revealed as completed?"[8] In other words, *the incarnation as an event is not complete until Jesus' death on the cross.* But this means that there is only *one*

---

[6] Barth, *CD* IV/1, 158.

[7] Barth, *CD* IV/2, 140-141.

[8] *Ibid*, 141.

historical event - and indeed, one indivisible event - in the final form of the pre-Easter Gospel narrative, so says Barth.[9]

Two propositions follow from this conclusion. The first is that there is only *one* historical truth-claim regarding Jesus in the pre-Easter narrative, namely, that cited above: God was in Christ reconciling the world to Himself (2 Cor. 5.19). (There are then according to Barth *two* historical events in the Gospel, the first corresponding the history of the atonement culminating in the crucifixion and the second corresponding to the resurrection-appearances history.)

The second is this. According to Barth Christological doctrine is in essence a historical truth-claiming doctrine. This is quite clear from the assertion that the atonement is ontically Jesus' own history. It followed therefore that there was only *one* Christology in the four Gospel narratives.[10] For Barth this Christology must fundamentally be in

---

[9] Barth speaks of the indivisibility of God in *CD* II/1. See Barth, *CD* II/1, 457ff. While he eschews the tendency of the older Reformed Dogmatics to think in terms of mathematical indivisibility, this seems to me to a subject where logic and analytic philosophy could be brought to bear genuinely and fruitfully on the concept of historical truth-claiming, and in particular, the historical event of God in Christ reconciling the world. To speak of the incomplete event of God reconciling the world to Himself seems fraught with conceptual difficulties, as if God could begin but cease for essentially accidental or arbitrary reasons: as if for example, the human agents in the story - Pilate, Judas, etc - could have done otherwise than they did. The one indivisible event of God reconciling the World to Himself entails that Pilate, Judas, etc could not have stood in Jesus' way: Pilate, for example, could not have insisted that Jesus go free and not be crucified. (This does not entail that they were not free to act otherwise, though it is to agree with Acts 2.23 and Acts 4.28 that God foreknew that Pilate and Judas, etc. would do what each did. I am confident there is no contradiction here but it is beyond the scope of the book to go into the reasons why). When I speak of the event being an indivisible event I do not mean that it comes ready-made, complete, and therefore indivisible in that sense. The intuition behind the concept is more that there is one event which is irreducibly identifiable as the above, and that the event that is God reconciling the world then and there, as it were, is not that event if it is not completed in the sense of the aspect of accomplishment (rather than mere activity). God cannot be reconciling the world (activity) but *not* reconcile the world (accomplishment). We are in the realm of the grammar of aspects (rather than mere tense), of the philosophy of event and of God.

[10] The evidence for this claim can, I submit, be found in *CD* IV/2, 139-140. The key passage that would be developed at length in this respect, had I the space, would be the following: "…. the Early Church was quite right when it did not hesitate to set [John's Gospel] alongside the other three [the Synoptic Gospels]. Must we prefer its Christology to that of the others? Or must we complain that it is a misunderstanding and misrepresentation? Both courses have been adopted. But surely it is better not to see any real distinction, but confidently to maintain that in the Fourth Gospel the deductions are drawn which are necessarily forced upon the reader by the text of the other three. If

conformity with that affirmed by the *homoousios* clause in the Nicene creed although he is clear that such doctrinal decisions are to be regarded as "guiding lines" rather than the fundamental ontological categories themselves.[11] There is no incarnational *account* that can be understood apart from an incarnational *narrative*. And there is no incarnational narrative independent of the *historical truth-claim* that God was in Christ reconciling the world to Himself.

### 2. "Quite So, Strauss, Schweitzer, and Bultmann! Any Interpretation That Has Nothing To Do with the Resurrection-Appearances History Has Nothing to do with God!"[11]

For Barth a theological interpretation of the pre-Easter Gospel narrative is one that affirms one historical truth-claim that 'God was in Christ reconciling the world to Himself' as one unitary completed event. But, as Barth is aware, there is little explicit interpretation of this kind in the Synoptic Gospels. As he puts it in *CD* IV/1: "It is obvious in these Gospels [the Synoptics] there is

---

we do not see it for ourselves, then perhaps this oldest comparative picture will show us that in respect of its character as revelation the story of Jesus before and after Easter is not merely a whole but is one in substance. Conversely, it is not really possible to read the comparative representation in John intelligently unless we are reminded by the synoptic pictures what is the problem which it answers: the step from the relative concealment of the being of Jesus Christ to its absolute manifestation: the historicity, even in this respect, in which His being is revealed before no less than after, but after differently from before." *Ibid*, 139-140.

[11] For Barth the fundamental ontological category is *event*, and indeed, *historical event*. Historical event in turn, and one unitary continuous completed historical event in particular – God in Christ reconciling the world to Himself – constitutes the *hypostasis*, *subsistentia*, or *identity* of the Son of God. The identity of the Son of God cannot be understood apart from this one completed historical event (Frei was right to understand Barth in this manner though Barth derived such conclusions from a historical truth-claiming narrative; he did not apply them as literary insights to the category of realistic narrative). Even to say that God was in Christ reconciling the world in such a way that it was God speaking and acting and going to His death on the cross – Christology understood ontologically rather than merely functionally - can only be said from the perspective of the completed historical event. The latter is always logically superordinate. Barth is the most thorough-going historical truth-claiming theologian who ever existed. Every theological doctrine is of the nature of a historical truth-claim. Truth-claims about the trinity, economic and immanent, are of the nature of a historical truth-claim, as are truth-claims regarding the eternal election of Jesus Christ. And one could list more. Jüngel's *The Doctrine of the Trinity* is one example of an analysis of Barth which rightly makes the concept of event central to Barth's theology.

little express mention of significance of the Christ event which took place there and then."[12] Instead: "It is content simply to tell the story - this is how it was, this is how it happened. There is interpretation only in the lightest and sometimes rather alien strokes."[13] And later on in *CD* IV/1 he says: "The Gospel story ... does not offer any theological explanation. It says hardly anything about the significance of the event."[14] But then he goes on: "But in telling us what it had to tell us, and the way in which it does, it testifies that we are dealing with the event which at bottom cannot bear any other theological explanation than that which we have tried to give it in actual agreement with every Church which is worthy of the name of Christian."[15] In other words, the story that is told, and the way in which it is told (the latter is quite crucial for Barth) entails that theological explanation (one can substitute here 'theological interpretation'), is the only valid alternative; which is to say, among other things, that one cannot affirm the history in the final form of the Gospel narratives without affirming a theological interpretation. And the reason is, to reiterate: not only is the atonement "noetically the history about Jesus Christ"; it is also "ontically, Jesus Christ's own history." What does all this mean?

    Whatever fundamental disagreement exists between, on the one hand, Barth, and, on the other, the tradition of Strauss to Schweitzer to Bultmann, there is no fundamental disagreement on the question of the narrative structure of the Gospel. All agree that the final form of the Gospel story could be broken down into three sub-parts: the history of Jesus proclaiming the Kingdom of God in Galilee; His passion history in Jerusalem; His resurrection-appearances history.[16] But crucial to Barth's thesis that "we are dealing with an event which cannot bear any other theological explanation" than the incarnational one is whether the first two histories were fundamentally in harmony with each other or whether they were fundamentally at odds with each other.[17] Fundamental conflict between Barth and Schweitzer, for example, existed on this point.

---

[12] Barth, *CD* IV/1, 224.

[13] *Ibid*, 227. One "rather alien stroke" is precisely the softening of the contradiction and reversal between Jesus' history in Galilee and his passion history.

[14] *Ibid*, 239

[15] *Ibid*, 239-240.

[16] Famously, Barth, *CD* IV/1, 224-228. Barth locates the division between the first part and the second part in the following way: "The sections from the record of the entry into Jerusalem up to and including the last supper can be regarded as belonging to the first of the second part, or as the transition from the one to the other. But from the description of Gethsemane at any rate the second part forms a self-contained whole." *Ibid*, 226.

[17] When I speak of theological interpretation I mean *Christian* theological interpretation!

The significance of the conflict cannot be underestimated. According to Barth harmony and continuity are absolutely vital in a logical sense to the validity of theological interpretation. Three propositions are essential to understanding Barth on this point.

1) One could not affirm a theological interpretation of the Gospel narrative and not affirm harmony and continuity between the two histories. Or putting the same point differently: to argue that the two histories were fundamentally (not just apparently) at odds with each other was *ipso facto* to rule out theological interpretation. To affirm a theological interpretation is to affirm fundamental harmony and concord.

But even more crucially perhaps is the second proposition: 2) One could not affirm harmony and not affirm the third part, the resurrection-appearances history. *In other words, for Barth what was crucial to which view should prevail - harmony or conflict - was whether or not one affirmed the historicity of the third part, the resurrection-appearances history.*

And since theological interpretation relied logically on harmony and the unified purpose of God in the two histories, a third proposition followed: 3) *One could only affirm a theological interpretation - the historical truth-claim that God was in Christ reconciling the world to Himself - if one affirmed the resurrection-appearances history.* To reject the resurrection-appearances history committed one to rejecting harmony between the two earlier histories and morally obliged one to jettison theological interpretation.

History had corroborated him on this. The nineteenth century adopted an increasingly sceptical attitude toward the stories, explaining them - in line with its understanding of nature as a closed continuum of cause and effect - as nothing more than the products of a first-century Palestinian mythological consciousness.[18] It was precisely because of this in the end that the tradition from Strauss to Weiss to Schweitzer (and one should include Ritschl in this) testified to a progressive diminution of the theological importance of the second half of the pre-Easter story - the passion story. The tradition did not deny that a man Jesus had died on a cross, but it did deny that in this event - *not merely as interpretation of this event* - God was acting, going to the cross Himself, reconciling the world to

---

[18] One view that gained increasing currency from the middle of the eighteenth century onward was the view that Bible itself is a product of a particular cultural-historical consciousness. According to this broadly 'history of religions' approach, the books of the Bible were viewed by emerging modernity as the products of a mentality awash in mythology. Strauss noted such a context to his own discernment of myth in the Gospel narratives. Strauss, *The Life of Jesus Critically Examined*, 52-59. It was in this context that Strauss understood the resurrection appearances. *Ibid*, 709-744.

Himself. It accepted that Jesus had been executed on a cross as historical fact but did not attach any theological significance to this. Simultaneously, there occurred a corresponding concentration on, and elevation of, the first half of the story, the historical kernel that could be identified with Jesus' proclamation of the kingdom of God in Galilee.[19]

When the tradition put the two parts together again, on the hand, the man Jesus proclaiming the kingdom of God in Galilee, and, on the other, the man Jesus crucified on a cross outside the gates of Jerusalem by the civil authorities at the invitation of the religious authorities, what increasingly imposed itself on the minds of such interpreters was the impression of utter contradiction between the two histories. Jesus' passion and death was seen as an alien element in His work in the sense that it completely contradicted his earlier work of proclaiming the kingdom of God in Galilee. The passion of Jesus was a catastrophe which burst unexpectedly into his life. Jesus' mission in proclaiming the kingdom of God ended in failure and death on the cross. The kingdom did not come. *In effect, the tradition of Strauss, culminating in Schweitzer (and beyond), felt morally bound on the grounds of historical rationality to dispense with the final form of the story and produce its own historical reconstruction of events, the real history of Jesus which, as Schweitzer has it, told of a reversal of fortune ending in defeat and ignominious death.*

Barth agreed that to consign the resurrection appearances stories to the category of mythology was necessarily to be committed to a relation of reversal and contradiction between the two earlier histories. Once one had assimilated the stories to mythology one merely had the death of a man on a cross. *Once one had eliminated the sequel one could not with any kind of rationality affirm the final form of the two earlier histories. The approach to the Gospels that one finds in Strauss, Schweitzer and Bultmann is not a theological interpretation precisely because it is not committed to the final form of the first two parts of the Gospel histories* (though clearly it is committed to literal sense). But given it had rejected the resurrection-appearances history, the position was utterly rational and inevitable, and indeed highly moral.

However, once one affirmed the sequel to the two earlier histories, it was quite different. For it was *only* in the light of Jesus' self-declaration that events which seemed to speak of reversal, contradiction and defeat

---

[19] To be sure, on the basis of an eschatological-apocalyptic understanding of the kingdom of God, Johannes Weiss criticised Ritschl's affirmation of an ethical understanding of the kingdom of God as a basis of dogmatic theology. Notwithstanding this, it remains the case that both concentrated on the first half of the pre-Easter story. See Johannes Weiss, *Jesus' Proclamation of the Kingdom of God*, trans. R H Hier and D L Holland (Philadelphia: Fortress, 1971), 57.

could be seen as the one unified purpose of God they were: the perfect harmony and accord, between, on the one hand, the first half of the pre-Easter story in which Jesus proclaims the kingdom of God, and, on the other, the second half of the pre-Easter story in which Jesus goes to His death on the cross. The sequel to the first two histories - the resurrection-appearances history - is absolutely crucial in distinguishing between the validity of *historical reconstruction* as against the validity of *theological history*. Historical reconstruction was perfectly rational as long as one did not affirm the historicity of the resurrection appearances and Jesus' self-declaration. Given this presupposition, historical reconstruction was the only moral course to undertake. If the resurrection-appearances history could not be affirmed historically then the harmony and accord intrinsic to the final form of the two earlier histories could not but be a departure from historical truth. As Barth said, perhaps with Schweitzer in mind, without His self-declaration in His resurrection-appearances history

> Jesus would certainly have gone through world history, or rather gone under in world history, only as an obscure and unsuccessful Jewish eccentric and revolutionary like so many others.[20]

In other words, one could affirm the history of *God in Christ reconciling the world to Himself* only if one affirmed the resurrection-appearances history. According to the historical truth-claiming narrative itself, *without* the short sequel to the passion history, the Evangelists would not have been in a position to say that in the pre-Easter history God was in Christ going to the cross, reconciling the world to Himself in his journey of obedience even unto death on the cross. Instead, the story would have been what it was at the point of the cross, one of hopes raised in Galilee by Jesus' proclamation of the kingdom of God and dashed on the cross outside the gates of Jerusalem.

But, according to Barth, once one affirmed Jesus' self-declaration in His resurrection-appearances history, one was not merely re-interpreting the death of a man on a cross (with the degrees of freedom that come with interpreting), one was telling His passion and death as it actually was. One was telling of a *theological* history which had unfolded in harmony and in identity with the 'Logos' of God. One was not adding to the history as in interpretation; rather, one was acknowledging it: the being of Jesus Christ as the One in whom God is and therefore the One who is God. This is the sense in which Barth affirmed that the atonement is, ontically, Jesus Christ's own history. There is *one* history, and this one history is

---

[20] Barth, *CD* IV/2, 168.

constituted by *one* historical event: God in Christ reconciling the world to Himself. One indivisible historical event.

### 3. "The Easter story is the Gospel story in its unity and completeness as the revealed story of redemption": the Judicial Work (IV/1) and the Kingly Office (IV/2)

One can affirm a theological interpretation - and therefore harmony and accord - only if one affirms the resurrection-appearances history. One can affirm one completed unitary indivisible event rather than two (or more) discrete incongruous divided events only if one affirms this history. Without this history, one only had the death on the cross of a man, the tragic end and failure of the man Jesus on the cross. It is for this reason that Barth understands "the Easter story as the commentary on the Gospel story in the unity and completeness of its first two parts."[21] The "commentary" of the resurrection-appearances history tells us that God was in this man in his pre-Easter history, or more precisely, the man Jesus revealed Himself as God. God was in Christ.

Clearly, 'God was in Christ' is an essential presupposition of 'God was in Christ reconciling he world to Himself.' The latter cannot be true unless the former is true. Nevertheless, they do not say the same thing. Though 'God was in Christ reconciling he world to Himself' entails 'God was in Christ', the converse is not true. The former is a necessary condition or presupposition of the latter, but not a sufficient condition. This means that the resurrection-appearances history is not a sufficient condition of 'God was in Christ reconciling the world to Himself' though it is a sufficient condition of 'God was in Christ'. What is a sufficient condition is *the threefold office of the work of Christ* in the context of the resurrection-appearances history.[22]

The concept of the threefold office, as was said, is a christological term referring to the threefold work of Christ as prophet, priest and king. It was taught by Calvin and became standard among the Reformed in the sixteenth century.[23] When one first examines Barth's employment it looks very much that he is affirming a threefold office in exactly the same way that Calvin is.

---

[21] Barth, *CD* IV/1, 228.

[22] In what follows I will focus only on the priestly office and the kingly office, not the prophetic office. Barth's exposition of the prophetic office is found in *CD* IV/3. I leave it to one side since it does not appear necessary to the argument that I make in this chapter on behalf of Barth against the nineteenth century.

[23] See Robert E Peterson Sr, *Calvin and the Atonement* (Ross-shire: Mentor, 1999) for a lucid introduction to Calvin's understanding of the threefold office of Christ.

First, like Calvin, Barth understands Christ as the fulfilment of the Old Testament offices of prophet, priest and king. He is the definitive prophet, the definitive priest and the definitive king. Second, like Calvin, he understands the threefold office as intrinsic or essential to the identity of Jesus Christ. For Calvin, the threefold office is not only true of the earthly Christ, it is also true of him in his heavenly life after the resurrection appearances and ascension. In other words, it is not something Christ ceases to be when he has left his earthly existence. Barth too says that the threefold office tells you who Jesus Christ is, who he is in his intrinsic identity.[24]

But when one looks closer at Barth's employment one sees that, as was said, there is a curious twist in the tale that he tells of the threefold office, and it is to do primarily with the priestly office. He does not affirm the priestly office directly but only indirectly - only insofar as he first affirms what he calls the judicial work of Christ. Though Barth does not speak explicitly of Christ's judicial office in IV/1, he does speak explicitly of Christ's "judicial work."[25] There are two important clues that I think are indicative of this fact. First: whereas Barth has a section in *CD* IV/2 where he affirms the Kingly Office directly under the title 'The Royal Man', no such title corresponds to a section on the Priestly Office. Instead in IV/1 we have the section entitled 'The Judge Judged in Our Place.' This is a simple and unmistakable asymmetry in Barth's presentation of the doctrine of Reconciliation that we cannot simply ignore. Second: the priestly office itself is treated almost as an appendix at the end of the section entitled 'The Judge Judged in Our Place' - only after Barth has provided exposition of some sixty pages on the judicial work of Christ.[26]

Why did he affirm the priestly office only indirectly - only insofar as he affirmed the judicial work of Christ? Barth says that he chose the judicial framework over other possible frameworks because of "the actual importance of this way of thinking and its particularly good basis in the Bible."[27] And more resonantly: he says that he refrained from presenting the Gospel narrative in the priestly framework for one main reason. He finds that he is able to see the narrative "better and more distinctly and more comprehensively" under the judicial framework than would be possible had he committed himself radically to the priestly framework.[28]

The question is: Why is it that Barth is able to see the Gospel story "more distinctly and more comprehensively" when he employs the judicial

[24] Calvin, *Institutes*, vol 1, 494-503; Barth, *CD* IV/1, 137-138; Barth, *CD* IV/3, 5-6, 275.
[25] Barth, *CD* IV/1, 277.
[26] *Ibid*, 211-283.
[27] *Ibid*, 273
[28] *Ibid*, 275.

framework rather than the priestly framework? The first answer might be: because then he can view the Gospel story as one continuous comprehensive whole. But this will not do. For if we look at Calvin's *A Harmony of the Gospels*, for example, we see too that he views the Gospel story as one continuous whole. Yet he does not employ the judicial framework in the manner in which Barth does. Why then? The answer I think is this. It is within the judicial framework that Barth can most successfully affirm the first two parts of the Gospels story as a unified whole. For Barth, as was said, the Gospel narrative is constituted of three essential parts. The first part is Jesus proclaiming the kingdom of God in Galilee. The second part is Jesus' passion history culminating in his death on the cross. And the third part is the resurrection-appearances history. What Barth is essentially doing with the judicial framework is affirming a unified narrative pattern connecting across the first two parts, and corresponding to the judicial work of Christ.

In doing this he does something which has no precedent in Calvin nor, as far as I can see - in the Reformed tradition as a whole. He understands the first part of the Gospel story - Jesus proclaiming the kingdom of God in Galilee - in terms of Jesus as the Judge. Now, Calvin certainly affirmed the presence of Christ's judicial work in the second part of the Gospel narrative. In both his 1555 commentary on the Synoptic Gospels and the 1559 *Institutes* he speaks of Jesus Christ judged before the judgement seat of Pilate: Jesus Christ as the judged who takes on the judgement that was ours.[29] But Jesus Christ as the Judge in the first part of the Gospel receives no real narrative emphasis from Calvin at all. Or, to be more precise: for Calvin the presence of Jesus Christ as the Judge in the first part is to be understood in the context of a salvation history framework: Jesus Christ as the Judge is construed as an anticipation or a prefigurement of the future Jesus Christ, the Jesus Christ who will judge the living and the dead on judgement day.[30]

For Calvin, as for the Reformed tradition in general, Jesus as the Judge in the first part of the Gospel narrative is understood entirely in terms of Jesus Christ the "Judge of the quick and the dead", as referred to in Acts 10 and the apostles' creed - and this was on the whole taken to be an exercise of His Kingly Office. Barth reversed the direction of this understanding: the judge of the living and the dead is understood in terms of the earthly Jesus. He is

---

[29] Calvin, *A Harmony of the Gospels*, vol 3, 179; Calvin, *Institutes*, 509.

[30] Calvin refers to Jesus in the first part of the Gospel story as "the severe Judge" whose judgement then and there is only a prefigurement of "the final day" - judgement day. Calvin, *A Harmony of the Gospels*, vol 1, 123, 128-129. For Barth, insofar as Jesus' judgement is a prefigurement of anything, it is, as we shall see, of His own judgement on the cross. It is precisely as this judged and crucified person that He is the judge of the 'quick and the dead' in the traditional sense.

completely identical with Jesus the Judge during his days in Galilee and Jerusalem, and his end on the cross.[31]

In other words, almost certainly Barth introduced something new in relation to Calvin and the Reformed tradition. When explaining the rationale behind the title of the section 'The Judge Judged in Our Place', he says that he first thought of Question 52 of the *Heidelberg Catechism*. There the 'Christ of last times' is called the judge "who has represented me before the judgement of God and has taken away all cursing from me."[32] But if one were expecting to find exposition in the traditional sense of 'the Judge of the quick and the dead' in Barth's exposition of Christ as the Judge in the section 'The Judge Judged in Our Place,' one's expectation would be unfulfilled. For the Judge there is Jesus Christ in the first part of the Gospel story proclaiming in Galilee the eschatological judgement of the kingdom of God who dies on the cross. Or more precisely: Barth affirms the traditional understanding of eschatology as found in the credal reference to Jesus 'the judge of the living and the dead on judgement day,' but he identifies this Jesus with the one who proclaims the judgement of the kingdom of God in the first (and second) parts of the Gospel story.

How does Jesus as the Judge proclaiming eschatological judgement in the first part of the Gospel story provide for unity and completeness with the second part? The answer Barth gives is essentially the one to which I have already referred when speaking of Calvin on the judicial work of Christ. For Barth, as for Calvin, it is essential to focus on Jesus Christ judged as a criminal before the judgement seat of Pilate. For Barth the narrative of Jesus' passion in Jerusalem understood in the context of the judicial framework corresponds to "... an arrest, a hearing, a prosecution in various courts, a torturing, and then an execution and burial."[33] In other words, Jesus is the Judge in the first part of the Gospel story proclaiming in Galilee the judgement of the kingdom God and He is the judged - and indeed the fulfilment of His own earlier judgement - in the second part. (Hence, in part, the rationale behind the title of the section 'The Judge Judged in Our Place.' )

The relative inadequacy of the priestly framework in this respect is readily apparent. The reason it is less successful in satisfying the criterion of

---

[31] Speaking of the aspect of the *munus sacerdotale* known as the *intercessio Christi*, Barth writes that Christ "not only did but does stand before God for us - not in a different form but in exactly the same form as He stood before Him for us 'in the days of His flesh' as the Judge judged and the priest sacrificed." Barth, *CD* IV/1, 314. Hence, for Barth, the Judge who proclaims eschatological judgement in the Gospel story is also the Judge intervening at the right hand of the Father for our sins. But he is the latter only as the former. Calvin affirms the reverse.

[32] Barth, *CD* IV/1, 211. See Barth, *The Heidelberg Catechism for Today*, translated by Shirley Guthrie, (London: The Epworth Press, 1964), 81-83,

[33] Barth, *CD* IV/1, 226.

comprehensiveness is that it receives scant reference in the narrative history of the first part of the Gospel story. Barth would have agreed with Calvin's insight that even then - during the first part - hidden in Christ's person was his identity as priest. But the fact that there are no striking narrative details in the first part of the Gospel story corresponding to the priestly office render it less able to hold together in narrative unity the first two parts of the Gospel story. In the Gospel of John, John the Baptist may refer to Jesus as "the lamb of God who takes away the sin of the world" as early on in the narrative as John 1.29, but this is not a claim made in response to Jesus enacting or executing the priestly office on the surface of the narrative. The priestly office as regards the narrative is almost completely concentrated on the second part of the story and, in particular on Jesus' death. Indeed, when Barth affirms the priestly office indirectly through the judicial work of Christ, it is strikingly apparent that he makes no connection between Jesus the Judge of the first part of the Gospel and Jesus the definitive priest. The reason is of course that Jesus the eschatological judge of the first part of the narrative has very little in common with Jesus the definitive sacrifice on the cross.

What I have said of the judicial work of Christ can be further corroborated if one looks at Barth's exposition of the kingly office in *Church Dogmatics* IV/2. There one sees the same impulse at work, the same desire to hold together the first and second parts of the Gospel story in unity and completeness in a comprehensive kingly framework. Barth discerns in the first part of the Gospel narrative a tradition which emphasises another aspect of the kingdom of God. As well as judgement, Jesus proclaims and enacts in Galilee the good news of the kingdom of God, both in his ethical teaching (e.g. the beatitudes) and in his deeds (the miracle tradition). In his proclamation and deeds Jesus Christ fulfils the unmediated will of God to be for humanity, to be for the good of humanity. This is in essence the ethics of the kingdom of God. In the second part of the Gospel narrative Barth discerns that this narrative pattern continues in the deepest kingly concealment in the striking narrative details of Jesus' passion. As he puts it:

> The sport or mockery which the Roman soldiers made of Jesus before his crucifixion, decking Him with the royal purple and the crown of thorns (Mk 15.16f and par.), is a drastic confirmation [of Jesus as King], as is also the taunting cry at the cross: 'He saved others; himself he cannot save. If He be the King of Israel, let him now come down from the cross, and we will believe him.....'[34]

And to this he adds the narrative detail of the title above Jesus Christ's head on the cross where Jesus is referred to as 'The King of the Jews.'

---

[34] Barth, *CD* IV/2, 168.

Together they all add up, for Barth, to the fact that the good news of the kingdom of God is fulfilled on the cross and in this sense the work of the kingly office fulfilled. The salvation and homecoming of humanity is accomplished in the inauguration of the kingdom of God on the cross. In other words, as in the Judicial framework, Barth is able to affirm the narrative unity of the first and second part of the Gospel story within the framework of the Kingly Office. And he is able to do this directly with the Kingly Office which he therefore affirms directly and not as in the case of the priestly office, indirectly.

Thus far I have provided the rationale behind Barth's employment of the threefold office. But my main aim, as always, is to present the details of Barth's exposition of this employment. In what way does Barth, through the judicial and the kingly work of Christ, affirm that God was in Christ reconciling the world to Himself? How *in fact* does the judicial and the kingly work hold together the first two parts of the Gospel narrative in "unity and completeness"? If one asks why Barth presented the Jesus of the first part of the Gospel story as proclaiming eschatological judgement, the answer might well be that Jesus as the eschatological Judge is where he saw the emphasis of the narrative pattern of the first part of the Gospel to lie. Undoubtedly this is true. But the question, why he saw it this way and Augustine, Aquinas, or Calvin did not, remains a begged question. Unquestionably, Barth's application of the concept of eschatology in *Church Dogmatics* IV/1 and IV/2 is derived from the nineteenth century, and in particular from Weiss and Schweitzer.[35] Though Barth affirms the traditional understanding of eschatology as found in the credal reference to Jesus 'the judge of the living and the dead' on judgement day, he quite clearly identifies

---

[35] McGrath implies that the central position that Barth gives the concept of 'eschatology' in *Romans* II is ultimately due to the influence of the 'consistent eschatology' as espoused by Weiss and Schweitzer. See McGrath, *The making of Modern German Christology*, 81, 99. But I would argue that the influence here is more Overbeck's rejection of the possibility of contemporary eschatological Christianity due to the unfulfilled hopes in the *parousia*, in Jesus' imminent return. However, to my mind there is no doubt that Barth's use of the concept in *CD* IV/1 and IV/2 is aligned to that of Weiss's and Schweitzer's. The difference is that: he agrees with Weiss and Schweitzer in locating Jesus' eschatological proclamation in the first part of the Gospel story (where before in *Romans* II he was quite willing to acknowledge that because 'last *things*' [end-*time*] were not '*last* things' [*end*-time] it followed that imminent eschatology properly understood was not within the reach of the critical-historical method); he disagrees with them in arguing that this proclamation of judgement is, precisely, fulfilled in the second part of the Gospel story on the cross. (Barth speaks of the "eschatological act of salvation, to use our modern jargon" occurring in Jesus' history culminating in his death on the cross. Barth, *CD* IV/1, 160.)

this Jesus with the one who proclaims the judgement of the kingdom of God in the first part of the Gospel story. (One finds in the pre-critical tradition reference to Jesus the judge *only* in the traditional eschatological sense.)

As was said, a close reading of the section entitled "The Judge Judged in Our Place" and the section entitled "The Royal Man" reveals that, throughout these pages, what is crucial for Barth is that – as against the reversal, conflict, and ultimate division claimed by such as Schweitzer between (crucially) Jesus' proclamation of the kingdom of God in Galilee and his death on the cross outside of the gates of Jerusalem - there is utter continuity and absolute harmony. This leads me to infer that Barth was, in his usual ironic way, affirming a central affirmation of the Enlightenment legacy only to turn the tables on this same legacy: 'Quite so, Weiss and Schweitzer, the Jesus of the first part of the Gospel story proclaimed the eschatological judgement of the kingdom of God!" He accedes to a central feature of the Enlightenment legacy on the historical Jesus   only to demonstrate that it in no way caused any great consternation for the great classical Christological tradition to which he belonged: 'Quite so, Weiss and Schweitzer, the Jesus of the first part of the Gospel story proclaimed the eschatological judgement of the kingdom of God!   This judgement was fulfilled on the cross!"[36]

## 4a. The Judicial Work:
## the Second Part Understood in Indivisibility with the First Part

Jesus judges in the first part. If the second part is to be understood in indivisibility with the first part it follows that he judges in the second part. Barth invokes a hermeneutical criterion congenial to those who would affirm the historicity of Jesus proclaiming eschatological judgement: "We must understand the first part of the story as a commentary on the second, and *vice-versa*."[37] That is to say, not only is the second half of the pre-Easter narrative to be a commentary on the first half, the first half is to be a

---

[36] To be sure, Barth is often referred to, rightly, as the first narrative theologian. But it is not just his concern with narrative unity which explains his affirmation of Jesus the eschatological judge. If this were the case all other theologians who affirmed the narrative as a continuous whole - and here I  am thinking of the pre-critical tradition - would also have affirmed Jesus in this way. But they did not. According to my argument, then, it is more than a coincidence that Barth's understanding of the first part resembles the essentially eschatological figure of the critical tradition - the critical tradition of such as Weiss and Schweitzer who saw Jesus precisely as proclaiming in Galilee the eschatological judgement of the kingdom of God.

[37] Barth, *CD* IV/1, 235.

commentary on the second half. How is Barth's theological analysis able to affirm the historicity of Jesus' eschatological judgement in continuity with the passion history?

In affirming the resurrection-appearances history Barth affirms continuity and accord between the first half and the second half. But more: the third part (the resurrection-appearances history) and the first part of the Gospel story (Jesus' proclamation of the eschatological judgement of the kingdom of God) together impose a constraint on the identity of the harmony and accord existing between the first two parts. To read the first part as a commentary on the second part means that Jesus' proclamation of judgement is part of the single unitary indivisible event completed on the cross. There is one event and this one event must necessarily be continuous with the event of Jesus' judgement in Galilee. The first half of the pre-Easter narrative cannot be re-interpreted far less made to shrink to insignificance as part of Jesus' history once he has died on the cross. It must be taken seriously as part of Jesus' historical identity, as part of the identity of God in Christ reconciling the world to Himself. It must therefore have a bearing on what it is that is completed on cross. Barth is committed to this conclusion.

According to Schweitzer, Jesus' proclamation of judgement in the wake of the kingdom of God is an instantiation of imminent or consistent eschatology.[38] According to C H Dodd, Jesus' proclamation pertains to realised eschatology: Jesus taught the reality of the kingdom of God as realized in His own ministry.[39] For Barth Jesus' proclamation is fulfilled on the cross. One might say that for Barth imminent eschatology prevails in the first half of the pre-Easter narrative, and realised eschatology in the second half. It follows therefore that if Jesus' proclamation is part of this one unitary continuous event, the judgement of Jesus must be fulfilled on the cross since the cross is the completion of this one continuous event. Jesus proclaims judgement: 'Repent for the kingdom of God is at hand!' Therefore, even in his arrest, trial, torture, and execution on a cross as a criminal, he precisely continues to judge those who judge him. In revealing Himself as the crucified one, Jesus revealed Himself as the one who had proclaimed the judgement of God in Galilee and indeed in Jerusalem.[40] The fulfilment of the one indivisible event that is the first part is indivisible with the second part. This means that Jesus continues to judge even as he is

---

[38] See Norman Perrin, *The Kingdom of God in the Teaching of Jesus* (London: SCM, 1966), 28-36.

[39] *Ibid*, chapter IV.

[40] See Barth, *CD* IV/1, 217-218, 235. It is not merely that Jesus proclaims the Father's judgement in Galilee, He is the Son of God proclaiming the judgement of God the Father. In this sense, He is God proclaiming the judgement of God.

judged in the second part. This is the sense in which Barth concurs with Weiss and Schweitzer's implicit claim that Jesus proclaiming the judgement of God in Galilee must be taken seriously in any historical analysis.[41]

How does Jesus continue to be the Judge in the second part of the Gospel story? Two conditions are pivotal. 1) The judgement on Jesus in the second part of the Gospel story is a judgement of which Jesus remains *subject*. 2) The judgement on Jesus is the *self-same eschatological judgement* of the first part of the Gospel story.

1) *He remains the subject of judgement even as He is its object.* How does this come to be the case? Jesus *allows* Himself to be the object of the eschatological judgement that He had declared on the world.[42] In this sense He is the subject of this judgement even as He becomes its object. *The fact that He intentionally executed becoming its object entails that He remains the subject of the eschatological judgement that He declared on the world.* This is the sense in which He remains subject. As Barth puts it, "Jesus Christ Himself ... was the Judge ... who *allowed* [*my italics*] Himself to be judged in execution of His judgement."[43] Jesus *allowed* Himself to be judged when "He was sought out and arrested as a malefactor, when he was accused as a blasphemer before the Sanhedrin and as agitator against

---

[41] It should be noted at this point that, in thinking this, Barth seems to diverge from Frei. Frei writes: "... if Jesus rendered directly accessible in depiction is joined to fact claims about what happened, then it will have to be in the sequence depicted in the last stage of the story, from the passion through the resurrection or ascension, not in his teachings." Frei, *The Identity of Jesus Christ*, 141. What Frei means by this is that "Jesus' identity comes to focus directly in the passion-resurrection narrative rather than the account of his person and teaching in his earlier ministry." *Ibid*, 142. And he concludes: "All this is not to say that we are bound to ignore the story of Jesus' ministry in identifying him. It is simply to affirm that Jesus, in his unique identity, is not available to us directly or unambiguously - either as a character in a story or historically - in the portion of the Gospel accounts describing his ministry." *Ibid*, 143. Frei's point is a highly original, complex one. But it is not Barth's view. To be sure, Barth would say that Jesus as the Son of God is more himself there than He is during His ministry (the relation between intentional execution and identity is closer). See Barth, *CD* IV/2, 252. But notwithstanding this, he is adamant that the first part of the Gospel story is intrinsic to Jesus' identity as the 'Judge who is judged in our place.' Hence who Jesus is in the second part of the Gospel story must be measured against the first part in which Jesus proclaims eschatological judgement. The latter must have a decisive bearing on who Jesus is in the second part.

[42] Jesus judges in the first part. Jesus is judged in the second part. Has Barth finished the task he has set himself against the nineteenth century culminating in Weiss and Schweitzer (and indeed in Bultmann)? No! Barth is conscious that these two statements together do not move the conclusion that Jesus *allowed* Himself to be judged.

[43] Barth *CD* IV/1, 227.

Caesar before Pilate, in both cases being prosecuted and found guilty."[44] He allowed Himself to be judged "when He refrained from saving Himself, from defending and justifying Himself, from making even the slightest move to evade the prosecution and verdict."[45] Jesus allows Himself be the object of judgement: he therefore remains the subject of judgement.[46] This does not entail an active "resolve to suffer" in the sense of Schweitzer.[47] For Barth, Schweitzer's famous understanding of Jesus' actions as 'the deliberate bringing down of death upon himself'[48] is logically incompatible with the historical truth-claim of Jesus' passion history, a history which begins in the Gospel narrative with Gethsemane. Schweitzer makes Jesus' passion history too *active* to be a *passion* history:

> What we have called [Jesus'] self-determination to this end and outcome [execution as a criminal on the cross] is also the divine order which controls His life and its course. He fulfils voluntarily that which is resolved concerning Him. And the divinity of that which is resolved emerges in the fact that its execution is not suffered by Him as a burdensome constraint of destiny or a chance misfortune, but in this readiness and willingness, as the content of *His own self-determination* [my italics].[49]

---

[44] *Ibid*, 239.

[45] *Ibid*, 239. That Jesus resisted the cross would for Barth contradict the historical truth-claim that: Jesus allowed Himself to be judged, that he allowed Himself to be subjected to what He was subjected to by, for example, Pilate, that he did not actively resist His fate in some sense or another. Such a claim of course could be true of any man, which is really all that Barth asks from the historical sceptic in a positive sense. There is no intellectual sacrifice in affirming this as a historical truth-claim,. But in the context of Jesus having revealed Himself as God, this historical truth-claim is replaced by another - *God* allowed Himself to be judged in our place. The crucial question is: how much historical detail is sufficient to entail the conclusion that Jesus allowed Himself to be judged? It may very well be that, collectively, the historical detail is over-determining such that one does not have to be committed to it all historically. But, equally, it may be that "refraining from saving Himself, from defending and justifying Himself, from making even the slightest move to evade the prosecution and verdict" is both necessary and sufficient in this respect - no matter whether a trial by night in front of the Sanhedrin took place or not. What is essential is that Jesus refrained from defending Himself against the charges brought against Him, and in particular, intentionally submitted to Pilate's judgement of death. If He did not, the truth-claim of the Obedience of the Son of God - Jesus' obedience - even unto death on the cross would be ruled out.

[46] As Barth puts it: Jesus "is the subject and not the object of what happens - the subject even when He is object." *Ibid*, 235.

[47] Schweitzer, *The Quest of the Historical Jesus*, 387.

[48] *Ibid*, 387, 391.

[49] Barth, *CD* IV/2, 259.

That is, Jesus determines Himself as subject of the events that befall Him. The identity of his divinity in the context of the resurrection-appearances history concerns *what it is* He intentionally executed in the context of the actions of the religious and civil authorities culminating in the judgement and verdict of Pilate. If God was in Christ reconciling the world to Himself then it must follow that the passion events are "not suffered by Him as a burdensome constraint of destiny or a chance misfortune, but in this readiness and willingness, as the content of His own self-determination." in the fact that he neither resists the things that happen to Him in His passion nor exhibits surprise or offence toward them.[50]

To affirm that Jesus intentionally executed Himself as the object of judgement in the narrative - and therefore remained its subject - entails that He was not surprised by what happened to Him in Jerusalem, did not perceive the fate that befell him as a chance misfortune:[51]

> we cannot find a single trace of his expecting or envisaging or desiring or seeking any other outcome than which was actually the case. *It cannot be said, then, that when it had this outcome He was surprised or disillusioned or offended* [*my italics*]. On the contrary, there are clear signs that His whole existence was prepared and armed for this outcome and directed toward it.[52]

The crucial sentence is the italicised one. The crucial question is: *as it happened to Him* did He respond otherwise than "refraining from saving Himself, from defending and justifying Himself, from making even the slightest move to evade the prosecution and verdict"? For then he did not intentionally execute allowing Himself to be judged.[53] Barth in fact

---

[50] This is the sense in which the passion predictions are true historical truth-claims; or more precisely, such are the historical truth-claims that have to hold if we are to understand the passion predictions as historical truth-claims. What does not have to hold is that Jesus actually made them in the sequence of events described in the Gospel narrative. "The passion of Christ is not for [the Gospels] a catastrophe which burst unexpectedly into His life. It is the necessary result of it. It is thus essential that it should be announced in it." *Ibid*, 253. That is the historical truth-claim made by the claim of Jesus' passion predictions.

[51] That Jesus allowed Himself to be judged in our place rules out the possibility that He was surprised by what happened to Him in Jerusalem, that He perceived the fate that befell him as a chance misfortune (though the latter does not mean that He foreknew the fate that would befall Him).

[52] *Ibid*, 258.

[53] What is also ruled out is the kind of active intentionality not derivable from - and indeed, in conflict with - Jesus' intentional execution as the Gospel narrative has it. The

pioneered an insight made explicit in Hans Frei's understanding of the Gospel narrative as realistic narrative (Barth would speak of a historical truth-claiming narrative that employs the literary devices, or tools, of realistic narrative). Frei's reference to Henry James' literary dictum is central here: 'What is character but the determination of incident? What is incident but the illustration of character?'[54] For Frei, Jesus' identity was not be identified with His private consciousness, His private self-understanding, His private hopes and fears, so to speak. It was to be identified with who He was in *His intentional execution in encountering incident.*[55] This means that it is to be identified with who He was in His intentional execution in encountering the circumstances in   which the Sanhedrin placed Him, who He was in His intentional execution in encountering the circumstances in which Pilate placed Him, and so on.[56]

---

latter rules out the kind of intentionality attributed to Jesus by Schweitzer when he speaks of "[Jesus'] deliberate bringing down of death upon himself." Schweitzer, *The Quest of the Historical Jesus*, 392. Schweitzer's attribution to Jesus of a continuity of intention which begins while in Galilee, and endures to the very end of his life, only *appears* to entail continuity  between the first and second parts of the Gospel story. Continuity of *intention* is compatible with non-continuity of *intentional execution*, the test of continuity between the first and the second part of the Gospel story.  Since Jesus' life ends in failure on the cross, Schweitzer cannot but share the perspective of the disciples at the time of Jesus' death:  Jesus' passion is a tragic reversal of his earlier proclamation of the kingdom of God.

[54] Frei, *The Identity of Jesus Christ*, 88.

[55] It almost goes without saying that the phrase "intentional execution" should not be confused with Jesus' own execution on the cross. It refers more broadly to Jesus' identity identifiable in his intentional action. His execution on the cross is one of many events that Jesus intentionally executes (his arrest in Gethsemane, and his trial by Pilate, are others). See the foot-note following.

[56] The concept of *intentional execution* - especially, intentionally executing becoming the object of the self-same judgement proclaimed in the first part - is integral to the rational status of Barth's affirmation that the final form of the historical truth-claiming narrative is sufficient for affirming the Jesus of the narratives as the historical Jesus. It is integral to the rational status of this affirmation because it does not imply - as *intending to execute* does - knowledge of Jesus' intentions, beliefs, inner states, etc. (It is above all Wolterstorff who has pointed out the importance of this distinction for both hermeneutics and the philosophy of action. See Wolterstorff, *Divine Discourse*, 149. Though he applies the distinction to the field of hermeneutics, he takes the view that it is no less applicable to the philosophy of action: there is a distinction to be made between intentionally kicking a ball and intending to kicking a ball.) The historical truth-claim of what Jesus intentionally executed does not imply any historical truth-claim about his intentions, beliefs and inner states. One can see that this is so in Barth's exposition of what it means to say that Jesus intentionally executed His own judgement on Himself. Insofar as we can call this an action of Jesus', it is an action that emerges out the

2) *The judgement on Jesus is the self-same eschatological judgement of the first part of the Gospel story.* What makes the judgement of which He intentionally executed becoming the object - and therefore of which he is the subject - His own judgement, the eschatological judgement that He declared in the first part of the Gospel story? How does he become the object of His own judgement in this sense? The object of His own eschatological judgement on the world?[57] Barth asserts that the Gospel story in its "unity and completeness" narrates a story in which

---

interaction of character and incident without reference to intentions, beliefs or inner states. As Frei put it of realistic narrative: "The story renders the subject-matter ... by the interaction of character and happening. Persons and publicly accessible circumstances are indispensable to each other, even as they are irreducible to each other. In their interaction they form the story and thereby render the subject-matter." Frei, *The Identity of Jesus Christ*, xvi. As was said, Jesus is to be identified with who He was in *His intentional execution in encountering incident.* He is to be identified with who He is in His intentional execution in encountering the circumstances in which the Sanhedrin placed Him, who He is in His intentional execution in encountering the circumstances in which Pilate placed Him, and so on. All of these historical truth-claims are in the narrative. None of them presupposes claims about Jesus' intentions, beliefs and inner states 'off the page' as it were - in the fashion of *Religionsgeschichte*. It is doubtless the case that Jesus intentionally executed many things that are not narrated in the Gospel. But if what he is described as intentionally executing *in the narrative* at crucial points can be rationally affirmed as historical truth, it can be argued that this is *sufficient* to move the conclusion that God was in Christ reconciling the world to Himself. Barth's claim, that the final form of the historical truth-claiming narrative is sufficient for affirming the Jesus of the narratives as the historical Jesus, is a rational one. And if it is sufficient then *Religionsgeschichte* and, in particular, the methodology of historical reconstruction as regards intention is, in the strict logical sense, unnecessary. Whatever its weaknesses, the classic interpretative tradition of Augustine, Calvin and Luther cannot be impugned for a lack of awareness of, or interest in, the extratextual realities pertaining to the Gospel narrative. The pre-critical tradition's position in this respect was not unwarranted. The question of intentional execution versus intending to execute, historical truth-claim and final form raises complex issues and I do not pretend to have dealt with it comprehensively here. Instead I have drawn attention to what I think are the main parameters of Barth's thought on this question.
[57] To say that Jesus was reconciling the world to Himself implies that Jesus' eschatological judgement in the first part of the Gospel story is a judgement on the world. It is this judgement - and no other - to which he must submit if he is to reconcile the world to Himself. But Barth says that the judgement that Jesus proclaimed in the first part of the Gospel narrative was a judgement on Israel. Barth, *CD* IV/1, 224. Does it then follow that God only reconciles Israel to Himself? (He proclaims judgement on Israel and it is this judgement to which he submits in the passion history; *ergo* only Israel is reconciled, not the world.) No. Barth does not say that Israel was the *sole* object of such eschatological judgement. To be sure, in intentionally executing becoming the object of this judgement (and therefore remaining the subject of this

the divine subject of the judgement on man as which Jesus appears in the first part of the evangelical record becomes the object of this judgement from the episode of Gethsemane onwards. If this judgement is fulfilled at all - and that is what the Evangelists seem to be trying to say in the second part of their account - then it is with this reversal.[58]

Implicit in this passage is the fact that Jesus becomes the object of the *self-same* eschatological judgement in the second part of the Gospel story that He issued in the first part of the Gospel story. But He can only become the subject of the same judgement if this same judgement - God's judgement - coincides with Pilate's judgement. This is indeed what Barth says. According to Barth, the rationale behind the narration of Jesus' agony in Gethsemane is precisely that the good will of God is absolutely at one with the evil will of the Sanhedrin and of Pilate. Gethsemane marks the beginning of the forsakenness of God that culminates in Jesus' cry of dereliction on the cross. "The Lordship of God is concealed under the lordship of evil and evil men."[59] The will of God is "indistinguishably one with the evil will of men and the world and Satan. It was a matter of the triumph of God being concealed under that of His adversary, of that which

---

judgement) in the second part, Jesus, as the embodiment of Israel - Jesus the Israelite (see *Ibid*, 172) - intentionally executes becoming the object of the judgement on Israel that He proclaimed in the first part. But He also proclaims judgement on the world in the first part of the Gospel story (*Ibid*, 225-226) and, ultimately, He intentionally executes becoming the object of this judgement in the second part (*Ibid*, 271). Eschatological judgement is a judgement on the whole world, the whole human race. Alluding to Mat. 3.10, Barth says that, by the end of the first part of the Gospel story, "there are no good trees left to stand" (*Ibid*, 225) meaning that, by the end of this part of the evangelists' record, Jesus' judgement has encompassed the whole world: "His judgement falls on all flesh with the coming of the kingdom." *Ibid*, 225. It is noteworthy that Weiss's account does not disagree with Barth's view that Jesus judges the world in the first part of the Gospel story. See Weiss, *Jesus' Proclamation of the Kingdom of God*, 98. Moreover, Barth speaks of: "the judgement to which (according to Israel's mission) the whole world as well as Israel is liable". Barth, *CD* II/2, 213. Israel is "a mirror held up to the men of all peoples. The Son of God in His unity with the Israelite Jesus exists in direct and unlimited solidarity with the representatively and manifestly sinful humanity of Israel." Barth, *CD* IV/1, 172. That is to say, Israel's relation to the rest of humanity as regards judgement is one of representation and mission. For these reasons Barth holds that the identity of the judgement in both parts of the Gospel story is a judgement on the world, not merely a judgement on Israel. As will be seen, a similar symmetry applies in the case of the Kingly office: Jesus is not merely reconciling Israel, he is reconciling the world.

[58] *Ibid*, 238.
[59] *Ibid*, 269.

is not, of that which is supremely not."[60]This means in the 'judicial' context
that:

> It was a matter of the divine judgement being taken out of the hands of
> Jesus and placed in those of His supremely unrighteous judges and
> executed by them upon Him.[61]

This is a crucial claim. The self-same judgement that he had declared in
the first part of the Gospel narrative is "taken out of the hands of Jesus."
Pilate's judgement on Jesus coincides with God's judgement - Jesus'
eschatological judgement - exercised in the first part of the Gospel story. Or
more precisely perhaps: Pilate's freely chosen judgement *is* Jesus'
judgement in the first part, a judgement of which Jesus is subject as object
precisely because he intentionally executes this judgement. Jesus "executes
the divine judgement by undergoing it himself."[62] And because Jesus is the
subject of His own judgement narrated in the first part He can be described
as being "ready to pronounce this sentence Himself and therefore on
Himself."

Jesus proclaims eschatological judgement. It is this judgement which is
"taken out of the hands of Jesus and placed in those of", pre-eminently,
Pilate. This means that  Pilate's judgement on Jesus is Jesus' own
eschatological judgement. Jesus is the object of eschatological judgement.

As regards this claim, Barth once more, utterly ironically, accepts the
first part of the Gospel story as Weiss, Schweitzer, and Bultmann
understand it. Jesus proclaims eschatological judgement in the first part and
it is this self-same judgement to which he is subjected as subject in the
second part. There is in fact a  historical truth-claim in the narrative itself
corresponding to the latter. The deep literal sense of the historical truth-
claim of Jesus' agony in the garden of Gethsemane is that Jesus undergoes
the self-same eschatological judgement of the first part. But this means that
He is the object of judgement declaring absolute final end on Him - the end
that eschatological judgement in the first part would have brought down on
the heads of sinners. According to Barth, if it is the self-same eschatological
judgement then it is not merely ordinary death that threatens Jesus:

> We are not dealing merely with any suffering, but with the suffering of
> God and this man in the face of the destruction which threatens all

---

[60] *Ibid*, 271.

[61] Barth, *CD* IV/1, 271. What makes these people sinners - the Sanhedrin, Pilate, etc. - is
the brute fact that they act against God in the person of Jesus. See *Ibid*, 499. Jesus,
remember, reveals Himself as God in the resurrection-appearances history.

[62] *Ibid*, 271.

creation and every individual .... We are dealing with the painful confrontation of God and this man not merely with any evil, not merely with death, but with eternal death, with the power of that which is not.[63]

We are dealing with *das Nichtige* - absolute nothingness.[64] In the context of Jesus' death this means that we are dealing with the *deuteros thanatos* - the apocalyptic 'second death' of Revelation 20.14.[65] It is death as absolute eschatological end, as the execution of *eschatological judgement*. The *deuteros thanatos* is death as the wages of sin. It is what man would suffer through freely chosen sin *without the reconciliation wrought by God through Jesus taking our place*. It is not merely dying, it is dying apart from God and Christ. In this sense it is absolute nothingness. Ordinary, non-eschatological' death is not absolute nothingness. Ordinary, 'non-eschatological' death is dying to God and Christ, not dying to ourselves (Rom. 14.2f.).[66] Ordinary death is what pre-fall man would have died prior to the fall.[67] Jesus does not die this death. He dies the death that was the rightful sentence of sinners. He dies apart from God so that we can die to the Lord.[68] (Dying apart from God is, for Barth, the deep literal sense of the historical truth-claim of the cry of dereliction on the cross: "My God, my God, why have you forsaken me" [Mar. 15.34].)[69] Jesus faces execution of the judgement of eternal, final, eschatological death. It is this which threatens Him in Gethsemane. This is the terrible awesome nature of His taking on the judgement! This is why He is precisely the object of eschatological judgement - real absolute end! What the execution of this judgement means we cannot know or comprehend except in what is revealed in what happens to Jesus. Thus, to reiterate: Barth affirms the eschatological judgement affirmed by historical analysis. He takes it utterly seriously and sees it brought to bear on Jesus in the second part: the self-same judgement on the world.

What or who makes Pilate's judgement the self-same eschatological judgement exercised by Jesus in the first part? It is, Barth says, God

---

[63] *Ibid*, 247.

[64] Note that Barth says that the concept of nothingness should be "developed in many different ways .... We can and must ask and say what real evil is, real death, the real devil and real hell [is] ...." Barth, *CD* III/3, 305. In other words, it is the context of the concept of nothingness that the biblical concept of Satan ought to be developed.

[65] Barth, *CD* III/2, 628-629, 633-634. See also *Ibid*, 603-607.

[66] Barth, *CD* IV/1, 295.

[67] Barth, *CD* III/2, 632.

[68] Barth, *CD* IV/1, 295.

[69] *Ibid*, 238-239, 264, 306.

Himself.[70] It is "according to the plan of God Himself", a plan that God has in fact decreed from eternity. This means, among other things, that "... the sinful men at whose hands Jesus will suffer and die - all of them from Judas to Pilate - will all actively take part in the event of His self-giving to death which takes place for the reconciliation of the world with God." That is to say: "Even as His enemies, His accusers, His judges and His executioners they will actively take part in it. They are no longer merely wicked men, but in their very wickedness they are involuntary instruments of God." As Barth puts it, it was a matter of these men "having and exercising by divine permission and appointment the right, the irresistible right of might" in their judgement and execution of Jesus.

The one indivisible historical event of God reconciling the world to Himself implies that Pilate could not have done otherwise: it is not as if God's will could be stopped in his tracks by human obstacle, as if Pilate could let Jesus escape the cross, as if he himself and the others who act against Jesus could be other than "agents and executors of 'the determinate purpose and foreknowledge of God.'" Given the one indivisible event of God in Christ reconciling the world to Himself, Pilate cannot avoid doing what he does - although he freely chooses.[71] This is what Barth means when

---

[70] Is this the one unavoidable fideistic claim that Barth makes in his understanding of the Gospel narrative? For, clearly, Pilate's judgement does not look much like the eschatological judgement that Jesus proclaims in the first part of the narrative. They look like distinctly unlike judgements - and one might say that they *are* distinctly unlike judgements. But if Jesus is to take our place in the sense Barth intends, there must be real identity between the two. However, no matter that John 19.13 is a tantalising intimation of this, it still falls short of providing an argument for identifying Pilate's judgement with God's judgement. According to Barth, the Gospel narrative makes the simple affirmation that it is *God* who makes the judgement on Jesus in the second part, and particularly Pilate's, the same eschatological judgement as the first part. (The way in which God does this must include His turning away from Jesus at His crucifixion and death. This has the consequence that Jesus dies apart from the God of Israel, and therefore dies the *deuteros thanatos*.) However, I suspect that Barth could minimise, or at least reduce, the fideistic nature of this claim as follows. Given that it is God who proclaims eschatological judgement (we know this from the resurrection-appearances history), it must follow that this judgement is fulfilled in the second part (it doesn't just evaporate into thin air, put aside in the second part as it were). But if it is fulfilled in the second part, where is it to be found? Barth would point to the judgement seat of Pilate. Is this an argument from analogy? Does God reveal to us that Pilate's judgement, and the execution thereof, is His own? Barth's answer remains to be worked out in detail.

[71] It may be argued that God's foreknowledge is part of the indivisible event that is God in Christ reconciling Himself. To say that this event is indivisible implies that it cannot but be executed and fulfilled as an event. If (a) God's decision of God in Christ reconciling the world to Himself is true in eternity and (b) this event is an indivisible event in the sense outlined then it follows of this very event that God knows what Pilate

he says that his actions were "determined and effected in divine necessity and freedom."[72]  What is true of Pilate is true of everyone else who is involved. Jesus' passion "could not be prevented. It had to take place, and it did take place. Not by the reign of chance, nor in consequence of a human nexus of guilt and destiny." As Barth puts it elsewhere:

> In what happens to Jesus, the participants, both Jews and Gentiles,  are [accurately] described in ... Acts  2.23. and Acts 4.28 as - for all the obvious and supreme guilt and reprehensibility of their actions - only instruments in the hands of God, agents and executors of 'the determinate counsel [purpose] and foreknowledge of God.'[73]

It may be said that one did not need to understand or explain what happened in both Galilee and Jerusalem, and finally on Golgotha as the execution of God's purpose. A purely human determination was sufficient in principle to have brought Jesus' life to the cross. Barth had absolutely no argument with this. The patterns that he discerned at the heart of the unity of the first two parts of the Gospel narrative could just as easily be coincidence of human interaction. But in this context Jesus' death on the cross could be no more than a life ending in tragic failure. In the context of the resurrection-appearances history in which this man Jesus revealed Himself as God, these patterns coincided with the one indivisible event of God reconciling the world to Himself. Hence, in the face of an event which could not but be fulfilled,[74] both the Sanhedrin and Pilate could not but

---

will do, but not in any causative sense. Pilate is no more compelled to do as he does with Jesus as he is with anything else in his life: he freely chooses. But in the case of sentencing Jesus he was not free to choose otherwise.

[72] *Ibid*, 239. Note Barth's juxtaposition of necessity and freedom, two concepts traditionally taken as contradictories. In the context of the biblical concept of God they are not.

[73] The event of God is Christ reconciling the world to Himself is one indivisible event. This has consequences for our understanding of the actions of the religious and civil authorities who close in on Jesus and act decisively against Him. Pilate freely chooses his verdict - he is under no duress far less the compulsion of causative determinism to decide as he does. Pilate is not coerced by God. He is free in his judgement. Yet he is an involuntary instrument of God's purpose. One may even add that God foreknows that Pilate will send Jesus to his death, but this does not mean that Pilate's judgement is causally determined. Indeed, that God foreknows - that there is divine foreknowledge proper - implies that his actions are not causally determined. Otherwise, God's foreknowledge would be no different from a Laplacean demon who predicts every future event given the initial conditions of a linear deterministic system.

[74] If it is God's judgement in the first part of the Evangelical record, and God's judgement as God's judgement cannot be thwarted or frustrated (and, in particular, it is

have been giving way to it even when their actions were crucial to determining that Jesus would end up on a cross. One may even say that it was when they were at their most determining that they were giving way to God's purpose - though that such a thing had happened was, without revelation, absolutely undetectable.

## 4b. The Judicial Work: Jesus the Judge Judged *in Our Place*

The fact that the judgement of the second part of the Gospel story is the self-same eschatological judgement of the first part is the fundamental rationale behind Barth's claim that Jesus is judged *in our place.*[75] It is because of this fact that Jesus can be said to be judged in place of those who were the object of eschatological judgement in the first part of the Evangelical record. Were it not the self-same judgement, Jesus - God - could not have taken our place. For then it would be the case that Jesus had suffered a different judgement. And if he suffered a different judgement he could not have taken our place as the object of the judgement declared in the first part of the Gospel story. This is the deep literal sense of the story of Barabbas' release (Mk 15.6-15). As Barth puts it: "... a murderer is in every respect acquitted instead of Jesus, and Jesus is condemned to be crucified in his place."[76] More expansively, he writes: "... the accusation, condemnation, and punishment to which [the second part of the Gospel story] refers all fall on the very One on whom they ought to fall least, and not at all on those on whom they ought to fall."[77] But Barth can only say this because he understands Pilate's judgement on Jesus as identical to -

---

fulfilled by the time of the cross), then it follows that God's judgement is fulfilled in Jesus' arrest, trial, torture, and execution as a criminal on the cross. As a logical corollary of this one might also say the following. If it is God's judgement in the first part of the Evangelical record, and God's judgement as God's judgement cannot but be fulfilled in one indivisible event then it must follow that God's judgement is fulfilled in Jesus' arrest, trial, torture, and execution as a criminal on the cross.

[75] Barth also claims that Jesus takes our place as the Judge. We take it on ourselves - unrighteously - to be the judge of each other. Jesus' judging rightfully takes this 'right' away from us, in effect judging our judging. Barth, *CD* IV/1, 231-235. This Barth says is the "explanation of the terrible address to the scribes and Pharisees who let themselves be called rabbis, fathers, and teachers (Mt. 23. 1f)." *Ibid*, 235. In taking our place in this way, Jesus can be said to be taking the place of sinners, i.e., unrighteous judges, in a straight-forward 'logical' substitution of identity. *Ibid*, 235. But Barth is clear that the fundamental rationale behind this substitution is that Jesus intentionally executes becoming the object of His own judgement. *Ibid*, 236-240.
[76] *Ibid*, 224.
[77] *Ibid*, 224.

continuous with - the eschatological judgement that Jesus proclaims in Galilee. The obedience and therefore sinlessness or righteousness of Jesus consists in His willingness to take our place as sinners. And this is what He did in His intentionally executing becoming the object of a judgement which is, in fact, the one He proclaimed on the world.[78] Given that it is God who declares us to be sinners in the first part of the Gospel story, that, Barth would say, is the fact of it: we are sinners.[79] But in becoming the object of the self-same eschatological judgement as subject, Jesus Christ the Judge justifies us - sets us free from judgement, in effect, declares us innocent - by taking on Himself the judgement that was proclaimed on the world in the first part of the Gospel narrative.[80]

In effect, Barth claims that the *substitionary* aspect of atonement is a historical truth-claim in the narrative itself. Atonement understood as reconciliation is not a theory or interpretation of the narrative. It is there, Barth claims, in the narrative itself. And it is there precisely because Barth takes utterly seriously the historical truth-claim that Jesus proclaimed the eschatological judgement of God in the first part of the Gospel story. "Quite so, Weiss and Schweitzer!"

### 4c. The Judicial Work:
### the First Part Understood in Indivisibility with the Second Part

Jesus is judged in the second part. If the first part is to be understood in indivisibility with the second part then Jesus must be judged in the first part. To reiterate: "We must understand the first part of the story as a commentary on the second, and *vice-versa*."[81] How does Barth satisfy this criterion in the latter respect, when measuring the second part against the first?

The resurrection-appearances history and the second part of the Gospel story (Jesus' passion history) together impose a constraint on the identity of the harmony and accord existing between the first two parts. Jesus revealing Himself in His resurrection-appearances history as the one who had been crucified, dead and buried is precisely what it means for it to be true that Jesus revealed Himself "in the mode of God." So says Barth. By this exegetical means he affirms, along with Luther and Moltmann, God

---

[78] *Ibid*, 258.
[79] Barth rejects a 'natural theology' of knowledge of sinful man on the basis that it implies that we can judge, or have an independent criterion of, *what it is* sinful man is. This is only revealed to us in Jesus Christ. See Barth, *CD* IV/1, 241-242.
[80] *Ibid*, 276.
[81] Barth, *CD* IV/1, 235.

crucified. But since 'God in Christ crucified' is the historical truth-claim of the passion history, 'God in Christ crucified' must in some sense be continuous with the first part of the Gospel story (the resurrection-appearances history provides for harmony and accord where up until that history there had only been reversal and conflict between the first and second parts of the Gospel story).

Jesus Christ declares Himself to the one they had encountered in His pre-Easter story as the One who had been crucified, dead and buried, and in doing so He reveals Himself 'in the mode of God.' In revealing Himself as the crucified one, Jesus revealed Himself as the one who had been arrested, tried, tortured and executed in the sequence of events of a judicial process, in the sequence of events constituting and fulfilling a judicial judgement "under Pontius Pilate", as the Apostles' creed has it. This means that the fulfilment of the one indivisible event that is the second part is indivisible from the first part, not only in terms of Jesus the judge, but also in terms of Jesus the judged. Is Jesus the judged present in the first part? Yes.

There is in the first part a dimension of judgement against Jesus even as He judges: Jesus is judged precisely as violating the law, for example, in his offence against the prevalent rules concerning the observation of the Sabbath in healing the man with the withered hand (Mk 3.6.).[82] The judgement on Jesus in the first part is fulfilled in the judgement in the second part that nails Jesus to the cross in fulfilment of Pontius Pilate's 'judicial judgement' against him. Barth like Schweitzer affirms the historicity of Jesus proclaiming the imminence of the eschatological judgement of God: "Repent for the kingdom of God is nigh!" But Jesus is also judged in the first part and this represents the spectre of Jesus' own impending judgement at the hands of the authorities, religious and civil.

That is to say: ominously, in the first part of the Gospel story - even at this stage in his history - Jesus is judged even as he judges. He is judged by the religious authorities, 'the Pharisees, the scribes', even as He proclaims judgement in the first part of the Gospel story. It is this strain of opposition which provides the background context to Jesus' own proclamation of judgement, a background which will become increasingly foregrounded as we approach the final judgement that sends him to his death on the cross as a criminal. Jesus is judged in the first part of the Gospel story even as He is judged in the second part of the Gospel story.[83]

---

[82] It is to be noted that Strauss accepts the historicity of the enmity against Jesus in the first part of the Gospel narrative. See Strauss, *The Life of Jesus*, 599-600.

[83] According to Barth, the Synoptic narratives make it clear that John the Baptist stands in the closest relationship to the person and work of Jesus. And John the Baptist is no less than the one who first proclaims the judgement of God and then is executed (unjustly we may say) for making judgement such as he did. Barth, *CD* IV/1, 217-218.

To summarise: Jesus continues to judge in the second part of the Gospel story even as He judged in the first part. He continues to be judged in the second part of the Gospel story even as he was judged in the first part. To repeat: "We must understand the first part of the story as a commentary on the second, and vice-versa."IV/1, 235. In other words, Jesus is judged as He judges is true of both the first part and the second part of the Gospel story.

To conclude on the matter of the Judicial Office. Barth's emphasis on the judicial office over the priestly office is motivated by one main consideration. He wishes to affirm a historical truth-claiming narrative of the one indivisible event of God in Christ reconciling the world to Himself. He wishes as against the nineteenth century position to hold the first two parts of the Gospel story together in one indivisible historical whole. If such a historical whole existed in the historical truth-claiming narrative it seemed only to be discerned in Jesus' judicial work, the particulars of which were manifest in both parts of the pre-Easter narrative. The Priestly Office seemed more suited to explicating the meaning of Jesus' death on the cross since the narrative particulars that might have motivated such a framework (such as arrest, trial, torture, and execution in the case of the judicial office) were absent in the case of the priestly office. The biblical rationale behind the *munus sacerdotale* is, almost without exception confined to the New Testament epistles; there are a few notable exceptions such as John 1.29, but even this reference does not lend itself to narrative treatment, and crucially does not lend itself naturally to the task of uniting the first two parts of the Gospel story into a single historical whole. Though Barth is able to explicate each part of the judicial office in terms of the priestly office (for example, Jesus Christ gave Himself to be offered up as a sacrifice to take away our sins says the same thing as Jesus Christ was the One who was accused, condemned and judged in the place of us sinners), it is clear that the latter is simply not comprehensive enough - as the judicial Office is - to render the first two parts of the Gospel story as one historical whole.

### 5. The Kingly Office, IV/2: Jesus the Royal Man Who Fulfils the Good News of the Kingdom of God and Christ (Ephesians 5.5.) and Who is Man Exalted to Fellowship with God

The judicial office as Barth understands it coincides with a decidedly more complex historical phenomenon in the Gospel narrative than does the Kingly Office. By comparison with the Judicial Office the Kingly Office is continuous across the first two parts of the Gospel story in a single historical dimension. Hence, in contrast to my exposition of the Judicial Office there is no need to have two separate sub-sections treating respectively the first half in terms of the second half and the second half in terms of the first. This is not to say that Barth's exposition of the Kingly Office is not equally extensive an exposition as that of the Judicial Office. It is: it encompasses a great deal of exegetical analysis covering for example, Jesus' teaching in the beatitudes, and his actions as narrated in the miracle tradition. Moreover, it remains the case as regards the redemptive nature of the kingdom of God fulfilled on the cross that, as ever, against the tradition culminating in Schweitzer, Barth's primary motivation is to affirm harmony and accord. (The essence of Schweitzer's case in this respect is that the good news of kingdom of God did not come and Jesus died a tragic failed figure on the cross.)

The tradition of Weiss and Schweitzer affirmed the historicity of Jesus' proclamation of the kingdom of God in the sense of the imminence of eschatological judgement. It did this in conscious rejection of Albrecht Ritschl's ethical interpretation of Jesus' proclamation. Nevertheless there was a crucial aspect or thematic of Jesus' ethical teaching about the kingdom of God to which Ritschl's formulation better approximated than the Weiss-Schweitzer *Interimsethik*. As Norman Perrin put it of the 'new questers for the historical Jesus' exemplified by such as Günther Bornkamm:

> They point out that the Weiss-Schweitzer *Interimsethik* breaks down when applied to the teaching of Jesus because the ethical demands of Jesus are not, in fact, derived from the proclamation of the nearness of the Kingdom, but from the unmediated will of God. Although the general challenge to repent is set in the context of the imminence of the kingdom (Mark 1.5), all the specific ethical demands for love, purity, faithfulness, truth are rooted in the direct will of God.[84]

And, indeed, Bornkamm did assert that Jesus' proclamation of the kingdom of God in the form of judgement is set in the context of a prior decision and action in manifesting the kingdom as redemption in Jesus.[85] Barth did not disagree with the substance of Bornkamm's view. First, it is clear that he thought there was a second narrative tradition other than the judgement theme attached to Jesus' proclamation of the kingdom of God in the first part of the Gospel story: Jesus' proclamation of the good news of the kingdom of God as manifest for example in his proclamation - most

---

[84] Perrin, *The Kingdom of God in the Teaching of Jesus*, 127-128.
[85] Günther Bornkamm, *Jesus of Nazareth,* translated by Irene and Fraser McLuskey with James M Robinson, (London: Hodder and Stoughton, 1960), 224-225.

especially perhaps the beatitudes, and his actions - most especially the miracles.[86] Second, he thought that the ethics of this good news was grounded in the "prior decision" of the "unmediated will of God", not in imminent eschatology.[87]

For Barth the substance of Bornkamm's assertion (and Perrin's characterisation of this assertion) is borne out by the fact that Jesus' proclamation of the good news of the kingdom of God is never tied to a prior decision of repentance of sin on the part of the individual in response to judgement. That it is the poor, the meek, the peace-makers who are blessed in the beatitudes never has anything to do with any fact that they alone have repented and turned away from sin, or are better able to turn away from sin in response to judgement. They may be better able to respond to judgement but this capacity is palpably not the point of the blessings in the stories.[88] For Barth, Jesus' sayings pertaining to the good news of the kingdom of God proclaim the unconditional glad news of the kingdom to everyone.[89]

---

[86] Barth, *CD* IV/2, 181, 166-247. Norman Perrin's historical analysis also affirms that Jesus' teaching and actions in relation to the kingdom of God follows two themes: the kingdom of God as eschatological judgement and as redemption and salvation. See Perrin, *The Kingdom of God in the Teaching of Jesus*, 168-185. It is noteworthy that Bultmann too affirms these two themes as corresponding to the historicity of the first part of the Gospel story. Bultmann, *Jesus Christ and Mythology*, 17-18.

[87] Just as judgement in both parts of the Gospel story is a judgement on the world, not merely a judgement on Israel, then so Jesus' - God's - unmediated will is to be for the good of humanity, not merely Israel. See, for example, Barth, *CD* IV/2, 168-171. To be sure, Barth says that the Word became Jewish flesh. Barth, *CD* VI/1, 166-172. To say that the Word became Jewish flesh means, of course, that the people of Israel are reconciled to God. But 'the Word made Jewish flesh' entails the 'Word made flesh' so, on this ground alone, there is no exclusion of the rest of humanity from God's reconciliation. Moreover, Barth is clear that the Noachic covenant (Gen. 9.1-17) - God's covenant with the human race as a whole - constitutes an outer concentric circle to the inner concentric circle that is the Abrahamic covenant (Gen. 14) - God's covenant's with Israel only. *Ibid*, 26. This, together with the canonical relationship between Genesis 1-11 and Genesis 12 onwards - "the astonishing fact ... that the Old Testament should have considered the race prior to and outside of Abraham in this way ...." - imply that the whole human race is in covenant with God. *Ibid*, 27. In other words, God's covenant with Israel is not a end in itself but has "a provisional and provisionally representative significance." *Ibid*, 28. It is a means to the end of witness: through Israel, "the redemptive will of God is to be declared to all humanity." *Ibid*, 28 Though God in Christ is reconciling Israel to Himself, He is not merely doing this. God is not merely reconciling *Israel* to Himself, He is pre-eminently reconciling the *world* to Himself.

[88] Barth, *CD* IV/2, 187-191.

[89] *Ibid*, 181-187.

The point that Barth makes about the beatitudes and Jesus' sayings in general in this respect is even more accented in the miracle stories. One of the distinctive things about Barth's view of the miracle stories is that he thinks we misunderstand them if we think them more miraculous than the sayings, the sayings less miraculous than the miracles.[90] In effect, the historical truth-claim made in each is essentially the same historical truth-claim concerning the same incomparable, unique event: the nearness of the good news of the kingdom of God. This means that, for Barth, the substance of Bornkamm's assertion is best borne out by a "remarkable and offensive feature of the miracle stories" though this feature is no less apparent in other narrative traditions which represent the good news of the kingdom of God. This is that

> in these stories it does not seem to be of any great account that the men who suffer as creatures are above all sinful men .... No, the important thing is not that they are sinners but that they are sufferers. [...] It is tacitly presupposed that those who were healed were sinners and ought not to continue in sin. But this has no thematic significance in the texts. In the true sense, their transgressions are not imputed to them by Jesus (2 Cor. 5.19). What is imputed to them is that they are poor and tragic and suffering creatures. In the strict sense, it is only as such that they are taken seriously[91]

Again:

> ... Jesus is the God who is always directly interested in man as His creature. Beyond or above or through his sin He is interested in man himself in his being in the cosmos as limited and determined by Him. He is interested in him as this specific cosmic being. He has not forgotten him

---

[90] "It is to be noted that as the tradition sees [the miracle stories] the same is true of the words of Jesus. Those who heard Him, whether they believed or not, were confronted with the same new thing, the same alien will and unknown power .... The Sermon on the Mount ... was no less a miraculous Word, the irruption and occurrence of something incomprehensible to man, than the raising of the young man at Nain (Lk. 7.11f) was a miraculous act. [...] Those who try to throw doubt on the distinctive action of Jesus, as recorded in the Gospels, by referring to it as the sphere of mythology must ask themselves whether in the first instance it is not His teaching that must be referred to this sphere. For it leaves no less to be desired - and perhaps much more - in terms of normal apprehension." *Ibid*, 211 This is in effect Barth's response to the nineteenth century's rejection of the miracle stories. One can only reject them if one rejects the sayings tradition *on the same grounds*.
[91] *Ibid*, 222-223. Barth cites John 9.2f and Luke 13.1 as corroborative passages of his position.

or left himself to himself. In spite of his sin He has not given him up. He maintains His covenant with him. He is always faithful to him. He takes his sin seriously. But He takes even more seriously, with a primary seriousness, the fact that he is His man even as a sinner, and above all that He Himself is the God even of this sinful man.[92]

As Barth puts it: "God does not will that which troubles and torments and disturbs man." And Finally:

> ... the fact that man is a sinner and therefore the enemy of God is not taken into account or imputed to man .... ... Jesus is not really concerned with what from the anthropological view is the cause of human suffering, but only with the misery itself and as such. In these passages it is not at the side of the bad man but the suffering man that He, God Himself, sets Himself. It is to the help of the sufferer that He comes. And that He does so is quite undeserved by him, the creature ... It is simply and exclusively the good will of God for him.[93]

Jesus does not shun to act as He did in these actions - to heal - on account of the sin of the sufferer. He does not impute the individual's sin to him at the time of His actions. He wills the good of the person in spite of or rather regardless of sin. As Barth puts it: the activity of Jesus "as an actualisation of His Word and commentary on it, necessarily has the crucial and decisive form of liberation, redemption restoration, normalisation. [...] He goes right past sin, beyond it and through it, directly to man himself: for His purpose is always with man."[94]  These then are the reasons that Barth would concur with an analysis of such as Bornkamm's.

Let me state again the nineteenth-century position (inclusive of Ritschl) culminating in Schweitzer on the first part of the Gospel story in respect of the above. Notwithstanding the fact that on the whole it rejected on

---

[92] *Ibid*, 224

[93] *Ibid*, 232. Barth is not slow to raise the question how it was that the Reformation, including Luther and Calvin could "overlook this dimension of the Gospel which is so clearly attested in the New Testament" *In nuce*, how could Protestantism "as a whole, only too faithful to Augustine, the 'father of the West' orientate itself in such a way which was so one-sidedly anthropological (by the problem of repentance instead of by its presupposition - the kingdom of God)." *Ibid*, 233. The point that Barth is getting at is that the Reformers by and large ignored the fact that Jesus does not make repentance a pre-condition of His saving action, that He does not focus on the anthropological aetiology of the individual's physical or mental condition and seek to have the individual focus on that as the cause of his suffering and make himself whole again through repentance.

[94] *Ibid*, 225-226.

rationalistic grounds the historicity of the miracle tradition, it did affirm the historicity of Jesus proclaiming the imminence of the good news of the kingdom of God. It therefore insisted that this historicity be taken seriously in any historical analysis. To be sure, there was the question of Bornkamm's augmentation of the original position but Schweitzer would have argued that this made no difference to the substance of his case. To reiterate: Jesus' passion and death was seen as an alien element in His work in the sense that it completely contradicted his earlier work of proclaiming the kingdom of God in Galilee. The passion of Jesus was a catastrophe which burst unexpectedly into his life. Jesus' mission in proclaiming the kingdom of God ended in failure and death on the cross. *The kingdom of God as proclaimed in the good news of Jesus did not come.*

Barth did not disagree with the claim that the first part of the Gospel story had to be taken seriously in any historical analysis. Further he agreed that it made a crucial difference whether one affirmed the resurrection-appearances history or not. If one chose, as Schweitzer did, to designate the stories as mythology then one was necessarily committed to a relation of reversal and contradiction between two earlier histories. Once one had assimilated the stories to mythology one merely had the death of a man on a cross.

In affirming the resurrection-appearances history Barth affirms continuity and accord between the first half and the second half. To reiterate: the Easter story is "the commentary on the Gospel story in the unity and completeness of its first two parts." But this means in practice that: "We must understand the first part of the story as a commentary on the second, and vice-versa."[95] To read the first part as a commentary on the second part and vice-versa means that Jesus' proclamation and action manifesting the good news of the kingdom of God is part of the single unitary indivisible event completed on the cross: one completed unitary indivisible event rather than two (or more) discrete incongruous divided events.[96] There is one event and this one event must necessarily be continuous with the event of Jesus in Galilee proclaiming the good news of the kingdom of God. To repeat: as in the case of the judicial office, the first half of the pre-Easter narrative cannot be re-interpreted far less made to

---

[95] Barth *CD* IV/1, 223.

[96] "... the standpoint from which they [the Evangelists] saw Jesus and told us about Him lie beyond the temporal limits of His life. From this standpoint [the resurrection-appearances history] they saw and represented the totality of His life as that of a royal man, not with the intention of adding something to the truth of His historical existence, or in any way glossing it over, but with the intention of causing *the one and only truth of His historical existence* [my italics], as it later disclosed itself to them, to shine out in the only way that is commensurate with it." Barth, *CD* IV/2, 248.

shrink to insignificance as part of Jesus' history once he has died on the cross. It is part of Jesus' historical identity, part of the identity of God in Christ reconciling the world to Himself. It must have a bearing on what it is that is completed on cross. It follows therefore that if Jesus' proclamation is part of this one unitary continuous event, the good news of the kingdom of God must be fulfilled on the cross since the cross is the completion of this one continuous event. Jesus manifests in both word and deed the good news of kingdom of God. But then he is crucified.

Accordingly: "What the disciples originally saw at this point was either nothing at all or only the frightful paradox of a radical contradiction and destruction of the Son of the Man ...." But, in the wake of the Easter history, "they now realised that it was really His radical activation and affirmation. They now realised it was His coronation as the Royal Man He was ...." The crown of thorns, the royal purple robe, the title on the cross: 'This is Jesus of Nazareth, the king of the Jews', Pilate's unconscious witness to the truth of this with his famous dictum "I have written what I have written." - all indicative of the fact that the kingdom of God and Christ (Ephesians 5.5) had been fulfilled on the cross.[97] In opposition to the Catholic modernist Loisy's famous aphorism 'Jesus proclaimed the kingdom of God and it was the church that came' (which Loisy meant positively), Barth juxtaposes another: 'Jesus proclaimed the kingdom of God and it was the cross that came'. The kingdom of God is fulfilled in Jesus' coronation as the Royal Man, as the Kingly Man on the cross, a kingdom that is emphatically not of this world.

How then do the Judicial Office and the Kingly Office relate to one another as the one indivisible event of God in Christ reconciling the world to Himself, that is to say, from the perspective of the resurrection-appearances history? Barth notes that in John's Gospel as well and in Mark and Luke we are told that when Jesus healed on the Sabbath, healed those who suffered, he was  judged by the scribes and Pharisees, "those who watched and criticized him"[98] for breaking the law of the sabbath. This is the first part of Gospel story. Jesus proclaims the good news of the kingdom of God even as He is judged. The relationship at the time is one of mere correlation. In the second part it becomes one of  convergence. The fulfilment of the kingdom of God comes to fulfilment only as God the judge allows Himself to be judged in our place. Therefore Jesus' inauguration and fulfilment of the kingdom of God can only occur in the context of his arrest, trial, torture, and execution. This is what happens. As Barth puts it:

---

[97] *Ibid*, 254-256.
[98] *Ibid*, 226.

The sport which the Roman soldiers made of Him before his crucifixion, decking Him with the royal purple and the crown of thorns (Mk 15.16f and par.), is a drastic confirmation of this reflection [of Jesus as the Royal Man], as is also the taunting cry at the cross: "He saved others; himself he cannot save. If He be the King of Israel, let him now come down from the cross, and we will believe him. ...."[99]

God the judge who allowed Himself to be judged in our place implies the obedience of the Son of God even unto death on the cross. But the man Jesus who reveals Himself in the resurrection-appearances history as the One who had allowed Himself to be judged in our place is precisely that: a man. Or rather: He is man who as God is obedient even unto death on the cross.[100] Indeed, this is the sense in which He is true man, true man who can only be reconciled to God by God. There is no reconciliation that can be achieved by man without God. This is the deep sense of the Reformers' insight that obedience and justification cannot be accomplished by anything we do through our works. There are two points to be noted here. First, there is Barth's argument on logical grounds that :

.... What became and is in the divine act of the incarnation is, of course, a man. It is the man Jesus of Nazareth. But its object, that which God assumed into unity with Himself and His being and essence and kind and nature, is not 'a man', i.e. one of many who existed and was actual with all his fellow-men in a human being and essence and nature and kind as opposed to other creatures, but who was and is also this one man as opposed to other men. For this would necessarily mean either that the Son of God, surrendering His own existence as such, had changed Himself into this man, and was therefore no longer the Son of God .... Or that He did not exist as One but in a duality, as the Son of God maintaining His own existence, and somewhere and somehow alongside this individual man.[101]

Barth's argument is clearly recognisable as an example of classical deductive logic. If God had assumed into identity with Himself 'a man' then it would logically follow "either that the Son of God, surrendering His own existence as such, had changed Himself into this man, and was therefore no longer the Son of God .... Or that He did not exist as One but in a duality, as the Son of God maintaining His own existence, and

---

[99] *Ibid*, 168.
[100] *Ibid*, 167.
[101] *Ibid*, 48-49.

somewhere and somehow alongside this individual man."[102] But since both logical consequences are untenable according to Barth, it must follow that the antecedent proposition from which these consequent propositions follow is false too.[103] It is false that God assumed into identity with Himself 'a man.' Therefore it follows that that which God assumed into unity with Himself is the 'essence of man.'[104] What Barth means is that God incarnate is God assuming into unity with Himself 'man' in the 'generic' sense rather a specific instantiation of the generic sense i.e. a specific man or individual.[105] It is on these grounds that Barth feels compelled to affirm the distinction between *enhypostatos* and *anhypostatos*.[106]

---

[102] *Ibid.*, 49. An example of the former position would be that of the neo-Lutheran kenotic Christology of Gottfried Thomasius in which God changed into the man Jesus and in doing so ceased to be God. The fifth century Antiochene theologian Nestorius was charged (probably wrongly) with the latter affirmation.

[103] The principle of logical reasoning is in fact one known as *modus tollendo tollens*: If p then q; not-q; therefore not-p. A simple example would be: If Jones is six feet tall then he is taller than five feet; Jones is not taller than five feet; therefore Jones is not six feet tall.

[104] Barth appears to make the assumption that the two alternatives - God assuming into unity with Himself 'a man' or God assuming into unity with Himself 'man' in the generic sense - are logically exhaustive. I have not the space to examine whether this assumption is correct (though I think is). I merely present it descriptively as Barth's argument.

[105] Nevertheless this generic sense is first and foremost a *sui generis* theological sense; it is itself particular in itself even though it is particular to every human being. The essence of man of which Barth speaks is this: "To be a man is to be with Jesus, to be like Him. To be a man is thus to be with the One who is the true and primary elect of God. To be a man is to be in the sphere where the first and merciful will of God toward His creatures, His will to save and keep them from the power of nothingness, is revealed in action. [...] To the extent that he is with Jesus and therefore with God, man himself is a creature elected in the divine election of grace, i.e., elected along with or into Jesus." Barth, *CD* III/2, 145. Man is he who has been elected in Jesus Christ; man is he who is incarnate in Jesus Christ. These identity statements are constitutive of Barth's general definition of man. The primary identity of man is not sinful man though it is sinful man who - included in Jesus Christ's obedience even unto death on the cross - is included in true man. In this context one should remember Barth's supralapsarian credentials. The object of election is not sinful man - *homo lapsus* - (as in infralapsarianism) but unfallen though fallable man (indeed, very fallable man) - *homo labilis*.

[106] This is the doctrinal apparatus which affirms, in continuity with Alexandrian Christology, that the hypostasis or identity of Jesus Christ enhypostatised an essentially anhypostatic human nature. In contrast to a position that holds that the Word became a particular human being with their own hypostasis, such a doctrine holds that the humanity of Christ has no independent hypostatic existence apart from the hypostasis that is the Son of God. The terms *anhypostatos* and *enhypostatos* affirm the Chalcedonian formula "in two natures" but interpret it along lines that preserve the Alexandrian emphasis on the

This means that the history of God the judge who allows Himself to be judged in our place is also the history of the 'homecoming of man.' Both are inseparable though distinct aspects of the one indivisible event of God in Christ reconciling the world to Himself, reconciling man to Himself. The movement of God toward the cross is also the movement of man reconciled by God to God:

> The atonement as it took place in Jesus Christ is the one inclusive event of this going out of the Son of God and this coming in of the Son of Man ... It was God who went into the far country and it was man who returns home. Both took place in the one Jesus Christ. *It is not therefore a matter of two different and successive actions, but of a single action in which each of the two elements is related to the other and can be known and understood only in this relationship* [my italics]: the going out of God only as it aims at the coming in of man; the coming in of man only as the reach and outworking of the going out of God.[107]

In other words, the fulfilment of the kingdom of God is fulfilled on the cross insofar as the judicial work is fulfilled on the cross. The fulfilment of the judicial work *is* at the same time the fulfilment of the kingdom of God. Jesus coronation on the cross is a real coronation since the kingdom of God is a real kingdom. There is no kingdom of God that is inaugurated other than by Jesus' coronation on the cross. For it is only by means of this particular and unique inauguration that the "coming in of man" - the reconciliation of man - is accomplished: a coronation that is embedded in a sequence of events signifying an arrest, a trial, torture, and finally and inevitably, execution as a criminal on a cross. The intentional execution of the judge who is judged in our place is at the same time the intentional execution of the fulfilment of the kingdom of God. But the former has the latter as its aim, it is its objective. *God wills the former because He wills the latter.* His allowing Himself to be judged in our place is at the same time the fulfilment of God's good will for man. His coronation on the cross is the fulfilment of the kingdom of God because His coronation on the cross is at the same time for the good of man.

---

priority of the person of the Son of God and the unity of the Son of God made flesh. To be sure, the humanity of Christ has to have a hypostasis but it does not have to have its *own* hypostasis. Its hypostasis is the hypostasis that is the Son of God. See U M Lang, "Anhypostatos-Enhypostatos: Church Fathers, Protestant Orthodoxy and Karl Barth" *Journal of Theological Studies* (49) 1988, 630-657 for a comprehensive account of the history of the term.
[107] Barth, *CD* IV/2, 21.

## Concluding Remarks

What lesson emerges from Barth's analysis of the historical truth-claiming Gospel narrative? Juxtaposed to the tradition of Strauss through Weiss to Schweitzer, and indeed through to Bultmann, one learns that affirming the resurrection-appearances history - the man Jesus revealing Himself as God - makes a decisive difference whether one can affirm the first two parts of the Gospel story as narrating two divided events or as one indivisible event: God was in Christ reconciling the world to Himself. One also learns how one can affirm the pre-Easter history as one indivisible historical event by affirming the historical truth-claim of respectively Jesus Christ's Judicial work and His Kingly work, God's Kingly work in the context of His Judicial work, God's Kingly work in the context of His Judicial work. If the resurrection-appearances history is necessary in this respect then the historicity of these historical truth-claims constitutes sufficient conditions for holding the first two parts of the Gospel history together as one continuous indivisible historical whole. The historical truth-claiming Gospel narrative ultimately makes two historical truth-claims, lays claim to two historical events: God in Christ reconciling the world to Himself and the resurrection-appearances history.

There is an epistemological moral here of course. Epistemologically, one could only affirm the former event if one affirmed the latter event. Both, to be sure, were *geschichtlichen* events but the latter was a *sui generis geschichtlichen* event, in particular, a historical event whose only means of measurement was it itself. Therefore to affirm God in Christ reconciling the world to Himself presupposed affirming a historical event whose only means of measurement is it itself. There was nothing in principle wrong with historical analysis *per se* but it had to draw the epistemic consequences of dealing with a historical event whose only means of measurement is it itself. I sought to show what they were in Chapters 8 and 9. Barth never deviates from the path of historical truth but it is historical truth seen through the lens of the strange new world within the Bible. In the case of the resurrection-appearances history this meant *sui generis* historical truth.

I end with what is perhaps the general moral of the chapter. Barth's commitment to literal sense, the final form of the text, and historical truth entailed the utterly ironic fact that the Jesus he had retrieved from the Gospels had no less a claim to be the historical Jesus than the Jesus who had been the quarry of those who had participated in the quest for the historical Jesus in the sense of seeking a historical reconstruction of the real

Jesus, the Jesus behind the Gospels.[108] It can truly be argued that Barth was no less committed to 'the quest of the historical Jesus' than any of these quests. The question with which Barth is most concerned to answer is the *same question* that in essence preoccupied the minds of those who made the most stringent historical enquiries into the Jesus behind the Gospel, the historical Jesus: the question between the Bible and historical reality.

The claim that Barth and the critical-historical school shared a common objective, namely the truth about the historical Jesus, is further corroborated by the following fact. That Barth was just as interested in the historical Jesus as the critical-historical school meant that he was *no more interested than it in the Christ of faith defined as the Christ myth or as 'what Christ means for us.'* The reason is clear. The 'Christ of faith' defined in terms of the 'Christ of myth' or in terms of 'what Christ means for us' - and in such a way that it *excluded* the historical Jesus - could not be reconciled with Jesus Christ as he was rendered by the literal sense of the Gospel, in particular, by the resurrection appearance stories. Barth had to reject an understanding of the Gospel that, on the one hand, identified the pre-Easter story (or at least the non-miraculous parts of it) with truth-claims about the historical Jesus, *and*, on the other, identified the resurrection stories - the Easter story - with truth-claims about the Christ of faith in this sense. For Barth, *both* the pre-Easter story and the Easter story make truth-claims about the one unitary figure, the historical Jesus. This is not contradicted one whit by the fact that the historical Jesus Barth discovered in the Gospel itself was a historical Jesus who had revealed Himself as God, not merely in a historical event, but in a *sui generis* historical event. "Quite so! Any Christ Who is not Absolutely and Utterly the historical Jesus has Absolutely and Utterly Nothing to Do with Christianity!"

---

[108] For Barth the historical Jesus is the Jesus of *Geschichte*. Clearly then Barth does not identify the Jesus of *Geschichte* - *his* historical Jesus - with the Jesus of *Historie* - the historical Jesus reconstructed on the basis of critical-historical methodology. For the Jesus who reveals Himself as reconciler in the resurrection-appearances history reveals Himself as such in an event whose only means of measurement is it itself. This Jesus, Barth would say, is not measured by Troeltsch's principle of analogy (for example). Barth argues that his Jesus - inclusive of the third part of the Gospel narrative - has just as much claim to be historical (and therefore part of the events of *Geschichte*) as the Jesus of *Historie*. In this sense Barth is no less interested in the historical Jesus than the critical-historical school.

# PART V

## Wittgenstein and Barth:

## From the Enlightenment to Hegel

# Chapter 12
# The Later Wittgenstein

## 1. Introduction

In Chapter 3, I drew unashamedly on Janik and Toulmin's book *Wittgenstein's Vienna* to show that Wittgenstein's *Tractatus* belonged to a tradition exemplified by such as Karl Kraus, Arnold Schoenberg and Adolf Loos - key figures of "Wittgenstein's Vienna." Barth's *Romans* II was then assimilated into the tradition of Wittgenstein, and, at one remove, other key figures of "Wittgenstein's Vienna." There was: Kraus and the metalinguistic dilemma, Schoenberg and the metamusical dilemma, Loos and the meta-architectural dilemma, the *Tractatus* and the metaphilosophical dilemma, and, finally, *Romans* II and the metatheological dilemma. Yet though the concept of "Wittgenstein's Vienna" provides a less immediate context to the Wittgenstein's later philosophical work,[1] there can be little question that the later Wittgenstein, in continuity with his *Tractatus* self, was just as concerned to preserve the autonomy of philosophy or at least the continued existence of philosophy as a separate subject. This is especially apparent in the *Philosophical Investigations* in which Wittgenstein made numerous remarks of a metaphilosophical nature.[2] The autonomy of philosophy and of theology was, respectively, a central theme in the later Wittgenstein's and the later Barth's attempt to resolve their respective metadilemmas.

But the historical parallel goes deeper than this. The later Wittgenstein is often construed as affirming an 'anthropological-phenomenological' approach to philosophical problem-solving: philosophical problems are clarified by observing communities and their cultural-linguistic systems phenomenologically, more or less to the exclusion of any other kind of

---

[1] Janik and Toulmin, *Wittgenstein's Vienna*, ch.7.
[2] Wittgenstein, *PI, § 1-133*.

investigation.[3]  One such affirmation of this interpretation is found in the work of the philosopher of religion, D Z Phillips.[4] According to this view, central to the later philosophy is a plethora of language-games each with their own respective logic and rationality.  A similar view is held in mainstream theological circles. There the Wittgenstein of George Lindbeck's *The Nature of Doctrine* holds sway.[5] In common with Phillips' 'internalist' approach, Lindbeck's 'intratextual' interpretation of Wittgenstein advocates a Wittgenstein who maintained that philosophy was limited to describing the grammar of each individual 'language-game' or 'form of life'. 'Grammar' in this context coincided with rules of truth, intelligibility, reality and rationality, whose final court of appeal was how these rules were used in each (communal) language-game. Since these rules were different for different language-games, no external critical perspective was possible, each language-game was 'self-authenticating', and rationality was an 'internal' matter.[6]

---

[3] The religious philosopher D Z Phillips' interpretation of Wittgenstein is another example of a 'cultural-linguistic' approach. Phillips undoubtedly construes the latter as a 'philosophical' cultural anthropologist, albeit an enlightened one. See, for example, D. Z. Phillips, "Primitive Reactions and the Reactions of Primitives", *Wittgenstein and Religion* (London: MacMillan Press, 1993), 103-122.

[4] D Z Phillips, *Belief, Change and Forms of Life* (London: MacMillan, 1986); *Faith After Foundationalism* (London: Routledge, 1988); *Faith and Philosophical Enquiry* (London: Routledge and Kegan Paul, 1970); *The Concept of Prayer* (Oxford: Basil Blackwell, 1981); Religion in Wittgenstein's Mirror", in *A Phillips Griffiths (ed), Wittgenstein Centenary Essays* (Cambridge: Cambridge University Press, 1991), 135-150.

[5] George Lindbeck, *The Nature of Doctrine. Religion and Theology in a Postliberal Age* (London: SPCK, 1984), 24. He calls his approach "faithfulness as intratextuality". Intratextuality entails that "meaning is constituted by the uses of a specific language rather than being distinguishable from it. Thus the proper way to determine what 'God' signifies, for example, is by examining how the word operates within a religion and thereby shapes reality and experience, rather than first establishing its propositional or experiential meaning and reinterpreting or reformulating its uses accordingly." *Ibid,* 114.

[6] According to the 'Reformed' interpretation I offer, the distinction between 'intratextuality' and 'extratextuality' is essentially an eisegetical reading of the later philosophy. The logic, and therefore rational status, of Wittgenstein's 'measure of faith' does not operate within the confines of an 'intratextual' or 'internal' boundary. Wittgenstein's argument can be evaluated by the canons of critical argument. Hence, though the 'grammar' of his philosophical *analogia fidei* has a definite theological precedent, this grammar is not susceptible to the charge of fideism as made by such as Kai Nielsen and Ernest Gellner. This, I believe, is also true of Barth. See Kai Nielsen, "Wittgensteinian Fideism", *Philosophy* XLII 161 (1967), 191-209. As Gellner famously put it: "By destroying philosophy, Wittgenstein made room for faith ... religious

The understanding I will propose implicitly disputes whether this 'cultural-linguistic' 'anthropological-phenomenological' conception of philosophy is the whole or, indeed, the most important truth about the later Wittgenstein. It does not dispute D Z Phillips' claim that, after philosophy has sought to clarify the grammar of our forms of life, its job is over.[7] But it implicitly questions whether Wittgenstein could not have intended something more by the *clarification* of grammar than a purely phenomenological *description* of our forms of life.

What I wish to argue is that, just as the distinction between *means of measurement* and *object of measurement* is central to the later Barth, so it is to the later philosophy, and it is in a sense that, logically speaking, renders a community conception of rule-following unnecessary in the strict logical sense. Wittgenstein's dissolution of philosophical problems extrapolates from the insight that rule-following presupposes measurement against a norm or standard of measurement - a means of measurement. Wittgenstein's key argument against philosophical scepticism, whether it be in epistemology, or about meaning itself, is that scepticism can only make sense against a pre-existing criterion of measurement. This implies that philosophical scepticism is in error since the latter presupposes that one's judgements *can* make sense outside of such a criterion of measurement. Wittgenstein's critique of philosophical scepticism is, at bottom, based on the observation that, in the act of doubt or criticism, the philosophical sceptic attempts to 'measure' - criticise - a very distinctive object of measurement, namely: *the object of measurement that constitutes the means of measurement itself*. One cannot have the means of measurement and not the object of measurement itself. This is precisely the position Barth reached in the *Church Dogmatics* as regards epistemology.

As a corollary of the conclusion that the distinction between means of measurement and object of measurement is central to the key argument of the later philosophy I wish to suggest a better analogy for the later philosophy than the 'anthropological-phenomenological' one. On the assumption that Wittgenstein does offer an argument of old-fashioned rational status, I suggest an unashamedly non-phenomenological ratiocinative *theological* analogy, that of the theological conception of the *analogia fidei*. Though there is more than one tradition of relevance in this

---

believers can find in Wittgensteinianism not merely a device for ruling out philosophic criticism, they can find in it a positive validation of their belief." E Gellner, "Reply to Mr. McIntyre", *Universities and Left Review*, 1958, 71-89. A J Ayer and A C Grayling implicitly commit themselves to the same position. Ayer, *Wittgenstein* (Harmondsworth: Middlesex, Penguin Books, 1985), 92; A C Grayling, *Wittgenstein* (Oxford: Oxford University Press, 1988), 103-4.
[7] D Z Phillips, *The Concept of Prayer* (Oxford: Blackwell, 1981), viii.

respect, the particular tradition I will cite is the Reformers' conception of the *analogia fidei*. The distinction between means of measurement and object of measurement is as fundamental to the Reformers' conception of the *analogia fidei* as it is to Wittgenstein's later philosophy. A distinctly non-Kantian *transcendental* argument emerges from Wittgenstein's philosophical recapitulation of the Reformers' doctrine of the *analogia fidei*. These are all quintessentially Barthian themes.

Lest I be accused of inviting confusion, I should point out that the analogy between Wittgenstein and the Reformed theological tradition does not take him from the camp of the enlightened phenomenological anthropologists and put him in the ranks of the Reformed epistemologists. That the later Wittgenstein is a kind of 'conceptual foundationalist' affirming a philosophical *analogia fidei*, if you will, does not make him a 'foundational' Reformed epistemologist, though neither is he an unreconstructed anti-foundationalist, contrary to what theologians of the 'cultural-linguistic' ilk have thought.[8]

One major feature of the 'anthropological-phenomenological' interpretation of the later Wittgenstein is a social or community conception of rule-following and of language in general. Intrinsic to such a conception are socially or community-based criteria for interpretation and understanding. Wittgenstein does not deny that such criteria exist; indeed, he affirms they are frequently used in successful communication. But he nowhere asserts that they are essential to the resolution of philosophical problems.

A major confusion among theologians is the confusion between the meaning of the term 'social' and the term 'public'. The terms do not mean the same thing in the later Wittgenstein. Wittgenstein's repudiation of the possibility of a private language is based not on the premise that language is a social phenomenon; it is based on the premise that language is a public phenomenon in the sense that the rules a person follows when communicating can be explained *in principle* to other people. 'Private' is not an antonym for 'social'; it is an antonym for 'public.'[9] The rules may or

---

[8] One can be assimilated to the Reformed theological tradition in the above respect without being incorporated into the tradition of Reformed epistemology. That the later Wittgenstein is not in fact a Reformed epistemologist is beyond the scope of this chapter. I shall say that the concept of basic belief is not fundamental to Wittgenstein's arguments. He may affirm them, but such affirmation does not constitute a premise of his central arguments. See also D Z Phillips, *Faith After Foundationalism* (London: Routledge, 1988) for additional reasons for rejecting the thesis that the later Wittgenstein is a Reformed epistemologist.

[9] The crucial insight that Wittgenstein did not hold language to be necessarily a social practice - it is not pleonastic to say that language *is* a social practice - has been made by two experts in the field of Wittgenstein scholarship. See G P Baker and P M S Hacker,

may not be agreed socially - though, in fact, for much the greater part they are - *but this fact is not itself the rationale behind Wittgenstein's repudiation of the concept of a private language*. The fact that rules have been agreed in a social context clearly entails that the rules can be explained *in principle* to other people. But the converse is not true: the fact that a rule can be explained in principle does not necessarily imply that it has been agreed in a social context. The two properties are logically separable.[10] Rules are not necessarily a matter of social practice, though they are necessarily in principle a matter of public practice.

The upshot of these comments is that the 'anthropological-phenomenological' emphasis in Wittgenstein is much less critical to his approach to philosophical problems than has been thought by theologians - which is why I believe that the emphasis in theology as regards the later Wittgenstein's resolution of philosophical problems must shift from the community conception to one orientated around the concept of means of measurement, around the concept of *analogia fidei*. The 'community' conception - emphasising a necessary social ingredient to Wittgenstein's resolution of philosophical problems which is simply not there - does an injustice to the stature of the originality of Wittgenstein's thought, just as it does Barth's. (I might go as far as to argue that the social dimension is neither a necessary nor a *sufficient* condition for Wittgenstein's philosophical problem-solving.) To compare the later Barth to the later Wittgenstein on the basis of a common 'cultural-linguistic' approach - citing concepts such as religious or ecclesial 'forms of life', theological 'language-games', or community-based theological 'grammar' - is to simplify the historical context in which each thought; it is to deal in generalities analytically insensitive to the 'Enlightenment' rigour intrinsic to the thought of each at its best.

Paradoxically, the 'anthropological-phenomenological' interpretation of the later Wittgenstein belongs to the lineage J P Stern considers the most appropriate for the *Tractatus*. Stern, it will be recalled from Chapter 3, wrote that "if Wittgenstein's philosophy is to be placed in a tradition, then the one summed up in the old story of the Austrian railway line - from Bolzano to Brentano, Meinong, and Husserl to *Endstation* Wittgenstein - is

---

*Wittgenstein: Rules, Grammar and Necessity, Volume 2 of an analytical Commentary on the Philosophical Investigations* (Oxford: Basil Blackwell, 1985), 154-181, esp. 179-180.

[10] The argument here can be compared with Donald Davidson's strictures against linguistic convention. He does not deny that convention is very frequently employed in communication. But he rejects the thesis that linguistic convention is necessary for it to take place. See Donald Davidson "Communication and Convention", *Inquiries into Truth and Interpretation* (Oxford: Blackwell, 1984), 265-280.

undoubtedly more relevant than any other."[11] What the *Tractatus* had in common with this Austrian scientific tradition was its espousal of a single 'language-game' of scientific (empirical) propositions. From this perspective, the later language-games of the *Philosophical Investigations* could be viewed, without contradiction, as the later additions to the original 'language-game'.[12] Notwithstanding the fact that under this interpretation logical analysis gave way to linguistic analysis, logical positivism to linguistic positivism, the implicit preservation of an analytical positivist 'language-game' emphasis rendered this particular later Wittgenstein the heir of an earlier Austrian scientific positivist self.[13] This latter self, as was shown in Chapter 3, is essentially an illusion. The actual continuity that exists between the early and later Wittgenstein resides in the fact that the themes of showing and metaphilosophical dilemma are also present in the later work, albeit less explicitly. The tradition of Austrian scientific positivism is singularly unimportant for understanding the later Wittgenstein.

Implicit in these arguments is another warrant for rejecting the 'cultural-linguistic' approach to the later Wittgenstein. It is a misconception to characterise the transition between the earlier and later Wittgenstein as one in which a Wittgenstein who believed that logic necessarily undergirded language developed into a Wittgenstein who took the view that that social practice and community provided the necessary context to language. Not only was the essence of the earlier Wittgenstein not the heir of nineteenth-century Austrian scientific positivism, the essence of the later Wittgenstein was not orientated around a social or community conception of language. That one cannot doubt without - independently of - a means of measurement of *what it is* doubt is, is for Wittgenstein, an example of a specifically philosophical truth not dependent on social norms. For Barth the logical ramifications of *sui generis* historical truth deliver a similar lesson: one cannot have the means of measurement of this historical event independently of the object of measurement - the historical event itself. This too has nothing to do with 'community' though its implications for 'the community' - the church and its existence - are great.

---

[11] Stern, "Wittgenstein in Context", 166.

[12] Paul Feyerabend, "Wittgenstein's *Philosophical Investigations*", in George Pitcher (ed), *Wittgenstein: The Philosophical Investigations* (London: MacMillan, 1986), 104-150.

[13] Haller, "Wittgenstein and Austrian Philosophy", 1-26; esp. 18-24. See also Haller, "Was Wittgenstein a Neopositivist?", in Nyíri (ed), *Austrian Philosophy: Studies and Texts* (Munich: Philosophia-Verlag, 1981), 27-43.

Is there a continuity between the earlier and the later philosophy as regards the concept of criterion?[14] The motivation behind the *Tractatus*, like that of Krausian polemics, can be assimilated to the "language-consciousness" of 'Grillparzer's Vienna' - the linguistic predecessor to 'Wittgenstein's Vienna' - in that it too took a stand against the twentieth-century "poetry of the market-place": prose in the service of science. A special subset of language is set aside as a criterion of meaning in which aesthetic and ethic coincide - integrate - and therefore, by extrapolation, possess integrity. In the later philosophy, no one 'language' is given preeminence over all others. Nevertheless, Wittgenstein pursues the same ethical and aesthetic ends - those which were originally vouchsafed by an ideal logical language - by means of the concept of *origin*, from whence the concept of *criterion*, so important to the later philosophy, derives. Though Goethe's model of biological genesis as expressed in his theory of the primal plant - the morphologically conceived *Urpflanze* - may be deserving of a small footnote in any history of the intellectual origins of Wittgenstein's thought (the concept of *Urpflanze* is not unlike Overbeck's model of historical genesis, as expressed in his concept of *Urgeschichte*),[15]

---

[14] It may be objected that the way in which I used the term *criterion* differs from the way Wittgenstein almost always uses it, that is, *as and when it occurs in his work explicitly*. Indeed, it may be argued that, as Wittgenstein uses the term, it is not central to the later philosophy. Joachim Schulte has pointed out that criteria "play a role in two main areas for Wittgenstein. The first concerns criteria of identity, which supposedly permit answers to questions such as whether we are dealing with one object or several. The second area concerns the attribution of states of consciousness, feelings, etc." Joachim Schulte, *Wittgenstein: An Introduction*, translated by William H Brenner and John F Holley, (Albany, State University of New York Press, 1992), 122. In the latter respect, it has been argued that the sense in which Wittgenstein uses "criterion" at *PI* § 580 - an "'inner process' stands in need of outward criteria [*Kriterien*]" - constitutes a 'verificationist' behaviourist solution to the sceptical problem of other minds (the relation between, for example, pain-behaviour and pain is one of 'criteria'). Whether Hanfling is right to say that construing *PI* § 580 in this way is a misinterpretation - and it seems to me he is right (Hanfling is undoubtedly correct to say that *PI* § 580 does not express Wittgenstein's solution to the sceptical problem of 'other minds', Hanfling, *Wittgenstein's Later Philosophy*, 121-123), the issue is quite simply irrelevant as I have used the term. The sense in which I have used the term is *as an explanatory concept*: hence, how Wittgenstein actually used the term is beside the point. I argue that, in the sense in which I have used it, it is central to the conceptual foundationalism at the root of his arguments on rule-following, the private language, and his position on epistemology. There may or may not be a superior explanatory concept in terms of accuracy; but whether that is so, is true regardless of what Wittgenstein actually meant at *PI* § 580.

[15] For some observations on the relation between Goethe's concept of *Urpflanze* and the later Wittgenstein, see Ray Monk, *Ludwig Wittgenstein: the Duty of Genius* (London: Vintage, 1991), 303-304, 509-512.

the fundamental rationale behind Wittgenstein's later philosophy recapitulates the Reformers' conception of the *analogia fidei* as described in the preceding chapter - the *analogia fidei* as explicated by such as Tyndale, Calvin, Bucanus, Charmier, and the Second Helvetian Confession. Though Wittgenstein was almost certainly *not* acquainted with the Reformed tradition's conception of the *analogia fidei*, the conception provides a decidedly theological precedent for the later philosophy.[16] Not only is the concept of criterion the fundamental rationale behind the later Wittgenstein's resolution of philosophical problems, it is essential in this respect precisely as a means of measurement. Philosophical scepticism (e.g., Cartesianism) can only be a viable option if doubt is possible without a 'measure of faith' against which to measure that doubt. The key argument of the 'Reformed' Wittgenstein is that scepticism can only make sense against a pre-existing criterion of measurement - a philosophical *analogia fidei* if you will. Meaning presupposes a foundational truth of some kind or another (hence the rationale behind the phrase *conceptual foundationalism* as a description of the later philosophy).

But not only was the concept of criterion manifest in the earlier Wittgenstein, at least in inchoate form; the idea of a object whose only criterion is it itself is fundamental to the doctrine of showing. As Wittgenstein himself indicated in his *Notebooks*,[17] the doctrine of showing was incompatible with the picture theory of meaning in the *Tractatus*. The relevant passage was quoted in Chapter 3. I cite it again:

> But is *language* the *only* language?
> Why should there not be a mode of language through which I can talk *about* language in such a way that it can appear in co-ordination with something else?[18]

That it is true "such a 'language' could not ... be contained in the language it talks about"[19] follows from the uniqueness of language. Language is unique precisely because nothing can stand in analogy or comparison to it. *It itself alone is its own criterion.* The consequence of all this is that, as Wittgenstein himself implied at the end of the *Tractatus*, a

---

[16] It appears that Wittgenstein's familiarity with Calvin and Calvinism was only of the most general sort. See M O' C Drury, "Conversations with Wittgenstein", in R Rhees (ed), *Recollections of Wittgenstein* (Oxford: Oxford University Press, 1984), 149, 180.

[17] Block, "'Showing' in the *Tractatus*: The Root of Wittgenstein and Russell's Basic Incompatibility", in S Shanker (ed), *Ludwig Wittgenstein: Critical Assessments*, vol I (London: Croom Helm, 1986), 136-149.

[18] Wittgenstein, *NB*, entry dated 29.5.15.

[19] *Ibid*, 148.

*theory* of meaning is impossible - not just the picture theory of meaning but any and all such theories. In the early philosophy the sense of a proposition shows itself without any help from any theory of meaning. This indeed must be the case since the picture theory of meaning is something that cannot be said. It is an attempt "to talk about language in such a way that it can appear in co-ordination with something else." The relation this had to the later philosophy can be stated thus:

> ... the idea that there can be no theory of language and no formal rules that explicate meaning was carried over in the later philosophy. It was no longer the concrete sentence that showed its meaning but rather the concrete situation in which the sentence was uttered that gave the sentence its significance. These situations he called 'language-games' and their concrete role in human thought and action or 'life' could not be formalized or justified, or grounded. [...] Nothing outside language can 'account' for language or explain it.[20]

---

[20] Block, "The Unity of Wittgenstein's Philosophy", in R Haller and W Grassl (eds), *Language, Logic and Philosophy* (1980), 233-236. Not only is the later philosophy in continuity with the early philosophy as Kenny shows, (Kenny, *Wittgenstein*), the way in which the *Tractatus* resolves the metaphilosophical dilemma is a fundamental key to understanding how the later philosophy resolves the dilemma (without incurring the charge of fideism). The continued presence of the doctrine of showing and saying testifies that the later philosophy is also (*inter alia*) an attempt to resolve the metaphilosophical dilemma. Most commentators on Wittgenstein would, I think, agree with the following observation: it is easier to prove that the showing and saying distinction is fundamental to the earlier philosophy than it is to prove it is fundamental to the later philosophy. Putting aside Wittgenstein's own remark that it constituted the 'cardinal problem of philosophy', the number of references to the distinction in the *Tractatus* make it abundantly clear to us that it is a central doctrine. In contrast, one might almost say of the later philosophy that there the distinction is conspicuous by its absence, such is the paucity of reference to it. Yet in the face of this apparent near absence there has been support for the abiding pervasive presence of the distinction in the later philosophy. Several commentators take the view, not merely that the distinction survives, but that it is central to an understanding of the later philosophy. For Kenny, the distinction between saying and showing was fundamental to both his earlier and his later philosophy. Kenny, *Ibid*, 45. McGuinness writes in the first part of his biography on Wittgenstein that the distinction is "a key notion, perhaps even throughout Wittgenstein's entire philosophical life." McGuinness, *Wittgenstein*, 199. Pears observes: "In the *Tractatus* this doctrine is presented in the rigid framework of logical atomism. The attachment of factual discourse to the world is achieved *au fond* through elementary sentences, each of which is linked to its own bit of reality and displays the simple possibility which it asserts to be realized. There is no way in which such possibilities can be described or explained; each one is a separate mystery, eluding the

But if nothing "could 'account' for language or explain it", it remained true in the later philosophy that one could not "talk about language in such a way that it can appear in co-ordination with something else." And the reason it remained true is that somewhere in each language-game, a philosophical *analogia fidei* was operative, but in such a way that could only be shown, not described: it itself was the means of the possibility of description.[21]

The comparison with Barth is striking. For Barth the means of measurement of respectively, Jesus Christ's self-revelation as reconciler (the resurrection-appearances history), and the God of Israel's self-revelation as creator (the creation history), cannot be had without or independently of the object of measurement itself. In other words, the object of measurement itself is the *means of the possibility* of the means of measurement itself. Both are logically prior to the church community constituting a community conception of the means of measurement. Hence, such a social or community analysis of Barth is not only historically incorrect if one is intent on getting to the fundamental rationale behind Barth, it also undersells the cogency of both Barth and Wittgenstein's position vis-à-vis a whole host of issues, including that of epistemology.

I begin with an account of Wittgenstein's non-Kantian transcendental argument (sections 2 and 3). Section 4 shows how Wittgenstein's *analogia fidei* resolves the argument between realism and idealism. Section 5 shows this *analogia fidei* to be the fundamental rationale behind Wittgenstein's position on epistemology in *On Certainty*. The final section, section 6 draws out some similarities between Wittgenstein and the Reformers on the possibility of private interpretation or meaning.

---

grasp of science. In the later system, this mystery did not disappear, but, rather, is spread over the whole surface of human language and behaviour." Pears, *Prison*, vol 1, 193.

[21] P M S Hacker gives an example of the logic of the showing-saying/description distinction: when we "explain what 'magenta' means by pointing at a patch on a table of colour samples and saying 'That - is magenta', we are not saying something *about* the patch, but explaining the meaning of the word." In other words, we are establishing a criterion of *what it is* magenta is, *what it is* "magenta" means, *what it is* "magenta" designates. Hacker continues: "[T]hen when we say of the curtains that they are that colour (pointing at the sample), we are using an element of our method of representation to say something about the world, namely that the curtains are magenta." Hacker, *Insight*, 186. In saying something about the world we are engaged in description, but the description is only possible on the condition that there is a criterion of *what it is* magenta is. The description has to measured against the latter. It cannot 'exist meaningfully' outwith this measure.

## 2. Wittgenstein and the Transcendental Argument

Erik Stenius takes the view that in the *Tractatus* what "Kant's transcendental deductions are intended to perform ... is performed by the logical analysis of language."[22] David Pears argues that the early Wittgenstein posits that the conditions of the possibility of logic "involve the possibility of elementary propositions, and the ultimate granulation of reality. Read in this direction the argument is a transcendental one."[23] Rüdiger Bubner, building on Stenius's insight, argues that the essential property of the transcendental argument in the *Tractatus* is that it is *self-referential*: logical analysis "reveals something, which it must presuppose if it intends to perform the task of clarifying meaningful statements. It must accept the relationship language and reality as one which exists prior to the analysis, and for this reason cannot be produced in arbitrary fashion."[24] Implicit in all these views is that when Wittgenstein affirms that logic is transcendental, he does not mean that the propositions of logic state "transcendental truths, it means that they like other propositions, shew something that pervades everything sayable and is itself unsayable."[25] That is, rather than manifesting a transcendental truth, Wittgenstein is alluding to the presence of a transcendental argument. The statement that propositions do *not* contain logical structure presupposes the very property the statement denies - that it does have logical structure (just like its contradictory "Propositions contain logical structure"); though, for reasons explained in Chapter 3, that this is so cannot be said, only shown. It is this type of transcendental argument that one finds in the later philosophy: though not a transcendental deduction in Kant's sense it is an argument which shows that the sceptical position self-destructs on the grounds that it assumes just what it denies.

As Derek Bolton notes, if the doctrine of showing what cannot be said (e.g., language can say nothing about the relation between itself and the world) no longer holds in the later philosophy, one cannot, as one could in the *Tractatus,* exclude a super-language on this ground.[26] The reason a super-language is excluded in the later work is that philosophy is now about

---

[22] Erik Stenius, *Wittgenstein's Tractatus: A Critical Exposition of its Main Lines of Thought* (Oxford: Basil Blackwell, 1960), 218.

[23] Pears, *Wittgenstein*, 83.

[24] Rüdiger Bubner, "Kant, Transcendental Arguments and the Problem of Deduction" *Review of Metaphysics* (28) 1975, 453-467.

[25] See Anscombe, *Introduction*, 166.

[26] Derek Bolton, *An Approach to Wittgenstein's Philosophy* (London: MacMillan, 1979), 128-130.

the *origin* of meaning.[27] But it does not then follow, as Bolton implies, that because there is no transcendental language for philosophy to use, there is no transcendental emphasis at all in the later philosophy. A transcendental argument does not require the "shared premise of the sceptic and Kantian, namely that we *know* our own experiences as expressed in such propositions as 'I am in pain', 'I seem to perceive ...', 'As I recollect ...'."[28]

Thus, though Hacker's criticism of Scruton's interpretation of the private language argument is valid,[29] it does not follow that Wittgenstein did not employ *some* species of transcendental argument. Though Kant defined a transcendental argument in terms of the conditions of the possibility of experience, which therefore were themselves transcendental, it does not follow that all transcendental arguments necessarily ask of the conditions of the possibility of *experience*.[30] This is because a "transcendental argument is one intending to prove that certain concepts or presuppositions are necessary for language or thought. The transcendental arguer is in position to point out to a sceptic that his claims are self-defeating: given a transcendental demonstration sceptical doubts are subject to a *reductio*, as they can be shown to assume just what they deny."[31] This

---

[27] *Ibid*, 128-129.

[28] Hacker, *Insight*, 213.

[29] *Ibid*, 211-212. Hacker's critique of Roger Scruton's interpretation of Wittgenstein's private language argument provides an excellent example of where Wittgenstein and Kant differ on the transcendental question. Scruton asserts: "Wittgenstein argues that there can be no knowledge of experience which does not presuppose reference to a public world. I can know my own experience immediately and incorrigibly, but only because I apply to it concepts which gain their sense for public usage. And public usage describes a reality observable to others beside myself." R Scruton, *Kant* (Oxford: Oxford University Press, 1982), 35. But Hacker's response is that this is not a correct account of the private language argument since "Wittgenstein emphatically denied that 'I can know my own experience immediately and incorrigibly', not because I can know my experience only mediately and corrigibly, but because there is no such thing as 'knowing my experience'." Hacker, *Insight*, 212. That is, I can neither know my own experience immediately and incorrigibly nor can I know my own experience only mediately and corrigibly; rather, both assertions are meaningless. Leslie Stevenson's interpretation of the private language argument is subject to the same criticism, namely that Wittgenstein's point of departure is not the incorrigible immediate knowledge of his own experience. L Stevenson, "Wittgenstein's Transcendental Deduction and Kant's Private Language Argument", *Kantstudien* (73), no.3 1982, 320-337.

[30] Kant, *Critique of Pure Reason*; B Stroud, "Transcendental Arguments and 'Epistemological Naturalism'", *Philosophical Studies 31* 1977, 105-115; T E Wilkerson "Transcendental Arguments", *Philosophical Quarterly (20)* 1970, 200-212; R Bubner, "Kant, Transcendental Arguments", 453-467.

[31] Charles Crittenden, "Wittgenstein and Transcendental Arguments", R Haller and W Grassi (eds), *Language, Logic and Philosophy* (1980), 259.

definition does not entail the shared premise of the sceptic and Kantian; it does not enquire into the conditions of the possibility of *experience*. It does, it is submitted,    encapsulate Wittgenstein's fundamental strategy of argument in the later philosophy. Therefore, Wittgenstein can be said to employ a transcendental argument. Speaking of the later philosophy, Fergus Kerr writes that forms of life and language-games

> cannot be explored or explained any more deeply because [they are] the foundation of every kind of exploration and explanation. If you like: the given cannot be discovered except by showing how it makes possible all that we do and suffer.[32]

Forms of life and language-games "cannot be explored or explained any more deeply because they are the foundation of every kind of exploration and explanation." This is not a *factual* foundation in the sense that corroborates philosophical realism. Forms of life and their accompanying language-games constitute the *conceptual foundations* of our epistemic norms of argument, investigation, explanation, etc. Hence, necessarily, they are already presupposed, logically, as the *origin, and therefore as the criterion,* of one's being able to criticise, doubt, etc., at all. One can quote Wittgenstein here:

> When philosophers use a word "knowledge", "being", "object", "I", "proposition" ... original home. What we do is bring words back from their metaphysical to their everyday use.[33]

To this list we could add: "true", "false", "explanation", "criticism", "exists" (although something like this is what Wittgenstein has in mind with "being") and "meaning". But the 'given' in Kerr's statement is expressed as a condition of possibility. This would indicate the opposite of that which Rudolf Haller implies, namely that a purely factual condition - a fact - cannot at the time be a condition of possibility.[34] Indeed, Kerr accords with Stanley Cavell here. Cavell holds that in this transcendental similarity to Kant the "differences light up the nature of the problems Wittgenstein set himself. For Wittgenstein it would be an illusion not only that we do know

---

[32] F Kerr, *Theology After Wittgenstein* (Oxford: Basil Blackwell, 1986), 69. Kerr goes on to write: "I discover myself, not in some pre-linguistic inner space of self-presence, but in the network of multifarious social and historical relationships in which I am willy-nilly involved." *Ibid*, 69. As regards philosophical problem-solving, I do not regard these alternatives as logically exhaustive for reasons given in this chapter.

[33] Wittgenstein, *PI*, § 116.

[34] Rudolf Haller, "Was Wittgenstein a Neo-Kantian?", *Questions on Wittgenstein*, 54.

things-in-themselves but equally an illusion that we do not (crudely, because the concept of 'knowing something as it really is', is being used without a clear sense, apart from its ordinary language game)."[35] Less crudely, one could say that the only criterion for the concept of "knowing something as it really is" is as the bench-mark against which we measure "not knowing something as it really is". That is, there is now no ideal (logical) language as Wittgenstein thought in the *Tractatus* (and which possibility he inveighed against in the *Investigations*);[36] nor is there a super-language pointing to what lies beyond the bounds of theoretical reason ("noumenon", "phenomenon", etc.).

Kerr's assertion, I would claim, manifests a transcendental condition in accord with Charles Crittenden's definition given above; it therefore makes no reference to a transcendental condition of the possibility of experience. The question is: where does Wittgenstein makes this species of argument in detail?

### 3. The Transcendental Argument Receives a Linguistic Turn

The type of transcendental argument Wittgenstein employs is inextricably linked with his concept of grammar. Wittgenstein's use of the term is not that of the traditional linguist's. Conventional grammar is concerned with parts of speech (nouns, verbs, adjectives, adverbs), distinguishing the correct from the incorrect combinations of word order, verb conjugation, noun pluralization, etc., in the form of rules. In contrast, when Wittgenstein calls philosophy a grammatical investigation, he means an activity which sets out to uncover certain conceptual relations between the different uses of language. Clarification of these conceptual relations - elucidation of grammar - will, it is held, resolve our philosophical problems. Articulating the grammar of our beliefs is a conceptual investigation of the use of language, not an empirical investigation of reality.

Central to Wittgenstein's clarification of philosophical problems is the proposition that rule-following presupposes measurement against a norm or standard of measurement - a means of measurement. Crucial to Wittgenstein's conception of rule-following is the concept of a public criterion which distinguishes between getting a rule right and getting it wrong. *The very concept of something being a rule entails that one can, in*

[35] Stanley Cavell, "The Availability of Wittgenstein's Later Philosophy", in G Pitcher (ed), *Wittgenstein. The Philosophical Investigations* (London: MacMillan, 1968), 176-177.
[36] See for example, Wittgenstein, *PI, § 120.*

*principle, get it wrong, fail to follow it.*[37] For Wittgenstein, the essential defect of a private language is that it does *not* have this characteristic. *One cannot - as long as one thinks one is following it - fail to follow the rule of a private language.* To think that one was following a rule would be the same thing as following a rule; to think that one was following a rule would be a *logically sufficient condition* of actually following the rule: "'Obeying a rule' is a practice. And to *think* one is obeying a rule is not to obey a rule. Hence, it is not possible to obey a rule 'privately': otherwise, thinking one was obeying a rule would be the same thing as obeying it."[38] Though it is possible to follow a rule privately, it is not possible to follow a private rule.[39]

To the objection that one *could* fail to follow a private rule Wittgenstein's reply is, but in that case, the rule would *not* be a private rule because then one could specify the rule one had failed to follow - one could in principle teach the rule to another person. As Pears puts it, Wittgenstein's objection to the notion of a private language is that it is without a "viable independent criterion which distinguishes getting [a rule] right from getting it wrong."[40] Only if there is such a criterion is there the possibility of failure. The possibility of failure - of missing the mark, so to speak - is essential to the concept of a rule. The possibility of failure implies that one's actions can be measured against a criterion or standard, a criterion or standard which measures whether one has followed, or not followed, the rule. In a private language there is no such means of measurement. The question is: what is the *nature* of this criterion or standard of measurement?

It is generally held that essential to Wittgenstein's conception of rule-following is a conception of norm or criterion defined in terms of inter-personal agreement. That is, it is generally held that, for Wittgenstein, rules are *necessarily social rules*. This, I will argue, is a mistake. Though such a criterion is not "'unimportant' or totally irrelevant" (to use the words of a relatively recent commentator) to Wittgenstein's account of rule-

---

[37] Anthony Thiselton may be alone among theologians in emphasising the importance of this insight in the later Wittgenstein. He writes: "Effective language presupposes a distinction between correct and mistaken application of words. For 'correct' has no substance unless it carries with it the concept of what being 'incorrect' in the same case might amount to. On this issue hangs even the capacity to identify, to recognise, to exercise, or to apply concepts." Anthony C Thiselton, *The Two Horizons: New Testament Hermeneutics and Philosophical Description with special reference to Heidegger, Bultmann, Gadamer, and Wittgenstein*, foreword by J B Torrance (Exeter: Paternoster Press, 1980), 380.

[38] Wittgenstein, *PI* § 202.

[39] Baker and Hacker, *Analytical Commentary* vol 2, 169-179.

[40] Pears, *The False Prison* vol ii, 523.

following,[41] it is not essential to it. Rule-following, for Wittgenstein, does *not* necessarily presuppose a norm of judgement as agreed by the community or, in other words, what Wittgenstein calls 'agreement in form of life' (*PI* §242) But it *does* necessarily presuppose what David Pears calls 'calibration on standard objects'.[42]

As Colin McGinn notes, it is the former conception that "has been endorsed by a great many, perhaps the majority of commentators" as a general interpretation of Wittgenstein's account of rule-following. Two recent influential commentators, Saul Kripke and Norman Malcolm, maintain that Wittgenstein endorses a community conception of rule-following. According to them, fundamental to Wittgenstein's conception is the idea that the individual *measures* his actions against those of the community in order to determine whether he is following correct usage. Malcolm was quite explicit about this: "the concept of following a rule implies the concept of a *community* of rule-followers."[43] According to Malcolm: "the actions of an individual, who believes that he is following a rule, must be *measured against* something other than his own actions."[44] The belief that one is following a rule can only be substantiated by measuring one's actions against a community of rule-followers.

If the concept of a rule implies a community of rule-followers it would follow that the latter is a logically necessary condition of the former. In other words, it would follow that, without a community of rule-followers against which to measure one's actions, there would be no sense in which one could be said to follow a rule. The question is whether this is Wittgenstein's own position on the concept of a rule. Does the distinction between getting a rule right and getting it wrong logically depend on the existence of a community of rule-followers?[45]

The two passages cited most frequently as evidence that a community conception of rule-following is essential to Wittgenstein's account of rule-following are *PI* §241 and §242. In answer to the imaginary interlocutor's question at *PI* § 241, "'So you are saying that human agreement decides what is true and what is false?'", Wittgenstein replies, "It is what human

---

[41] Colin McGinn, *Wittgenstein on Meaning: an Interpretation and Evaluation* (Oxford: Basil Blackwell, 1987), 91.

[42] David F. Pears, *The False Prison. A Study of the Development of Wittgenstein's Philosophy* vol ii (Oxford: Oxford University Press, 1987), 441-442.

[43] Norman Malcolm, *Wittgenstein: Nothing is Hidden* (Oxford: Basil Blackwell, 1986), 156.

[44] *Ibid*, 156.

[45] The tale I implicitly tell is that a social conception of meaning is not a necessary (and may not be a sufficient) condition of rule-following in the later Wittgenstein. But moreover: the community conception (in Malcolm's sense for example) is not a sufficient condition of philosophical problem-solving in the later philosophy.

beings *say* that is true or false; and they agree in the *language* they use. That is not agreement in opinions but in form of life."[46] In other words, as Colin McGinn puts it, Wittgenstein's claim "concerns the conditions for *meaningful* utterances, not the conditions for their truth."[47] Though there is no such thing as justifying grammar by reference to reality, this does not mean that "in making assertions, we are not really, or not successfully, making statements about the world. Nor does it express a commitment to some form of transcendental idealism according to which the mind, in some obscure sense, makes nature."[48] Neither does it entail a form of *linguistic* idealism in which it is our language-systems that determine reality instead of reality determining our language-systems.[49]

That is, Wittgenstein affirmed agreement in forms of life as a principle of metaphorical measurement, but he did not affirm a community conception of truth insofar as this is taken to mean that the community decides by consensus, as it were, what is true and what is false. Truth itself is not reducible to mere inter-personal agreement. This conclusion flies in the face of accepted wisdom, at least among certain theologians. According to George Lindbeck's *The Nature of Doctrine*, the lesson that one can draw from Wittgenstein is that correct usage of the predicate 'true', for example, in the religious community is necessarily - and merely - a matter of one's use conforming to the relevant rules of that community.[50] But, as McGinn says, such agreement is not what makes sentences true but, rather, merely a condition of being able to agree that such-and-such is true. 'Agreement in form of life' *constitutes* what counts as the stability it maintains. As Pears puts it: any such source of stability is a resource that stabilises language in the sense that it defines "what counts as the stability that it maintains."[51]

---

[46] Wittgenstein, *PI* § 241.

[47] McGinn, *Wittgenstein on Meaning: an Interpretation and Evaluation*, 54.

[48] P. M. S. Hacker, *Insight and Illusion. Themes in the Philosophy of Wittgenstein* 2nd ed., revised (Oxford: Oxford University Press, 1986), 186.

[49] Oswald Hanfling, *Wittgenstein's Later Philosophy* (London: MacMillan Press, 1989), 129.

[50] Lindbeck, *The Nature of Doctrine*, 33; 65-69. Lindbeck's account of truth within a religious form of life recognises that "the ontological truth of religious utterances ... is different as well as similar to what occurs within other realms of discourse." To be sure, D. Z. Phillips argues that Lindbeck's account is confused in that it sometimes seems as if the conception of truth deemed appropriate to the context of a religious form of life can be one derived from the grammar of physical objects. D. Z. Phillips, *Faith After Foundationalism*, 195-211; see esp. 205-206. But it is clear from Phillips' analysis of Lindbeck that insofar as there is such a confusion in Lindbeck, it does *not* derive from Wittgenstein. It remains true that Lindbeck's interpretation of Wittgenstein is a 'cultural-linguistic' one in which truth is relative to community rule and practice.

[51] Pears, *The False Prison* vol ii, 368.

This latter point is well-made in the other passage most often quoted in support of the necessity of a community conception of rule-following. Wittgenstein writes at *PI* §242:

> If language is to be a means of communication, there must be agreement not only in definitions but also (queer as this may sound) in judgements. This seems to abolish logic, but does not do so. - It is one thing to describe methods and another to obtain and state results of measurement. But what we call 'measuring' is partly determined by a certain constancy in results of measurement.[52]

In other words, if there is to be communication - if there is to be a shared use of what we call 'measuring' - there has to be agreement not only on the metaphorical unit of measurement,  but also agreement in the results of measurement.  If I am to be able to communicate my claim that  such-and-such is of a certain  length then there must be agreement between people on those two things. Only then does it make sense to speak of the other person confirming or disconfirming my assertion. The concept of 'agreement in form of life' gives no credence to the notion that truth-claims are justified by reference to a social standard or norm. Truth is not a question of consensus agreement in opinions. Instead, central to Wittgenstein's conception is the concept of '(metaphorical) means of measurement.' 'Agreement in form of life' is a necessary means of communicating that 'such-and-such is the case' in general (not merely of communicating the results of literal measurement).

Communication between two people presupposes agreement in form of life. What *PI* 241 and *PI* 242 do not say individually or collectively, however, is that agreement in form of life is necessary  for my claim to be meaningful *per se. That is, though one could only be said to be following a rule were it the case that, given agreement in form of life, another person could learn which rule one was following - what it was one meant - it does not follow that agreement in form of life is a necessary condition of following the rule itself, and hence of one's utterance being a meaningful utterance.* In other words, the elimination of the community of rule-followers does not entail the elimination of the distinction between getting a rule right and getting it wrong. The latter, if you recall, is logically internal to the very concept of something being a rule at all. G. P. Baker and P. M. S. Hacker cite Robinson Crusoe in isolation on his island and the last of the Mohicans (the last Mohican) as counter-examples to the assertion that the absence of the community - the social dimension - is a sufficient condition of a private language. The litmus-test for these individuals being rightly

---

[52] Wittgenstein, *PI* § 242.

said to follow rules or speak a language - of there being a distinction between getting the rule right from getting it wrong - is that the rule *could in principle* be taught to or learned by another person.[53]

As Baker and Hacker put it, Wittgenstein's "private language argument introduces 'private' to signify what *cannot* in principle be explained to another person, what cannot be understood by others."[54] This implies the further conclusion that Baker and Hacker are correct as against Kripke and Malcolm in another respect: "private" is not an antonym of "social". McGinn is correct to say that the central theme behind Wittgenstein's use of the term "private" is: "within the sphere of consciousness in logical independence of behaviour";[55] he does not mean something akin to an action that one does on one's own or a thought that one has on one's own.

Moreover, as Pears points out, *PI* §242 is quite explicit that agreement in judgements is necessary in order for language to be a means of communication.[56] The implication is not only the logical point that the identity of language *qua* language would not be compromised were it ever used other than as a means of communication, but that language - as a matter of empirical fact - can indeed be used other than as a means of communication. Ironically, those who argue that language is necessarily always a means of communication have succumbed to theory-building instead of looking at the particular case. To repeat: agreement in form of life is not a necessary condition of meaningfulness *per se*, it is a necessary condition of communication.

However, the fundamental basis of Wittgenstein's objection to the notion of a private language and, therefore, the basis of his critique of the classical conception of meaning in general, is that it is without a "viable independent criterion which distinguishes getting [a rule] right from getting it wrong."[57] To be able to learn the rule presupposes such a criterion. In the case of, for example, Robinson Crusoe, the question is: what constitutes such a criterion? Is there any such source of stabilisation of Crusoe's language in the sense that it defines "what counts as the stability that it maintains"?[58] David Pears argues that there is such a criterion in the form of 'calibration on standard objects'. Agreement in form of life is a necessary condition of

---

[53] G P Baker and P M S Hacker, *Rules, Grammar and Necessity: Volume 2 of an Analytical Commentary on the* Philosophical Investigations (Oxford: Basil Blackwell, 1995), 169-181.

[54] *Ibid*, 179.

[55] McGinn, *Wittgenstein on Meaning*, 47.

[56] Pears, *The False Prison* vol ii, 383.

[57] *Ibid*, 523.

[58] *Ibid*, 368.

communication between one person and another, but not of a person making a meaningful utterance.[59]

It is in this sense that the principle of *calibration - or measurement - on standard objects* can be said to be *more* fundamental than the principle of agreement in form of life. As Pears points out, a deficiency in terms of 'calibration on standard objects' would make a deficiency in terms of 'agreement in forms of life' inevitable.[60] But a deficiency of the latter sort would not make a deficiency of the former sort inevitable. It is "possible to imagine an intelligent wolf-child exploiting physical objects to set up a language for his own use without the help provided by a typical human family."[61] As long as the condition of calibration on standard objects held, the possibility of making a meaningful utterance existed. Pears devotes a whole chapter of *The False Prison* vol ii (chapter 14, 'The Disabling Effect of a Private Language') to the question of whether Wittgenstein came to the same conclusion. He argues that there is "strong reason for not taking his later view to be that, in default of other people, and, therefore, without any opportunity to exploit agreement in judgements, whatever was done could never be described as 'speaking a language'."[62] In other words, "there is strong reason for not taking his later view to be that" agreement in form of life is a necessary condition of meaningful utterance *per se*. However, there is no "strong reason for not taking his later view to be that" 'calibration of standard objects' *is* a necessary condition.

Moreover, as Pears puts it, it is "evident that purely coincidental agreement would not indicate that a group of people were following a rule [as opposed to seeming to follow a rule], and that agreement by direct imitation, without independent consideration of the objects described, would not do either. Therefore, even if agreement in judgements were the main resource, it could not be the only one, and in fact, there was also the possibility of calibration on standard objects, which is something that can be done without other people."[63] In other words, even in a language-using community in which agreement in form of life, or inter-personal agreement, is the main source of stability, there had to be another resource. Hence, given the possibility of coincidental agreement, agreement in form of life appears not even to be a *sufficient* condition of rule-following (though in fact it is - as a matter of empirical fact - a very important resource of

---

[59] *Ibid*, 367.

[60] "The second deficiency would make the first one inevitable, because the only way to get in a position to seek confirmation from other people is to establish communication with them through the physical world." *Ibid*, 362.

[61] *Ibid*, 362.

[62] *Ibid*, 367.

[63] *Ibid*, 434.

stabilization in language use). 'Calibration on standard objects', not 'agreement in form of life', is essential to Wittgenstein's concept of a rule.

*Contra* Kripke's interpretation of Wittgenstein as holding the 'sceptical' view that there is no objective fact of correctly following or incorrectly following the rule,[64] Wittgenstein's argument is that "the rule and nothing but the rule determines what it is correct to do."[65] Though Kripke's radical Humean translation of Wittgenstein's argument against the possibility of a private language - "there can be no such thing as meaning anything by any word" -[66] is tempered by a species-specific naturalism congenial to Wittgenstein, there would be no such thing as *seeming to* mean anything by any word were there no objective possibility of correctly or incorrectly following a rule. Not only is scepticism the very thing Wittgenstein rejects in his repudiation of the possibility of a private language, the principle behind this repudiation constitutes the rationale behind his critique of Cartesian scepticism in *On Certainty*. In other words, if Wittgenstein's account of rule-following is central to his position on classical epistemology in *On Certainty*, Kripke's interpretation must be false. In point of fact, Wittgenstein is philosophy's greatest arch anti-sceptic; and he is this precisely because he affirms the necessity of a philosophical *analogia fidei* in form of the concept of 'means of measurement'.[67]

As has been said, the distinction between means of measurement and object of measurement is central to the later philosophy. To repeat: Wittgenstein's dissolution of philosophical problems extrapolates from the insight that rule-following presupposes measurement against a norm or standard of measurement - a means of measurement. We have seen that the private language argument, claimed by at least one commentator to be the centre-piece of the *Investigations*,[68] undoubtedly depends on it. Now I wish to show in what way the distinction is fundamental both to (a) Wittgenstein's position on philosophical realism and solipsism in *Philosophical Investigations* and (b) his position on epistemology in *On Certainty*. I have already provided grounds for concluding that Wittgenstein held 'calibration on standard objects' to be a necessary condition of avoiding the pitfall of a private language. This conclusion, I will now argue, constitutes the rationale behind Wittgenstein's resolution of philosophical problems, in particular, his repudiation of philosophical scepticism. The

---

[64] Saul Kripke, *Wittgenstein on Rules and Private Language* (Oxford: Basil Blackwell, 1982).
[65] Hacker, *Insight*, 333-334.
[66] Kripke, *Wittgenstein on Rules and Private Language*, 55.
[67] See Hanfling, *Wittgenstein's Later Philosophy*, 152.
[68] Pears, *Prison* vol ii, 361.

sceptic's claim that one can, and should, doubt everything rests upon the possibility of meaning something *without* having to satisfy the principle of 'calibration on standard objects'. But since the latter is a necessary condition of meaning *per se*, the sceptic's claim is without foundation. In particular, rule-following in this instance implies that the concept of doubt occupies the role of metaphorical object of measurement; as such, it is measured against a metaphorical means of measurement which coincides with a norm or standard of measurement. Hence, to omit to measure in this sense is to succumb to a private language.

The objective of Wittgenstein's arguments is to show that, even under the condition of 'agreement in form of life', the sceptic is unable in principle to communicate the rule he or she claims to be following. In other words, 'agreement in form of life' - measuring one's actions against that of the community's - would have been implicated in the sceptic's communication of the rule had he or she, in fact, been following a rule; but it is not necessary to the constitution of the rule itself. As in the private language argument, 'calibration on standard objects' is necessary for following a rule at all; 'agreement in form of life' is logically presupposed in any successful communication of the rule being followed.

Making a measurement in the literal sense is one of the examples of language-games Wittgenstein cites in *PI* § 23. But clearly the concept of measurement is more than just an   example of a language-game for Wittgenstein. Wittgenstein will use an example of literal measurement to make an important philosophical point.  He writes at *PI* § 50:

> There is *one* thing of which one can say neither that it is one metre long, nor that it is not one metre long, and that is the standard metre in Paris. But this is not to ascribe any extraordinary property to it, but only to mark its peculiar role in the language-game of measuring with a metre-rule. - Let us imagine samples of colour being preserved in Paris like the standard metre. We define: "sepia" means the colour of the standard sepia which is there kept hermetically sealed. Then it will make no sense  to say of this sample either that it is this colour or it is not.[69]

The colour, like the metre, serves in the language-game as a "paradigm" [*ein Paradigma*]  - "something with which comparison is made."[70] Later, Wittgenstein will use the terms *Vergleichsobjectke*  (*"object of comparison"*)[71] and *Maßstab* (*"measuring-rod"*)[72] when referring to the

[69] Wittgenstein, *Philosophical Investigations*, ed. G. E. M. Anscombe (Oxford: Basil Blackwell, 1953), § 50. Hereafter referred to as *PI*.

[70] *Ibid*, § 50.

[71] *Ibid*, § 130.

role basic language-games have vis-à-vis more complicated ones. What is important about this passage is that it intimates the philosophical rationale behind Wittgenstein's employment of the concept of measurement. The reason one cannot say of the Paris metre that it is or is not one metre long is because it itself is the measure of *what it is* a metre is. It itself is the means of measurement and, as such, cannot be used to measure itself *other than in the sense in which no empirical discovery can be made.* (Clearly, there is an empirical measurement involved in using the measure of *what it is* a metre is to discover that something is, e.g., two metres long.) To attempt to measure the standard metre in Paris is to attempt to measure a very distinctive object of measurement, namely: the object of measurement that constitutes the means of measurement itself. As Wittgenstein said in the introduction to the *Investigations*, one of the weaknesses of the *Tractatus* was it thought of language as a ruler laid out against reality. In other words, it presumed that one had a pre-existent means of measurement against which to measure reality in terms of truth and falsity.

### 4. 'Calibration on Standard Objects' and Wittgenstein's Position on Philosophical Realism and Idealism (Solipsism): *PI* § 402

In the *Investigations* Wittgenstein makes only one remark bearing on the resolution of the realist-idealist controversy. At *PI* § 402 he writes:

> When ... we disapprove of the expressions of ordinary language (which are after all performing their office) we have a picture in our heads which conflicts with the picture of our ordinary way of speaking. Whereas we are tempted to say that our way of speaking does not describe the facts as they really are. As if, for example the proposition "he has pains" could be false in some other way than by that man's *not* having pains. As if the form of expression were saying something false even when the propositions *faute de mieux* asserted something true.
> For *this* is what disputes between idealists, [i.e.] Solipsists and Realists look like. The one party attack the normal form of expression as if they were attacking a statement; the others defend it, as if they were stating facts known to every reasonable human being.[73]

This passage follows the private language argument (or collection of such arguments, § 242-315). It is thus no surprise that it incorporates some

---

[72] *Ibid*, § 131.
[73] Wittgenstein, *PI* § 402.

of that argument's essential features. Wittgenstein steers the passage to a *reductio ad absurdum*. The last two sentences of the first paragraph tell of a situation which, to Wittgenstein, is manifestly impossible. Wittgenstein's point, I think, is this. What is meant by "a man having pains" (being true) is the bench-mark against which we measure what it is we mean by "a man not having pains" ("a man having pains" being false). But if "the man has pains" did not describe the facts as they really are then there could no such bench-mark. But in that case what would "the man does not have pains" mean? Unless we have a conception of what "the man has pains" means we cannot know what it is we mean by "the man does not have pains". If the sceptic wishes to evade the consequences of this argument, there is only one other route left for him to take. But it is precisely the one Wittgenstein believes is manifestly self-evidently absurd: the proposition "he has pains" could be false in some other way than by that man's *not* having pains. Only if this were possible could there be a concept of existence other than the one expressed in ordinary language. Knowing what it is for a man not to have pains presupposes knowing what it is for a man to have pains. The latter constitutes the means of measuring *what it is* a man not having pains is. It is the criterion, yardstick, standard or measure on which basis one establishes the truth of the man not having pains. It is in this sense that to know what it means for a man to have pains presupposes a rule governing the use of the sentence which, in turn, presupposes the phenomenon of stabilisation. In *PI* §402, this phenomenon coincides with 'calibration on standard objects'.

Wittgenstein's conclusion is this: *in order to be able to conceive of the possibility of non-existence, one has to have a criterion of existence against which to measure what it is one is conceiving is not the case.* There has to be an "external viable criterion" against which the applicability of the concept of non-existence makes sense. If it were not the one intrinsic to our ordinary way of conceiving what it is to exist, the absurd conclusion would follow that "x exists" could be false other than by x not existing. Hence, it could not but be the case that our way of speaking does describe the facts as they really are. For any assertion on the subject of 'the facts as they really are' cannot avoid measuring the concept of non-existence against a criterion of existence. There is no sense in which these concepts are in use for the pragmatic reason of 'for want of something better'. In that sense, the sceptic can be shown to assume just what he denies. He cannot really deny what he claims to deny since in order to do that he has to be able to assume what he denies, namely that his concept of non-existence has to take as its criterion the criterion of existence explicit in what it (ordinarily) means to say "the man has pains" is true.

What Wittgenstein describes as the "normal form of expression" is, in fact, the *norm* of expression. As such, it constitutes the means of measurement - the standard of measurement - against which to measure whether one is using the concept of x not being true (or x not actually existing) correctly or incorrectly. All disputes between philosophical realists and philosophical idealists are resolved by pointing out this conceptual fact. It is in this sense that one can say that, in his act of doubt or criticism, the philosophical sceptic attempts to measure a very distinctive object of measurement, namely: the object of measurement that constitutes the means of measurement itself of *what it is* non-existence means.

### 5. 'Calibration on Standard Objects' and Wittgenstein's Position on Epistemology in *On Certainty*

The distinction between means of measurement and object of measurement constitutes the underlying rationale of Wittgenstein's critique of classical epistemology (Cartesian and Humean scepticism, sense-data theory, etc.). That one should begin by doubting everything is a thesis that Western thought has taken as self-evident since the 1700s. But, according to Wittgenstein, it is a seriously misconceived thesis. For in order to conceive of the possibility of doubt one has to have a criterion of non-doubt - certainty - against which to measure *what it is* one conceives as doubt. "If you tried to doubt everything you would not get so far as doubting anything. The game of doubting itself presupposes certainty."[74] "To be sure, there is justification; but justification comes to an end."[75] "Doesn't testing come to an end?"[76] Wittgenstein says "This statement appeared to me fundamental; if it is false, what are 'true' or 'false' any more?"[77] The point is: since such statements are the means of measuring what it is 'true' and 'false' are, their truth is presupposed in the very act of making such judgements (they are objects of measurement whose means of measurement are them themselves). Similarly: it is not a question of having the right not to doubt, as if one's claim to know had justified one suspending one's willing faculty; rather, doubt only works in the context of what it is to be certain about something - just as being wrong can only make sense against a criterion of what it is to be right, and just as miscalculating can only make sense against the criterion of a correct calculation.

Justification - and criticism - comes to an end not because we reach rock-bottom facts about the external world which we know for certain (as, for example, the philosophical realist G. E. Moore thought), but because we

---

[74] *Ibid*, § 115.
[75] *Ibid*, § 192.
[76] *Ibid*, § 164.
[77] *Ibid*, § 514.

reach some point beyond which our concepts become detached from: the criterion against which we measure what it means to know something does not exist; the criterion against which we measure what it means to know what it is to make a mistake about the existence of something ("I thought it existed, as for example, this does, but I made a mistake"); the criterion against which we measure what it means to doubt whether something is the case. Wittgenstein writes:

> The idealist's question would be something like this: "What right have I not to doubt  the existence of my hands?" (And to that the answer can't be: I *know* that they exist.) But someone who asks such a question is overlooking the fact that a doubt about existence only works within a language-game. Hence, that we should first have to ask: what would such a doubt be like?, and don't understand this straight off.[78]

In what sense is it the case that "a doubt about existence only works within a language-game"? At *OC* § 52 Wittgenstein writes:

> [The] situation is not the same for a proposition like "At this distance from the sun there is a planet" and "Here is a hand" (namely my own hand). The second can't be called a hypothesis. But there isn't a sharp dividing line between them.[79]

But even though there is no sharp dividing line between them, it didn't follow, as Moore thought, that mistakes merely became increasingly improbable:

> For it is not true that a mistake merely gets more and more improbable as we pass from the planet to my own hand. No: at some point it has ceased to be conceivable.
> This is already suggested by the following: if it were not so, it would also be conceivable that we should be wrong in *every* statement about physical objects; that any we ever make are mistaken.[80]

Wittgenstein then considers this possibility:

---

[78] *Ibid*, § 24.

[79] Wittgenstein, *On Certainty*, ed. G. E. M. Anscombe and G. H. von Wright, trans. Denis Paul and G. E. M. Anscombe (Oxford: Basil Blackwell, 1969), § 52. Hereafter referred to as *OC*.

[80] *Ibid*, § 54.

So is the *hypothesis* possible, that all the things around us don't exist? Would that not be like the hypothesis of our having miscalculated in all our calculations?

His answer to this question is given in the next paragraph:

When someone says: "Perhaps this planet doesn't exist and the light-phenomenon arises in some other way", then after all one needs an example of an object which does exist. This doesn't exist, - as *for example* does ....[81]

As in *PI* § 402, Wittgenstein's point is that to be able to conceive of the concept of non-existence in this example presupposes that one has a criterion of existence against which to measure it. One cannot affirm the non-existence of something without knowing already what it is to exist, without having a criterion of what it is to exist. Otherwise, how could one judge whether something did not exist? The Cartesian sceptic's belief that one could be mistaken about the existence of everything one ordinarily took for granted comes to grief for precisely the same reason. The idea of the possibility of making a mistake every time is incoherent because knowing what it is to make a mistake presupposes knowing what it is not to make a mistake. Otherwise, we could not know what it is to make a mistake. Thus given the concept of making a mistake it is not possible that we are not certain about *some* things. Otherwise, we have no bench-mark against which to measure what it is to make a mistake.

Note what Wittgenstein is not saying. It is not that a person could not make a mistake, empirically speaking, every time! Wittgenstein accepts this as quite possible. His point is that knowing what it is not to make a mistake - knowing what it is to get it right - is presupposed even in this case just as it is in the case of someone who makes the occasional mistake. Otherwise we would have no criterion against which to measure his getting it wrong each time. Getting it wrong all the time presupposes a bench-mark of getting it right. In the *Meditations* Descartes uses the argument that one might be mistaken on every occasion about one's belief that there is a physical object (for example, a table) in front of one's eyes. In reality, being mistaken like this is no more powerful a proof for philosophical scepticism than being mistaken once.

The same strategy of argument occurs towards the end of *On Certainty* when Wittgenstein writes:

---

[81] *Ibid*, § 56.

Children do not learn that books exist, that armchairs exist, etc. etc. - they learn to fetch books, sit in armchairs, etc. etc.

Later, questions about the existence of things do of course arise. "Is there such a thing as a unicorn?" and so on. But such a question is possible only because as a rule no corresponding question presents itself. For how does one know how to set about satisfying oneself of the existence of unicorns? How did one learn the method for determining whether something exists or not?[82]

One can only determine whether something exists or not (and therefore know *what it is* for something not to exist) if one already has a criterion - the means of measurement - of *what it is* something existing is. This of course is true of children who are very likely to go on and develop the relatively more sophisticated skill of asking about the existence of vampires, ghosts, aliens from outer space, legendary places, etc. "Do you know the way to Xanadu?" "No, Xanadu does not exist." is a meaningful exchange only on the assumption that one already knows what it is to exist. It could not meaningful if it made sense to answer "Do you know the way to London? with: "I'm not sure London exists (because I'm not sure the external world exists)." For in that case one could have no criterion against which to measure what it is for Xanadu not to exist.

It is testimony to the importance Wittgenstein attaches to this argument that it is used in a similar epistemological context in *Zettel*. Doubt is not a matter of will precisely because the distinction between getting the concept of doubt right and getting it wrong logically presupposes a pre-existing means of measurement, a metaphorical act of calibrating on standard objects. Wittgenstein writes:

How does it come about that doubt is not subject to arbitrary choice - and that being so - might not a child doubt everything because it was remarkably talented?[83]

A person can doubt only if he has learned certain things; as he can miscalculate only if he has learned to calculate. In that case it is indeed involuntary.[84]

---

[82] *Ibid*, § 476.

[83] Wittgenstein, *Zettel*, ed. G. E. M. Anscombe and G. H. von Wright (Oxford: Basil Blackwell, 1981), § 409.

[84] *Ibid*, § 410.

Imagine a child was especially clever, so clever that he could at once be taught the doubtfulness of all things. So he learns from the beginning: "That is probably a chair."
And now how does he learn the question: "Is it also really a chair?"[85]

To begin by teaching someone "That looks red" makes no sense. For he must say that spontaneously once he has learnt what "red" means, i.e. has learned the technique of using the word.[86]

In other words, to teach someone "That looks red" presupposes they know *what it is red is*: "'It looks red to me.' - 'and what is red like?' 'Like *this*.' Here the right paradigm must be pointed to."[87] "Why doesn't one teach a child the language-game "It looks red to me" from the first? Because it is not yet able to understand the rather fine distinction between seeming and being?"[88] No, because it first has to know *what it is* red is in order to have something against which to measure what it is that looks red. One can doubt whether something looks red only if one already knows what it is that is red; the latter is the criterion against which the former is measured. Therefore doubt is not and cannot be a function of the human will; doubt cannot be a matter of choice; in this sense one is not free to doubt. One cannot will to doubt because one cannot, as a matter of logic, doubt anything and everything.

"If you tried to doubt everything you would not get so far as doubting anything. The game of doubting itself presupposes certainty."[89] Certainty about what? Norman Malcolm attributes to Wittgenstein the view that: "Certain propositions belong to my 'frame of reference'. If I had to give *them* up, I shouldn't be able to judge *anything*."[90] As Wittgenstein puts it himself: "... the *questions* we raise and our *doubts* depend on the fact that some propositions are exempt from doubt."[91] Again, he writes: "To be sure, there is justification; but justification comes to an end."[92] And again: "Doesn't testing come to an end?"[93] On G. E. Moore's claim to know certain fundamental facts such as he has two hands Wittgenstein writes: "Moore does not *know* what he asserts he knows, but it stands fast for

[85] *Ibid*, § 411.
[86] *Ibid*, § 418.
[87] *Ibid*, § 420.
[88] *Ibid*, § 422.
[89] *Ibid*, § 115.
[90] N. Malcolm, "The Groundlessness of Belief", in Stuart C. Brown (ed.), *Reason and Religion* (Ithaca: Cornell University Press, 1977), 74.
[91] Wittgenstein, *OC*, § 341.
[92] *Ibid*, § 192.
[93] *Ibid*, § 164.

him."[94] Examples of propositions Wittgenstein cites as 'standing fast' are: 'I know that I am a human being'; 'I know I have a brain';[95] 'The earth existed long before I was born';[96] 'I believe I have forebears, and that every human being has them'.[97] The importance of such propositions is that they - or propositions like them - constitute the metaphorical means of measurement against which, and only against which, one's use of the concept of doubt can be measured for correct usage, can be measured in terms of getting it right as opposed to getting it wrong.

Descartes' project of pure enquiry was motivated by a desire to put the science of his day on a firm foundation.[98] As if in anticipation of the later Enlightenment philosophers who drew extensively from the legacy of the Greek and Roman ideals of classical antiquity,[99] Descartes' *Meditations* was influenced by the arguments of the ancient Sceptics and Sextus Empiricus in particular.[100] Descartes sought to prove - as against the Sceptics - a proposition or propositions which could not conceivably be doubted.[101] Almost 150 years later philosophy was still lamenting the fact that a proof of the existence of the external world had not been found. "It still remains a scandal to philosophy and to human reason in general" Kant wrote "that the existence of things outside us (from which we derive the whole material of knowledge, even for our inner sense) must be accepted merely on faith, and if anyone thinks good to doubt their existence, we are unable to counter his doubt by any satisfactory proof."[102]

Wittgenstein demonstrates that it does not make sense to doubt those propositions which 'stand fast' in our system of knowledge precisely because they are intrinsic to the meaning of doubt itself. They constitute the means of measurement of the concept of doubt itself. In his act of doubt or

---

[94] *Ibid*, § 151.

[95] *Ibid*, § 4.

[96] *Ibid*, § 233.

[97] *Ibid*, § 234.

[98] Descartes, *Discourse on Method and the Meditations* (Middlesex: Penguin Books, 1968), 95. See also J. L. Watling, "Descartes", in D. J. O'Connor (ed.), *A Critical History of Western Philosophy* (New York: The Free Press of Glencoe, 1964), 171.

[99] Peter Gay, *The Enlightenment* vol i (New York: Alfred A Knopf, 1969), 9-10; 31-203.

[100] E. M. Curley, *Descartes Against the Sceptics* (Cambridge: Cambridge University Press, 1978); R. Popkin, *The History of Scepticism from Erasmus to Descartes* (Assen: Van Goram, 1964), 172-192.

[101] The first of Descartes' *Meditations* is in fact a rehash of ancient scepticism. M. Burnyeat, "Idealism and Greek Philosophy: What Descartes Saw and Berkeley Missed", in G. Vesey (ed.), *Idealism Past and Present*. Royal Institute of Philosophy Lecture Series: 13. Supplement to *Philosophy* 1982 (Cambridge: Cambridge University Press, 1982), 45.

[102] Immanuel Kant *Critique of Pure Reason*, 34.

criticism, the philosophical sceptic attempts to measure a very distinctive object of measurement, namely: the object of measurement that constitutes the means of measurement itself of *what it is* existence means.  In *On Certainty*, then, the concept of doubt is measured against a criterion, or measure, of *what it is* knowing something for certain is. Hence, to follow the rules involved in doubting this or that fact is, necessarily, to participate in a metaphorical act of measurement. But there is no sense in which we can metaphorically measure *what it is* knowing something for certain is; for, as I will show, as the means of measurement itself, it can only be measured against itself. In other words, 'justification comes to an end.'; we 'run up against the limits of language.' Wittgenstein's *conceptual foundationalism* posits the necessity of an origin or means of measurement of truth and meaning; *hence, if any such origin or means is to measured at all, it can be measured only in terms of itself.*

## 6. The Concept of a Private Language: Wittgenstein and the Reformers' *Analogia Fidei*

I said earlier that I would return to the similarity between, on the one hand, Wittgenstein's objection to the possibility of a private language, and, on the other, the Reformers' objection to the private interpretation of scripture. It would be helpful to summarise what I have said about Wittgenstein in this respect. The basis of Wittgenstein's objection to the notion of a private language is that it is without a "viable independent criterion which distinguishes getting [a rule] right from getting it wrong."[103] Wittgenstein writes: "'obeying a rule' is a practice. And to *think* one is obeying a rule is not to obey a rule. Hence, it is not possible to obey a rule 'privately': otherwise, thinking one was obeying a rule would be the same thing as obeying it."[104] In this connection Malcolm comments, "If the distinction between 'correct' and 'seems correct' has disappeared, then so has the concept *correct*."[105] Why? *What it is* to follow a rule correctly is the criterion against *what it is* to seem to follow a rule correctly is measured. The former is the criterion against which the latter is measured; the latter only makes sense in the context of the former. *In other words, there is a distinction between 'correct' and 'seems correct'.* They are not the same concept. The concept of a private language contradicts the existence of this distinction. In such a language there is no distinction between 'correct' and

---

[103] Pears, *Prison*, vol II, 523.

[104] Wittgenstein, *PI* § 202.

[105] N Malcolm, "Wittgenstein's *Philosophical Investigations*", in *Wittgenstein and the Problem of Other Minds* (New York: McGraw-Hill, 1967), 48.

'seems correct'. But since there is such a distinction, a private language cannot exist. That is to say, what does 'correct' mean in the context of 'seems correct' if 'seems correct' and 'is correct' mean the same thing?

Hence, though it is possible to follow a rule privately, it is not possible to follow a private rule.[106] One cannot will into existence a private language. All these themes are reciprocated in the Reformed *analogia fidei*. Tyndale quoted the words of 2 Peter 1.20 when he wrote: "no prophecy in the scripture hath any private interpretation. For the scripture came never by the will of man; but holy men of God spake as they were moved by the holy ghost."[107] Tyndale further asserted: "no place of scripture may have a private interpretation."[108] The Reformer, Hutchinson wrote: "open the scripture with the key, not with the picklock; that is, expound it by itself, not by private interpretation."[109] Private interpretation is, as in the later Wittgenstein, associated with man's will, in particular, with the individual will which imposes on scripture a sense that suits the individual's own desires. Such an individual is not, to use the words of Wittgenstein, following a rule privately; he is, rather, following a private rule.

The Reformers saw nothing remarkable about following a rule privately, for example, following the thirty-nine articles of the Church of England privately in one's interpretation of scripture. But the concept of following a private rule, for example, following the advice of a private revelation on interpretation of a particular passage of scripture, fatally compromised the fundamentals of the faith, the *analogia fidei*. Indeed, one reason that the individual will cannot be allowed to arbitrate on the meaning of scripture is precisely that such freedom sacrifices the independent criterion of meaning necessary for each individual to interpret scripture correctly. For such a sacrifice entailed that, in the words of Wittgenstein, there was no "viable independent criterion which distinguishes getting [a rule] right from getting it wrong"; or, in other words, no independent criterion distinguishing following a rule correctly from following it incorrectly. Instead, anarchy reigned.

The Reformer Calfhill opined: "if every man shall have the authority to give his verdict upon a controversy which shall seem and say that he hath the spirit, no certain thing shall be decreed; every man shall have his own way; no stable opinion and judgement to be rested on."[110] What the *analogia fidei* provided as an antidote to this precarious situation was

[106] Baker and Hacker, *Analytical Commentary*, vol 2, 169-179.
[107] Quoted by H C Porter, "The Nose of Wax: Scripture and the Spirit from Erasmus to Milton", *Transactions of the Royal Historical Society* (1963), 166.
[108] *Ibid*, 166.
[109] *Ibid*, 166.
[110] *Ibid*, 166.

precisely something 'on which stable opinion and judgement could rest'. To quote some of the Reformed conceptions of the *analogia fidei* from Chapter 6: (Tyndale) "Marke the playne and manyfest places of the scriptures, and in doubtfull places, see thou adde no interpretation contrary to them; but (as Paul saith) let all be conformable and agreynge to the faythe";[111] (Bucanus) "the constant and unchanging sense of Scripture expounded in the opening passages of Scripture and agreeing with the Apostles' Creed, the Decalogue and the Lord's Prayer";[112] (the Anglican Church) "... no sense bee received contrary to the ten commandements, Lords prayer, and the Articles of our beliefe." [113] These three elements "provided the basic 'analogie of faith' in plain, straightforward statements."[114]

What all these criteria or rules of meaning have in common is that they are independent of all individual interpreters. Moreover, they constitute viable points of reference against which all possible interpretations can be measured. If such criteria did not exist, there would be no such thing as being correct in one's interpretation. Hence, seeming to be correct would be the same as being correct - in which case, as was said above, there would be no such thing as, *no possibility of*, being correct.

To be sure, the question the Reformers did not raise explicitly was precisely the philosophical one - whether such criteria constituted a criterion of meaning or of interpretation. The question is a quintessentially modern one. Postmodernists would answer not: texts do not have a single authoritative meaning (no reading is privileged); there is a 'free play' of meaning; we are free to decide as we wish, since 'all interpretation is misinterpretation'. But Wittgenstein endorsed the Reformed position on this matter. Conceptual foundationalism could not be gainsaid. Otherwise, meaning and communication were impossible, semantic anarchy prevailed.

## Concluding Remarks

What conclusions should be drawn from my analysis of the later Wittgenstein's thought and its assimilation to the Reformers' conception of the *analogia fidei*? I do not claim that *no* part of the later Wittgenstein belongs amongst the cultural anthropologists. For example, his remarks on Sir James Frazer's *The Golden Bough* are clearly of some relevance to

---

[111] Quoted in Rivkah Zim, "The Reformation: the Trial of God's Word", 121-122.
[112] Quoted in Heinrich Heppe, *Reformed Dogmatics*, 35.
[113] Zim, "The Reformation: the Trial of God's Word", 74.
[114] *Ibid*, 74.

cultural anthropological investigations;[115] and much the same kind of observation can be made of *Lectures and Conversations on Aesthetics, Pyschology and Religious Belief.*[116] In the former, Wittgenstein challenged the assumption that magical rituals should be treated as though they were early forms of science. In the latter, he challenged the assumption that religious belief should be assimilated to the grammar of scientific belief. Each assumption in its respective field had, indeed, prevented the scientist from discovering the rules actually followed by the communities in question. Clearly, these communities - primitive, religious - were innocent of any charge of speaking a private language. The fact that the rules which they followed - magical and/or religious - were, and still are, passed down through the generations is testimony to this.

However, implicit in my analysis of the later Wittgenstein is that his greatest contribution to philosophy has been to show that some of most influential theories of modern philosophy are held captive in the shadow-land of a private language (unlike the religious community, for example, the community of philosophical sceptics does not have any rules to follow). This, however, means that there is more to Wittgenstein's resolution of philosophical problems than the kind of data provided by cultural anthropologists. The concept of 'agreement in form of life', for example, does not endorse any kind of cultural relativism. One's communication of one's use of terms like 'truth' presupposes agreement in form of life; but this is a completely different proposition from one which says that truth itself - what is true - is a question of mere inter-personal (cultural) agreement.

However, though 'agreement in form of life' is one of two metaphorical means of measurement in the later philosophy, it is the other such means of measurement - calibration on standard objects - which constitutes the fundamental rationale behind the resolution of the central philosophical problems of the later Wittgenstein. Removal of 'agreement in form of life' is not a sufficient condition of the sceptic speaking a private language. Removal of 'calibration on standard objects' is.

Stanley Cavell once criticised a certain interpretation of the later Wittgenstein for attributing to him a nanny-like posture toward what could and could not be said. Such a picture of the later Wittgenstein was, as

---

[115] Wittgenstein, *Remarks on Frazer's Golden Bough*, ed. R. Rhees (London: Brynmill, 1979).

[116] Wittgenstein, *Lectures and Conversations on Aesthetics, Psychology and Religious Belief*, ed. C. Barrett (Oxford: Blackwell, 1966).

Cavell clearly saw, a gross caricature.[117] But the opposite picture, that one was free to make up the rules - as Hans Küng, for instance, suggested - or that whole communities were free to make up the rules, is not even a gross caricature;[118] it is entirely contrary to the fundamental rationale behind the later philosophy. Simply put, one cannot do what one wants in the realm of language. One cannot do without 'means of measurement', without a philosophical *analogia fidei*. That I have discerned a comparable intellectual investment in the concept of 'means of measurement' among Reformed conceptions of the *analogia fidei* - among theologians whose respect for *regula fidei* was paramount - is indicative of the fact that, though Wittgenstein's later philosophy could not be said to defer to (pre-Enlightenment) tradition, orthodoxy or authority, certain kinds of truths had a certain 'absolute' authority, and were, indeed, sacrosanct.

To summarise the relation between the later Barth and the later Wittgenstein implicit in this chapter. Barth's position on epistemology in the *Church Dogmatics* owes something to Kant's transcendental argument; but the form it takes in Barth is not found in Kant. Although this makes Barth's problems the problems of the Enlightenment rather than the problems of Calvin's own era, Barth does not break with the legacy of Calvin. Barth ties the Reformers' *analogia fidei* to Kant's transcendental argument in his own unique way. The fundamental rationale behind Wittgenstein's later philosophy is his own unique philosophical variation of the Reformers' *analogia fidei* issuing in a non-Kantian transcendental argument: a philosophical 'measure of faith' whose only measure is it itself. Central to Wittgenstein's position on epistemology and on meaning is a species of conceptual foundationalism similar to that which one finds in the later Barth. Concepts such as *Quelle, Norm* and *Ursprung* are central to Barth's position on epistemology in the *Church Dogmatics*. They are also central to the later philosophy.

---

[117] Stanley Cavell, "The Availability of Wittgenstein's Later Philosophy", in George Pitcher (ed.), *Wittgenstein, The Philosophical Investigations* (New York: Anchor Books, 1966), 167.

[118] Hans Küng, *Does God Exist? An Answer For Today* (London: Collins, 1978), 461.

# Chapter 13
# Postscript to the Metadilemmas of the Enlightenment: Toward Hegel[1]

## 1. Introduction

As against the interpretation of Barth proposed in this book, it has been argued that intrinsic to Barth's theology is a form of post-modern desire motivated by *différance*.[2] Translated in terms of the epistemological categories of apologetic and fideism, the post-modern response to the Enlightenment is to 'argue', either that apologetic is no more 'rational' (or no less 'fideistic') than fideism, or fideism no less 'rational' (or no more 'fideistic') than apologetic. The consequence is that the term "fideism" is taken to be a misnomer on the grounds that it presupposes an (absolute or objective rather than relative) standard of rationality against which something can be judged (somewhat pejoratively) to be fideism. Now, were apologetic and fideism not just mutually exclusive, but exhaustive categories, then conceivably this might be a valid characterisation of Barth's epistemology. For either Barth's epistemology is apologetic or it is fideism. Since it is not the former, it must be the latter. Does this mean that the Enlightenment on the side of apologetic can dismiss Barth to the realm of fideism as it (counterwise pejoratively) understands this position? No, for as the post-modern response shows and Barth too (since, according to post-modernism, he makes this response), apologetic cannot be said to be more rational than fideism, or fideism less rational than apologetic. To do

---

[1] I offer the following tentative judgement. If the thesis in this chapter is valid then it follows that there is in Barth's theological epistemology a Hegelian emphasis that goes beyond Kant. Barth's epistemology cannot be understood within Kant alone. But since the particular Hegelian element articulated in this chapter is present in the later Wittgenstein in the same way as it is in Barth, I submit he may provide a more comprehensive intellectual context in which to understand Barth's epistemology given the thesis of the preceding chapter. But I offer this only as a tentative judgement.

[2] Graham Ward, *Barth, Derrida and the Language of Theology* (Cambridge: CUP, Cambridge, 1995).

so is to think in terms of an   anachronistic Enlightenment conceptual framework.

Whatever one makes of the argument (if argument it is), it is my belief that its proponents have been too hasty in attempting to understand Barth's epistemology  in terms of this response. For if apologetic (or Popperian criticism or other species of this kind of argument) and fideism are, under the old conceptual scheme, not exhaustive categories then another epistemological option emerges, one that does not reject the Enlightenment conceptual framework. As we have seen, Barth spoke approvingly of 'Enlightenment reason'.[3] And though, as we shall see, he acknowledged the failure of the grand Hegelian project, he did not think it necessary for the post-modern critique of apologetic to be ushered into theology. Barth had another epistemological option to offer, an argument in the old-fashioned sense, in the form of conceptual foundationalism.[4]

---

[3] See Chapter 1.

[4] Robert Jenson writes: "If there is such a thing as 'postmodernism' Barth may be its only major representative so far, for his work is a vast attempt to transcend not merely the Enlightenment but also 'modern' Protestantism's defining way of making that attempt. Jenson, "Karl Barth", in D F Ford (ed), *The Modern Theologians. An Introduction to Christian Theology in the Twentieth Century*, vol 1, (Oxford: Basil Blackwell, 1989), 25. To be fair to Jenson, if one takes his words literally, he does not say that Barth *is* a postmodern theologian. What is at issue, however, is whether the premises:  (1) "his work is "a vast attempt to transcend the Enlightenment",  (2) his work is a vast attempt to transcend 'modern' Protestantism's defining way of making that attempt" entail that Barth is a post-modern theologian. My answer is that they do not. The crucial issue is whether Barth jettisons argument in the old-fashioned 'Enlightenment' sense. He does not; *ergo* he is not post-modern. Postmodernism fails to discern a distinct, well-defined stage of 'philosophy' between the eras of apologetic and postmodern thinking. This stage of 'philosophy' is characterised by a thought-form that is neither rational in the apologetic sense nor in the post-modern sense (nor is it fideistic in the apologetic sense). Wittgenstein's later philosophy satisfies the properties of this stage in philosophical thought. It has been argued that Barth's later theology does too. In particular, conceptual foundationalism cannot be categorised as a form of apologetic reason precisely for the reason that the former cannot in principle be justified by the latter; rather, the objective of the former is to specify the conditions of the possibility of the latter: the criterion against which the meaningfulness of the latter is measured. Apologetic reason ignores the fact that the thing it wants to prove is the criterion for proving anything at all, including the thing itself. In that sense,  proof of the thing itself is redundant, since one has to presuppose what it is one purports to prove.

## 2. Wittgenstein too has an Argument in the Old-fashioned Sense

Like Barth, Wittgenstein, did not consider apologetic and fideism exhaustive categories. It is often thought that the intellectual ethos Wittgenstein characterised as 'the darkness of the age' was the spirit of science. There is, undoubtedly, a great deal of truth in this. But it is not the whole story. Most of Wittgenstein's remarks on the subject reveal a man who was against science only insofar as it sought to interpret philosophy and, in particular, his own later philosophy according to its own methods and laws.[5] Wittgenstein rejected scientism, not science.

More importantly, though Wittgenstein eschewed apologetic, he did not embrace dogmatic fideism. In the 1930s he made it clear how he viewed his later philosophy in relation to the previously existing path of philosophy. He claimed that philosophy as he was now practising it was not merely a stage in the continuous development of the subject but a new subject. He declared that his philosophy introduced a "kink" in the evolution of philosophy comparative to that which occurred in physics when Galileo invented dynamics.[6] He also said of the later philosophy: "One might say that the subject we are dealing with is one of the heirs that used to be called philosophy."[7]

It is on the basis of such a statement that G H von Wright can conclude: "The later Wittgenstein in my view has no ancestors in the history of thought. His work signals a radical departure from previously existing paths of philosophy."[8] And in a footnote to this comment he adds: "Wittgenstein's so-called later philosophy, as I see it, is quite different [from the philosophy expressed in the *Tractatus*]. Its spirit is unlike anything I know in Western thought and in many ways opposed to the aims and methods of traditional philosophy."[9]

Yet this by itself cannot be taken to entail that the later Wittgenstein's commitment is to pre-Enlightenment or post-Enlightenment thinking and not to the legacy of the Enlightenment. Hilary Putnam surely puts it perceptively when he says that Wittgenstein could neither be said to hold what could properly be called a "philosophical view" nor propose any argument "in any traditional philosophical sense".[10]

---

[5] See Chapter 3.

[6] L Wittgenstein, "Lectures 1930-1933", in G E Moore, *Philosophical Papers* (London: Allen and Unwin, 1959), 322.

[7] Wittgenstein, *BB*, 28.

[8] Von Wright, "Wittgenstein: A Biographical Sketch", 27.

[9] *Ibid*, 27-28.

[10] H Putnam, "Review of *The Concept* of a Person", in H Putnam, *Mind, Language and Reality*, (Cambridge: Cambridge University Press, 1975), 134.

However, neither of these views are intended to contradict Brian McGuinness's assertion that Wittgenstein:

exposes the weaknesses of traditional philosophies by a method which is itself a subtle differentiation of traditional philosophy.[11]

Though the later philosophy is, in the words of Bartley, "discourse-orientated", it does not follow - *pace* Bertrand Russell, and in our own time, Richard Rorty, D Z Phillips and most Popperians - that it is not "problem-orientated" in the old-fashioned sense of argument.[12] It is in fact both.[13]

---

[11] McGuinness, "Editor's Preface", McGuinness (ed), *Wittgenstein and His Times*, iii.

[12] In his otherwise fine essay "Philosophy and the Mirror of Rorty", P Munz appears to presume that the choice between "discourse-orientated" and "problem-orientated" philosophy is a mutually exclusive and exhaustive one. He rejects Richard Rorty's "discourse-orientated" Wittgenstein and traditional justificationism, which, to his mind, leaves only Popper's philosophy of criticism. P Munz, "Philosophy and the Mirror of Rorty", in Radnitzky and Bartley III (ed), *Evolutionary Epistemology, Rationality, and the Sociology of Knowledge* (Illinois: Open Court, 1987), 361.

[13] A Quinton's classic essay "Contemporary British Philosophy" was one of the first to distinguish Wittgenstein from the purely "discourse-orientated" Oxford ordinary-language philosophy: "[As against Wittgenstein] they believed that the job of philosophy was to set out the logical properties and relations of the various forms of discourse in a systematic way." A Quinton "Contemporary British Philosophy", in O'Connor (ed), *Critical History of Western Philosophy*, 546. Toulmin's recollection of Wittgenstein the philosopher in action makes for at least anecdotal evidence that Wittgenstein's later philosophy offered more than an explication of the correct uses of linguistic expressions over different domains of discourse - that in fact Wittgenstein was concerned with philosophical problems just as traditional philosophy was concerned with philosophical problems: "The difference in priorities that divided Wittgenstein from so many of his fellow philosophers in Britain after 1945 is well captured in a remark by the Oxford analyst, J L Austin. In the course of rebutting objections to the supposed triviality of his own laborious explorations of linguistic usage, Austin replied that he had never been convinced that the question, whether a philosophical question was an important question, was itself an important question. Like any pure scientist, the professional philosopher should begin by tackling problems that were technically 'sweet' and ripe for solution, whatever their extrinsic importance or unimportance. Pure philosophy must have priority; there would be time enough to apply its results to practical problems later. So, to go from Wittgenstein's Cambridge to the linguistic analysts of Oxford at the end of the nineteen-forties was to feel that philosophy had somehow or another lost its mainspring. Anyone who listened to Wittgenstein in person was conscious of a deeply philosophical thinker struggling to clear away intellectual obstacles to the free movement of their mind. At Oxford, meanwhile, similar looking techniques were being employed with the greatest skill but without any deeper or clearly philosophical purpose. it was like exchanging a real clock

Wittgenstein too, as we have seen, has an argument in the old-fashioned sense. His species of conceptual foundationalism is such an argument.

### 3. The Outstanding Problem of Hegel's Epoch: the Reconciliation of Reason and Will ('Desire')

That there is in both Barth and Wittgenstein an argument in the old-fashioned sense excludes the possibility of the presence of post-modern desire. According to post-modernism, since 'one reason is as good as any other', all that is left is intellectual decision as a function of desire. But Barth and Wittgenstein believe in dialectical reason, *ergo* they reject post-modern desire. But it should not be inferred from this that there is no place in their thought for desire *per se*.

The theology of Barth from the 1930s onwards and the later philosophy of Wittgenstein can be interpreted within the context of the resolution of the outstanding intellectual problem of Hegel's epoch, an epoch which began with Kant's *Critiques* and ended with the death of Hegel in 1831. This problem, which "insistently demanded the solution of the thinkers of the time"[14] was precisely that of the reconciliation of Enlightenment reason and Romantic will, feeling or desire. In what follows I will advance what I take to be the foundations of such a conclusion. Crucial in this respect is the finding that in the thought of Barth and Wittgenstein respectively, desire manifests itself as will-to-evil (not dissimilar to Nietzsche's 'will-to-power'), in a manner anticipated by Schopenhauer. Barth and Wittgenstein join the ranks of Freud and Marx as the 'heroes' of the radical Enlightenment in that they see the value of reason, or enlightenment, as a means of release from the pernicious effect of the will.[15]

To be sure, both Barth and Wittgenstein were born in the second half of the 1880s, Barth in 1886 and Wittgenstein in 1889. But this fact by itself does not preclude their being assimilable to the history of ideas of Hegel's epoch. Though the central problem of Hegel's epoch had originated in the intellectual history inaugurated by Kant and brought to a particular conclusion by Hegel, it does not follow that the epoch necessarily had the last word on the problem. It may indeed be the case that the epoch failed to

---

for a child's clock-face - which looks just the same at first sight but does not tell time." A Janik and S Toulmin, *Vienna*, 259.

[14] Charles Taylor, *Hegel* (Cambridge: Cambridge University Press, 1975), 3.

[15] Alex Callinicos has written that "Marx and Freud are the great heroes of the radical Enlightenment. Both discovered the dark underside of the *philosophes*' Empire of reason. [...] But unlike Nietzsche neither took the next step. Both viewed reason as an instrument of liberation." Callinicos, *Against Postmodernism*, 214.

resolve the problem. In other words, not only is it possible that what Barth and Wittgenstein had to say has some bearing on the problem, it may be that they succeeded in solving it where Kant, Fichte, Schiller, Schelling, Schleiermacher and, yes, Hegel himself failed. Notwithstanding this possibility, my objective is simply to show that their work can be understood within the context of this problem.

Barth once said, toward the end of his life, that he wondered whether "in a second life I might not turn completely to history, for which I have a secret passion."[16] There is no reason not to take this statement seriously: his first life gave vent to this passion in no small measure. The *Church Dogmatics* contains, *inter alia*, a history of theology and the development of theological ideas. He also wrote *Protestant Theology in the Nineteenth Century*, a book which, above all, set out the historical context to Barth's own theology.

One of Barth's fundamental historical beliefs was that the history of theology as an authentic discipline with its own *sui generis* potential had ground to a halt with the death of Hegel, with the consequence that the only authentic theologians thereafter were mavericks or nonconformists like Overbeck and Kierkegaard. It was not merely that the theology of the second half of the nineteenth century had turned its back on Hegel's grand project; it was that it had denied its truest and purest impulses in its attempt to align itself with the forces of progress of a practical, material kind. In other words, continuous with the prevailing positivist *bourgeois* nationalist ethos at this time was the theology of the German world of the second half of this century. This was a theology which, as was said in Chapter 3, betrayed - in the words of Paul Tillich - "an attitude of self-sufficient finitude".[17] As was said there, this attitude was the attitude of the self-satisfied *bourgeois* man, satisfied with who he is and what belongs to him as a member of this or that nation. In theology it was Albrecht Ritschl's theology which represented this tendency.[18] As Barth puts it, Ritschl is "the very epitome of the national-liberal German *bourgeois* of the age of Bismarck."[19] Moreover, Ritschl's theology conforms to "the pressure of the

---

[16] Quoted in Busch, *Barth*, 169.

[17] Welch, *Nineteenth Century Theology*, vol 1, 4.

[18] It is worth noting that Barth is in no doubt that Ritschl's world is *bourgeois*: "One thing ... is certain. Even before 1910 I was a stranger in my innermost being to the bourgeois world of Ritschl and his pupils." Barth, *The Theology of Friedrich Schleiermacher. Lectures at Gottingen, Winter Semester of 1923/4*, edited by D Ritschl, translated by G W Bromiley, (Edinburgh: T & T Clark, 1982), 262.

[19] Barth, *PT*, 656.

positivism prevailing in the second half of the nineteenth century."[20] It conforms to the positivist ethos prevailing in German (inclusive of Austrian) science. It is this ethos which Barth contrasted with the superior intrinsic value and dignity of the theology of the first half of the nineteenth century:

> We need only to compare the representative figures of the two eras in our field, the field of theology, the two church fathers, Schleiermacher and Ritschl, to be shocked at once at the era of meaner things, of smaller stature, which has manifestly arrived.[21]

To be sure, the Germany of Ritschl was Bismarck's, and not the Germany of the age of Wilhelm II which was to supersede Bismarck's. It was not, therefore, the world of the Pan-German movement. But the difference was only one of degree. The theological era which followed Ritschl was an era in which the prospect of grandeur and power took on the force of an entrenched value for a, hitherto, self-satisfied national-liberal bourgeois spirit. This spirit sought political and economic expansion: it wanted to extend its borders; it wanted new markets.

That Schleiermacher was more popular in 1910 than he had been in 1830 was the pre-eminent theological manifestation of these dreams of grandeur. The military and territorial ambitions of Imperial Germany had to be imbued with the universal civilising German cultural spirit. Ritschl was in the end considered too finite for this purpose. Ritschl could not stand shoulder to shoulder with Goethe and Beethoven; but Schleiermacher might just get away with it. The theological-cultural clothes of a former age had been restored to fashion for the occasion, had been taken out of the wardrobe, so to speak, to serve as the Emperor's new clothes. But the age superseding the historical "episode" of Ritschl's theology (as Barth called it),[22] had far more in common with Ritschl's time than with Schleiermacher's. Hence, Barth asked the question whether the will behind Ritschl's theology was not in fact the noumenal will of the whole century's theology, whether in fact Ritschl's theology was not the true picture of nineteenth-century theology.

> One could of course ask whether this will, soberly and honestly expressed by Ritschl, was not universally present, somewhere in the background of the theology of the whole century, except in certain outsiders, and whether

---

[20] Barth, "Evangelical Theology in the 19th Century", 56.

[21] Barth, *PT*, 386-387.

[22] *Ibid*, 654.

all else was not more like an artificial fog surrounding this will than actually another will.[23]

It is not that Schleiermacher culminates in Ritschl, that "theological romanticism" 'culminates' in positivism; it is rather that Schleiermacher's theology as "cultural theology, as exaltation of life in the most comprehensive sense, the exaltation, unfolding, transfiguration, ennobling of the individual and social human life, as religion which is the true object of theology",[24] is too a translation of theology into non-theology; as such it changes into a subject of inferior and smaller stature. In other words, Schleiermacher's theology cannot escape the fate that the meaner and smaller phenomenon of Ritschl is ultimately a more authentic description of its true identity than it is itself.

Yet Barth's partitioning of the nineteenth century into two halves prevails: Hegel's death in 1831 becomes a harbinger of the First World War, since coinciding with his demise is the emergence of the positivism and nationalism of the second half of the nineteenth century. Speaking of the nineteenth century's loss of interest in Hegel Barth wrote:

It was the first time that the new time was growing old, the first harbinger we might say of the catastrophe of 1914, the first hint that men were themselves beginning to doubt their own desires, when they became unfaithful to Hegel.[25]

The generation that came after Hegel's death judged his attempt to resolve the two apparently irreconcilable forces of his epoch to be a failure. Relinquishing any hopes of (nostalgic) fulfilment without sacrificing critical reason, this generation resigned itself to an apparently more modest *instrumental reason*, setting its sights on more practical political and economic ends. Yet Hegel's supreme self-confidence, superseded by the nationalist *bourgeois* spirit of the second half of the nineteenth century coincides with the birth of that which is designated by Marx's concept of 'false consciousness'.

Did it have to have been this way in theology? For Barth, it is precisely because of the way history had developed since Hegel that one had to be prepared to break with this history, and embrace, and make, the history that might have developed. (The idea of historical progress moving in a continuous straight line is thus repudiated.) Only then would the way "be

---

[23] *Ibid*, 655-656.
[24] *Ibid*, 434-435.
[25] *Ibid*, 386.

free for remembering forgotten things, resuming neglected things, facing the problems which have been suppressed, and in doing so honouring the truth."[26] Precisely "in this way will it then become possible really to become aware of the concern of the preceding age, in our case that of the age of Hegel, without failing to realize that that time is truly past."[27] But if such concerns are taken up again can Hegel's time truly be past?:

> Everything we have said so far must admittedly be put into parenthesis, for we do not know whether the age of Hegel is in fact entirely past, even if we should, in all seriousness, consider it to be so far as we ourselves are concerned. [...] It may be that the dawn of the true age of Hegel is still something that will take place in the future. But that would mean that we are in fact standing only at the beginning of the era.[28]

Barth wrote this in 1932, almost exactly a century after the demise of this age. The true age of Hegel, he suggested, was perhaps still to come. Who was to inaugurate it? Did he see himself standing at the beginning of this era? We have already noted his intimation that he, rather than Schleiermacher, is the true legatee of the Enlightenment. Was he also ready to step into Hegel's shoes? Not, of course, as Hegel, but as Barth, attempting to resolve the problems that the concerns of 'Enlightenment reason' and 'Romantic desire' posed for humanity?

It is indisputable that Barth held Hegel in high regard. It has often been remarked how pervasive is his influence in the *Church Dogmatics*.[29] Yet of greater historical significance is the fact that Barth himself recognised the reconciliation of the two apparently irreconcilable forces of Reason and Romanticism to be the problem with which Hegel was preoccupied, the objective of the grand Hegelian project. In the wake of Kant and the Enlightenment the central and defining problem of the generation to which Hegel (1770-1831) belonged was the re-unification of the two opposing impulses of the time: the ideal of radical freedom on the one side, and integral expression on the other. This opposition manifested itself between:

> thought, reason, morality, on one side, and desire and sensibility on the other; full self-conscious freedom, on one side, and life in the community on the other; self-consciousness and communion with nature; and beyond

---

[26] Barth, *PT*, 390.

[27] *Ibid*, 390.

[28] *Ibid*, 390.

[29] See, for example, R Roberts, "The Doctrine of Time in the Theology of Karl Barth", in S Sykes (ed), *Karl Barth: Studies of His Theological Method* (Oxford: Oxford University Press, 1979), 93.

this the separation of finite subjectivity from infinite life that flowed through nature, the barrier between the Kantian subject and the Spinozist substance, *Deus sive natura*, or in Lessing's phrase, the '*Hen kai pan*'.[30]

Hegel himself had come to see that the consequences of intellectual freedom required the breaking up of expressive unity, the original undivided wholeness within man and communion with other men and nature. Thus though the sense of fragmentation within, and of exile in, a dead mechanical universe was not an inexplicable and unmitigated loss of an earlier paradise, but was rather the result of an ineluctable development essential for the full realisation of man as rational and free agent,[31] the quintessentially modern tragedy of man was that he appeared to attain his self-conscious rational autonomy only at the cost of separating off from nature, society, fate - and God.[32]

The hope of Hegel's epoch was that a way would be found to unite these two ostensibly incompatible powerful aspirations. Man would be fulfilled as an expressive being through unity with nature, other men, himself or God without sacrificing the radical moral autonomy which had reached paradigm expression in Kant.[33]

Barth saw Hegel precisely in these terms. On the one hand, Hegel sought to satisfy the concerns of Romanticism:

If the eighteenth and nineteenth century formed a unity in such a way that the nineteenth century was the fulfilment of the eighteenth, then it was Hegel who represented this unity in his philosophy as no other man did. Is it not [Hegel] in whom the extremely vulnerable attempt to form an opposition to Kant's real or supposed one-sidedness, as it had been undertaken by Herder and others like him, came most legitimately into his own? Is it not he who is above all the systematiser and apologist of the concerns of Romanticism ....[34]

Yet, on the other hand, Hegel did not renounce "the reason known and available to everyone":[35]

Hegel takes up the inheritance of the Enlightenment: in fulfilment of the concern of the whole movement between himself and the Enlightenment,

---

[30] Charles Taylor, *Hegel*, 36.

[31] *Ibid*, 76.

[32] *Ibid*, 79.

[33] *Ibid*, 76.

[34] Barth, *PT*, 385.

[35] *Ibid*, 392.

but also criticising and correcting the courses it had taken acting in an independent direct relationship to the Enlightenment. In affirming this equivalence and final identity of things within and things without, of ego and non-ego, of the familiar and the unfamiliar, Hegel affirms the insights of romanticism. Of the minds we have studied here he is unquestionably most akin to Novalis. For just three years (Jena, 1801-3) he was closely associated with Schelling, the true philosopher of Romanticism, and even though he turned away from Schelling later this did not mean that he had rejected the things Romanticism wanted, but that he was attempting to provide for it a better system and apologetics than that of Schelling. He found the Romantic synthesis and identity to be lacking in a firm and universally valid basis. It seemed to him that the truth and force of this synthesis was imperilled by the mere appeal to poetry, to creative experience, to the individual genius. That was why he was also Schleiermacher's determined opponent and opposed his metaphysics of feeling, and the doctrine of faith which called this instance to witness. For him it is a question of understanding the synthesis which he also affirmed as Novalis, as Schelling, and as Schleiermacher wanted it to be, as solid knowledge, as a free, conscious and responsible act of the capacity of reason, which is in principle always and everywhere present in man and can be appealed to.[36]

In other words, Hegel's philosophy "does not allow itself to be surpassed in cold-blooded rationalising by any worldling, nor in the depth of feeling by the most pious."[37] That Barth, then, saw Hegel as attempting to resolve the two apparently irreconcilable forces of his time cannot seriously be doubted.

To be sure, none of this by itself answers the question whether Barth saw himself as inaugurating the new, or genuine, age of Hegel, far less whether he saw himself as resolving these two apparently irreconcilable forces when ushering in this age. Nevertheless, I want to suggest that emerging from his theology is a solution to the outstanding problem of Hegel's epoch.

## 4. Barth: the 'Desire' for Natural Theology

Before I proceed to show this, I want to ask the question, to what extent does post-modern desire resolve this problem? The answer is that post-modern desire has *no hope* of resolving the apparently irreconcilable forces. It is a species of Romanticism - a truth underlined by the fact that the art-

---

[36] *Ibid*, 392.
[37] *Ibid*, 395.

form of expressionism, claimed as the 'first post-modernism', is undoubtedly such a species.[38] And, like its Romantic predecessors - Schiller, Fichte, Schelling, and Schleiermacher - it refuses the all-encompassing necessity of reason, deprecating it as a form of totalitarian control and repression (from the critical perspective [the old conceptual framework], this refusal of reason could only be described as an old-fashioned kind of fideism). Postmodernism is, as earlier versions of Romanticism were, only interested in one side of the equation. *Unlike* them, it (apparently) changes the conceptual framework in such a way that, henceforth, there is no 'Enlightenment' case to answer.

As has been said: Barth did not jettison the old conceptual framework. But neither did he accept that apologetic and fideism were exhaustive categories. Hence, though Romanticism is alive in Barth's theology, *the desire that surfaces there manifests itself within this framework.* There it has a distinctly negative role of being the eternal impetus behind what Barth described as 'the anti-Christ': the phenomenon of *natural theology*! However exaggerated a claim it appeared at the time, to Barth it was the simple conclusion of an unassailable premise: the anti-Christ of Jesus Christ was *sin*. Accepting the premise, as did many of those who thought Barth had gone too far, meant accepting the conclusion.

To be sure, natural theology is superfluous because "from the very outset a theology of this kind looks in another direction than where God has placed Himself."[39] Natural theology is a solution to an illusory problem. As Robert Jenson puts it, natural theology is superfluous because "the attempt to reach God rests on the illusory supposition that he has ever left us."[40] Or, again, as Barth puts it:

Natural theology is not in any sense a partner of a theology of the Word of God [Jesus Christ] which has a true understanding of itself. From the point of view of this theology, it quietly drops away as superfluous.[41]

But natural theology obstinately refused to fall away in this fashion. There was something behind natural theology which ensured its durability. I turn to §26 of *CD* II/1:

Why then is all this not so simple and self-evident? Why then in spite of all the refutations like those we have just made, can a theology of this kind

---

[38] Patricia Waugh, *Practising Postmodernism, Reading Modernism*, (London: Hodder and Stoughton, 1992), ch. 1, esp., 13-18.
[39] Barth, *CD* II/1, 126.
[40] Jenson, *God After God*, 71.
[41] Barth, *CD* II/1, 168.

continually arise, announcing itself anew in ever new forms (as if nothing had been said against it and as if it had not been refuted), creeping into theological ventures which have quite different intentions, and like a rank weed clinging even to what is apparently the soundest talk, weakening and finally killing it? It cannot be disputed - there is no use shutting our eyes to it - that it actually can do this. And it can do this to a degree that we cannot rate too highly, and with a weight which once released, will generally sweep away all opposing considerations and even the most careful and complete refutations.[42]

Again:

Why is it, then, that our statement on the knowability of God is not so simple and self-evident that the question of a basis of our knowledge of God in ourselves and in our relationship to the world cannot be settled once and for all, but seems as though it must continually arise again in different forms and phases?[43]

Not only does natural theology refuse to lie down and die, it refuses to do so even when it has been decisively refuted (not only that, it sweeps away even the most careful and complete refutations). The question is, why, in the face of what Barth considers his own decisive refutation - not merely harangue or dogmatic assertion - does it continue to sweep all before it? Why does natural theology remain with us? Why can we not put an end to it for good? Why does it not quietly drop away as superfluous, at least over a longer time-scale? Why did it occur in the past, persist in the present, and will do so in the future? Why is a true understanding of the Word of God so difficult to maintain? As Barth himself puts it:

Wherein lies the eternal vitality of natural theology?[44]

He continues:

... the acknowledged vitality of natural theology must be explained in some other way, if it can be explained at all.[45]

---

[42] *Ibid*, 126-7.
[43] *Ibid*, 85.
[44] *Ibid*, 97.
[45] *Ibid*, 97.

He considers several possible explanations, all of which he will eventually find wanting (though it becomes clear that he did not give any of them serious consideration).[46]

First, he considers that the explanation may be that natural theology is actually successful.[47] But this, he thinks, is "rendered impossible" on the basis of God's self-revelation.[48] Hence Barth duly concludes: "The tenacity with which the hypothesis of natural theology obtrudes itself cannot be explained by its superiority."[49]

The second explanation is that natural theology is relied upon as a necessary preliminary or supplementary to Christian theology itself. According to this explanation "the introduction of natural theology into the foundation of the doctrine of God is for some reason unavoidable in our understanding of the knowability of God; ... out of respect for some hitherto unconsidered facts and necessities we are perhaps forced to accord it a place."[50] Are we then compelled to affirm natural theology in this albeit limited sense? Barth does not accept this conclusion: "the acknowledged vitality of natural theology must be explained in some other way - if it can be explained at all."[51] The search goes on.

The third possibility is the one that Barth appears to take most seriously, to which he devotes most time. It is that natural theology is "allowed, even authorised and necessitated" by Holy Scripture.[52] Passages from the Old and New Testaments are subjected to detailed and protracted analysis,[53] after which Barth delivers his judgement: "Holy Scripture neither imposes the necessity nor even offers the possibility of reckoning with a knowability of the God of the prophets and apostles which is not given in and with his revelation, or bound to it; and therefore to that extent with a "Christian" natural theology."[54] Hence, "in the present context this means that even this third explanation of the actual vitality of natural theology is not sufficient."[55]

The fourth explanation he considers is quite simple: it is that the vitality of natural theology is inexplicable or within the context of the Church an

---

[46] The issue is not whether Barth's grounds for rejecting all the explanations in question are justified. It is that he spends a great deal of time and effort to clear the way in order to assert something like the will as the motive-force behind natural theology.
[47] Barth, *CD* II/1, 85-8.
[48] *Ibid*, 88.
[49] *Ibid*, 88.
[50] *Ibid*, 97.
[51] *Ibid*, 97.
[52] *Ibid*, 98.
[53] *Ibid*, 97-128.
[54] *Ibid*, 125.
[55] *Ibid*, 125.

"unexplained phenomenon of Church history."[56] In other words, it can't be explained at all and the presupposition that it can be has to be abandoned. This explanation, like the previous ones, is rejected.

Though it would be harsh to accuse Barth of disingenuousness at this juncture in *CD* II/1, it is perfectly obvious that he did not give any of the above explanations serious consideration. What he has done is clear away competing hypotheses to leave the field open for the one he favours. This is that

the vitality of natural theology is the vitality [*Vitalität*] of man as such.[57]

He explains:

In the sphere of man as such his own vitality is the phenomenon controlling the whole field of vision. For this reason natural theology can recommend so impressively, and so powerfully intrude, a consideration which is seriously addressed to the sphere of man. For this reason it can always triumphantly produce in this sphere new arguments for its right to exist. For this reason it can here evade every counter-argument, however illuminating.[58]

What is the vitality of man in this context, the motive-force behind the eternal vitality of natural theology?

## 5. The *Vitalität* of Man as a Species of Schopenhauerian Expressivism[59]

*Vitalität* is a species of human expressiveness. It is as close to a concept of will as one might get. In the German philosophical tradition, *Vitalität* is rooted in the Romantic vocabulary of *Lebensphilosophie*. But, in Barth's theology it is associated with sin. It is an expression of a disease, an intellectual disease, an intellectual cancer - in Barth's phrase, it is "like a rank weed." However counterintuitive it may appear, that man possesses *Vitalität* in this respect, is not an intrinsically good thing, but an intrinsically

---

[56] *Ibid*, 126.

[57] *Ibid*, 165.

[58] *Ibid*, 165.

[59] Barth does not cite Schopenhauer in § 26 of the *Church Dogmatics*. But, as would be expected of someone opposed to the phenomenon of natural theology, he rejects Schopenhauer's pessimistic account of man as a picture of true man (though it is a picture of false man, natural man, vitality being an intrinsic property of natural man). See Barth, *CD* III/1-4 for various references to Schopenhauer in this vein.

bad thing. Its presence in the human condition is inimical to theological health.

*Vitalität* as sin is not hereditary sin [*Erbsunde*], which Barth rejects, but, rather, original sin [*Ursunde*] (it is "only in a very loose sense that something I cannot refuse to do can be regarded as my own act, something for which I am responsible");[60] it is not - and here we must be reminded of Barth's supralapsarian sympathies over and against infralapsarian views - indicative of *Homo Lapsus* but, rather, *Homo Labilis*.[61] Man is liable, indeed, easily inclined by his will, to do evil rather than good, in the sense that he is inclined to do what he wants to do, regardless of what God wants him to do. He is liable to fall only in the sense that it is of his own volition.

Much has been written in Western philosophy on the concept of will as it occurs in the contexts of the philosophical problem of volition and the philosophical problem of free will versus determinism. However, the metaphysical characterisation of the will as existing independently of the thinking self, as the fundamental ontological presence animating the human being, owes its more specialised conceptual identity primarily to the work of Schopenhauer and his *Die Welt als Wille und Vorstellung* (*The World as Will and Representation*). Barth's characterisation of *Vitalität* belongs to the Schopenhauerian tradition.

Schopenhauer's philosophy takes as its point of departure Kant's philosophy and his distinction between the phenomenon and the noumenon, between the world as it appears to us and the world as it is in itself. In Kant the knowing subject's world is comprised of his perceptions, which are the product of the understanding applied to the data of sense, together with his rational interpretations of these, which are the product of reason. This implies that the knower's apprehension of reality is conditioned throughout, that is to say, is relative to his sense, understanding, and reason, these being what the knower contributed to his experience. Reality cannot then be grasped as it is in itself but only through faculties which cannot but be imposed on experience. Thus arises the distinction between the phenomenal world as it is experienced and rationally understood, and the noumenal world, which lies beyond the boundaries of human experience and thought.

Although Kant concluded that the noumenal world was unknowable, he noted that a man is both a phenomenon and a noumenon, that is, in so far as he is both a perceivable body in space and time causally related to other bodies, and a subject that perceives, thinks, wills, and acts. In particular, he distinguished between man and a mere object such a stone. Man is a subject who wills. He is the ultimate architect of his own moral conduct. A stone does not will; therefore the concept of moral conduct is logically inapplicable to it.

---

[60] Barth, *CD* IV/1, 499-500.
[61] Barth, *CD* II/2, 127-145.

But this subject that perceives, thinks, wills, and acts, is not itself and cannot as subject be an object and, in particular, an object of experience. On the contrary, it is transcendental ego: it is only deducible *a priori* as a necessary accompaniment to the empirical self which Hume described as nothing but a flux of experiences. It is not itself something we encounter in our experience as a constituent of the world. The empirical self is an object of experience and as such is to be distinguished from the transcendental or metaphysical self. Therefore, Kant is able to reconcile the conception of subject as noumenal with the proposition that it is unknowable in the empirical sense.

Schopenhauer sharpened Kant's insight but in such a way as to turn it against Kant's declaration that the noumenal world was *in toto* unknowable. On the contrary, like Hegel, Schopenhauer asserts that the noumenal world is knowable, or at least an aspect of it is knowable, and this because we are identical with it and as such know ourselves, not indirectly, but directly as subjects who will. But, as Charles Taylor points out, although Schopenhauer *appears* to belong to a stream of expressivism that turned to an idea of fulfilment as the release of the instinctual or elemental depths beyond the ordered limits of conscious rationality, his own theory was

in a sense its pessimistic inversion. Schopenhauer's concept of the 'will' and of the body as its 'objectification' derive from the expressivist stream of thought, but there is no idea of fulfilment here.[62]

Quite the reverse: "the elemental force of the will brings man only suffering and degradation."[63] It is this that is borne out in Barth's analysis of *Vitalität*. There is no fulfilment. Analogous to a disease, a rank weed, it brings about (from a God's eye-view) intellectual suffering and corruption. But it is no genetically-determined illness, it is will expressed in temptation. In his famous encounter with Emil Brunner, Barth wrote that natural theology:

does not exist as an entity capable of becoming a separate subject within what I consider to be real theology - not even for the sake of being rejected. If one occupies oneself with real theology one can pass by so-called natural theology only as one would pass by an abyss into which it is inadvisable to step if one does not want to fall. All one can do is turn one's back upon it as upon the great temptation [*Versuchung*] and source of error, by having nothing to do with it and making it clear to oneself and to others why one acts that way. A real rejection does not differ from its

---

[62] Taylor, *Hegel*, 562.
[63] *Ibid*, 562.

acceptance only in the way in which 'No' differs from 'Yes'. Rather are our 'Yes' and 'No' said, as it were, on different levels. Really to reject natural theology is to refuse to admit it as a separate problem. Hence rejection of natural theology can only be a side-issue, arising when serious questions of real theology are being discussed.[64]

Can this assertion - as well as those quoted from *CD* II/1 - be interpreted within the context of postmodernist desire? In the 'post-modern' paradigm, real theology is associated with desire. But this is not what we find in Barth. In Barth, *Vitalität - desire* succumbing to temptation - is the causal force behind natural theology. It is because real theology is no such one-dimensional species of Romanticism that the way is open to interpret natural theology in such a way as to make the resolution of the outstanding problem of Hegel's epoch feasible. It is not real theology, but natural theology, which is the great temptation.[65] As was said before,

---

[64] "No!", in Brunner and Barth, *Natural Theology*, translated by Peter Fraenkel, introduction by John Baillie, (London: 1946), 14, 11, 75-6. To be sure, there is an apparent tension between this claim and the claim cited earlier, that within the sphere of man, the vitality of man is the phenomenon controlling the whole field of vision. If "one occupies oneself with real theology one can pass by so-called natural theology"; one is to "turn one's back on it as upon the great temptation and source of error"; one is to have "nothing to do with it", "making it clear why one acts that way." But if this all occurs within the sphere of man, then the vitality of man is the phenomenon controlling the whole field of vision. How then is it possible that man as such can occupy himself with real theology? Is he not hopelessly ensnared by natural theology? The resolution of this apparent inconsistency lies in the concept of temptation intrinsic to *Homo Labilis* (but not to *Homo Lapsus*). Once one succumbs to temptation - engendered by the vitality of man - one is in the sphere of man where the field of vision is occluded by illusion. There is however another sphere of man that is subsumed under the existence of Jesus Christ. In this realm, man can do real theology.

[65] It is to be noted that, for Barth, natural theology will not go away, even in the face of theological knowledge. In *FQI* he makes the following statement: "According to Anselm there are no theological problems that are finally settled, so surely must we, when we have prayed, pray again and continue to pray. But it would be prayer devoid of faith in the hearing of prayer (and therefore not prayer) if theological thinking in the act of its fulfilment were not entirely sure of its own case. Barth, *FQI*, 158-9. It is in conjunction with this sentiment that Barth notes Anselm "dares the bold statement that now he has clearly recognised that this knowledge would still remain to him even were he to refuse to believe." *Ibid*, 35-36, footnote 3. For Barth sees that Anselm perceived the real possibility of being unable to remain wedded to his knowledge, to the achieved *intelligere*, and so consoled himself with the observation that, once achieved, it would remain with him even if he could did not acknowledge it. In other words, there is little difference between Anselm and the fool of *Prosl. 4*. The passage quoted from pages 158-9 continues: "And it is exactly the same with the basis which Anselm describes as

postmodernism cannot, even in principle, resolve this problem since all it recognises is desire. Barth recognises both: desire and rationality proper - though this latter is assuredly not apologetic reason (nor, for that matter, 'fideistic' reason). To be sure, natural theology invokes thought too, but it is thought operating under illusion, it is thought operating under a controlling field of vision fundamentally in error; to that extent, it is not rational.

This pessimistic understanding of human vitality provides the perennial background threat to the possibility of theological epistemology proper. The error of natural theology is that "from the very outset a theology of this kind looks in another direction than where God has placed Himself."[66] But the reason it necessarily behaves in this way is because it is driven on by human vitality as Barth understands it. In the context of his theological epistemology as I have presented it in Chapters 7 and 8, this means that human vitality is the motive-force behind the perennial attempt to have what one cannot have: the means of measurement independently of its objects of measurement - the *sui generis* historical events of God's self-revelation in the creation history and the resurrection-appearances history.

But as was said in Chapter 8, one cannot have the means of measurement for measuring God's self-revelation independently of - without - the object of measurement itself, without God's self-revelation itself. This is because there is no means of measurement other than the object of measurement itself. There is no human capacity for knowledge of what it is God's self-revelation is independently of the event itself. The conceptual point of comparison against which to measure the truth of God's self-revelation originates in God's self-revelation and nowhere else, not, therefore, in an immanent 'measure of the divine'. Once we acknowledge this - see this - we will cease striving to measure God by our own resources and put ourselves completely at the mercy of God's revealing Himself through Himself. But natural theology driven on by human vitality will always occlude this insight, and we will once more seek to measure God with our own measure, conceive of God with our own conceptions, wish ourselves a God according to our own wishes[67]

---

the only possible basis for the statement *Deus non est*." Anselm will at times be unreconciled with God. Barth says of the statement *Deus non est* that it is "the statement of unbelief, of the corrupt will, of man unreconciled." *Ibid*, 161. But it will at times be no less true of Anselm who "realises that it is only by the grace of God that his solidarity with him [man unreconciled] has been ended." *Ibid*, 160. Anselm is just as much natural man as anyone else.

[66] Barth, *CD* II/1, 126.
[67] Barth, "The Strange New World Within the Bible", 47.

The same paradigm occurs in Wittgenstein. The causal force behind apologetic reason is identified as desire - *urge, feeling, will*. But reason - rationality proper - can also operate outside of desire. This is the realm of philosophy proper, real philosophy, if you will.  In Wittgenstein's later thought, there is the later philosophy - real philosophy - and traditional philosophy. The latter occupies the same role in the later philosophy that natural theology does in Barth's theology. As in the case of Barth - and for exactly the same reasons - postmodernism is too limited a *Weltanschaunng* to encompass the parameters of the later philosophy. The later philosophy has sufficient dimensions in it to resolve Hegel's great problem; postmodernisn does not (it only recognises a single dimension).

Wittgenstein interpreted traditional philosophy in terms of the same, or similar, metaphors. Traditional philosophy was a disease [*eine Krankheit*], an illness requiring therapy; it bewitched us as would a demon; it is original sin transposed to the realm of philosophy. But, as in Barth, it is interpreted as something entirely natural, something intrinsic to the human condition, something which "sweeps away even the most careful and complete refutations"; something that "must continually arise again in different forms and phases." It is a disease of the *will*. The presence of urge, feeling, will - *desire* - in traditional philosophy blinds us to the truth. Apologetic reason is motivated by desire; it too, in the realm of philosophy, blinds us to the truth. But it is precisely because argument in the old-fashioned sense is not restricted to apologetic alone that there is a place for desire in Wittgenstein's philosophy (though it is not desire in the post-modern sense).

## 6. Wittgenstein:
### the 'Vitality' of Traditional Philosophy as a Function of 'Desire'

In the preface to the *Tractatus* Wittgenstein declared that all the problems of philosophy were finally solved. To this extent the early Wittgenstein, like Hegel, had thought of himself as ushering in the final stage of philosophy, indeed, as having brought about the end of philosophy. Accordingly, if philosophers had any integrity at all they would have gone off and done something else - much as Wittgenstein had when, having made himself redundant, he went off to teach peasant children in the Austrian country-side.

It is, perhaps, the hall-mark of such eschatological philosophies that they reduce everything in the end to one essence (as has been said of that most eschatological character Ulrich in Robert Musil's *The Man Without Qualities*: "he reduces everything to essentials"). To be sure, to the extent that this essence, correctly apprehended, represented the dissolution of all philosophical problems, it also represented the end of philosophy. Yet, ironically, one of the cardinal faults of the *Tractatus,* as Wittgenstein later saw, was that it wanted to reduce all the various and diverse uses of language to one essence. This explains why an enlightened Wittgenstein could say of Hegel:

> Hegel seems to say that everything which looks different is really the same. I am saying that everything which looks the same is different.[68]

However, this difference between Wittgenstein and Hegel does not preclude the possibility that Wittgenstein's later philosophy coincides the final stage of philosophy. For in the later philosophy Wittgenstein still hankers after a dissolution of philosophy that leaves behind only one essence: forms of life and language-games. Yet, final essences notwithstanding, the later Wittgenstein did not share Hegel's supreme self-confidence that he had brought about the end of philosophy. The *Tractatus* is a young man's work, sure of itself and its conclusions. The later philosophy is the product of a more mature and realistic spirit. In the early work philosophy simply evaporates never to return; in the later work traditional philosophy will not oblige in this way: it will not go away because, as Wittgenstein learned as he got older, there is something in the human being which will not let go of it.

Anthony Kenny comments that Wittgenstein would note with approval a remark of Georg von Lichtenberg's: "Our whole philosophy is a rectification of linguistic usage: the rectification that is of a philosophy which is the most universal philosophy".[69] To be sure, Wittgenstein would have agreed that there were a great many human beings who were not subject to the temptations of philosophy. For instance, in a remark culled from one of his lectures he is reported as saying:

> A philosopher has temptations which an ordinary person does not have. We could say he knows better what the word means than the others do. But actually philosophers generally know less because ordinary people have no temptation to misunderstand language.[70]

However, the ordinary person was immune from misunderstanding and perplexity only insofar as he avoided thinking philosophically. Once he has

---

[68] Quoted in Kerr, *Theology After Wittgenstein*, 36.

[69] A Kenny, "Wittgenstein on the Nature of Philosophy", in B F McGuinness (ed), *Wittgenstein and His Times* (Oxford: Basil Blackwell, 1981), 13.

[70] Quoted in McGuinness, "Wittgenstein and Freud", in B F McGuinness (ed), *Wittgenstein and His Times* (Oxford: Basil Blackwell, 1981), 40; see esp. 39-41.

gone down this path, he was no less liable to the same mistakes as other philosophers. (Wittgenstein might well have said that G.E. Moore, 'the philosopher of the ordinary man's common sense', was the perfect example of such a phenomenon.)

Insofar as the temptation of which Wittgenstein speaks above is the temptation of the will, he must be understood as holding the view that the traditional philosopher is *Homo Labilis* rather than *Homo Lapsus*. *Homo Lapsus*, by definition, inhabits a psychological universe 'beyond temptation', since to speak of temptation at all presupposes the logical possibility of not doing what one is tempted to do.

The question is whether, in the realm of philosophy, one could finish with temptation *once and for all*. The temptation to tackle philosophical problems by traditional philosophical methods would exist only up to the point coinciding with their dissolution by Wittgenstein's methods. *Prima facie*, one might imagine that one would have to do the tour of traditional philosophy once and once only. The dissolution of all the problems of philosophy would simply be a question of time. One would cease doing philosophy: traditional philosophy, because all the problems had finally been solved; Wittgenstein's philosophy, because there was no longer any need for it. Is this how Wittgenstein thought of it? The answer is, no. It is too static, not to say, optimistic, a picture of the relation between his philosophy and traditional philosophy. Like Sisyphus, we are condemned *by the temptation of our own wills - an unavoidable part of the human condition* - to return to the same task again and again. There was no lasting release from the pernicious presence of the will.

It is certainly the case that Wittgenstein thought his philosophy brought peace. But it remains to be shown that he thought this a lasting state. In the *Investigations* he wrote:

> The real discovery is the one that makes me capable of stopping doing philosophy when I want to - The one that gives philosophy peace, so that it is no longer tormented [*gepeitscht*] by questions which bring itself into question. - Instead we now demonstrate a method, by examples; and the series of examples can be broken off. Problems are solved (difficulties eliminated), not a single method.
> There is not a philosophical method, though there are indeed methods, like different therapies.[71]

There is no question that he ever repudiated the substance of this remark. In 1944 he returned to the idea that the philosopher or one who philosophises seeks peace as the end of his endeavours: "Thoughts that are

---

[71] Wittgenstein, *PI* § 133.

at peace. That's what someone who philosophises yearns for."[72] However, there was something about *PI* § 133 which caused him disquiet. Rush Rhees describes a conversation he had with Wittgenstein: "He had found some feature of what he had being saying unsatisfactory. This was typical: he would come back to the same questions time and time again, often trying to see if they could not be done in another way. As he was leaving, this time, he said to me roughly this: 'In my book I say that I am able to leave off with a problem in philosophy when I want to. But that's a lie; I can't.'"[73]

That the admission is wholly autobiographical cannot be dismissed. But it can be argued that the remark does go beyond Wittgenstein's own personality. It says more about the nature of philosophy than it does about how Wittgenstein's own nature interacted with it. It should be noted that, after opening in the first-person, he writes: the one that gives *philosophy* peace, not: the one that gives *me* peace. He speaks of himself, certainly, but this does not prevent him from speaking of all others who do philosophy. Wanting to stop is one thing; being able to, given the state of *Homo Labilis*, is another. Indeed, it is clear he thought there was a sense in which we would question whether *any* of our methods and results had really dealt with the problem in question. He doubted whether we would ever attain peace such that philosophy - his own philosophy and its results - would cease to be "tormented" by questions which brought it - his own philosophy - into question. Why?

## 7. Schopenhauer Transposed to the Realm of Wittgenstein's Philosophy

While Wittgenstein did not postulate, and would never have postulated, the will as a noumenal ontological presence, he proposes a source of will underlying traditional philosophy which inclines, or urges on, the traditional philosopher in us. Its function is analogous to how the will operates in

---

[72] Wittgenstein, *CV*, 43.

[73] Quoted in Garth Hallett, *A Companion to Wittgenstein's "Philosophical Investigations"* (Ithaca: Cornell University Press. 1977), 230. I am not sure that the Wittgenstein of 1944 would have agreed with the remark he made to Drury in 1930 unless the two can be synthesised at a higher 'Hegelian' level!: "Yes, I have reached a real resting place. I know that my method is right. My father was a business man, and I am a business man: I want my philosophy to be business-like, to get something done, to get something settled." M O'C Drury, "Conversations with Wittgenstein", in Rush Rhees (ed), *Recollections of Wittgenstein*, (Oxford: Oxford University Press, 1984), 110.

Schopenhauer's philosophy.[74] In fact, it can be argued that Wittgenstein's discussion of volition in §611-628 of the *Investigations* is directly influenced by Schopenhauer. The thesis that willing is acting is, as Janaway puts it, "one of the most distinctively Schopenhauerian views to be found anywhere in Wittgenstein."[75] Janaway argues that the view Wittgenstein took in his later work on the willing subject was first developed in the *Notebooks* (1914-1916) alongside the material we have discussed above, and that the reason it did not emerge in the *Tractatus* (1922) was that it was logically incompatible with the idea of a purely metaphysical self. Janaway further argues that Wittgenstein would have been even more Schopenhauerian had he followed his later view at the time of the *Tractatus*.[76] But it is not will as volition with which we are primarily concerned here in our discussion of Wittgenstein's later work and, in particular, his view of the motive-force behind traditional philosophy. Our remit is will not as volition, but will as something to be overcome;[77] an

---

[74] There is little doubt that Wittgenstein's *Tractatus* proposed a concept of the metaphysical self heavily influenced by Schopenhauer's conception. See: P M S Hacker, *Insight and Illusion. Themes in the Philosophy of Wittgenstein*, revised edition, (Oxford: Oxford University Press, 1986), 81-107; C Janaway, *Self and World in Schopenhauer's Philosophy* (Oxford: Oxford University Press, 1989), 317-357; P Gardiner, *Schopenhauer* (Harmondsworth: Penguin Books, 1971), 275-282; A Janik, "Schopenhauer and the Early Wittgenstein", *Philosophical Studies (Ireland)* 15 (1966), 76-95; B Magee, *The Philosophy of Schopenhauer* (Oxford: Clarendon, 1983), 286-315; S Morris Engel, "Schopenhauer's Impact on Wittgenstein", *Journal of the History of Philosophy* 7 (1969), 285-302. Indeed, Schopenhauer was one of the few philosophers Wittgenstein had encountered early in life: according to G E M Anscombe he read Schopenhauer when he was sixteen: "As a boy of sixteen Wittgenstein had read Schopenhauer and had been greatly impressed by Schopenhauer's theory of the 'world as idea' (though not of the 'world as will'); Schopenhauer then struck him as fundamentally right, if only a few adjustments and clarifications were made." See G E M Anscombe, *Introduction to Wittgenstein's Tractatus*, 11. This would date the occurrence at 1905. What Wittgenstein read then was *Die Welt als Wille und Vorstellung*. See G H von Wright, "Wittgenstein, A Biographical Sketch", 18. Hacker has no doubt that Wittgenstein re-read this book while writing the last of the three extant notebooks. See Hacker, *Insight*, 18. McGuinness reports that Wittgenstein was also fond of quoting from *Aphorismen zur Lebensweisheit*. See McGuinness, *Wittgenstein*, 18. In particular, a detailed comparison of Wittgenstein's third and final surviving notebook with the *Tractatus* serves to reveal that Wittgenstein's remarks on both the metaphysical subject and the will are basically inherited from Schopenhauer. See: Hacker, *Insight*, 2; Janaway, *Self*, 320-321.

[75] Janaway, *Self*, 337.

[76] *Ibid*, 337-442; see also Peter Winch, "Wittgenstein's Treatment of the Will", *Ratio* 10 (1968), 38-53.

[77] Kenny,"Wittgenstein on the Nature of Philosophy", 14.

urge;[78] a feeling to be renounced.[79] That is, though our concern is will in terms of something we make happen in the world, it is also will as something that happens to us, will as something for which we are liable in the legal and culpable sense of the term. In a passage in which Wittgenstein discusses Tolstoy's criterion of art, he writes:

> Tolstoy: a thing's significance (importance) lies in its being something everyone can understand. That is both true and false. What makes a subject hard to understand - if it's something significant and important - is not that before you can understand it you need to be trained in abstruse matters, but the contrast between understanding the subject and what people want to see. Because of this the very things which are the most obvious may become the hardest to understand. What has to be overcome is a difficulty having to do with the will, not the intellect.[80]

Tolstoy believed it was the measure of a work of art's worth that it be universally understood, as in, for example, the case of the Bible. Wittgenstein was sympathetic to Tolstoy's aesthetic criterion but for the purpose of the point he wants to make, he qualifies Tolstoy in the following way. Even if understanding an object does not require that one be "trained in abstruse matters", it does not follow that one will understand the object in question: "the very things which are the most obvious may be the most difficult to understand". What makes a subject hard to understand - in this case the results of philosophy - is not a lack of knowledge of what is in the pages of the philosophical classics; knowledge of such things - metaphysics, epistemology, etc. - will not make a difference. The problem does not lie with the intellect; rather it lies with the will.[81] It lies with what people want to see, rather than what they do see. Wittgenstein writes elsewhere:

> As I have often said, philosophy does not call on me for any sacrifice, because I am not denying myself the saying of anything but simply giving up the certain combinations of words as senseless. But in another sense, philosophy demands a renunciation, but a renunciation of feeling, not of

---

[78] Wittgenstein, *PI*, 109.

[79] Kenny, "Wittgenstein on the Nature of Philosophy", 16.

[80] Wittgenstein , *CV*, 17.

[81] "Wittgenstein thinks that the task of philosophy is not to enlighten the intellect, or not directly, but to work upon the will, to strengthen one to resist certain temptations." A Kenny, "Wittgenstein on the Nature of Philosophy", 14.

understanding. It can be as hard to refrain from using an expression as it is to hold back tears or hold in anger.[82]

And, finally, to the following famous passage from the *Investigations*:

We must do away with all explanation, and description alone must take its place. And this description gets its power of illumination - i.e., its purpose - from the philosophical problems. These are of course not empirical problems; they are solved, rather, by looking into the workings of our language and that in such a way as to make us recognise those workings: *in despite of* our urge to misunderstand them [*entegen einem Trieb, es missverstehen*].[83]

Later in the same paragraph, Wittgenstein says that philosophy "is a battle against the bewitchment of our intelligence by language." *Urge, feeling, will* - all are terms which can be easily assimilated to the Romantic dimension of Hegel's problem.[84] But they occupy a place in Wittgenstein

---

[82] Quoted in Kenny, "Wittgenstein on the nature of Philosophy", 16.

[83] Wittgenstein, *PI*, 109.

[84] There is a sense in which the later Wittgenstein's repudiation of philosophical realism recapitulates Hegel. In other words, there is a sense in which the rational dimension recapitulates Hegel. Bartley writes that "the movement from the early Wittgenstein to the work of the later Wittgenstein is a movement from a pre-critical, pre-Kantian position to a post-Kantian, Hegelian-style position *without benefit of Kant*." Bartley, *Wittgenstein*, 47. Yet it is more accurate to say that he held an Enlightenment-style position *without benefit of Kant*, which, in the transition from the earlier to the later philosophy, culminated in 'a Hegelian-style position'. For in collapsing saying to showing through collapsing realism to grammatical truth (truths which merely tell us the meaning and usage of words, e.g., 'This is "a physical object"'), the later philosophy did away with the gap between thought and reality characteristic of philosophical realism. If Marx's dialectical materialism turned Hegel's idealist dialectic on its head, Wittgenstein's dissolution of philosophical theses to grammatical propositions is a historical recapitulation of Hegel's 'Great Idea' of the identity of thought and being. In dissolving philosophical problems the later philosophy collapses the gap between thought and reality characteristic of realism just as Hegel's identity dissolves the total diastasis in Kant between noumenon and phenomenon. To be sure, the gap between self and world is not an example of the gap between phenomenon and noumenon in Kant's philosophy (Kant believes a proof is possible in the former but not in the latter case). Yet Wittgenstein's dissolution of realism in the problem of the external world proceeds along Hegelian lines, that is, *as if* he were advancing the claim of *Speculative Reason*. Wittgenstein, like Hegel, attempts to neutralise the gap between the one who knows and the thing that is known. As Peter Singer has written, Hegel "set himself an extraordinary task. Beginning with a powerful critique of knowledge taken by Kant (and not only Kant, but all philosophers who start off by assuming a division between one who knows

only insofar as they signify a negative force whose intellectual products, at least in philosophy, are nothing more than obstacles to the truth. It is in this way that Schopenhauer's pessimism - *the pessimistic inversion of the Romantic tendency*, to cite Taylor again - surfaces in Wittgenstein.

This 'unhappy' Romantic context is the context to which the later Wittgenstein resigned himself in his resolution of philosophical problems as described in Chapter 12. It was precisely the will which drove the philosophical sceptic, for example, in his act of doubt or criticism to separate what cannot be separated: the means of measurement from the object of measurement. The sceptic attempted to use the means of measurement to measure the very object of measurement from which the means itself originated. Or putting it another way: the sceptic attempted to measure a very distinctive object of measurement, namely, the object of measurement that constituted the possibility of  using the means of measurement itself in the first place! This is the error of traditional philosophy. And Wittgenstein employed a distinctive non-apologetic species of reason to reveal the error.

As was said in Chapter 12: 'justification comes to an end'; we 'run up against the limits of language.' Wittgenstein's *conceptual foundationalism* posits the necessity of an origin or means of measurement of truth and meaning; *hence, if any such origin or means is to measured at all, it can be measured only in terms of itself.* Once we see this - so Wittgenstein thinks - our philosophical perplexities will vanish: we will see rightly.  But the insight is only temporary, victory only temporary, because of the unceasing urge of the will on the philosophical mind to posit its own independent measure.

Can it really be argued that Wittgenstein belongs, with Barth, to what the latter called "the true age of Hegel"? Against this idea, it might be said that Wittgenstein did not share Barth's passion for history. As J P Stern put it:

> Wittgenstein wrote within a highly history-conscious culture, and in a massively politicised age. Yet the very few political reflections he confided to his letters and diaries are quirky  rather that illuminating, and compared to everything else he wrote, unremarkable. And what he says

---

and the thing that is known", (P Singer, *Hegel* [Oxford: Oxford University Press, 1983], 52), he reaches a point in the *Phenomenology* where "knowledge is no longer compelled to go beyond itself, where reality will no longer be an unknowable beyond, but instead mind will know reality directly and be at one with it. Now we can understand what all this meant: absolute knowledge is reached when mind realises that *what it seeks is itself.*" *Ibid*, 70. Thus, identity instated, the divide between thought and reality is eliminated. The philosophical problem is not so much solved as dissolved.

about history (again mainly from the diaries, and in the prefaces to some of his works) are little more than expressions of a heartfelt regret for the passing of more dignified and more *decent* ages.[85]

And Jacques Bouveresse writes:

Though in different places in his manuscripts, he expresses his antipathy to modern civilisation and his feeling of belonging to a world which is condemned to disappear, and had practically already disappeared, one would look in vain for some trace of that in his philosophical texts that he intended for publication.[86]

Yet one can say in reply that what little Wittgenstein did say, on how he thought he related to history, suggests that he assimilated his philosophy to the history of European ideas from the late Enlightenment to the era brought to an end by the death of Hegel. For instance, he writes:

I often wonder whether my cultural ideal is a new one, i.e. contemporary, or whether it derives from Schumann's time. It does at least strike me as continuing that ideal, though not in the way it was actually continued at the time. That is to say, the second half of the nineteenth century has been left out. This I ought to say has been a purely instinctive development and not the result of reflection.[87]

Although Wittgenstein did not say explicitly that a meaner age had ushered in the end of the great golden European past of Mozart, Goethe, Schiller and Beethoven, it is clear that this is what he thought. McGuinness observes that Wittgenstein was not obsessed with the thought that the culture which he himself represented was a thing of the past. He accepted it more simply - as the medium in which to form his understanding of life.[88] Wittgenstein, like Barth, felt compelled to acknowledge the distinction between the historicist and the historical, between the first half of the nineteenth century as it could or might have developed on the one hand and the way it in fact did on the other.[89] In other words, Wittgenstein would

---

[85] Stern, "Wittgenstein in Context", 153.
[86] J Bouveresse, "'The Darkness of this time': Wittgenstein and the Modern World", in A Phillips Griffiths, *Wittgenstein Centenary Essays* (Cambridge: Cambridge University Press, 1991), 12.
[87] Wittgenstein, *CV*, 2.
[88] B F McGuinness, *Wittgenstein: A Life. Young Ludwig, 1899-1921*, 33.
[89] Barth, like Wittgenstein, was more impressed by the culture of the first half of the nineteenth century than by the second. In all respects - philosophy, literature, music and

have been utterly sympathetic to Barth's call, cited above,[90] for our being "free for remembering forgotten things, resuming neglected things, facing the problems which have been suppressed, and in doing so honouring the truth." The cultural ideal Wittgenstein affirmed opposed the scientific positivism and materialism of the second half of the nineteenth century. Both the earlier and the later philosophy opposed the spirit of scientific positivism. Accordingly, for the reasons cited above, it could be argued that the later philosophy belongs to the earlier rather than the later nineteenth century (though this is not to say that this is not true of the *Tractatus* too). Philosophy and truth coincided, but the truth could only be shown, not said. It could not be said by means of language. This, as we have seen, is a central insight of both the early and later philosophies.

It also, as will be seen, coincides with his aesthetic ideal. In retrospect, the facets of the first half of the nineteenth century to which Wittgenstein warmed had more in common with the late eighteenth century than with the second half of the nineteenth. The first half is, in this sense, an epilogue to the story of the Enlightenment rather than a prologue to the later epoch. Juxtaposed to the challenge of the Romantic movement - dedicated to the cult of the subjective elements of individuality, genius and originality - its art appears to some as intransitively enclosed in a complacent aesthetic of artistic autonomy and perfection. Such art was charged at the time with being an enemy of progress, for refraining from serving the great progressive ideals of the time, principally German nationalism. This is why Hegel asserted that the "epoch of art" or *Kunstperiode* was drawing to a close and, henceforth, art was obliged to serve in the social and political spheres.[91] The apogee of the aesthetic criterion implicit in Wittgenstein's doctrine of showing and saying had been reached; henceforth it was in decline.

Philosophy too, genuine philosophy, could exist only insofar as it participated in this criterion. Otherwise, it was philosophy-as-science, and therefore non-philosophy. Whether intentional or otherwise, Wittgenstein's definition of philosophy pointed philosophy in the direction it had to take if

---

theology - the first half was the second's superior: "Can there be any question that the intellectual atmosphere of the first half of the century was distinguished from the second not only by a far greater sense of self-importance but also by a far higher standard, intrinsic value and dignity?" Barth, *PT*, 386.

[90] See this chapter, page 313.

[91] Richard Freidenthal writes: "With the deaths of the poets and writers of the Older generation of, Weiland, Schiller, Herder, Lavater and many more, Goethe is left as the only survivor of an age which, to the younger generation, has already passed into history." R Freidenthal, *Goethe* (London: Weidenfeld and Nicholson, 1965), 405.

Hume's metaphilosophical dilemma was to be resolved, and philosophy were to survive.

## 8. Wittgenstein and Barth:
## The Aesthetic as an Epiphenomenon of Non-Apologetic Reason

Far from aesthetics invading the sphere of reason, as post-modernism envisages,[92] the aesthetic dimension itself is an epiphenomenon of the sphere of the reason in both Barth and Wittgenstein. This is the final piece in the jigsaw assembling a picture of both as modernist Enlightenment thinkers attempting to resolve Hegel's 'great problem' of reason and feeling. That art is an epiphenomenon in this sense in both is no coincidence. For, in Schopenhauer it is art that releases one from the bondage to the will. Kant's intimation of an aesthetic totality that yet provokes limitlessness is inversely correlated to an infinitesimal (willing) subject, i.e., a non-willing subject. (Aesthetic experience is the only means to [the intellect's] release from bondage to the will.) In other words, Hegelian identity is invoked in the losing of oneself completely in the object when "it is as if the object alone were there, without anybody who perceives it."[93]

The principal Hegelian thesis animates Wittgenstein's showing and saying distinction in a *Schopenhauerisch* way. Transposed to the realm of art, saying collapses to that which shows, shows wholeness, *integritas*, indeed, all the things that satisfy the hunger of nostalgia. In other words, like theology, art is not necessarily sidelined, even condemned, to the realm of privatised subjective experience even though it appears to be above the social and political fray. Aesthetic autonomy has not yet dissolved into the realm of the self;[94] on the contrary it constitutes no less than the formal pattern of thought with which any such resolution of the problem central to Hegel's philosophy would have to accord. To the fore is the fact that aesthetic autonomy can and does reveal *itself* to the self but on its own terms and without giving itself away; rather it is the self that 'gives itself away'.

It is this that shows itself in Ludwig Uhland's poem "Grafs Eberhardts Weisshorn". The poem may be absolutely insulated from issues of progress, political, economic and social, but such must be the case if it is to satisfy its identity as art.[95] Indeed, it must satisfy the *sui generis* identity proper to art if

---

[92] Waugh, *Practising Postmodernism, Reading Modernism*, ch.1, esp. 3-7, 16-18.
[93] Schopenhauer, *Will*, vol. 1, 178.
[94] See Waugh, *Practising Postmodernism, Reading Modernism*, ch. 7.
[95] Written in the Goethean lyrical tradition, this poem is a most striking example of the Goethean tradition of self-enclosed *sui generis* artistic autonomy. See A Closs, *The Genius of the German Lyric: an historical survey of its formal and metaphysical values*

it is to elucidate by way of analogy Wittgenstein's metaphilosophical 'thesis' of the nature and identity of *sui generis* philosophical truth. (However, there is no simple identity: philosophy is not art, nor art philosophy; rather, art or the aesthetic is a parable, exemplifying by analogy, the *sui generis* nature of philosophy separate from all other disciplines.) In what is the single most extensive written remark Wittgenstein made on a work of art, he enthused:

> The poem by Uhland is really magnificent. And this is how it is: if only you do not try to utter what is unutterable then nothing gets lost. But the unutterable will be - unutterably - contained in what has been uttered.[96]

Wittgenstein's reaction testifies that he perceived the distinction between showing and saying - the cardinal doctrine of the *Tractatus* - could be made manifest in art, in this case in a poem, if the art adhered to certain principles of form and content. Just as in the *Tractatus*, where propositions show their sense but cannot say what this sense is, and, just as in the *Tractatus* where propositions cannot say what it is they have in common with reality to be able to represent it, so the distinction carries over into the artistic realm.[97] There is no doubt that the distinction between showing and saying, as embodied in art, became, and remained, for him the criterion for great and profound art. A remark he made in 1946 corroborates this view:

---

(London: Cresset Press, 1962), 232ff. It has often been observed just how much Wittgenstein's aesthetic sense is a classical measured one, one that extols the virtues of a perfect fit between what is said and what is felt, between form and content. See for example P Engelmann, *Letters from Wittgenstein*, (Oxford: Basil Blackwell, 1967), 86. It is submitted that Wittgenstein's positive orientation towards this type of art is guided by the principle that also guided his philosophy: showing and saying.

[96] Letter dated 9 April 1917. Engelmann, *Letters*, 7.

[97] Thus Engelmann, who in fact sent Uhland's poem to Wittgenstein, comments: "The positive achievement of Wittgenstein which has so far met with complete incomprehension, is his pointing to what is manifest in a proposition. And what is manifest in it, a proposition cannot state explicitly. The poet's sentences, for instance, achieve their effect not through what they say but through what is manifest in them and the same holds for music, which also says nothing. [...] It seems to me indeed that his discovery of what a proposition cannot make explicit because it is manifest in it - in my view the essential core of the *Tractatus* although only adumbrated in the book - has found a lasting expression in this letter." *Ibid*, 84-85. McGuinness notes that in this poem Wittgenstein's feeling for literature is wedded to one of the central ideas of his philosophical work - what is shown by a proposition cannot also be stated explicitly. McGuinness, *Wittgenstein*, 251.

An observation in a poem is overstated if the intellectual points  are nakedly exposed, not clothed from the heart.[98]

This also explains Wittgenstein's remark to Norman Malcolm:

When Tolstoy just tells a story he impresses me infinitely more than when he addresses the reader. When he turns his back to the reader then he seems to me most impressive .... It seems to me that his philosophy is most true when it is latent in the story.[99]

Art which preached - didactic art, art for propagandistic purposes, etc. - did not satisfy this criterion. It sought to highlight what it was it was about: it spoke about itself, if you like - something  ruled out by both Wittgenstein's early and later philosophy. Great and profound art, as measured by this criterion, did not preach, did not overstep its limits. It did not violate its own autonomy as art and become something else, something that threatened this identity: it did not become, e.g., an intellectual tract or a piece of overt propaganda. When Tolstoy does not turn his back on the reader he produces infinitely inferior art. This is because by not turning his back he upsets the balance between aesthetic object and subject - the human subject - in the direction of the latter. He compromises the integrity, autonomy, and unique identity of the aesthetic object, sending it out from behind its own lines, so to speak, from behind the boundaries circumscribing its autonomy as art. The aesthetic object thus comes to the nonaesthetic  realm to which we as human subject belong. It comes to us, we do not come to it. Art has become non-art or at least corrupted with elements of non-art.

This is of course good Schopenhauerian philosophy, remembering what Schopenhauer says about the effect of art. One as it were 'disappears' into it:

by ... losing oneself completely in the object [the aesthetic object] i.e., forgetting precisely one's individual ego, one's will, and remaining only as pure subject, as clear mirror of the object; so it is as if the object alone were there, without anybody who perceives it. The subject is no longer an individual, but rather: pure, will-less, painless, timeless subject of knowledge.[100]

---

[98] Wittgenstein, *CV*, 54.

[99] N Malcolm, *Ludwig Wittgenstein: a Memoir*, 2nd edition, (Oxford: Oxford University Press, 1984), 43.

[100] Schopenhauer, *Will*, vol. 1, 178.

Wittgenstein's criterion of great and profound art uncannily turns out to have the same consequences as in Schopenhauer's philosophy. Aside from the metaphysical implications of Schopenhauer's description of what happens when we contemplate art, there is the same balance between aesthetic object and human subject, wholeness (totality) and non-wholeness[101] - in the direction of the aesthetic object - that one finds in Wittgenstein.

Further, Wittgenstein identified art as the beautiful and the beautiful as that which makes one happy:

Is it the essence of the artistic way of looking at things that it looks at the world with a happy eye?

Life is serious, art is gay (Schiller)

For there is certainly something in the idea that the end of art is the beautiful.

And the beautiful is what makes one happy.[102]

This is an eminently Schopenhauerian sentiment. Happiness converges with peace and releases us from the strivings of the will:

the joy of contemplation ... consists in the fact that we are freed from the misery of *willing*. We are pure subject of knowledge and so celebrate a holiday from the penal labour of willing ....[103]

In Wittgenstein too there is a moment of peace. The aesthetic experience as a turning toward the aesthetic object on the terms of the latter's own reality is also what makes one happy. A moment of peace then is also a moment of tranquillity, of contentment, of happiness, of release and freedom from the will.

---

[101] Engelmann perceives the importance of the totality and wholeness of Uhland's poem: "... I was deeply moved. Something in the poem struck me as completely new: taken singly, no line had ... the beauty and conspicuous depth of a verse, say of ... the unromantic verbal magic of a Moerike (*'Gelassen steig die nacht an's Land'* - 'With measured step night strode ashore'). Each one of Uhland's verses was simple - not ingenuous, but tersely informative ('On Holy errand steered to Palestina's strand') - so that none of them taken by itself, would cause delight. But the poem as a whole gives in 28 lines the picture of a life. [...] Wittgenstein's letter showed to me to my delight that he shared my reaction. Naturally he grasped the matter more deeply than I had done, and I attach immense significance to the way in which he formulated his impression." Engelmann, *Letters*, 84.

[102] Wittgenstein, *NB*, 86.

[103] Schopenhauer, *Will*, 129.

For Wittgenstein, great art and solutions to philosophical problems possess the following property in common: no points of comparison are available other than them themselves. The criterion of showing that Wittgenstein believes intrinsic to great art is counterposed to the concept of saying, which latter is motivated by the will. The tension between showing and saying coincides with the tension between Wittgenstein's later philosophy and traditional philosophy - between non-apologetic reason and apologetic reason. The objective of non-apologetic reason is, precisely, to demonstrate that the claim of apologetic reason is an illusion. And since it is the will which imposes on us the claim of apologetic reason and, in particular, the belief that one has to satisfy apologetic reason, it follows that non-apologetic reason releases us from the strivings of the will. But the only object that can release one from the will-to-apologetic (or will-to-saying or will-to-description) is one that embodies the showing and saying distinction (embodies showing but not saying). Non-apologetic reason requires that its 'object' of reason (viz. the concept of criterion, norm or source) embodies the property of showing what cannot be said (described). (Apologetic reason assumes that it possesses a point of comparison independently of the object itself.)

Being released from the will is to be released from feeling (in particular, the driving feeling that philosophical problems have to be resolved by description). One's understanding is freed from the clutches of the will. Understanding is precisely *understanding what cannot be described, understanding what is shown.*[104] (Accordingly, philosophical writing had to

---

[104] Central to Wittgenstein's concept of understanding - *Verstandniss* - is the concept of an *Übersicht*. An *Übersicht* produces understanding. Wittgenstein, *PI*, § 122. It embodies a clear view of the use of our words. *Ibid*, § 122. It is complete clarity. *Ibid*, § 133. G E M Anscombe's English translation of the original German *übersichtlichen Darstellung* is "perspicuous representation". The stem of *übersichtlichen* is *Übersicht*. *Übersicht* means overview or survey. Both P M S Hacker and G P Baker and P M S Hacker prefer what appears to be an amalgam of these two words: surview and its related terms 'to survey', 'surveyable', etc. G P Baker and P M S Hacker, *An Analytical Commentary on Wittgenstein's "Philosophical Investigations"*, vol 1, (Oxford: Basil Blackwell, 1980), 531-2. But P M S Hacker acknowledges there has been a variety of translations: "The terms *Übersicht, Übersichtlichkeit*, and the related verb *übersehen* have given Wittgenstein's translators much trouble. They have chosen to translate it non-systematically in conformity with the demands of English style, thereby partially obscuring the significance and pervasiveness of the concept in Wittgenstein's work, e.g., "command a clear view" (*übersehen PI* §122); "perspicuous representation" (*übersichtlichen Darstellung, PI*, § 122); "synoptic account" (*übersichtlichen Darstellung, Z*, § 273); "Survey" (*Übersicht, Z*, § 273); "synoptic view" (*Übersichtlichenkeit, Z*, § 464; "perspicuity" (*übersichtlichenkeit, RFM*, 95); "capable of being taken in" (*übersehbar, RFM*, 170)." P M S Hacker, *Insight and Illusion*, 2nd edition, 151, #6. Baker and Hacker had earlier reached the same conclusion. Baker and

be written in the form of poetic composition precisely because it attempts to convey what cannot be said.)[105] Since 'showing but not saying' is, for Wittgenstein, an aesthetic property, *understanding that something can only be shown but not said* brings its wake its own aesthetic experience. It is not the cause of the temporary quiescence of the will, as in Schopenhauer (the aesthetic property *per se* does not release one from the will). But insofar as it is an aesthetic property ultimately governed by the reason intrinsic to the 'philosophical object',[106] the aesthetic experience will be one of 'pure' feeling, feeling appropriate or proper to its object (feeling refined by reason).[107] There is, in Wittgenstein, an aesthetic of philosophical knowledge precisely because the 'philosophical object' itself possesses the property essential to great and profound art. In a comment he wrote down in 1937 he spoke of the enlightenment his work brings to the understanding:

the light work sheds is a beautiful light, which however, only shines with real beauty [*wirklich schön*] if it is illuminated by yet another light.[108]

---

Hacker, *An Analytical Commentary on Wittgenstein's "Philosophical Investigations"*, vol 1, 531. Were it not for a variety of non-systematic or unrelated translations giving the impression of not necessarily related concepts, we would have seen that Wittgenstein means the same thing at all these points in his work where he uses *Übersicht* or the related terms *Übersichtlichkeit* and *übersehen*. A. Kenny has written: "Translators of Wittgenstein have been criticised for failing to adopt a uniform translation of the word *übersehen* and its derivatives, given the importance of the notion of *übersichtlichen Darstellung* in Wittgenstein's later conception of philosophy." A Kenny, 'Translator's Note to *Philosophical Grammar*', 1973, 491.

[105] In 1933-4 Wittgenstein wrote: "I think I summed up my attitude to philosophy when I said: philosophy ought to be written as *poetic* composition." Wittgenstein, *Ibid*, 24. But he added: "... I cannot quite do what I would like to be able to do." *Ibid*, 24. What did Wittgenstein mean? That he had failed to write poetic composition when writing philosophy? That he had, for example, failed to imbue his philosophical writing with the qualities he discerned in Uhland's poem? But he only says "he cannot *quite* [my italics] do what he would like to be able to do" (as opposed to saying he cannot do what he would like to be able to do). But why did he think that the point he wanted to convey should be conveyed in the form of poetic composition? Because only poetic composition had at its disposal the rhetorical armoury capable of conveying a point which could not be directly stated, which could only be insinuated.

[106] Even in art, the realm of feeling, of emotion, has its limits drawn by the rational, by the understanding. Wittgenstein's response to Uhland's poem is precisely that it possesses feeling tempered by the understanding, by intellect, by reason.

[107] I have in mind Wittgenstein's comment in *Culture and Value*: "The greater purity of objects which don't affect the senses, numbers for instance." Wittgenstein, *CV*, 26.

[108] *Ibid*, 26.

It is unclear, at least to me, what he means by an enlightenment that "shines with real beauty only if it is illuminated by yet another light."[109] But what might have been at work in Wittgenstein's mind was the idea that one sees the beauty of the enlightenment only if one perceives the aesthetic property intrinsic to the showing and saying distinction. In this sense, one only sees the beauty of the 'philosophical object' if one perceives the showing and saying distinction as the aesthetic property it is. In this sense the aesthetic sense is an epiphenomenon of reason. It does not participate in the argument itself (made by non-apologetic reason), but it is a consequence of it.

What of Barth in the above respect? If one looks at the nature of Barth's comments on Mozart, Bach and Beethoven, one sees at once that he measured great art, in this case music, by the same set of criteria. Great music did not preach nor was it personal confession; it was itself, *sui generis*, just as authentic theology was.[110] That said, does he speak of an aesthetic sense which, though not part of the argument itself, is a phenomenological consequence of it, and, in this sense, an epiphenomenon? Though, by comparison, Barth wrote very little on how aesthetics related to theology, his most interesting comments do focus on the aesthetic dimension as an epiphenomenon - an epiphenomenon of the imparting of theological knowledge. It is in this sense that theological knowledge has a phenomenological aesthetic presence. Barth at no time allows the realm of the aesthetic to invade the cognitive. In *CD* II/1 Barth asserts that:

---

[109] There is another comment in *Culture and Value* (written 11 years later, in 1948) in which Wittgenstein speaks of a "light shining on his thoughts from behind." But is not clear that he is thinking specifically of his philosophical thinking. Indeed, since the comment speaks of thoughts that occur in the context of a poetic mood, the implication is that the thoughts are a function of the mood rather than the other way round. Given this, it may be that the thoughts are of a more purely artistic nature, in other words, not philosophical in the sense in which his thoughts in *Philosophical Investigations* are: "In a letter (to Goethe I think) Schiller speaks of a "poetic mood". I think I know what he means, I believe I am familiar with it myself. It is a mood of receptivity to nature in which one's thoughts seem as vivid as nature itself. It is strange that Schiller did not produce anything better (or so it seems to me) and so I am not entirely convinced that what *I* produce in such a mood is really worth anything. It may be that what gives my thoughts their lustre on these occasions is a light shining on them from behind. That they do not *themselves* glow. *Ibid*, 66. The phrase, "vivid as nature", undoubtedly pays homage to Goethe's view of nature as an absolute criterion of beauty.

[110] For the case that Barth's comments on Mozart, Bach, and Beethoven stand in point-to-point similarity with Wittgenstein on, for example, Uhland. I refer you to Chapter 3, note 33.

reflection and discussion of the aesthetics of theology can hardly be counted a legitimate and certainly not necessary task of theology.[111]

But he augments this seeming restriction with the following thought:

Yet it must not be forgotten that there is actually something here which must be perceived rather than discussed and that the theologian has good cause for repentance if he has not perceived it.[112]

Few would disagree with Jüngel's comment that "the architecture of the *Church Dogmatics* demonstrates that Barth knew how to put what Anselm called the beauty of theology into practice."[113] The classical symmetry of the loci structure is preserved down beyond the division of dogmatics into its various doctrines, within each individual locus.[114] Yet it is not this particular aesthetic property that Barth speaks of when he speaks of an *aesthetic of theological knowledge*. This aesthetic Barth perceived as intrinsic to the course and practice of the ratiocinative element of theology. Though the aesthetic sense does not participate in the theological argument itself, it is, Barth thinks, a consequence of it. In *Anselm: Fides Quaerens Intellectum* Barth writes:

It ought to be noticed first of all that this is not the only result of *intelligere* that all the way through Anselm recognises and has before him. As *intelligere* is achieved, it issues - in joy. The dominating factor in Anselm's mind is that even the Church Fathers wrote about it in order to give the faithful joy in believing by a demonstration of the *ratio* of their faith. This reason which the *intelligere* seeks and finds, possesses in itself not only *utilitas* (by which Anselm may have been thinking of a polemical proof) but also *pulchritudo*. It is *speciosa super intellectus hominum*.[115]

According to Barth, Anselm's proof not only possesses 'Enlightenment' *utilitas*; the ensuing joy "possesses in itself ... *pulchritudo*" - beauty. It is "*speciosa super intellectus hominum*." It is clear that Barth envisages the phenomenological presence of the aesthetic as a secondary phenomenon in the wake of theological knowledge (in *CD* II/1, Barth says that the "insight" that there is such an aesthetic "depends too much on the presence of the

[111] Barth, *CD* II/1, 657.
[112] *Ibid*, 657.
[113] Jüngel, *Karl Barth: a Theological Legacy*, 47.
[114] See Jungel's diagram of the symmetry of the doctrine of Reconciliation, *Ibid*, 48-49.
[115] Barth, *FQI*, 15.

necessary feeling to allow of theoretical development").[116] Barth goes on in *FQI*:

> Is it mere coincidence that in a work like *Cur Deus Homo*, which on its own admission, is so set on proving, its chief end should be given as, first, this *delectari*, and secondly, the polemical obligation of *1 Peter 3.15*? It is evident here that a strong foundation is combined with a genial inclination to please, and this fact may well remind us that early Scholasticism was contemporary with the heyday of the Romanesque style of cathedral art. And it might well be a first test of our understanding of Anselm to ask ourselves whether we are capable of appreciating that the despair with which, as he says in the prologue of the *Proslogion*, he sought that *unum argumentum*, could not be taken less seriously, because in addition to the fighting spirit obviously indispensable to one engaged in theological work, he still had some freedom left to admit other spirits, one of them clearly being the aesthetics of theological knowledge. And indeed, why not? Why not just that? At least we have to take this second aim of Anselm's *intelligere* very seriously and we cannot evade the prior question - what exactly does 'to prove' mean, if it is the result of the same action which may also lead straight to *delectatio*?[117]

The fact that, for Barth, proving in Anselm's sense leads to *delectatio* implies that Anselm's sense of *probare* is to be understood not in an apologetic sense - in the traditional 'ontological' sense - but in a non-apologetic sense. In other words, the presence of *delectatio* as a secondary aim is testimony to the validity of Barth's own non-apologetic interpretation of Anselm. If (corrupt) will is the motivating force behind apologetic, it is very likely that, as in Wittgenstein, the only object that can release one from the will-to-apologetic (or will-to-saying or will-to-description) is one that embodies the showing and saying distinction (embodies showing but not saying). Were this not the case, apologetic, saying, and description would be appropriate representations of the reality in question. However, according to Barth, such representations are distortions of the reality in question since God as 'object' (subject as object) does embody the showing and saying distinction.

What is certain is the conclusion that Barth thought of the aesthetic sense as a epiphenomenon of reason. Why not just an aesthetics of theological knowledge? Jüngel remarks that Barth could make the point of his theology in two words: "Ah, yes!": "Everything depends on, and everything

---

[116] Barth, *CD* II/1, 657.
[117] *Ibid*, 15-16.

must return to, this small sigh in which we say to God 'Ah, yes!'."[118] "Everything depends upon", "everything must return to": 'In the end' we might say; the last word is 'Ah, yes!' - a small sigh - the last word of Barth's theology when all argument is past. But did he think that the 'Ah, yes!' ought to be said in the voice of a man who, having had mislaid his razor prior to his morning shave, has now happened upon it? Did he, in other words, think that the 'Ah, yes!' was delivered with the inflection of man making a discovery? Or was it rather, simultaneously, the quiet voice of acknowledgement coinciding with enlightenment, a 'small sigh' - 'Ah, yes!'? Is there not also in this latter reflection a hint of where an aesthetic enters into Barth's theology, not as part of Barth's theological arguments, but at the end, converging with the moment of understanding?

Schiller had sought the unity between thought and will in beauty. Barth and Wittgenstein sought humanity's release from the strivings of the will in reason, a reason not without the accompanying emotional sense that one had, indeed, been released.

## Concluding Remarks

This chapter has attempted to show how Barth and Wittgenstein can be (intellectually and culturally) assimilated to the epoch of history continuing on from the Enlightenment, the age of Hegel. The argument that this is so adds further credence to the view that the Enlightenment provides the point of departure for both thinkers. *Contra* post-modern proposals, Barth and Wittgenstein can be understood within the context of the age of Hegel and its own attempt to resolve the conflict between two ostensibly opposing historic aspirations. One is represented in the moral autonomy and critical attitude of the Enlightenment epitomised by Kant's declaration *Sapere Aude!* The other is represented by the Romantic impulse and desire for integration with the Infinite, with God. Barth and Wittgenstein, like Hegel before them, attempt to maintain and hold the two forces together, to acknowledge the claims of both in their respective theology and philosophy. Will or 'desire' is perceived by both thinkers as a kind of bondage of the intellect, preventing the intellect from acknowledging the truth. It is arguable that, in both, being released from the will coincides with a feeling or sense that can be described as aesthetic in nature.

---

[118] Quoted in Jüngel, *Barth's Theological Legacy*, 52.

# Chapter 14
# Epilogue

1920 was, as Busch tells us in his biography of Barth, "the year in which Barth subjected the view he had presented in *Romans* I to new criticism, and rethought it after varied and intensive study."[1] Above all, it was, as we know, Overbeck's critique of theology which precipitated rewriting Barth's *Romans* I. In the midst of this study, Busch also tells us, Barth "found the painter Matthias Grünewald illuminating."[2] The extent of the illumination can be measured from the fact that for the rest of his life Barth worked with a copy of Grünewald's painting of the crucifixion - the centre-piece of the famous Isenheim Altar-piece - hanging above his desk.

Barth expressed the following famous thought on the figure of John the Baptist in a lecture he presented in April 1920 entitled "Biblical Questions, Insights and Vistas":

> We think of John the Baptist in Grünewald's crucifixion with his hand pointing in an almost impossible way. It is this hand which is in evidence in the Bible.[3]

Yet it is clear that it is Christ on the cross and not John the Baptist who is the central presence in the painting. Grünewald's painting of the crucifixion conveys with utmost realism the suffering of Christ on the cross. As Kenneth Clark put it in his book *The Nude*:

> ... Grünewald's Isenheim altar-piece where the scars and blood-stains made familiar in popular wood-cuts or *biblia pauperum* are overwhelmingly magnified. This is the most corporeal of all Crucifixions, in which every line contributes to the image of an organism in torment.

---

[1] Busch, *Barth*, 114.
[2] *Ibid*, 144.
[3] Barth, "Biblical Questions, Insights and Vistas", 65.

Never before or since have the sufferings of Christ been made so real to us.[4]

The dimensions of every detail of his body on the cross are "overwhelmingly magnified" according to Clark. This is realism and yet it is not realism. E H Gombrich discerns just such a paradox at the centre of the painting:

> In this picture in which reality seems to be depicted in all its unmitigated horror, there is one real and fantastic trait: the figures differ greatly in size. We only have to compare the size of the hands of Mary Magdalene under the cross with those of Christ to become fully aware of the astonishing difference in their dimensions.[5]

The painter known as Grünewald (real name now thought to be Mathis Gothardt-Nithardt) lived in the sixteenth century, a century after the Italian Renaissance artist and architect Brunellesco who may still be reckoned the inventor (or discoverer) of mathematical perspective. Yet Grünewald's painting, as Gombrich will tell us, is painted without utilising this theory of mathematical perspective (a theory he would have known). In fact, like the Greeks before him who understood foreshortening, and the Hellenistic painters who were skilled in creating the illusion of depth but did not know the mathematical laws of perspective, Grünewald draws near or important things large and distant things small; but unlike them, he draws out of proportion *fully aware of mathematical perspective*. The rationale behind this conscious artistic decision is the text behind John the Baptist's pointing hand. It is taken from John 3.3 and says: "He must increase, while I must decrease." Grünewald's decision to represent the figure of Jesus as disproportionately larger than John the Baptist has a strictly theological rationale.

Though God's grace grants the figure of John the Baptist a place within the theological realm, the presence of the fantastic realism intimates there is no logical space for him. As Barth himself put it:

> Near the steadily pointing figure of his John are the words, *Illum oportet crescere, me autem minui*. The prophet, the man of God, the seer and hearer, ceases to be, as that to which he unwaveringly points begins to be.[6]

---

[4] K Clark, *The Nude: a Study of Ideal Art* (London: Murray, 1956), 226.
[5] E H Gombrich, *Art and Illusion: a Study in the Psychology of Pictorial Representation* (London: Pantheon Books, 1960), 104.
[6] Barth, "Biblical Questions, Insights and Vistas", 75.

There is no possibility of a 'reference to the fulfilment of revelation; rather only of the fulfilment itself, allowing the actuality speak for itself'. Accordingly, the human element is eliminated from the picture, leaving only God in Christ. John "points in an almost impossible way" at a 'measure of faith' whose only measure is it itself. He has no means of measurement of *what it is* God's self-revelation is, other than God's self-revelation itself. The fact that there is no such means of measurement other than the object of measurement itself is testimony to the Godness of God. Man must set himself aside and rely utterly on God revealing Himself: "He must increase, while I must decrease." Saying collapses to showing; both *sui generis* historical truth and the resolution of the metatheological dilemma are preserved.

"Christ must increase, while I must decrease." On his deathbed Wittgenstein uttered the words, "Tell them I had a wonderful life!" To say that Wittgenstein said this in the 'sure and certain hope of being with Christ' is too fanciful, not to say pretentious. Yet Wittgenstein was a man who lived religiously rather than morally; and the pride of Lucifer notwithstanding he would, I think, have been more than prepared to give up the ghost to 'be in the presence of the Lord.'

"Christ must increase, while I must decrease." Barth's time came in the middle of the night. His wife found him the next morning, as if asleep, his hands clasped from his evening prayers. Is it too fanciful to imagine that the Mozart playing in the background, with which she had wanted to wake him, was the second movement, the 'Prayer for Peace' from Mozart's *Exaltate Jubilate*?

# Select Bibliography

## 1. Primary Literature

### a. Works by Barth

#### i. Book and Book-length lecture series

Barth, Karl, *Church Dogmatics*, edited by G W Bromiley and T F Torrance, (Edinburgh: T&T Clark, 1936-1969).

-, *Credo*, translated by J S McNab, (London: Hodder and Stoughton, 1936).

-, *Dogmatics in Outline*, translated by G T Thomson, (London: SCM Press, 1949).

-, *Evangelical Theology: an introduction*, translated by G Foley, (London: SCM Press, 1963).

-, *Kirchliche Dogmatik*, vols I-IV, (Zurich: Evangelischer Verlag A G Zollikon, 1932 *et seq*).

-, *Fides Quaerens Intellectum: Anselms Beweis der Existenz Gottes im Zusammenhang seines theologischen Programms*, edited by E Jüngel and I U Dalferth, (Zurich: Theologischer Verlag Zurich, 1981).

-, *Anselm: Fides Quaerens Intellectum. Anselm's Proof of the Existence of God in the Context of his Theological Scheme* (London, 1960; reprinted Pittsburgh: The Pickwick Press, 1975).

-, *Protestant Theology in the Nineteenth Century. Its Background and History*, translated by B Cozen and J Bowden, (London: SCM Press, 1972).

-, *Der Römerbrief* (Munich: Chr Kaiser Verlag, 1922).

-, *Romans 1922*, translated by E Hoskyns, (London: Oxford University Press, 1933).

-, *The Faith of the Church: A Commentary on the Apostles' Creed According to Calvin*, edited by Jean-Louis Leuba, translated by Gabriel Vahanian, (New York: Meridian, 1958).

-, *The Heidelberg Catechism for Today*, translated by Shirley Guthrie, (London: The Epworth Press, 1964).

-, *The Göttingen Dogmatics: Instruction in the Christian Religion*, vol 1, edited by H Reiffen, translated by G W Bromiley, (Grand Rapids: Eerdmans, 1991).

-, *The Resurrection of the Dead*, translated by H J Stenning (London: Hodder and Stoughton, 1933).

-, *The Theology of Friedrich Schleiermacher. Lectures at Gottingen, Winter Semester of 1923/4*, edited by D Ritschl, translated by G W Bromiley, (Edinburgh: T & T Clark, 1982).

## ii Shorter Articles, Essays and Addresses

-, "Biblical Questions, Insights and Vistas", *The Word of God and the Word of Man*, translated by D Horton, (New York: Harper, 1957), 51-96.

-, "Biblische Fragen, Einsichten und Ausblicke" [Lecture delivered at the 24th Aarau Student Conference, April 17, 1920], *Das Wort Gottes und die Theologie* (Munich: Chr Kaiser Verlag, 1924), 70-98.

-, "Das Wort Gottes als Aufgabe der Theologie" [Lecture delivered on October 3, 1922], *Das Wort Gottes und die Theologie* (Munich: Chr Kaiser Verlag, 1924), 156-178.

-, "Die neue Welt in der Bible" [Lecture delivered on February 6, 1917], *Das Wort Gottes und die Theologie* (Munich: Chr Kaiser Verlag, 1924), 18-32.

-, "Evangelical Theology in the 19th Century", *Scottish Journal of Theology Occasional Papers*, No 8, translated by J S McNab, (Edinburgh: Oliver and Boyd, 1959), 53-74.

-, "Introductory Essay", translated by J Luther Adams, in L Feuerbach, *The Essence of Christianity* (New York: Harper Torchbooks, 1957), x-xxxii.

-, "No!", in Brunner and Barth, *Natural Theology*, translated by Peter Fraenkel, introduction by John Baillie, (London: 1946).

-, "Rudolf Bultmann, An Attempt to Understand Him", in H-W Bartsch (ed), *Kerygma and Myth: A Theological Debate*, translated by Reginald Fuller, (London: SPCK, 1972), 83-132.

-, "The Christian's Place in Society", *The Word of God and the Word of Man*, [Lecture delivered September 25, 1919], translated by D Horton, (New York: Harper, 1957), 272-327.

-, "The Christian Understanding of Revelation", *Against the Stream. Shorter Post-War Writings, 1946-52*, edited by R G Smith, (London: SCM press, 1954).

-, *The Germans and Ourselves*, translated by R G Smith, (London: Nisbet and Co.), 1945.

-, "The Humanity of God", *Scottish Journal of Theology Occasional Papers No. 8*, 29-52.

-, "The Need of Christian Preaching", *The Word of God and the Word of Man*, translated by Douglas Horton, (New York: Harper, 1957), .

-, "The Strange New World Within the Bible", *The Word of God and the Word of Man*, translated by Douglas Horton, (New York: Harper, 1957), 28-50.

-, "The Word of God and the Task of the Ministry", *The Word of God and the Word of Man*, translated by Douglas Horton, (New York: Harper, 1957), .

-, "Unsettled Questions in Theology Today", *Theology and Church*, with an introduction by T F Torrance, translated by L Pettibone Smith, (London: SCM Press Ltd, 1962), 55-73.

-, "Wolfgang Amadeus Mozart", translated by W M Mosse, in W Leibrecht (ed), *Religion and Culture: Essays in Honour of Paul Tillich* (London: SCM Press, 1959), 61-78.

## iii. Autobiographical material

-, *How I Changed My Mind*, translated by M E Bratcher, (Edinburgh: Saint Andrew Press, 1969).

### iv. Collected Letters

-, *Letters 1961-1968*, translated by G W Bromiley, (Edinburgh: T & T Clark, 1981). Jaspert, Bernd (ed), *Karl Barth-Rudolf Bultmann: Letters 1922-1966*, translated and edited by G W Bromiley, (Edinburgh: T & T Clark, 1982).

### v. Works by Karl Barth and Eduard Thurneysen

Barth, Karl and Eduard Thurneysen, *Revolutionary Theology in the Making*, translated by J D Smart, (Richmond, Virginia: John Knox Press, 1964).

### b. Works by Wittgenstein

### i Books

-, *Blue and Brown Books. Preliminary Studies for the 'Philosophical Investigations'* (Oxford: Basil Blackwell, 1978).
-, *Culture and Value*, edited by G H von Wright in collaboration with H Nyman, (Oxford: Basil Blackwell, 1980).
-, *Lectures and Conversations of Aesthetics, Psychology and Religious Belief*, edited by C Barrett, (Oxford: Basil Blackwell, 1966).
-, *Notebooks 1914-1916*, edited by G H von Wright and G E M Anscombe, translated by G E M Anscombe, (Oxford: Basil Blackwell, 1961).
-, *On Certainty*, edited by G E M Anscombe and G H von Wright, translated by Denis Paul and G E M Anscombe, (Oxford: Basil Blackwell, 1969).
-, *Philosophical Grammar*, edited by R Rhees and translated by A Kenny, (Oxford: Blackwell, 1974).
-, *Philosophical Investigations*, edited by G E M Anscombe, (Oxford: Basil Blackwell, 1953).
-, *Philosophical Remarks*, edited by R Rhees, translated by R Hargreaves and R White, (Oxford: Basil Blackwell, 1975).
-, *Remarks on Frazer's Golden Bough*, ed. R. Rhees (London: Brynmill, 1979).
-, *Tractatus Logico-Philosphicus*, translated by D F Pears and B F McGuinness, (London: Routledge and Kegan Paul, 1961).
-, *Zettel*, edited by G E M Anscombe and G H Von Wright, (Oxford: Basil Blackwell, 1981).

### ii. Collected Letters

-, *Letters to Russell, Keynes and Moore*, edited with an introduction by G H von Wright, (Oxford: Basil Blackwell, 1974).

## 2. Secondary Literature

### a. Barth

von Balthasar, Hans Urs, *The Theology of Karl Barth*, translated by J Drury, (New York: Holt, Rinehart and Winston, Inc, 1971).

Beintker, Michael, Die Dialectik in der 'dialektischen Theologie' Karl Barths (Munich: Chr Kaiser Verlag, 1987).

Blandshard, Brand, "Critical Reflections on Karl Barth", in J Hick, (ed), *Faith and the Philosophers* (London: MacMillan, 1964), 159-200.

Bowden, John, *Karl Barth: Theologian* (London: SCM Press, 1983).

Bromiley Geoffrey W, *An Introduction to the Theology of Karl Barth* (Grand Rapids: Eerdmans, 1979).

Busch, Eberhard, "God is God: The Meaning of a Controversial Formula and the Fundamental Problem of Speaking About God", *The Princeton Seminary Bulletin*, 7, (1986), 101-113.

-, *His Life From Letters and Autobiographical Texts*, translated by J Bowden, (London: SCM Press, 1976).

Dalferth, Ingolf, "Karl Barth's Eschatological Realism", in S Sykes (ed), *Karl Barth: Centenary Essays* (Cambridge: Cambridge University Press, 1989), 14-45.

Fergusson, David, Review Article, *The Scottish Journal of Theology* 42 (1989), 454-455.

Fisher, Simon, Revelatory Positivism? Barth's Earliest Theology and the Marburg School (Oxford: Oxford University Press,1988).

Foley, Grover, "The Catholic Critics of Karl Barth." *Scottish Journal of Theology*, 14, (1961), 136-155.

David Ford, *Biblical Narrative and the Theological Method of Karl Barth* Studies on the Intercultural History of Christianity 27, (Frankfurt am Main and Bern: Verlag Peter Lang, 1981).

-, "The Interpretation of the Bible", in S Sykes (ed), *Karl Barth: Studies of His Theological Method* (Oxford: Oxford University Press, 1979), 55-87.

Frei, Hans, "An After-Word: Eberhard Busch's biography of Karl Barth", in H Martin Rumscheidt (ed), *Karl Barth in Review* (Pittsburgh: Pickwick Press, 1981), 95-116.

-, "Niebuhr's Theological Background" in P Ramsey (ed), *Faith and Ethics* (New York: Harper, 1957), 9-64.

Gill, Theodore A, "Barth and Mozart", *Theology Today*, vol XLIII, No 3, (1986), 403-411.

Godsey, John D, *Karl Barth's Table Talk* (Edinburgh: Oliver and Boyd, 1963).

Gunton, Colin E, *Becoming and Being: The Doctrine of God in Charles Hartshorne and Karl Barth* (Oxford: Oxford University Press, 1978).

-, "Article Review. David Ford: Barth and God's Story", *Scottish Journal of Theology*, vol 37, (1984), 375-380

Hendry, George S, "The Transcendental Method in the Theology of karl Barth", *The Scottish Journal of Theology*, (1984), 213-227.

Hunsinger, George, "Beyond Literalism and Expressivism: Karl Barth's Hermeneutical Realism", *Modern Theology* 3: 3, (1987), 209-223.

Hunsinger, George, *How To Read Karl Barth. The Shape of His Theology* (New York: Oxford University Press, 1991).

Jeanrond, Werner, "Karl Barth's Hermeneutics" in N Biggar (ed), *Reckoning With Barth. Essays in Commemoration of the Centenary of Karl Barth's Birth* (Oxford: A R Mowbray & Co, 1988), 80-97.

Jenson, Robert W, *God After God: the God of the Past and the God of the Future, Seen in the work of Karl Barth* (Indianapolis and New York: Bobbs-Merrill, 1969).

-, "Karl Barth", in D F Ford (ed), *The Modern Theologians. An Introduction to Christian Theology in the Twentieth Century*, vol 1, (Oxford: Basil Blackwell, 1989), 23-49.

Jüngel, Eberhard, "Die theologischen Anfänge. Beobachtungen", in Eberhard Jüngel, *Barth-Studien* (Gütersloh: Gütersloh Verlagshaus Gerd Mohn, 1982), 61-126.

-, *Karl Barth. A Theological Legacy*, translated by G Paul, (Pennsylvania: Westminster Press, 1986).

-, *The Doctrine of the Trinity. God's Being is in Becoming*, translated by H Harris, (Edinburgh: Scottish Academic Press, 1976).

Lang, U M, "Anhypostatos-Enhypostatos: Church Fathers, Protestant Orthodoxy and Karl Barth" *Journal of Theological Studies* (49) 1988, 630-657.

Lindbeck, George, "Barth and Textuality", *Theology Today*, XLIII (3), 1986, 361-376.

McAfee Brown, George, "Introduction", in G Casalis, *Portrait of Karl Barth* (Garden City: Doubleday and Company, 1963), 1-17.

Macken S.J., John. The Autonomy Theme in the Church Dogmatics. Karl Barth and his Critics (Cambridge: Cambridge University Press, 1990).

McCormack, Bruce L, *Karl Barth's Critically Realist Dialectical Theology*, (Oxford: Oxford University Press, 1995)

McCormack, Bruce L, "A Scholastic of a Higher Order: The Development of Karl Barth's Theology, 1921-31", PhD. dissertation, (Princeton University: 1990).

-, "Review Article: Graham Ward's *Barth, Derrida, and the Language of Theology*", *Scottish Journal of Theology* 44 (1991), 260-264.

., "Review of *Barth's Ethics of Reconciliation* by John Webster", *The Scottish Journal of Theology* 49 4, 273-274.

McLelland, Joseph C, "Philosophy and Theology - A Family Affair (Karl and Heinrich Barth)", in H Martin Rumscheidt (ed), *Footnotes to a Theology: The Karl Barth Colloquium of 1972* Sciences Religieuses Supplements, 1974, 30-52.

Putin, Philip, "Two Early Reformed Catechisms, the Threefold Office and the Shape of Karl Barth's Christology" *The Scottish Journal of Theology* (44) 1991, 195-214.

Roberts, Richard H, "The Ideal and the Real in the Theology of Karl Barth" in S Sykes and D Holmes (ed), *New Studies in Theology 1* (London: Duckworth, 1980), 163-180.

-, "Barth and the Eschatology of Weimar: A Theology on its Way?", in R H Roberts, *A Theology on its Way? Essays on Karl Barth* (Edinburgh: T & T Clark, 1991), 169-199.

Robinson, James M, (ed), *The Beginnings of Dialectical Theology* (Richmond: Virginia, John Knox Press, 1968).

Rogers , Jr, Eugene, "Thomas and Barth in Convergence on Romans I?" *Modern Theology* 12:1, 1996, 57-83.

-, *Thomas and Karl Barth: Sacred Doctrine and the Natural Knowledge of God* (Indiana: Notre Dame Press, 1998).

Rosato S. J., Philip, *The Spirit as Lord: The Pneumatology of Karl Barth* (Edinburgh: T & T Clark, 1981).

Rumscheidt, H Martin, *Revelation and Theology. An Analysis of the Barth-Harnack Correspondence of 1923* (Cambridge: CUP, 1972).

-, *The Way of Theology in Karl Barth: Essays and Comments* (Alison Park, P A: Pickwick Press, 1986).

Runia, Klass, *Karl Barth's Doctrine of Holy Scripture* (Grand Rapids: Eerdmans, 1962).

Smart James D, *The Divided Mind of Modern Theology: Karl Barth and Rudolf Bultmann 1908-1933* (Philadelphia: Fortress Press, 1967).

Sykes, Stephen W, "The Centre of Barth's Theology", in S Sykes (ed), *Karl Barth: Studies of His Theological Method* (Oxford: Oxford University Press, 1979), 17-54.

- (ed), *Karl Barth: Studies of His Theological Method* (Oxford: Oxford University Press, 1979).

Torrance, Thomas F, *Karl Barth: Biblical and Evangelical Theologian* (Edinburgh: T & T Clark, 1990).

-, *Karl Barth: An Introduction to His Early Theology, 1910-1931* (London: SCM Press, 1962).

Ward, Graham, *Barth, Derrida and the Language of Theology* (Cambridge: Cambridge University Press, 1995).

Webber, Stephen H, *Re-Figuring Theology: The Rhetoric of Karl Barth* (New York: University of New York, 1991).

Williams, Rowan, "Barth on the Triune God", in S Sykes (ed), *Karl Barth: Studies of His Theological Method* (Oxford: Oxford University Press, 1979), 147-193.

## b. Wittgenstein

Aidun, Deborah, "Wittgenstein on Grammatical Propositions", in S Shanker (ed), *Ludwig Wittgenstein: Critical Assessments*, vol ii, (London: Croom helm, 1986), 142-149.

Anscombe, G E M, *An Introduction to Wittgenstein's Tractatus*, 3rd edition, (London: Hutchinson, 1967).

Ayer, A J, *Wittgenstein* (Harmondsworth: Penguin Books, 1985).

Baker, G P and P M S Hacker, *An Analytical Commentary on Wittgenstein's "Philosophical Investigations"*, vols 1-2, (Oxford: Blackwell, 1980, 1985).

-, *Scepticism, Rules and Language* (Oxford: Blackwell, 1984).

-, *Wittgenstein, Meaning and Understanding* (Oxford: Blackwell, 1982).

-, *Wittgenstein: Rules, Grammar and Necessity, Volume 2 of an analytical Commentary on the Philosophical Investigations* (Oxford: Blackwell, 1985).

Bartley, III, William Warren, "A Popperian Harvest" in P Levinson (ed), *In Pursuit of Truth: Essays on the Philosophy of Karl Popper on the Occasion of his 80th Birthday* (New York: Humanities Press, 1982), 249-290.

-, "Non-justificationism: Popper *versus* Wittgenstein", in Epistemology and Philosophy of Science, Proceedings of the 7th International Wittgenstein Symposium (Vienna: Hölder-Pichler-Tempsky, 1983), 255-261.

-, *Wittgenstein* (London: Quartet Books, 1977).

Black, Max, *A Companion to Wittgenstein's 'Tractatus'* (Cambridge: Cambridge University Press, 1964).

Block, Irving, "'Showing' in the *Tractatus*: The Root of Wittgenstein and Russell's Basic Incompatibility", in S Shanker (ed), *Ludwig Wittgenstein: Critical Assessments*, vol I, (London: Croom helm, 1986), 136-149.

-, "The Unity of Wittgenstein's Philosophy", in R Haller and W Grassl (eds), *Language, Logic and Philosophy* (1980), 233-236.

Bolton, Derek, *An Approach to Wittgenstein's Philosophy* (London: MacMillan, 1979)

Bouveresse, Jacques, "'The Darkness of this time': Wittgenstein and the Modern World", in A Phillips Griffiths (ed), *Wittgenstein Centenary Essays* (Cambridge: Cambridge University Press, 1991), 11-40.

Bubner, Rüdiger, "Kant, Transcendental Arguments and the Problem of Deduction" *Review of Metaphysics (28)* 1975, 453-467.

Cavell, Stanley, "The Availability of Wittgenstein's Later Philosophy", in G Pitcher (ed), *Wittgenstein. The Philosophical Investigations* (London: MacMillan, 1968), 151-185.

Crittenden, Charles, "Wittgenstein and Transcendental Arguments", in R Haller and W Grassl (eds) *Language, Logic and Philosophy*, (1980), 259-261.

Engel, S Morris, 'Schopenhauer's Impact on Wittgenstein', *Journal of the History of Philosophy* (7) 1969, 285-302.

Engelmann, Paul, *Letters from Wittgenstein*, edited by B F McGuinness, translated by L Furtwiller, (Oxford: Basil Blackwell, 1967).

Feyerabend, Paul "Wittgenstein's *Philosophical Investigations*", in George Pitcher (ed), *Wittgenstein: The Philosophical Investigations* (London: MacMillan, 1986), 104-150.

Fogelin, Robert, "Wittgenstein and Classical Scepticism", in S Shanker (ed), *Ludwig Wittgenstein: Critical Assessments*, vol ii, (London: Croom helm, 1986), 163-182.

Grayling, A C, *Wittgenstein* (Oxford: Oxford University Press, 1988).

Griffin, James, *Wittgenstein's Logical Atomism* (London: Oxford University Press, 1964).

Hacker P M S, *An Analytical Commentary on Wittgenstein's "Philosophical Investigations"*, vol 3, (Oxford: Basil Blackwell, 1993).

-, *Insight and Illusion. Themes in the Philosophy of Wittgenstein*, 2nd edition, revised, (Oxford: Oxford University Press, 1986).

Haller, Rudolf, *Questions on Wittgenstein* (London: Routledge, 1988).

Hallett, Garth, *A Companion to Wittgenstein's "Philosophical Investigations"* (Ithaca: Cornell University Press. 1977).

Hanfling, Oswald, *Wittgenstein's Later Philosophy* (London: MacMillan, 1989)

Hudson, W Donald, *Wittgenstein and Religious Belief* (London: MacMillan, 1975).

Janik, Allan, "Schopenhauer and the Early Wittgenstein" *Philosophical Studies (Ireland)*, 15 (1966), 76-95.

-, "Wittgenstein: an Austrian Enigma", in J C Níyiri (ed), *Austrian Philosophy: Studies and Texts* (Munich: Philosophia-Verlag, 1981), 75-89.

-, "Wittgenstein and Weininger", in E Leinfeller, W Leinfellner, H Berghel, and A Hübner (ed), *Wittgenstein And His Impact On Contemporary Thought* (Vienna: Hölder-Pichler-Tempsky, 1978), 25-30.

- and Stephen Toulmin, *Wittgenstein's Vienna* (London, Weidenfeld and Nicholson, 1973).

Keightley, Alan, *Wittgenstein, Grammar and God* (London: Epworth Press, 1976).

Kenny, Anthony, "Wittgenstein on the Nature of Philosophy", in B F McGuinness (ed), *Wittgenstein and His Times* (Oxford: Blackwell, 1981), 1-26.

-, *Wittgenstein* (Harmondsworth: Middlesex, Penguin Books, 1975).

Kerr, Fergus, *Theology After Wittgenstein* (Oxford: Basil Blackwell, 1986).

Kripke, Saul, *Wittgenstein on Rules and Private Language* (Oxford: Basil Blackwell, 1982).

Luckhardt, C G, "Wittgenstein on Paradigms and Paradigm Cases: problems With *On Certainty*" in E Leinfellner, W Leinfeller, H Berghel, and A Hübner (ed), *Wittgenstein And His Impact On Contemporary Thought* (Vienna: Hölder-Pichler-Tempsky, 1978), 379-385.

Malcolm, Norman, *Ludwig Wittgenstein: a memoir*. 2nd edition, (Oxford: Oxford University Press, 1984).

-. *Wittgenstein: Nothing Is Hidden* (Oxford: Basil Blackwell, 1986).

Mays, Wolfe, "Recollections of Wittgenstein", in K T Fann (ed) *Wittgenstein: the Man and his Philosophy* (New York: Dell Publishing, 1967), 79-88.

McGinn, *Wittgenstein on Meaning: an Interpretation and Evaluation*, (Oxford: Basil Blackwell, 1987).

McGuinness, Brian F, *Wittgenstein: A Life. Young Ludwig, 1899-1921* (London: Duckworth, 1987).

McGuinness, "Wittgenstein and Freud", in B F McGuinness (ed), *Wittgenstein and His Times* (Oxford: Basil Blackwell, 1981), .

McGuinness, Brian F and Rudolf Haller, *Wittgenstein in Focus* (Amsterdam: Rodopi, 1989).

Moore, George Edward, "A Defence of Common Sense", *Philosophical Papers* (London: Allen and Unwin, 1959), 32-59.

-, "Proof of an External World", *Philosophical Papers*, 127-150.

- , "Wittgenstein: Lectures 1930-1933", *Philosophical Papers*, 252-324.

Mounce, H O, *Wittgenstein's Tractatus: An Introduction* (Oxford: Blackwell, 1981).

Monk, Ray, *Wittgenstein: The Duty of Genius*, (London: Vintage, 1991).

Morawetz, Thomas, *Wittgenstein and Knowledge: the Importance of On Certainty* (Amherst: Massachusetts University Press, 1978).

Nielsen, Kai, "Wittgensteinian Fideism" *Philosophy* XLII 161 (1967), 191-209.

Nyíri, J C, "Wittgenstein 1929-31: The Turning Back", in Shanker (ed), *Ludwig Wittgenstein: Critical Assessments*, vol iv, (London: Croom Helm, 1986), 29-59.

-, "Wittgenstein's Later Work in Relation to Conservatism", in B F McGuinness (ed), *Wittgenstein and His Times* (Oxford: Basil Blackwell, 1981), 44-68.

-, "Wittgenstein's New Traditionalism", in *Essays in Honour of G H Von Wright, Acta Fennica* 28 (1976), 501-12.

Drury, M O' C, "Conversations with Wittgenstein", in R Rhees (ed), *Recollections of Wittgenstein* (Oxford: Oxford University Press, 1984), 97-171.

Pears, David F, *The False Prison. A Study of the Development of Wittgenstein's Philosophy*, 2 vols, (Oxford: Oxford University Press, 1987).

-, *Wittgenstein* (Glasgow: Fontana, 1971).

Phillips, D Z, *Belief, Change and Forms of Life* (London: MacMillan, 1986).

-, *Faith After Foundationalism* (London: Routledge, 1988).

-, *Faith and Philosophical Enquiry* (London: Routledge and Kegan Paul, 1970).

"Primitive Reactions and the Reactions of Primitives", *Wittgenstein and Religion* (London: MacMillan Press, 1993), 103-122.

"Religion in Wittgenstein's Mirror", in *A Phillips Griffiths (ed), Wittgenstein Centenary Essays* (Cambridge: Cambridge University Press, 1991), 135-150.

-, *The Concept of Prayer* (Oxford: Basil Blackwell, 1981).

Rhees, Rush, "Miss Anscombe on the *Tractatus*" *Philosophical Quarterly* 10 (1960), 21-31.

Shanker, Stuart G, "Wittgenstein and the Problem of Hermeneutic Understanding", in S Shanker (ed), *Ludwig Wittgenstein: Critical Assessments*, vol iv, (London: Croom Helm, 1986), 104-115.

Schulte, Joachim, "Wittgenstein and Conservatism". in S Shanker (ed), *Ludwig Wittgenstein: Critical Assessments*, vol iv, (London: Croom Helm, 1986), 60-69.

-, *Wittgenstein: An Introduction*, translated by William H Brenner and John F Holley, (State University of New York Press: Albany, 1992).

Schwyzer, Hubert, "Thought and Reality: The Metaphysics of Kant and Wittgenstein", in S Shanker (ed), *Ludwig Wittgenstein: Critical Assessments*, vol ii, (London: Croom Helm, 1986), 150-162.

Stern, Josef Peter, "Wittgenstein in Context", in E Timms and R Robertson (ed), *Vienna 1900: from Altenberg to Wittgenstein*, (Edinburgh: Edinburgh University Press, 1990).

Stevenson, Leslie, "Wittgenstein's Transcendental Deduction and Kant's Private Language Argument", *Kantstudien* (73), no.3 1982, 320-337.

Thiselton, Anthony C, *The Two Horizons: New Testament Hermeneutics and Philosophical Description with special reference to Heidegger, Bultmann, Gadamer, and Wittgenstein*, foreword by J B Torrance (Exeter: Paternoster Press, 1980).

Von Wright, Georg Henrik, "Ludwig Wittgenstein: A Biographical Sketch", in G H von Wright, *Wittgenstein* (Oxford: Basil Blackwell, 1982), 13-34.

-, "The Origin of the *Tractatus*", in G H von Wright, *Wittgenstein* (Oxford: Basil Blackwell, 1982), 65-109.

-, "Wittgenstein on Certainty", in G H von Wright, *Wittgenstein* (Oxford: Basil Blackwell, 1982), 165-182.

Waismann, Friedrich, *Ludwig Wittgenstein and the Vienna Circle*, edited by B F McGuinness, translated by B F McGuinness and J Schulte, (Oxford: Blackwell, 1979).

### c.  General

Alter, Robert, *The Art of Biblical Narrative* (London: Allen and Unwin, 1981)

Auerbach, Erich, *Mimesis: The Representation of Reality in Western Literature*, translated by William R Trask (Princeton: Princeton university Press, 1953).

Audi, Robert, "Direct Justification, Evidential Dependence, and Theistic Belief", in Audi, Robert, and William J Wainwright, *Rationality, Religious Belief, and Moral Committment* (Ithaca: Cornell University Press, 1986), 139-166.

Augustine, *The Literal Meaning of Genesis*, vol I, translated by John Hammond Taylor, SJ, (New York: Newman Press, 1982).

Ayer, A J, *Language, Truth and Logic*, 2nd edition, (London: Victor Gollancz, 1946).

Barrow, John D and Frank J Tipler, *The Cosmological Anthropic Principle* (Oxford: Clarendon, 1986).

Bartley III, William W, *Morality and Religion* (London: Macmillan, 1971).

-, "A Refutation of the Alleged Refutation of Comprehensively Critical Rationalism", in Radnitzky and Bartley III (ed), *Evolutionary Epistemology, Theory of Rationality, and the Sociology of Knowledge* ( Ilinois: Open Court, 1987), 313-341.

-, *Retreat from Commitment*, 1st edition, (London: Chatto and Windus, 1962).

-, *Retreat from Commitment*, 2nd edition, (la Salle, Illinois: Open Court Publications, 1984).

-, "Theories of Rationality", in Radnitzky and Bartley, III (ed), *Evolutionary Epistemology, Theory of Rationality, and the Sociology of Knowledge* (Ilinois: Open Court, 1987), 205-214.

Berlin, Isaiah, *The Age of Enlightenment: the Eighteenth Century Philosophers* (Oxford: Oxford University Press, 1979).

Bornkamm, Günther, *Jesus of Nazareth,* translated by Irene and Fraser McLuskey with James M Robinson, (London: Hodder and Stoughton, 1960).

358                                                                 Select Bibliography

"The Theology of Rudolf Bultmann", in C W Kegley *The Theology of Rudolf Bultmann* (London: SCM Press, 1966), 3-20.

Brecher, Robert, *Anselm's Argument. The Logic of Divine Existence* (Aldershot: Grover Publishing Ltd, 1985).

Bultmann, Rudolf, *Jesus Christ and Mythology*, trans. S M Ogden, (London: SCM, 1958)

-, *History of the Synoptic Tradition*, trans. John Marsh (Oxford: Blackwell, 1968).

-, *New Testament & Mythology and Other Basic Writings*, selected, edited and translated by S M Ogden, (London: SCM Press, 1985).

Burnyeat, Miles F, "Idealism and Greek Philosophy: What Descartes Saw and Berkeley Missed", in G Vesey (ed), *Idealism Past and Present*. Royal Institute of Philosophy Lecture Series, 13. Supplement to *Philosophy* 1982 (Cambridge: Cambridge University Press, 1982), 19-50.

Callinicos, Alex, *Against Postmodernism. A Marxist Critique* (Cambridge: Polity Press, 1989).

Calvin, John, *A Harmony of the Gospels, Matthew, Mark, Luke*, vols I-III, translated by A W Morrison, edited by David F Torrance and Thomas F Torrance, (Edinburgh: St Andrew Press, 1972).

-, *The Epistle of Paul the Apostle to the Romans and to the Thessalonians*, trans. Ross MacKenzie, eds. David W. Torrance and Thomas F. Torrance (Edinburgh: Oliver and Boyd, 1961).

-, *The Gospel According to St John, 11-21*, translated by T H L Parker, edited by David W Torrance and Thomas F Torrance, (Edinburgh: Oliver and Boyd, 1961).

Carr, William, *A History of Germany, 1815-1945* (London: Edward Arnold, 1987).

Cassirer, Ernst, *The Philosophy of the Enlightenment*, translated by F C A Koelln and J P Pettigrew, (Princeton: Princeton University Press, 1951).

Cavell, Stanley, *Quest of The Ordinary: Lines of Skepticism and Romanticism* (Chicago: The University of Chicago Press, 1988).

-, *The Claim of Reason: Wittgenstein, Skepticism, Morality, and Tragedy* (Oxford: Clarendon Press, 1979).

Charlesworth, M J, *St. Anselm's Proslogion: with A Reply on Behalf of the Fool by Guanilo and The Author's Reply to Guanilo*, translated with an introduction and philosophical commentary by M J Charlesworth, (Oxford: Oxford University Press, 1965).

Childs, Brevard, *New Testament Canon: an Introduction* (London: SCM, 1985).

Clayton, John Powell (ed), *Ernst Troeltsch and the Future of Theology* (Cambridge: Cambridge University Press, 1976).

Clark, Kenneth, *The Nude: a Study of Ideal Art* (London: Murray, 1956).

Clement, Keith, *Schleiermacher, Pioneer of Modern Theology* (London: Collins, 1987).

Closs, August, *The Genius of the German Lyric: a Historical Survey of its Formal and Metaphysical Values* (London: Cresset Press, 1962).

Conant, James, "Introduction", in Putnam, *Realism with a Human Face*, edited by J Conant, (Massachussets: Harvard University Press, 1990), xv-lxxiv.

Cranfield, C E B, "*Metron Pisteos* in Romans XII.3", *Journal of New Testament Studies* 8, 345-351.

-, *The Epistle to the Romans*, vol ii, (Edinburgh: T and T Clark Ltd, 1979).

Craig, Gordon A, *Germany 1866-1945* (Oxford: Oxford University Press, 1981).

Crowther, Paul, *The Kantian Sublime* (Oxford: Oxford University Press), 1989).

Cupitt, Don, *The Sea of Faith* (London: British Broadcasting Corporation, 1984).

Curley, Edwin M, *Descartes Against the Sceptics* (Cambridge: Cambridge University Press, 1978).

Dalferth, Ingolf, *Theology and Philosophy* (Oxford: Basil Blackwell, 1988).

Davidson, Donald, "Reality Without Reference", in D Davidson, *Enquiries into Truth and Interpretation* (Oxford: Clarendon Press, 1984), 215-225.

Davies, Brian, "*Quod Vere Sit Deus:* Why Anselm Thought That God Truly Exists", *New Blackfriars (199)*, 1995, 212-221.

Descartes, René, *Discourse on Method and the Meditations* (Harmondsworth: Penguin, 1968).

Dibelius, Martin, *From Tradition to Gospel*, trans. Bertram Lee Woolf (London: Ivor Nicholson and Watson, 1934).

Diem, Herman, *Kierkegaard's Dialectic of Existence*, translated by H Knight, (Edinburgh: Oliver and Boyd, 1959).

Ebeling, Gerhard, "The Significance of the Critical Historical Method of Church and Theology in Protestantism", *Word and Faith*, translated by J Leitch, (London: SCM Press, 1963), 17-61.

Engel, S Morris, "Schopenhauer's Impact on Wittgenstein", *Journal of the History of Philosophy*. (7) 1969, 285-302.

Evans, Donald D, *The Logic of Self-Involvement: a Philosophical Study of Everyday Language* (London: SCM Press, 1963).

Fackenheim, Emil L, "Immanuel Kant", in N Smart, J Clayton, S T Katz, P Sherry (eds), *19th Century Religious Thought in the West vol 1*, (Cambridge: Cambridge University Press, 1985).

Field, Frank, *The Last Days of Mankind: Karl Kraus and his Vienna* (London: St. Martin's Press, 1967).

Flew, Antony, *David Hume: Philosopher of Moral Science* (Oxford: Blackwell, 1986).

- (ed), *A Dictionary of Philosophy* (London: Pan Books, 1979).

-, *Hume's Philosophy of Belief: a Study of his First 'Inquiry'* (London: Routledge and Kegan Paul, 1961).

Frei, Hans W, *The Eclipse of Biblical narrative. A Study in Eighteenth and Nineteenth Century Hermeneutics* (New Haven: Yale University Press, 1974).

-, *The Identity of Jesus Christ* (Philadelphia: Fortress Press, 1975).

-, "The Literal Reading of the Biblical narrative: Does It Stretch or Will It Break?", in F D O'Connell (ed), *The Bible and the Narrative Tradition* (Oxford: Oxford University Press, 1986), 36-77.

-, *Theology and Narrative*, edited by G Hunsinger, introduction by W C Placher (Oxford: OUP, 1993).

-, *Types of Christian Theology*, edited by G Hunsinger and W C Placher, (New Haven: Yale University Press, 1992).

Friedenthal, Richard, *Goethe: His Life and Times* (London: Weidenfeld and Nicholson, 1965).

Gardiner, Patrick, *Schopenhauer* (Harmondsworth: Penguin, 1971).

Garvie, A E, *The Ritschlian Theology* (Edinburgh: T & T Clark, 1899).

Gay, Peter, *The Enlightenment: An Interpretation*, 2 vols, (New York: Alfred A Knopf, 1969).

Gellner, Ernst, "Reply to Mr. McIntyre", *Universities and Left Review*, 1958.

Gerrish, Brian, *A Prince of the Church, Schleiermacher and the Beginnings of Modern Theology* (London: SCM, 1984).

360                                                                        Select Bibliography

-, *Tradition and the Modern World: Reformed Theology in the Nineteenth Century* (Chicago: University of Chicago Press, 1978).

Goethe, *Selected Verse*, edited and translated by D Luke, (Harmondsworth: Penguin, 1964).

Gollwitzer, Helmut, *The Existence of God as Confessed by Faith*, translated by J Leitch, (London: SCM, 1965).

Gombrich, Ernst Hans, *Art and Illusion: a Study in the Psychology of Pictorial Representation* (London: Pantheon Books, 1960).

Grant, C K, "From World to God", *Proceedings of the Aristotelian Society* Symposium, Suppl. XLI 1967, 153-62.

Green, G, "Fictional Narrative and Scriptural Truth", in G Green (ed), *Scriptural Authority and Narrative Interpretation* (Philadelphia: Fortress Press, 1987), 79-96.

Gunkel, Herman, *Genesis*, translated by Mark E Biddle, foreword by Ernest W Nicholson (Macon: The Mercer University Press, 1987).

Güttgemanns, Erhardt, *Candid Questions Concerning Gospel Form Criticism: A Methodological Sketch of the Fundamental Problematics of Form and Redaction Criticism*, translated by William G Doty (Pittsburgh: Pickwick Press, 1979).

Habermas, Jürgen, "Modernity - An Incomplete Project", in H Foster (ed), *Postmodern Culture* (London: Pluto Press, 1985), 3-15.

Hannay, Alastair, *Kierkegaard* (London: Routledge and Kegan Paul, 1982).

Hartshorne, Charles, *Anselm's Discovery. A Re-examination of the Ontological Proof For God's Existence* (La Salle, Illinois: Open Court, 1965).

Harvey, Austin van, *The Historian and the Believer: the Morality of Historical Knowledge and Christian Belief* (London: SCM, 1966).

-, *A Handbook of Theological Terms* (London: G Allen and Unwin, 1966).

Heald, David, "Grillparzer and the Germans", *Oxford German Studies* 6 (1971-72), 61-73.

Hebblethwaite, Brian, *The Ocean of Truth: A Defence of Objective Theism* (Cambridge: Cambridge University Press, 1988).

Heimbeck, Raeburn S, *Theology and Meaning: A Critique of Metatheological Scepticism* (London: Allen and Unwin Ltd, 1969).

Heller, Erich, *The Disinherited Mind: Essays in Modern German Literature and Thought*, 4th edition, (London: Bowes and Bowes, 1975).

-, *The Importance of Nietzsche* (Chicago: University of Chicago Press, 1988).

Hendel, Charles W, *Studies in the Philosophy of David Hume* (New York: Bobbs-Merrill, 1963).

Heppe, Heinrich, *Reformed Dogmatics*, ed. Ernst Bizer, trans. G. T. Thompson (London: Allen and Unwin, 1950).

Hick, John, *Arguments for the Existence of God* (London: Macmillan, 1970).

Holmer, Paul L, *The Grammar of Faith* (San Francisco: Harper and Row, 1978).

Hopkins, Jasper, *A Companion to the Study of St. Anselm* (Oxford: Oxford University Press, 1972).

- and Herbert W Richardson (ed), *Anselm of Canterbury. Volume 1: Monologion, Proslogion, Debate with Guanilo and a Meditation on Human Redemption*, translated by J Hopkins and H Richardson, (London: SCM Press, 1974).

Hume, David, *Enquiries concerning Human Understanding and concerning the Principles of Morals, 1777*, edited by P H Nidditch, (Oxford: Oxford University Press, 1975).

Iggers, Wilam Abeles, *Karl Kraus: a Viennese Critic of the Twentieth Century* (The Hague: Martinus Nijhoff, 1967).

Janaway, Christopher, *Self and World in Schopenhauer's Philosophy* (Oxford: Oxford University Press, 1989).

Johnson, Roger A, *The Origins of Demythologising: Philosophy and Historiography in the Theology of Rudolf Bultmann* (Leiden: E J Brill, 1974).

Kann, Robert A, The Multinational Empire: Nationalism and Natural Reform in the Habsburg Monarchy 1848-1918, 2 vols, (New York: Octogon, 1950).

Kant, Immanuel, *Prolegomena to Any Future Metaphysics*, translated by P G Lucas, (Manchester: Manchester University Press, 1953).

-. *Foundations of the Metaphysics of Morals* and *What is Enlightenment?*, translation with an introduction by L W Beck (New York: Bobbs-Merril, 1959).

-. *Religion Within the Limits of Reason Alone*, translated with an Introduction and Notes by Theodore M Greene and Hoyt H Hudson, (New York: Harper Torchbooks, 1960).

-. *The Critique of Pure Reason*, translated by N Kemp Smith, (London: MacMillan, 1933).

Kemp Smith, Norman (ed), *Hume's Dialogues Concerning Natural Religion*, 2nd ed., edited with an introduction by N Kemp Smith, (New York: Social Science Publishers, 1948).

Kenny, Anthony, "Descartes on Ideas" in W Doney, *Descartes*, (New York: MacMillan, 1967), 227-249.

-, *The God of the Philosophers* (Oxford: Clarendon Press, 1979).

-, *The Five Ways. St Thomas Aquinas' Proofs of God's Existence* (London: Routledge and Kegan Paul, 1969).

Kierkegaard, S, *Kierkegaard's Concluding Unscientific Postscript*, translated by D S Swenson, (Princeton: Princeton University Press, 1968).

-, *Philosophical Fragments; Johannes Climacus*, translated by H V Hong and E H Hong, (Princeton: Princeton University Press, 1985).

-, The Instant, Nos I to X, in *Kierkegaard: Attack Upon Christendom" 1854-1855*, translated by W Lowrie, (London: Oxford University Press, 1946), 77-293.

Klemke, E D, *The Epistemology of G E Moore* (Evanston: Northwestern University Press, 1969).

Kolakowski, Leszek, *Positivist Philosophy. From Hume to the Vienna Circle*, translated by N Guterman, (Harmondsworth: Penguin Books Ltd, 1972).

Konyndyk, Kenneth, "Faith and Evidentialism", in Audi, Robert, and William J Wainwright, *Rationality, Religious Belief, and Moral Committment* (Ithaca: Cornell University Press, 1986), 82-108.

Körner, S, *Kant* (Harmondsworth: Penguin Books, 1955).

Küng, Hans, *Does God Exist? An Answer for Today*, translated by Edward Quinn, (London: Collins, 1980).

-, *Theology for the Third Millenium: an ecumenical view*, translated by P Heinegg, (London: HarperCollins, 1991).

Kuschel, Karl-Josef, *Born Before All Time? The Dispute over Christ's Origin*, translated by J Bowden, (London: SCM, 1992).

Lear, Jonathan, "The Disappearing 'We'", *The Aristotelian Society* Suppl vol 58 (1984),219-242.

Lindbeck, George A, *The Nature of Doctrine. Religion and Theology in a Postliberal Age* (London: SPCK, 1984).

-, "Postcritical Canonical Interpretation: Three Modes of Retrieval", C Seitz and K Greene-McCreight (ed), *Theological Exegesis: Essays in Honour of Brevard Childs* (Grand Rapids: Eerdmans, 1998), 26-51.

Lunn, Eugene, *Marxism and Modernism* (Berkeley: University of California Press, 1982).

Luther, Luther, *Lectures on Romans*, Vol. 45, ed. Hilton C. Oswald (Saint Louis: Concordia Publishing House, 1972),

Lyotard, Jean-Francois, *The Postmodern Condition: a Report on Knowledge*, foreword by F Jameson, translated by G Bennington and B Massumi, (Minneapolis: University of Minnesota Press, 1984)

Magee, Bryan. *The Philosophy of Schopenhauer*, (Oxford: Clarendon, 1983).

Malcolm, Norman, "Anselm's Ontological Arguments", *Philosophical Review LXIX*, 42-52.

Malcolm, "George Edward Moore", *Knowledge and Certainty. Essays and Lectures* (Englewood Cliffs: Prentice-Hall, 1963), 163-183.

McCartney, C A, *The Habsburg Empire 1790-1918* (London: Weidenfeld and Nicholson, 1968).

-, *The House of Austria: The Later Phase, 1790-1918* (Edinburgh: Edinburgh University Press, 1978).

McGinn, Marie, *Sense and Certainty* (Oxford: Blackwell, 1989).

McGrath, Alister, *The Making of Modern German Christology* (Oxford: London, 1986),

McIntyre, J. *St Anselm and His Critics* (Edinburgh: Oliver and Boyd, 1954).

McQuarrie, John M, "Philosophy and Theology in Bultmann's Thought" in C W Kegley (ed), *The Theology of Rudolf Bultmann*, 127-143.

Milbank, John, *Theology and Social Theory. Beyond Secular Reason* (Oxford: Blackwell, 1990).

Minear, Paul S, *The Obedience of Faith: The Purposes of Paul in the Epistle to the Romans* (London: SCM, 1971).

Mondin, Battista, *The Principle of Analogy in Protestant and Catholic Theology* (The Hague: Martinus Nijhoff, 1963).

Moore, G E, *Philosophical Studies* (London: Routledge and Kegan Paul, 1960).

Nagel, Thomas, *Mortal Questions* (Cambridge: Cambridge University Press, 1991).

Neill, Stephen and Tom Wright, *The Interpretation of the New Testament 1861-1986* 2nd ed. (Oxford: Oxford University Press, 1988),

Norris, Christopher, *What's Wrong With Postmodernism. Critical Theory and the Ends of Philosophy* (Hemel Hempstead: Harvester Wheatsheath, 1990).

Noxon, James, *Hume's Philosophical Development. A Study of his Methods* (Oxford: Oxford University Press, 1973).

O' Connor, D J, *A Critical History of Western Philosophy* (New York: The Free Press of Glencoe, 1964).

Oechli, Wilhelm, *History of Switzerland, 1499-1914*, translated by E and C Paul, (Cambridge: Cambridge University Press, 1922).

O'Neill, John C, *The Bible's Authority. A Portrait of Thinkers from Lessing to Bultmann* (Edinburgh: T & T Clark, 1991).

Pannenberg, Wolfhart, *Anthropology in Theological Perspective*, translated by M J O' Connell, (Edinburgh: T & T Clark, 1985).

-, *Jesus - God and Man*, translated by L Wilkins and D Priebe (London: SCM, 1968).

-, "The Later Dimensions of Myth in Biblical and Christian Tradition" in Pannenberg, *Basic Questions in Theology* (London: SCM Press, 1973), 1-79.

-, *Introduction to Systematic Theology*, translation by M J O' Connell, (Edinburgh: T & T Clark, 1991).

-, *Theology and the Philosophy of Science*, translated by F McDonagh, (Philadelphia: Westminster Press, 1976).

Papineau, David, *Reality and Representation* (Oxford: Basil Blackwell, 1987).

Parides, C A, *The Grand Design of God: the Literary Form of the Christian View of History* (London: Routledge and Kegan Paul, 1972).

Pelikan, Jaroslav, "Alas Theology, Too", *The Christian Tradition. A History of the Development of Doctrine. Christian Doctrine and Modern Culture (since 1700)*, vol 5, (Chicago: The University of Chicago Press, 1989), 1-8.

Perrin, Norman, *The Kingdom of God in the Teaching of Jesus* (London: SCM, 1966).

Peterson Sr, Robert, *Calvin and the Atonement* (Ross-shire: Mentor, 1999).

Phillips, D Z, *Belief, Change and Forms of Life* (London: MacMillan, 1986).

-, *Faith After Foundationalism* (London: Routledge, 1988).

-, D Z, *Faith and Philosophical Enquiry* (London: Routledge and Kegan Paul, 1970).

-, *The Concept of Prayer* (Oxford: Basil Blackwell, 1981).

Plantinga, Alvin, "Coherentism and the Evidentialist Objection to Belief in God", in Audi, Robert, and William J Wainwright, *Rationality, Religious Belief, and Moral Committment*), 109-138.

-, "Is Belief in God Rational?" in C F Delaney (ed), *Rationality and Religious Belief* (London: University of Notre Dame Press, 1979), 7-27.

-, "Reason and Belief in God" in A Plantinga and N Wollenstorff (ed), *Faith and Rationality* (Notre Dame: University of Notre Dame Press, 1983), 16-93.

-, "Reformed Epistemology Again", *The Reformed Journal* vol 32 issue 7, 3-14.

Popkin, Richard H, *The History of Scepticism from Erasmus to Descartes* (Assen: Van Goram, 1964).

Popper, Karl Raimund, *Postscript to the Logic of Scientific Discovery*, vol 1, edited by W Bartley III, (London: Hutchison, 1983).

-, *Unended Quest: An Intellectual Autobiography* (Glasgow, Fontana: 1976).

Porter, H C, "The Nose of Wax: Scripture and the Spirit from Erasmus to Milton", *Transactions of the Royal Historical Society* (1963), 155-174.

Putnam, Hilary, "Review of *The Concept* of a Person", in H Putnam, *Mind, Language and Reality*, (Cambridge: Cambridge University Press, 1975), 129-143.

Quine, Willard Van Orman, "Two Dogmas of Empiricism", *From a Logical Point of View: Nine Logico-Philosophical Essays*, revised edition, (New York: Harper Row Publishers, 1961), 20-46.

-, *Word and Object* (Massachussets: M I T Press, 1960).

Quinton, A M, "Contemporary British Philosophy", in O'Connor (ed), *A Critical History of Western Philosophy* (New York: The Free Press of Glencoe, 1964), 531-556.

Von Rad, Gerhardt, *Genesis*, translated by John H Marks, (London: SCM, 1963).

Radner, Ephraim, "The Absence of the Comforter: Scripture and the Divided Church", C Seitz and K Greene-McCreight (ed), *Theological Exegesis: Essays in Honour of Brevard Childs* (Grand Rapids: Eerdmans, 1998), 355-394.

Ree, Jonathan, *Descartes* (London: Allen Lane, 1974).

Riddle, M B, Introductory Essay to Augustine's *De Consensu Evangelistarum*, vol vi *Augustine* The Nicene and Post-Nicene Fathers, First Series (Grand Rapids: Eerdmans, 1956).

Rorty, Richard, *Philosophy and the Mirror of Nature* (Princeton: Princeton University Press, 1980).

Rupp, George, *Culture-Protestantism: German Liberal Theology at the Turn of the Twentieth Century* AAR Studies in Religion 15 (Montana: Scholars Press, 1977).

Russell, Bertrand, "Logical Atomism", *The Monist* 1918-1919, nos 28-29, in B Russell, *The Collected Papers of Bertrand Russell*, vol 8, (London: G Allen & Unwin Ltd, 1986), 160-244.

-, *My Philosophical Development* (London: Allen and Unwin, 1959).

-, "On Scientific Method in Philosophy", *Mysticism and logic and other essays* (London: Longmans Green, 1918), 95-119.

Ryle, Gilbert, *The Concept of Mind*

de Salis, J R, *Switzerland and Empire: essays and reflections*, translated by A and E Henderson, (London: Wolff, 1971).

Schacht, Richard, *Classical Modern Philosophers: Descartes to Kant* (London: Routledge and Kegan Paul, 1984).

Schweitzer, Albert, *The Quest of the Historical Jesus: a Critical Study of Its Progress from Reimarus to Wrede*, introduction by F C Burkitt, translated by W Montgomery (Baltimore: John Hopkins University Press, 1998).

Scruton, Roger, *Kant* (Oxford: Oxford University Press, 1982).

Sherry, Patrick, *Religion, Truth and Language-games* (London: MacMillan, 1977).

Schilpp, Paul Arthur (ed), *The Philosophy of G E Moore* (Menasha: Banta Publishing, 1942).

Schleiermacher, Friedrich, *On Religion: Speeches for the Cultured Despisers of Religion*, translated by R Crouter, (Cambridge: Cambridge University Press, 1988).

-, *The Christian Faith*, edited by H R Mackintosh and J S Stewart, (Edinburgh: T and T Clark, 1928).

Schopenhauer, Arthur, *Essays and Aphorisms*, selected and translated with an introduction by R J Hollingdale, (Harmondsworth: Penguin Books, 1970).

-, *The World as Will and Representation*, 2 vols, translated by E F J Payne, (New York: Dover Publications, 1969).

Soloveytchik, George, *Switzerland in Perspective* (Oxford: oxford University Press, 1954).

Steiner, George, Review Article of Bruce McCormack's *Karl Barth's Critically Realistic Dialectical Theology, Times Literary Supplement*, May 19, 1995, 7.

Stern, Josef Peter, "Grillparzer's Vienna", in *German Studies presented to W H Bruford* (London: George G Harraps, 1962), 176-192.

-, *Re-Interpretations: Seven Studies in Nineteenth Century German Literature* (London: Thames and Hudson, 1964).

Sternberg, Meir, *The Poetics of Biblical Narrative* (Bloomington: Indiana University Press, 1987).

Strauss, David Friedrich, *The Life of Jesus Critically Examined*, translated by George Eliot, edited with an introduction by Peter C Hodgson (London: SCM, 1973).

Strawson, Peter, *Scepticism and Naturalism: Some Varieties* (London: Menthuen, 1985).

Streetman, Robert F, "Romanticism and the *Sensus Numinus* in Schleiermacher", in D Jasper (ed), *The Interpretation of Belief: Coleridge, Schleiermacher and Romanticism* (London: MacMillan, 1986), 104-125.

Stroud, Barry, *Hume* (London: Routledge and Kegan Paul, 1981).

-, *The Significance of Philosophical Scepticism* (Oxford: Oxford University Press., 1984).

-, "Transcendental Arguments and 'Epistemological Naturalism'", *Philosophical Studies 31* 1977, 105-115.

Swinburne, Richard, *Faith and Reason* (Oxford: Oxford University Press, 1981).

-, *The Coherence of Theism*, revised edition, (Oxford: Clarendon Press, 1993).

-, *The Existence of God* (Oxford: Clarendon Press, 1979).

Taylor, A E, *Philosophical Studies* (London: MacMillan, 1934).

Taylor, A J P, *The Habsburg Monarchy, 1809-1918: A History of the Austrian Empire and Austria-Hungary*, 2nd edition, revised, (Harmondsworth: Penguin Books, 1981).

Taylor, Charles, *Hegel* (Cambridge: Cambridge University Press, 1975).

Taylor, Vincent, *The Formation of the Gospel Tradition* (London: MacMillan, 1933).

Thürer, Georg, *Free and Swiss: the Story of Switzerland*, adapted and translated by R P Heller and E Long, (London: Wolff, 1970).

Timms, Edward, *Karl Kraus, Apocalyptic Satirist: Culture and Catastrophe in Habsburg Vienna* (New Haven: Yale University Press, 1986).

Torrance, Thomas F, *The Hermeneutic of John Calvin* (Edinburgh, Scottish Academic Press, 1988) *Theological Science* (London: Oxford University Press, 1969).

"Knowledge of God and Speech about Him according to John Calvin", *Theology in Reconstruction* (London: SCM Press, 1965), 76-98.

-, "Theological Realism", in B Hebblethwaithe and S Sutherland (ed), *The Philosophical Frontiers of Christian Theology* (Cambridge: Cambridge University Press, 1982), 169-196.

Troeltsch, Ernst, "Historical and Dogmatic Method in Theology", *Religion in History*, translated by J Luther Adams and W F Bense, introduction by James Luther Adams, (Edinburgh: T & T Clark, 1991), 11-32.

Vanhoozer, Kevin, *Biblical Narrative in the philosophy of Paul Ricoeur: a Study in Hermeneutics and Theology* (Cambridge: Cambridge University Press, 1990).

Vesey, Godfrey (ed), *Idealism Past and Present*. Royal Institute of Philosophy Lecture Series: 13. Supplement to *Philosophy* 1982 (Cambridge: Cambridge University Press, 1982).

Ward, Keith, *The Concept of God* (Oxford: Basil Blackwell, 1974).

Waugh, Patricia, *Practising Postmodernism, Reading Modernism* (London: Hodder and Stoughton, 1992).

Watling, J L, "Descartes", in O'Connor, (ed), *A Critical History of Western Philosophy* (New York: The Free Press of Glencoe, 1964), 170-186.

Weiss, Johannes, *Jesus' Proclamation of the Kingdom of God*, trans. R H Hier and D L Holland (Philadelphia: Fortress, 1971).

Welch, Claude, *Protestant Thought in the Nineteenth Century*, 2 vols, (New Haven: Yale University Press, 1972-85).

Wenham, John, *Easter Enigma: Do the Resurrection Stories Contradict One Another?* (Exeter: Paternoster Press, 1984).

White, Alan R, "G E Moore", in O'Connor (ed), *A Critical History of Western Philosophy* (New York: The Free Press of Glencoe, 1964), 464-472.

-, *G E Moore. A Critical Exposition* (Oxford: Oxford University Press, 1958).

White, Roger, "Notes on Analogical Predication and Speaking about God", in Hebblewaithe and Sutherland (ed), *The Philosophical Frontiers of Christian Theology* (Cambridge: Cambridge University Press, 1982), 197-226.

Wilkerson, T E, "Transcendental Arguments", *Philosophical Quarterly (20)* 1970, 200-212.

Elizabeth M Wilkinson, *Goethe's Conception of Form* (London: Oxford University Press, 1951).

Williams, Bernard, *Descartes: The Project of Pure Enquiry* (Harmondsworth: Penguin, 1978).

Wolterstorff, Nicholas, *Divine Discourse: Philosophical Reflections on the Claim that God Speaks* (Cambridge: CUP, 1995).

-, "The Migration of the Theistic Arguments: From Natural Theology to Evidentialist Apologetics", in Audi, Robert, and William J Wainwright, *Rationality, Religious Belief, and Moral Committment* ( Ithaca: Cornell University Press, 1986), 38-81.

Wood, Allen W, *Kant's Rational Theology* (Ithaca: Cornell University Press, 1978).

Zim, Rivkah, "The Reformation: the Trial of God's Word", in Stephen Prickett (ed), *Reading the Text. Biblical Criticism and Literary Theory* (Oxford: Blackwell, 1991), 64-135.

Zohn, Harry, *Karl Kraus* (New York: Twayne Publishers, 1971).

Zuckmayer, Carl, *A Late Friendship, the letters of Karl Barth and Carl Zuckmayer*, translated by G W Bromiley, (Grand Rapids: Eerdmans, 1983).

# Name Index

Alter, Robert, 142
Anscombe, Elizabeth M, 34, 35, 37
Anselm, 20, 26, 103, 109, 123, 124, 125, 137, 194, 197-199, 201, 322, 341, 342
Aquinas, Thomas, 81, 98, 103, 137-139, 159, 162
Auerbach, Erich, 98, 99
Augustine, 50, 99, 100, 102, 103, 104, 106, 108, 109, 137, 140, 142, 145, 170, 177, 239, 246, 259
Austin, J L, 308
Ayer, A J, 4, 5, 11, 271

Bach, Johann Sebastian, 49, 50, 340
Baker, G P, 273, 283, 286, 287, 300, 338
Bartley, William, 32, 34, 64
Beethoven, Ludwig van, 44, 47, 49, 50, 311, 332, 340
Beintker, Michael, 57
Bismarck, Otto von, 28, 45, 310, 311
Black, Max, 31, 35, 36, 41
Bloch, Ernst, 51
Block, Irving, 276, 277
Bolton, Derek, 279, 280
Bolzano, Bernard, 32, 273
Bonhoeffer, Dietrich, 189, 190
Bornkamm, Günther, 256, 257, 258, 259, 260
Bouveresse, Jacques, 332
Brahms, Johannes, 47
Brentano, Franz, 29, 30, 32
Brod, Max, 51
Bromiley, Geoffrey W, 136, 143, 146
Brunner, Emil, 25, 26, 216, 321, 322

Bubner, Rüdiger, 279, 280
Bucanus, Wilhelm, 129, 276, 301
Bultmann, Rudolf, 25, 26, 51, 84, 85, 89, 91-93, 96, 97, 182, 216, 229, 230, 232, 242, 248, 257, 265
Burnyeat, Miles, 298
Busch, Eberhard, 11, 24, 44, 45, 52, 53, 54, 55, 56, 59, 63, 64, 67, 75, 80

Calvin, John, 93, 98, 99, 100-101, 102-103, 104, 106, 107, 108, 109, 127-129, 130, 132, 135, 136, 137, 139, 140, 142, 162, 163, 170, 174, 177-179, 180, 183, 185, 209, 211, 223, 224, 226, 227, 234, 235, 236, 237, 238, 239, 246, 259, 303
Carnap, Rudolf, 30
Cassirer, Ernst, 49
Cavell, Stanley, 281, 282, 302, 303
Childs, Brevard, 98, 101, 102, 105, 131, 132, 142, 143, 152, 153, 170
Clark, Kenneth, 345, 346
Cranfield, C E B, 127, 130
Crittenden, Charles, 280, 282

Darwin, Charles, 40
Davidson, Donald, 273
Descartes, René, 19, 199, 214, 216, 295, 298
Dibelius, Martin, 182
Dodd, C H, 241
Dostoyevsky, Fydor, 54

Ebeling, Gerhard, 25, 26
Ehrenstein, Albert, 46

# Subject Index

aesthetic:
  and Barth, 340-343
  and Wittgenstein, 334-340
*analogia fidei*, 115, 120, 122-126,
  127, 128, 129, 174, 182, 183, 185,
  186, 191 209-210, 216-221, 224;
  Reformed, 127-130, 221-223, 224,
  271, 272, 276, 279-301; and
  Wittgenstein, 273, 278, 289, 303
analogy, 167, 191, 216-218; and
  Hume, 12, 167-168; and Troeltsch,
  125, 135, 164, 167-168, 177, 191,
  199, 203
angelology, 71, 80-89
autonomy:
  of philosophy, 33, 38, 269, 333-
  334
  of theology, 1, 17-18, 74-75, 80,
  86-89

basic belief, 93, 100-101, 103; and
  non-basic belief, 105, 137-138

creation history, 135-162, 163; as the
  coming into being of created
  reality, 146-148; first narrative of,
  148-152; God reveals Himself as
  creator in the, 136, 138, 146-152,
  156; in time, 144-145; second
  narrative of, 152-159
critical-historical method, 93, 104,
  105, 124-125, 164-165, 177

demythologising, 84, 85, 91, 97
dilemma:
  metaphilosophical, 3-7, 27, 32-40,
  269, 274

metatheological, 3-4, 7-18, 27, 50-
  59, 71-72, 107-108, 112, 140,
  170, 194, 202, 203, 269, 347
  other, 41-50, 65, 269

Enlightenment, 3-4, 7-8, 81-82, 93, 95,
  135-136, 163, 164, 169, 190-192,
  305-306, 309, 313, 314
epistemology:
  and Barth, 59-64, 167, 174, 184,
  186, 187-188, 210, 224, 305-306
  and Wittgenstein, 293-299
eschatology, 53, 57-59, 64, 71-72, 73,
  74, 81, 163-164
event:
  creation history as, 146, 147, 149,
  154
  whose only means of measurement
  is it itself, 109, 111, 112, 115, 125,
  143-144, 147-148, 151, 154, 157,
  162, 164-168, 173-192; specific
  identity of, 193-201
  reconciliation as, 228, 229
  resurrection-appearances history as,
  163-164
Expressionism, 42, 45, 50, 51, 52, 53,
  54, 316

fallen man, 152-159; as *homo lapsus*,
  156, 159, 263
fideism, 270; and apologetic, 305-308,
  323
*fin-de-siècle* Vienna, 23-24
foundationalism:
  classical, 297-298
  conceptual, 115, 224, 272, 276,
  298, 302, 306, 309, 331

# Paternoster Biblical and Theological Monographs
*(Uniform with this Volume)*

## Eve: Accused or Acquitted?
*An Analysis of Feminist Readings of the*
*Creation Narrative Texts in Genesis 1–3*
Joseph Abraham

Two contrary views dominate contemporary feminist biblical scholarship. One finds in the Bible an unequivocal equality between the sexes from the very creation of humanity, whilst the other sees the biblical text as irredeemably patriarchal and androcentric. Dr. Abraham enters into dialogue with both camps as well as introducing his own method of approach. An invaluable tool for anyone who is interested in this contemporary debate.

*2000 / 0-85364-971-5*

## Deification in Eastern Orthodox Theology
*An Evaluation and Critique of the Theology of Dumitru Staniloae*
Emil Bartos

Bartos studies a fundamental yet neglected aspect of Orthodox theology: deification. By examining the doctrines of anthropology, Christology, soteriology and ecclesiology as they relate to deification, he provides an important contribution to contemporary dialogue between Eastern and Western theologians.

*1999 / 0-85364-956-1 / 386pp*

## The Weakness of the Law
Jonathan F. Bayes

A study of the four New Testament books which refer to the law as weak (Acts, Romans, Galatians, Hebrews) leads to a defence of the third use in the Reformed debate about the law in the life of the believer.

*2000 / 0-85364-957-X*

## The Priesthood of Some Believers
*Developments in the Christian Literature of the First Three Centuries*
Colin J. Bulley

The first in-depth treatment of early Christian texts on the priesthood of all believers shows that the developing priesthood of the ordained related closely to the division between laity and clergy and had deleterious effects on the practice of the general priesthood.

*2000 / 0-85364-958-8*

## Paul as Apostle to the Gentiles
*His Apostolic Self-awareness and its Influence
on the Soteriological Argument in Romans*
Daniel J-S Chae

Opposing 'the post-Holocaust interpretation of Romans', Daniel Chae competently demonstrates that Paul argues for the equality of Jew and Gentile in Romans. Chae's fresh exegetical interpretation is academically outstanding and spiritually encouraging.

*1997 / 0-85364-829-8 / 392pp*

## Parallel Lives
*The Relation of Paul to the Apostles in the Lucan Perspective*
Andrew C. Clark

This study of the Peter-Paul parallels in Acts argues that their purpose was to emphasize the themes of continuity in salvation history and the unity of the Jewish and Gentile missions. New light is shed on Luke's literary techniques, partly through a comparison with Plutarch.

*2000 / 085364-979-0*

## Baptism and the Baptists
*Theology and Practice in the Twentieth Century*
Anthony R. Cross

At a time of renewed interest in baptism, *Baptism and the Baptists* is a detailed study of twentieth-century baptismal theology and practice and the factors which have influenced its development.

*1999 / 0-85364-959-6*

## The Crisis and the Quest
*A Kierkegaardian Reading of Charles Williams*
Stephen M. Dunning

Employing Kierkegaardian categories and analysis, this study investigates both the central crisis in Charles Williams's authorship between hermeticism and Christianity (Kierkegaard's Religions A and B), and the quest to resolve this crisis, a quest that ultimately presses the bounds of orthodoxy.

*1999 / 0-85364-985-5 / 278pp*

## The Triumph of Christ in African Perspective
*A Study of Demonology and Redemption in the African Context*
Keith Ferdinando

This book explores the implications for the gospel of traditional African fears of occult aggression. It analyses such traditional approaches to suffering and biblical responses to fears of demonic evil, concluding with an evaluation of African beliefs from the perspective of the gospel.

*1999 / 0-85364-830-1 / 439pp*

## Suffering and Ministry in the Spirit
*Paul's Defence of His Ministry in 2 Corinthians 2:14 – 3:3*
### Scott J. Hafemann
Shedding new light on the way Paul defended his apostleship, the author offers a careful, detailed study of 2 Corinthians 2:14 – 3:3 linked with other key passages throughout 1 and 2 Corinthians. Demonstrating the unity and coherence of Paul's argument in this passage, the author shows that Paul's suffering served as the vehicle for revealing God's power and glory through the Spirit.

*1999 / 0-85364-967-7 / 276pp*

## The Words of our Lips
*Language-Use in Free Church Worship*
### David Hilborn
Studies of liturgical language have tended to focus on the written canons of Roman Catholic and Anglican communities. By contrast, David Hilborn analyses the more extemporary approach of English Nonconformity. Drawing on recent developments in linguistic pragmatics, he explores similarities and differences between 'fixed' and 'free' worship, and argues for the interdependence of each.

*2001 / 0-85364-977-4*

## One God, One People
*The Differentiated Unity of the People of God in the Theology of Jürgen Moltmann*
### John G. Kelly
The author expounds and critiques Moltmann's doctrine of God and highlights the systematic connections between it and Moltmann's influential discussion of Israel. He then proposes a fresh approach to Jewish–Christian relations, building on Moltmann's work and using insights from Habermas and Rawls.

*2000 / 0-85346-969-3*

## Calvin and English Calvinism to 1649
### R.T. Kendall
The author's thesis is that those who formed the Westminster Confession of Faith, which is regarded as Calvinism, in fact departed from John Calvin on two points: (1) the extent of the Atonement and (2) the ground of assurance of salvation. 'No student of the period can ignore this work' – *J.I. Packer.*

*1997 / 0-85364-827-1 / 224pp*

## Karl Barth and the Strange New World within the Bible
### Neil B. MacDonald
Barth's discovery of the strange new world within the Bible is examined in the context of Kant, Hume, Overbeck, and, most importantly, Wittgenstein. Covers some fundamental issues in theology today; epistemology, the final form of the text and biblical truth-claims.

*2000 / 0-85364-970-7*

## Attributes and Atonement
### *The Holy Love of God in the Theology of P.T. Forsyth*
### Leslie McCurdy
*Attributes and Atonement* is an intriguing full-length study of P.T. Forsyth's doctrine of the cross as it relates particularly to God's holy love. It includes an unparalleled bibliography of both primary and secondary material relating to Forsyth.

*1999 / 0-85364-833-6 / 323pp*

## Towards a Theology of the Concord of God
### *A Japanese Perspective on the Trinity*
### Nozomu Miyahira
This book introduces a new Japanese theology and a unique Trinitarian formula based on the Japanese intellectual climate: three betweennesses and one concord. It also presents a new interpretation of the Trinity, a co-subordinationism, which is in line with orthodox Trinitarianism; each single person of the Trinity is eternally and equally subordinate (or serviceable) to the other persons, so that they retain the mutual dynamic equality.

*1999 / 0-85364-863-8*

## Your Father the Devil?
### *A New Approach to John and 'The Jews'*
### Stephen Motyer
Who are 'the Jews' in John's Gospel? Defending John against the charge of anti-Semitism, Motyer argues that, far from demonising the Jews, the Gospel seeks to present Jesus as 'Good News for Jews' in a late first century setting.

*1997 / 0-85364-832-8 / 274pp*

## Origins and Early Development of Liberation Theology in Latin America
*With Particular Reference to Gustavo Gutierrez*
Eddy José Muskus

This work challenges the fundamental premise of Liberation Theology: 'opting for the poor', and its claim that Christ is found in them. It also argues that Liberation Theology emerged as a direct result of the failure of the Roman Catholic Church in Latin America.

*2000 / 0-85364-974-X*

## 'Hell': A Hard Look at a Hard Question
*The Fate of the Unrighteous in New Testament Thought*
David Powys

This comprehensive treatment seeks to unlock the original meaning of terms and phrases long thought to support the traditional doctrine of hell. It concludes that there is an alternative – one which is more biblical, and which can positively revive the rationale for Christian mission.

*1999 / 0-85364-831-X / 500pp*

## Evangelical Experiences
*A Study in the Spirituality of English Evangelicalism 1918–1939*
Ian M Randall

This book makes a detailed historical examination of evangelical spirituality between the First and Second World Wars. It shows how patterns of devotion led to tensions and divisions. In a wide-ranging study, Anglican, Wesleyan, Reformed and Pentecostal-charismatic spiritualities are analysed.

*1999 / 0-85364-919-7 / 320pp*

## Is World View Neutral Education Possible and Desirable?
*A Christian Response to Liberal Arguments*
(Published jointly with The Stapleford Centre)
Signe Sandsmark

This thesis discusses reasons for belief in world view neutrality, and argues that 'neutral' education will have a hidden, but strong world view influence. It discusses the place for Christian education in the common school.

*1999 / 0-85364-973-1 / 205pp*

## The Extent of the Atonement
*A Dilemma for Reformed Theology from Calvin to the Consensus*
G. Michael Thomas

A study of the way Reformed theology addressed the question, 'Did Christ die for all, or for the elect only?', commencing with John Calvin, and including debates with Lutheranism, the Synod of Dort and the teaching of Moïse Amyraut.

*1997 / 0-85364-828-X / 237pp*

## The Power of the Cross
*Theology and the Death of Christ in Paul, Luther and Pascal*
Graham Tomlin

This book explores the theology of the cross in St Paul, Luther and Pascal. It offers new perspectives on the theology of each, and some implications for the nature of power, apologetics, theology and church life in a postmodern context.

*1999 / 0-85364-984-7 / 368pp*

## Constrained by Zeal
*Female Spirituality amongst Nonconformists 1825–1875*
Linda Wilson

*Constrained by Zeal* investigates the neglected area of Nonconformist female spirituality. Against the background of separate spheres, it analyses the experience of women from four denominations, and argues that the churches provided a 'third sphere' in which they could find opportunities for participation.

*1999 / 0-85364-972-3*

## Disavowing Constantine
*Mission, Church and the Social Order in the Theologies of
John Howard Yoder and Jürgen Moltmann*
Nigel G. Wright

This book is a timely restatement of a radical theology of church and state in the Anabaptist and Baptist tradition. Dr. Wright constructs his argument in dialogue and debate with Yoder and Moltmann, major contributors to a free church perspective.

*1999 / 0-85364-978-2*

**The Voice of Jesus**
*Studies in the Interpretation of Six Gospel Parables*
Stephen Wright
This literary study considers how the 'voice' of Jesus has been heard in different periods of parable interpretation, and how the categories of figure and trope may help us towards a sensitive reading of the parables today.

*2000 / 0-85364-975-8*

**The Paternoster Press**
**P O Box 300**
**Carlisle Cumbria**
**CA3 0QS UK**

**Web: www.paternoster-publishing.com**